Also by Claudia Roden

A Book of Middle Eastern Food

Everything Tastes Better Outdoors

CLAUDIA RODEN

Illustrated by Alta Ann Parkins

A Fireside Book
Published by Simon & Schuster Inc.
New York London Toronto Sydney Tokyo Singapore

Fireside
Simon & Schuster Building
Rockefeller Center
1230 Avenue of the Americas
New York, New York 10020

Originally published in Great Britain as *Picnic* by
Jill Norman and Hobhouse, Ltd., London
First Fireside Edition 1991
Published by arrangement with
Alfred A. Knopf, Inc.
201 East 50th Street
New York, New York, 10022

FIRESIDE and colophon are registered trademarks
of Simon & Schuster Inc.

Manufactured in the United States of America
1 3 5 7 9 10 8 6 4 2 Pbk.

Library of Congress Cataloging in Publication Data
Roden, Claudia.
[Picnic]
Everything tastes better outdoors/Claudia Roden;
illustrated by Alta Ann Parkins.—1st Fireside ed.
p. cm.
"A Fireside book."
Reprint. Originally published: Picnic. New York: Knopf:
Distributed by Random House, © 1984.
Includes bibliographical references and index.
1. Outdoor cookery.   I. Title.
TX823.R57   1991
641.5'78—dc20   90-13976
CIP
ISBN 0-671-73263-3

Grateful acknowledgment is made to the following for permission to reprint previously published material:

M. Evans & Co.: "Carne Fiambre" from *The Complete Book of Caribbean Cooking* by Elisabeth Lambert Ortiz. Copyright © 1973 by Elisabeth Lambert Ortiz. "Fiambre Potosino" from *The Complete Book of Mexican Cooking* by Elisabeth Lambert Ortiz. Copyright © 1967 by Elisabeth Lambert Ortiz.

James Beard: Fifteen recipes from *The Complete Book of Outdoor Cookery* by James Beard and Helen Evans Brown. Copyright © 1955 by James Beard and Helen Evans Brown.

Madhur Jaffrey: For "A Picnic in the Himalayas."

Alfred A. Knopf, Inc.: Recipes and passages from six sources. "Beef Consommé" and description by Revival Week with recipes for "Boiled Virginia Ham" and "Sweet Potato Pie" from *The Taste of Country Cooking* by Edna Lewis. Copyright © 1976 by Edna Lewis. "Three Salads to Serve with Sushi" from *At Home with Japanese Cooking* by Elizabeth

(permissions cont. on p. 417)

In ample space under the broadest shade,
A table richly spread in regal mode,
With dishes piled and meats of noblest sort
And savour—beasts of chase, or fowl of game,
In pastry built, or from the spit, or boiled,
Gris-amber-steamed; all fish, from sea or shore,
Freshet or purling brook, of shell or fin
And exquisitest name, for which was drained
Pontus, and Lucrine bay, and Afric coast,
Alas! how simple, to these cates compared,
Was that crude apple that diverted Eve!
And at a stately sideboard, by the wine,
That fragrant smell diffused, in order stood
Tall stripling youths rich-clad, of fairer hue
Than Ganymede or Hylas; distant more
Under the trees now tripped, now solemn stood,
Nymphs of Diana's train, and Naiades
With fruits and flowers from Amalthea's horn,
And ladies of th' Hesperides, that seemed
Fairer than feigned of old, or fabled since
Of fairy damsels met in forest wide
By knights of Logres, or of Lyonese,
Lancelot, or Pelleas, or Pellenore.
And all the while harmonious airs were heard
Of chiming strings or charming pipes; and winds
Of gentlest gale Arabian odours fanned
From their soft wings, and Flora's earliest smells.
Such was the splendour; and the Tempter now
His invitation earnestly renewed:—
    "What doubts the Son of God to sit and eat?
    These are not fruits forbidden."

—*John Milton,* Paradise Regained

Contents

Contents

Preface

This book is divided broadly into three sections which represent three aspects of cooking and eating outdoors. The first is about food that is prepared in the kitchen and then transported, to be eaten outdoors on a picnic, in a garden, or on a terrace. It deals with unusual as well as traditional picnic fare, from soups and sandwiches, cold meats and fish, pies, salads and dips, to desserts and drinks. The second is about food that is cooked outdoors on a backyard grill, over a campfire, or in a barbecue pit. The last, for travelers using galley kitchens on boats or in campers or dining in the wilderness, includes provisions and impromptu meals as well as more elaborate ones. There are ideas for freshly caught fish, details of primitive ways of cooking, and descriptions of equipment. Each section also contains some special menus such as those for Indian and Japanese meals.

Many dishes are suitable for different kinds of events, and recipes can be taken from one section, combined with those from another, and used for a different occasion. The index has been planned to be helpful in making these selections.

Flexibility is intended in using the book just as improvisation is encouraged in cooking. Browse through the whole book for inspiration, for that is its nature. The style in which recipes are given varies deliberately from the formal with precise measures to informal or even mere suggestions when they are to be used away from the home kitchen.

In the belief that the last thing one wishes in field or boat is strict measures and dogmas, I have allowed myself and readers a certain freedom from standard recipes and precise measurements. Without scales and measuring equipment you can forget the arbitrary measures which have been forced onto an old art whose principal quality is the personal touch.

True gastronomy is making the most of what is available, however modest. It has little to do with following recipes. And the leisurely atmosphere of vacation cooking is the best time to learn to trust your own taste and common sense, to weigh with eyes and hands, to feel and taste and dream a little. I have given precise measures only where they are required and when the preparation is likely to be done in the kitchen. Otherwise I have given enough information for a moderately accomplished cook, with encouragement toward self-assurance.

The object of the book is to inspire those who like to eat well and who love to be out among the trees. It is for those who travel all over the world, who camp and sail, who enjoy good food and cannot always afford the prices of restaurants and prefer to pack a picnic meal or cook on the spot. It is not a hiker's primer, nor a woodsman's textbook, about how to dress game and skin deer and overcome the harsh rigors of outdoor life, nor is it a cooking school. It assumes a certain knowledge of basic cooking skills, an ease of transport, the availability of ingredients and equipment consistent with light cruising and comfortable camping. Most important, it assumes an enthusiasm for experimenting and attempting different styles of cooking and a desire for ease and pleasure rather than a bent on roughing it.

Acknowledgments

This book was drawn from many people's experiences of cooking out-of-doors. The most pleasant part of working on it for me was sharing their memories, capturing their ideas, and recording their knowledge. I cannot name everyone who helped me and added a part of themselves, and although some have been acknowledged in the text, I take the opportunity here of expressing my gratitude to all of them.

Of those who gave professional information, I thank especially James Marks, Frank Odell, and Brian Lee of the barbecue trade, Paul Breman, who gave advice about drinks, and Kumar Chowdhary, father of a family very dear to my own, who revealed the secrets of the tandoor at his Akash Restaurant.

I am particularly indebted to three friends: Sami Zubaida, whose kitchen was the setting of many joyful gastronomic events and who read the manuscript in draft and made many suggestions; Clint Greyn, who lent his experience as a camping gourmet; and Barbara Maher, whom I cannot thank enough for her enthusiastic involvement, her much appreciated advice, and her constructive criticism.

I owe an affectionate debt to Elizabeth David, who first inspired me to write, and to Jane Grigson, whose scholarship has brought a new dimension to cookery writing, for it is from them that I have learned the ways and joys of the trade. I am especially grateful to Jane for the literary picnics she brought to my attention and to Maxime Rodinson, the French Orientalist, for historical references.

I have a great debt to my publisher in England, Jill Norman, who fostered the idea of the book and encouraged and guided me. She has been sympathetic and deeply involved in every stage, and it has been a pleasure to work with her.

I thank my children Simon, Nadia, and Anna, who have gracefully eaten their way through the recipes, for their patience and their willingness to taste everything.

I have looked for ideas and information in many cookbooks. The principal ones are listed in the bibliography.

For this American edition I have included recipes from several Americans, including Edna Lewis, Linda Gassenheimer, Bruce Aidells—and Madhur Jaffrey. James Beard, the great pioneer of outdoor cooking whom I have long and much admired, generously offered a selection of favorite barbecue recipes. My dear friends Judith and Evan Jones have contributed much; Evan his kind and important collaboration, Judith her flair and expert guidance as well as a wealth of knowledge and information. I thank them warmly.

Everything
Tastes Better
Outdoors

Note: The recipes in this book are intended to provide six servings except where otherwise specified.

INTRODUCTION

Everything tastes better outdoors.

There is something about fresh air and the liberating effect of nature which sharpens the appetite and heightens the quality and intensity of sensations. It is enough to see the contented expression of someone sitting at a sunny outdoor café to realize it. The sense of smell especially is extraordinarily keen, and every little perfume from a nearby blossom or resinous bark adds to the flavor of the most banal sandwich filling.

Brillat-Savarin gives his support to a cliché when he describes a picnic party: "Seating themselves on the green sward, they eat while the corks fly and there is talk, laughter and merriment, and perfect freedom, for the universe is their drawing room and the sun their lamp. Besides, they have appetite, Nature's special gift, which lends to such a meal a vivacity unknown indoors, however beautiful the surroundings."

Visions of paradise have always been of the great outdoors, of trees laden with luscious fruit and rivers flowing with milk and honey, and many, like Milton, have been moved to eloquence by the first dining room of man.

My own experience of the Garden of Eden was in the Seychelles islands. The smell of pork roasting on a fruitwood fire and the Indian Ocean Creole mixture of garlic, spices, and chilies frying in coconut oil still fill me with sudden bursts of happiness, summoning as they do the primeval forest, the tropical climate mitigated by the sea breeze, and the waters so clear that you could see the multicolored fish and the shells and corals rocking gently on the white sands at the bottom.

Every day at noon, after a morning swim, I scrambled between clumps of fern and granite rocks up the hill slopes, lured by the smell of cooking which wafted around the lush vegetation. Light clouds of smoke rose beside corrugated iron-roofed huts nestling behind rocks and between coconut palms. They emanated from burning husks over which large heavy pots were sitting firmly on sturdy grills, the local outdoor kitchen arrangement.

Whiffs from ripe mangoes and papaws, still hanging on trees, mingled with the smell of bananas simmering in coconut milk and the fermenting juice of sugar cane. It was difficult to tell if the scent of vanilla came from the fragile pods dangling on their climbing stalks or from the sweet potato and yam pudding in the pot.

Scents became confused with colors and sounds. A hundred shades of green were pierced by scarlet-flowered flamboyants and pale mauve bougainvillaeas. The gentle bubbling of the daube and the crackling of the fire were accompanied by the rustling of palms and the chattering chorus of little red cardinals, warblers, and sunbirds.

Lunch was prepared in the open, for all to see. Exchanges were shouted about the contents of the pots, which were fondly watched over by the women. To constant giggling and laughter I accepted every invitation to taste. I tried a peppery fish soup, the contents of which had been found caught in the twisted bamboo trap now resting by the fire. A coconut fallen not far away had provided the liquor for the breadfruit daube. Black freshwater shrimp, caught in the stream by a little boy, were turning red on dying embers. A sweet potato melted in the ashes. Indian Ocean Creole food, amid the trees and the birds, was an assault on all the senses; I had to hold my breath to eat. Today the smell is still in my nostrils, the taste still on my tongue.

The pleasures of outdoor food are those that nature has to offer, as ephemeral as they are intense. A bird will sing his song and fly away, leaves will flutter and jostle the sunlight for a brief second—sky, flowers, and scents have each their small parts to play in the perfect happiness of those enchanted moments. They serve, as Jean Jacques Rousseau said, to "liberate the soul."

My adventure in what has been called "the last paradise on earth" is long past, but still, whether I have a sandwich with my family beneath a tree of rustling leaves on nearby Hampstead Heath, or breakfast in the garden watched over by an inquisitive squirrel, the food and the drink taste much better than they do indoors, and that too is a little bit of paradise.

Despite the gray and drizzly weather, picnics have become a British institution. Forever endearing is the romantic nostalgia and sublime recklessness with which people continue to indulge in the national passion at great social events like Henley Regatta and Glyndebourne, the Chelsea Flower Show, Goodwood and Ascot and on Epsom Downs on Derby Day. Race meetings, agricultural shows, sports days, and regattas see thousands of enthusiasts eating their lunch in rain and snow. City parks on chilly spring days are full of office workers at lunchtime. Glorious weather or not, bank holidays bring crowds to Hampstead Heath, and every summer scores of people set off with hampers and picnic baskets to the sea, the woods, or the fields. The more energetic make picnics occasions of activity, devoted to watching birds, sketching, hunting for fossils, or collecting wild flowers, shells, and pebbles. There are rowing and climbing expeditions, pony trekking, mushroom gathering, strawberry picking, and learned societies on architectural, archaeological,

or botanical outings often combine their scientific research with a little joyful reveling.

Americans, of course, are no less imaginative in their reasons for dining in the open. Kentucky Derby Day in Louisville is only one of the gala occasions for picnics before or during sports events. The big U.S. contribution to celebrating of this kind may be the tailgate feast—some plain, some fancy. A few years ago a Chicago newspaper published this report after a college football game:

"The Illinois version of the parking-lot picnic looked like something right out of 'The Great Gatsby.' One group of two dozen football fans ate a catered dinner that included silver plates, candelabra, a string quartet playing Mozart, lobster flown in from Maine, and waiters in tuxedos imported from Chicago at a cost of $300. Another group of about 12 had the same formal setting with gold plates and chateaubriand." For such extravagant doings a crisp fall day is the ideal foil.

Georgina Battiscombe says in *English Picnics* (1951) that the English picnicker is a hardy species, above the vagaries of the weather. It does require stoicism to defy fate and bring out knives and forks at the risk of being rained and blown upon. But it is also true that the gastronomic rigors of British hotels and restaurants are usually worse than those of the British climate, and there seems to be a particular, grim, English pleasure in a cold, wet, uncomfortable picnic. Jane Grigson has remarked that often the success of a picnic depends on disaster. Judging by the abundance of catastrophes described with glee in English diaries and fiction, it must be so. Stories abound of rain and umbrellas blown away, of wet, wasp-infested fields, of pots fallen in the fire, and soggy bread. Even John Betjeman in *Trebetherick* writes nostalgically:

Sand in the sandwiches, wasps in the tea,
Sun on our bathing-dresses heavy with the wet,
Squelch of the bladder-wrack waiting for the sea,
Fleas round the tamarisk, an early cigarette.

All things taken into account, it is not surprising that eating outdoors has had an uneven history in England. Coming in and out of fashion as pilgrims' wayside snack, hunting feast, and garden party, alfresco eating was at its most popular in Victorian times. In their heyday, picnics were great social events, opportunities for matchmaking and introductions, with music and singing and kettles boiling for tea and fashionable ladies in bonnets, with sketchbooks, watercolors, and pencils in hand. Remarkable, as all things Victorian, for their size and solidity, they were perfectly planned. Nothing was forgotten, with menus immensely varied and quantities to feed an army. The profusion of foods set in gelatin in highly decorative molds bore tribute to this by-product of the Industrial Revolution and to the sophisticated and decorative tastes that had arrived with the fugitive cooks of the French Revolution. Until then the fare had remained the same since the Middle Ages, when English and French picnics were as similar as were the manners and social habits of the two countries. The picnic outside Valenciennes, described by the fourteenth-century French poet Froissart in *Espinette Amoureuse*, "Lo! a place made for our pleasant repose; here let us break our fast! Then with one accord we brought out the meats, pastries, hams, wines and bakemeats and venison packed in heather," might have been a May-time picnic in the meadows of Kent or Surrey.

Mrs. Beeton's picnic menus, lavish and extravagant as they were, followed the same tradition. Here is a bill of fare for forty persons in her *Book of Household Management:*

A joint of cold roast beef, a joint of cold boiled beef, 2 ribs of lamb, 2 shoulders of lamb, 4 roast fowls, 2 roast ducks, 1 ham, 1 tongue, 2 veal and ham pies, 2 pigeon pies, 6 medium sized lobsters, 1 piece of collared calveshead, 18 lettuces, 6 baskets of salad, 6 cucumbers.

Stewed fruit well sweetened and put into glass bottles well corked, 3 or 4 dozen plain pastry biscuits to eat with the stewed fruit, 2 dozen fruit turnovers, 4 dozen cheese cakes, 2 cold cabinet puddings in moulds, a few jam puffs, 1 large cold Christmas pudding (this must be good), a few baskets of fresh fruit, 3 dozen plain biscuits, a piece of cheese, 6 lbs of butter (this of course includes the butter for tea), 4 quartern loaves of household bread, 3 dozen rolls, 6 loaves of tin bread (for tea), 2 plain plum cakes, 2 pound cakes, 2 sponge cakes, a tin of mixed biscuits, 1/2 lb of tea. Coffee is not suitable for a picnic, being difficult to make.

It was these Victorian picnics, with their formal rituals, and their cold lamb, roast chicken, veal and ham pies, puddings and jellies, which the English transported all over the world and which became a favorite pastime and a remembered feature of colonial life. In Calcutta and Madras, Jamaica, Aden, and Egypt (where I saw them), the English entertained each other in their gardens, the desert, and the wild countryside like their relatives at home, only with considerably more pomp. In the early days of the Empire, picnics were often stately, formal affairs which required arranging. Servants were sent ahead with tents and provisions to start preparations, but the fare was the same as it was back home. No one, it seems, took any notice of the large saucepans bubbling with curries for the "idle and unintelligible" servants. Nor had they much interest in the culinary ways of the high-caste natives they met at shoots and hunting expeditions. The little morsels pierced by skewers roasting over dying embers in their Arab protectorates, and the spare ribs glistening in their sweet-and-sour sauce in Hong Kong also went unnoticed. Ironically it has taken more than a century for all these things to appear in suburban English back gardens at sunny weekend lunches. Indian tandoori chicken, spare ribs, and kebabs have become party favorites with the new-found fashion for barbecues. And when a *déjeuner sur l'herbe* is planned, it is jambon persillé and poulet en croûte which summon idyllic visions immortalized by Tissot and Manet, Renoir and Léger.

While old traditions waned in Europe a new impetus for eating in the open came from across the Atlantic. Much of today's enthusiasm for outdoor eating and the fashion for barbecuing which has swept through all corners of the world in the last fifteen years has come from America. My friend Evan Jones says that barbecuing is in the American blood. M. F. K. Fisher writes that the feeling for nature is in their bones and their flesh. The wilderness is everybody's background, and the campfire remains part of the pioneer heritage. It may be through atavism and nostalgia that cooking and eating out-of-doors have become part of the American dream, but certainly natural beauty, a mild, agreeable climate, and an abundance of good local products have combined to make alfresco meals one of the richest and most rewarding experiences of American life.

The wondrous tales of the pioneers and early settlers who set out in covered wagons through shimmering deserts and vast fertile plains, across mountains and mighty rivers, are still fresh, and people look back at their culinary efforts with awe and with affection. Before the wilderness was tamed and the plow turned the soil, foods were mainly gathered and hunted. There were bountiful supplies of game, including beaver, moose, elk, deer, antelope, buffalo, rabbits, hares, prairie chickens, wild turkeys, grouse, ducks, and geese. Wild fruits and berries such as strawberries, currants, elderberries, and grapes were plentiful, as were mushrooms, walnuts, hickory, and hazelnuts. Trout, salmon, sturgeon, shad, and smelt along with a hundred other fish could be drawn from the rivers.

The flavor of an animal free to select its own food changes with the seasons. It carries the memory of moist woodlands and sunny fields, the taste of new berries and ripe fruits which may be heightened with the same fruits in a sauce. The memory of these things is still on the American palate, and the knowledge of how to take advantage of them is a national heritage. Food that you do not have to pay for has a special attraction. And when it comes as Nature's bounty, as those who know the pleasures of fresh berries, wild fruits, good game, and the delicacy of fish caught in a cold mountain stream will tell you, it is even more attractive. There is the fun of the hunt, the pleasure in foraging, the promise of unexpected flavors which are no less engaging for being hazardous, all of which bring an intimacy with Nature. Whichever way you cook them, there is little to beat the special flavor of mushrooms gathered in fields, except perhaps the watercress discovered by chance in a stream, eaten with nuts and oranges, the wild sorrel found in rock crevices or on the dark, barren floors of conifer woods, the thistle dressed in oil and lemon and served with yogurt, or the cockles winkled out from the sand after the tide has gone out and fried the same night with bacon. Who has had elderflower, stirred into beaten egg, fried by the tablespoon and eaten with plenty of sugar? I have heard ecstatic accounts of mussels cooked in a pail on the beach, of game birds encased in clay, gypsy fashion, and baked in the open fire. Few things have been as tasty or as much fun. Whether a snail or a berry, there is something unforgettable about food which has not been reared or grown for eating and which has just happened to be there. Memory clothes it with very special virtues. It is like manna, the food which the Israelites found and ate during their sojourn in the desert between Egypt and Canaan. It seems probable that it was a sweet, resinous substance which exudes from the desert tree, *Tamarix manifera,* when it is punctured by the insect *Gossyparia mannipara.* It can be ground or pounded like meal, boiled and made into cakes, but it has none of the other properties attributed to what was called the "grain of heaven" and the "bread of the mighty," and one would imagine the Jews must have grown very weary of it. Nevertheless, the memory of this food was expanded in Jewish tradition into the regular diet of all Israel and was endowed with marvelous features. It was said to have fallen on the ground like frost, white and sweet, but never on the Sabbath, and to have melted when the heat of the morning sun reached it. It was wonderful in every way, like our wild mushrooms and buckets of strawberries and the fish from the thundering waterfall which grows larger in our memories.

Americans know the pleasures of open spaces. They cherish memories of hunting and fishing trips and of wild forests and peaceful prairies. Everyone has spent magical moments at the beach or the countryside, and everyone loves the rituals that gather people outdoors, clambakes, oyster roasts, election barbecues, race day picnics, football games, church suppers, and Fourth of July celebrations; all these are important and joyful events. And sitting in the balcony or the backyard, sandwich in hand, surrounded by clouds of smoke emanating from a great roast turning slowly around a spit means happiness.

There are no more lost horizons in America, and the last frontier has been won a long time ago, but the pioneer spirit lives on. The trail is in the minds of many who dream of the wilderness and the cooking that has the wild and zestful ring of the American past. The methods of the western trappers and hunters and of the Indians, the planked fish, the animal buried in its hide in a smoldering pit, the bird covered in clay still with its feathers on and the biscuit dough wound like a ribbon on a stick have been handed down. Cooking on the trail, primitive equipment and the plain and simple meals of the past—sweet corn, flapjacks, the three Bs (bacon, beans, and bannock), hush puppies, apple pie, and stewed huckleberries—are deep in people's affections.

A nation that is still constantly on the move has developed food on the run and food cooked with speed to the point of an art. Dishes have been adopted from each wave of immigrants from England, Holland, Italy, France, Spain, Scandinavia, Germany, and many other countries of Europe and the Orient, and they have been given an American stamp. The Spaniards introduced the barbecue and its peppery sauces at their fiestas, the hamburger and the hot dog originate in Germany, and many salad dishes come from Scandinavia. Swedes brought meatballs, Jews influenced the style of the American sandwich through the delicatessen trade, Italians brought pizzas, and pâtés and terrines come from France. Very many countries have contributed cold and portable foods and foods that can be cooked on the spot to the American picnic barbecue and cook-out menus. Some of these dishes have acquired new flavors and trimmings, and a few have become American pop foods and international snacks-in-the-hand.

The object of this book is to add to the melting pot and nostalgic favorites the enormous variety of foods from all over the world which are traditionally eaten or cooked outdoors. Every culture and every country has its outdoor specials to which it remains attached. It is these classic dishes, whether they be simple regional snacks or elaborate festive meals, which have been brought together here. There is usually some sense in custom, but this book is inevitably mainly concerned with the casual and unpretentious cooking most suited to the carefree and relaxed atmosphere of outdoor eating. It reflects my taste and the preferences of friends and acquaintances on whose experience I have drawn.

Planning the menu for an outdoor meal, whether it is an elaborate banquet prepared at home the day before, a camper's cook-out, a sailor's luncheon, or an improvised meal put together with what there is in the larder, is one of the most creative parts of the affair. The choice of food is wide. It lies between what is easily transportable and holds well, what can be eaten cold or easily kept hot, and what can be cooked on the spot. A wide range of equipment makes it possible to transport most things, and there are many types of cooking arrangements.

You may decide simply to plan around one special dish with cheese and fruit to follow, or make it a grander affair with three or four courses: a simple first dish such as a chilled soup, a nobler second one, cheese, and a light dessert. For a larger party it is best to have a variety of dishes as for a buffet, or it may just be some good sandwiches with a hearty wine to wash them down.

You can prepare a first course and a cake at home the day before and cook the main part of the meal on the barbecue, or you can do everything from beginning to end on the fire.

Whether you are going forth gun in hand for game or merely having a picnic spread in the garden, look all through the book for ideas. You will find them in unexpected places.

Mrs. Beeton had a word of advice:

Watch carefully not to provide too much of one thing and too little of another; avoid serving plenty of salad and no dressing; two or three legs of lamb and no mint sauce; an abundance of wine and no corkscrew; and such like little mistakes. Given a happy party of young people, bent on enjoyment, these are trifles light as air, which serve rather to increase the fun than diminish it. But, on the other hand, the party may not all be young and merry; it may be very distasteful to some to have to suffer these inconveniences.

The easiest way to arrange that there should be nothing wanting, is to make out a menu, adding all the little etceteras. It is advisable to estimate quantities extravagantly, for nothing is more annoying than to find everything exhausted and guests hungry.

If the party is very large, and resources and efforts are to be pooled, it is best to plan the menu together. Whatever it is to be, it is worth remembering that appetites are sharper in the open air and it is advisable to estimate generous quantities. Whether it is a wayside snack or an elegant luncheon, an open-air meal should always be an occasion for good food.

Food to Take Out

SOUPS

A good way to begin an outdoor meal is with soup, chilled on a hot day, steaming hot and heart-warming on a cold one, especially if the rest of the food tends to be dry. A wide-necked thermos bottle with a screw top is ideal for carrying it in.

Remember that after a soup is chilled, its seasoning usually needs adjusting. Heat or cool your thermos by rinsing it with boiling or cold water before pouring in the soup either as hot or as cold as possible. Slip in a few pieces of ice with a cold one. The soups will remain hot or cold for up to 6 hours.

Minestrone

This soup provides a sustaining meal in itself for cold and windy occasions.

Every region of Italy and indeed every cook has his own version of this vegetable soup. Make it with the vegetables available. The following ingredients make a rather large quantity, enough for 12 servings.

1 onion
2 carrots
3 ribs celery
3 potatoes
2 fennel stems
3 zucchini
A few green beans
A few shelled green peas
2 cabbage leaves
2 cloves garlic, crushed
4 tablespoons oil
14-oz. (400-g.) can peeled tomatoes
10 cups (3 liters) chicken or
    meat stock

Salt and pepper
A few sprigs (finely chopped) of
    thyme, parsley, basil, marjoram,
    and mint*
1 1/8 lb. (1/2 kg.) coarse boiling
    sausage, skin removed and cut in
    thick slices, or 9 oz. (250 g.)
    bacon cut in thin strips
9 oz. (250 g.) white haricot beans
Chickpeas or large brown lentils
    cooked beforehand without any
    salt (canned may be used)
Juice of half a lemon
2 oz. (60 g.) grated Parmesan

*Use all or only 2 or 3 of these.

Peel or wash and trim the vegetables and chop them small. Warm the oil in a large saucepan and throw the vegetables in, in the order they are listed, allowing 2 minutes between each addition and stirring so they do not stick to the bottom. Now add the peeled tomatoes, stock, salt, and pepper. Cook gently for at least 2 hours, adding the herbs toward the end. Add the sausage or bacon, the beans, and the chickpeas or lentils. Add the lemon juice, adjust the seasoning, and cook until everything is soft and tender.

This quantity will fill several thermos bottles, so you may find it simpler to carry it in a large container in an insulated box with a hot pack. Put the grated Parmesan in a small screw-top jar to pass around when serving.

Lentil Soup with Bacon

Another heart-warming and sustaining soup.

1 large onion, finely chopped	2 qt. (2 liters) water or stock
2 tablespoons oil	Salt and pepper
3–4 slices bacon cut into very small strips	1 teaspoon ground cumin (optional)
	1 teaspoon ground coriander
1 1/8 lb. (1/2 kg.) red lentils	

Fry the onion gently in the oil in a large saucepan until well colored, stirring occasionally. Add the bacon and fry. Add the lentils and cover with water or stock. Bring to the boil and cook for an hour or until the lentils have disintegrated. Add salt and pepper and the cumin and coriander. Mash with a fork or with a potato masher. These lentils do not generally need to be pressed through a sieve. Add water or stock if too thick.

Harira / Moroccan Bean Soup

This makes a sustaining meal to take out on a cold day for 15 to 20 people. You may also like to add some meat cut into cubes. Carry in an insulated box with a hot pack or reheat on the spot.

1/2 lb. (225 g.) chickpeas	1 tablespoon turmeric or to taste
1/2 lb. (225 g.) haricot or other beans	Juice of 1 large lemon or more
1/2 lb. (225 g.) lentils	3–4 tablespoons flour
1 3/4 lb. (793 g.) peeled canned tomatoes	1 small bunch fresh coriander, finely chopped
1 1/8 lb. (1/2 kg.) onions, coarsely chopped	1 small bunch parsley, finely chopped
Salt and pepper to taste	1 teaspoon harissa (optional)

Pick over, wash, and soak the chickpeas, beans, and lentils for a few hours or overnight. Drain. Bring the first two to the boil in fresh cold water in a large pan and simmer until tender. Add the lentils and continue to cook until these are just tender. Add the tomatoes, cutting them up into small pieces, the onions and more water. Season to taste with salt and pepper. Add turmeric (some people use saffron instead) and lemon juice and simmer a further half hour.

In a small pan stir a pint of cold water gradually into the flour, beating constantly so as not to have any lumps. Add some strained liquid from the hot soup and stir over low heat until it begins to boil. The flour gives the soup a velouté (velvety) texture much loved in Morocco. Add the chopped coriander leaves and parsley and pour back into the soup.

Continue to cook until the pulses are soft and the taste is rich. Adjust the seasoning and add water if necessary. Add harissa if you like.

Cauliflower and Leek Soup with Cheese

1 medium cauliflower	Salt and pepper
3 leeks	A few sprigs of parsley, finely chopped
3 medium potatoes	1/4 lb. (100 g.) grated Cheddar
1 1/2 qt. (1 1/2 liters) chicken stock or water	A grating of nutmeg

Wash the cauliflower, remove the leaves, and cut into flowerets. Trim the leeks and wash them very well to remove all grit. Cut into pieces. Peel the potatoes and chop coarsely. Put the vegetables into a saucepan, cover with stock, and season with salt and pepper. Bring to the boil, then simmer for 20 to 30 minutes until the vegetables are tender. Put through a sieve or a blender and return the mixture to the pan. Add the parsley, the grated cheese, and nutmeg and heat up until the cheese has melted. (Milk may be used instead of the stock for a creamier version.)

Pour into a warmed thermos bottle.

Race Day Picnic

In *The Taste of Country Cooking* (Knopf, 1976), Edna Lewis remembers the good beef consommé they always made for a Race Day picnic.

Beautiful Montpelier, nestling in the Shenandoah Valley, surrounded by an oak forest, was the most perfect spot to have a great fall picnic lunch. Everyone would be dressed in the latest fashions to attend the races, even the handsome guest horses wearing the colorful silks of their stables. There was always excitement in the fresh November air and the good, hot, beef consommé seemed to build an appetite for all the good things to follow. There would be a cold roast of aged pheasant, a salad of lentils, fresh-picked scallions from the garden, and ham biscuits. And for dessert, thin slices of white pound cake, tangy ginger cookies, a basket of delicious Winesap apples, sweet dessert grapes, and juicy Kieffer pears, with a thermos of good, hot, black coffee.

Here is Edna Lewis's Virginia Country-Style Beef Consommé.

Virginia Country-Style Beef Consommé

5 1/2 lb. (2 1/2 kg.) bottom
   round beef
1 knuckle and shinbone
2 1/2 qt. (2 1/2 liters) cold water
2 chicken backs plus necks
1 large onion stuck with 4 cloves
2 carrots, sliced
1 large leek, top removed

1 bunch celery
1 tomato, peeled, seeded, and
   finely chopped
4 peppercorns
1 bouquet parsley and bay leaf
1/4 teaspoon thyme, fresh or dry
1 tablespoon salt

Preparing a good consommé today requires careful cooking of the ingredients. Meat hasn't the same flavor of years gone by. The best ingredients should go into a pot that you are going to cook in for 6 hours.

Place the beef and bones in a pot containing the water. Cover and bring to a slow simmer without ever letting the pot come to a boil. A gray scum will rise on the surface as it begins to heat up. This you skim off and discard. Continue to skim until it is no more. At this point add the chicken and vegetables, peppercorns, and herbs. About halfway through add salt. Cover loosely and barely simmer for 6 hours. Remove from burner, strain, and leave to cool. When cold, skim off all fat. This consommé can be served clear or used as the base for other soups, onion soup in particular.

After 2 hours of cooking, the celery may be removed and reserved for later. When the consommé has finished cooking, the meat may be removed and served later for supper with the celery.

Yogurt Soup

In the Middle East and India people love drinking yogurt diluted with iced water. With the addition of chopped cucumber, the drink becomes a soup.

1 cucumber, peeled and chopped	Pepper
Salt	6 fat spring onions, finely chopped
1 qt. (1 liter) plain yogurt	A sprig of mint, finely chopped
1 1/2 cups (450 ml.) water	A sprig of parsley, finely chopped

Sprinkle the cucumber with salt and let the juices drain away in a sieve for an hour. Beat the yogurt and water together with a fork. Season to taste with salt and pepper and add the rest of the ingredients. Chill, then pour into a cold thermos bottle, adding a few cubes of ice.

Variation: A less common alternative, which is a favorite of mine, is to make a mixture of 1 part sour cream and 3 parts yogurt. You may like to add, as they do in Iran, a handful of raisins.

Gazpacho

One of the most delightful and best-known iced soups, it is as popular in Portugal as it is in Spain.

1 1/8 lb. (1/2 kg.) tomatoes	2 cloves garlic, crushed
1 cucumber	4 tablespoons olive oil
2 green peppers	3 tablespoons wine vinegar
3 slices whole wheat bread, crusts removed (optional) or 3–4 tablespoons ground almonds (optional)	Salt and pepper
	3 tablespoons tomato purée
	Parsley, chives, mint, or sweet marjoram, finely chopped
1 small onion or a small bunch spring onions, chopped	1–2 cups (1/4–1/2 liter) water

Peel the tomatoes by pouring boiling water over them in a bowl. Wash the cucumber and the peppers; there is no need to peel them unless the cucumbers are waxed. Chop them up roughly, removing the seeds from the peppers. Bread gives the soup a more filling and peasantlike quality. If you are using it, soak it in water and squeeze dry. Put in the blender or food processor with the rest of the ingredients. Add only enough fresh cold water to blend to a light smooth cream (3 or 4 tablespoons of ground almonds are a good alternative to the whole wheat bread as a thickening). Chill. Pour into a cooled thermos bottle, adding a few ice cubes.

The usual garnish of finely chopped tomatoes, onions, cucumbers, and peppers may be dispensed with at a picnic, but you can always take them separately in a plastic box or screw-top jar.

Iced Cucumber Soup

1 1/2 cucumbers
1 medium onion or 5 spring onions
3 tablespoons butter
3 tablespoons flour
1 qt. (1 liter) jellied chicken stock

2/3 cup (150 ml.) light cream
Salt and pepper
2 tablespoons chives or mint, finely
    chopped (optional)

Peel and chop the cucumber coarsely, or you may leave the peel on for a greener appearance unless it is waxed. Chop the onion or spring onions. Melt the butter in a large saucepan and gently sauté the onions until they are soft but not colored. Add the flour and stir until well blended. Add the stock, a little at a time, beating vigorously with a wooden spoon. Bring to the boil, stirring constantly, and simmer for 15 minutes. Put in the blender or food processor with the cucumber and cream and blend to a smooth cream. Season to taste with salt and pepper and stir in the herbs. Chill before putting into a cold thermos bottle with a few ice cubes.

Cream of Avocado Soup

3 large avocados
Juice of 1 or 2 lemons
3 tablespoons butter
3 tablespoons flour

1 qt. (1 liter) jellied chicken stock
1 cup (1/4 liter) light cream
Salt and pepper

Purée the avocados with the lemon juice in a blender. Melt the butter in a large saucepan. Add the flour and stir until well blended. Add the stock gradually, stirring constantly until thickened and smooth. Remove from the heat and add the avocado purée and the cream, beating well. Season with salt and pepper. Chill and pour into a cooled thermos bottle just before you are ready to leave.

SANDWICHES

Bread has always proved a useful foundation for other food. In Tudor times meat was given out on thickly cut pieces, but it was not until 1762 that a filling was first pressed between two thin slices. The occasion was a 24-hour gambling session when John Montagu, fourth Earl of Sandwich, found this was a clean and handy way of eating without soiling the cards. At the beginning of the nineteenth century sandwiches left the card tables for the great outdoors. Easily wrapped and carried, they made the perfect meal in the pocket, so perfect that they soon became the ubiquitous horrors described by Osbert Sitwell as "slimy layers of paste like something out of the Ancient Mariner."

Most countries now have their own types of sandwiches with favorite breads and fillings, but nowhere are they as important or as varied as in America. A hurried nation, too busy to stop, has developed the ideal fast food into the perfect meal for luncheon, supper, and in between. Behind the counter as part of the delicatessen trade sandwiches also symbolize the Americanization of ethnic foods.

Although limp and soggy, "sawdust and spongy plastic" types are still turned out, there is no reason why a sandwich should not always be a delicious as well as a healthful gastronomic event. Every type of bread may be used: white, whole wheat, and grain, rye, pumpernickel and sourdough, white crusty rolls and soft egg rolls, toast, baps, sesame buns, long French baguettes, brioche, Italian bread, Indian naan, and Greek or Syrian pita, as well as nut and fruit breads. The secret is to use fresh bread, cut it carefully, and spread it with slightly softened, unsalted butter, and to be very generous with the filling. Sandwiches are best eaten as soon as they are made, but they keep well if wrapped in foil or plastic or in a damp towel.

English Sandwiches

Roast beef. In the old days they used to pound it. "What can be more appalling," said Mrs. Gardiner and Mrs. Steel in *The Complete Indian Housekeeper and Cook,* "than a bite at the usual sandwich, which either lands you with no meat at all, or leaves two disconsolate pieces of mustard-patched bread to lament the slice of tough beef which you are struggling to conceal from your neighbour."

In truth there is nothing better, provided that it is very juicy, tender, and rare, than a slice of roast beef. Mash some mustard or grated horseradish into the butter and garnish with cress or lettuce.

Salt beef or tongue may be treated in the same way.

Poach a fat kipper in water for 5 minutes. Drain, skin, and flake it. Mash it with 2 tablespoons lemon juice, 2 tablespoons butter, and 3 tablespoons light cream.

American Sandwiches

Americans have revolutionized the sandwich. They have turned the making of this item of diet which best suits their hurried lifestyle into an art. Their success lies in the generosity and quality of the filling, the happy marriage of meat, fish, salad, and all manner of ingredients, with condiments and sauces such as mayonnaise to keep them moist and juicy, and the variety of breads used.

Here is a selection of popular favorite fillings to press between two slices of good fresh well-buttered bread.

Corned Beef Sandwich. Pile 3 or 5 very thin slices of corned beef, cut while still warm, on buttered rye bread. Serve with mustard and dill pickle.

You may also add a slice of Swiss cheese or a tablespoon of chutney.

Tongue Sandwich. Pack several thin slices of tongue in buttered rye bread and serve with mustard or horseradish and dill pickle or chutney.

Hot Pastrami Sandwich. Pile 4 or 5 thin slices of pastrami, cut while still warm, on well-buttered pumpernickel or rye bread. Serve with mustard. If you are going far, wrap it in foil and carry it in an insulated bag or box, as it is best eaten warm.

Roast Beef Sandwich. This is much like the English version above, only much more generous with the slices of meat. Serve with mustard pickles.

Ham Sandwich. Use 2 or 3 slices of good, well-flavored ham cut thin, and spread if you like with English or French mustard or with Russian or thousand island dressing. Rye bread with caraway seeds is particularly compatible.

You may also cut the ham into shreds and combine it with mild cream cheese or grated Cheddar cheese.

For a deviled ham sandwich mix shredded ham with mayonnaise and if you like a little mustard and chopped pickles.

Chicken or Turkey Sandwich. Season 3 slices of chicken or turkey with salt and pepper and spread with mayonnaise. Top if you like with a lettuce leaf or watercress or with thinly sliced cucumber (salted and allowed to lose its juices for 30 minutes).

You may also chop the chicken or turkey, combine it with 1 tablespoon finely chopped celery, 1/2 hard-boiled egg, a few capers, and 2 chopped olives, and bind it with 2 tablespoons mayonnaise. It is also nice to add 1/4 teaspoon curry powder and 1 teaspoon chutney.

Bacon, Lettuce, and Tomato Sandwich. Use toasted white bread spread with mayonnaise. Fill with 3 slices of crisply fried bacon drained on a paper towel, topped with 4 tomato slices and a crisp lettuce leaf.

Salami, Mortadella, Bologna, or Liverwurst Sandwich. Pile 3 or 4 slices of one of these meats on dark, buttered rye or whole wheat bread. You may also spread with 1 teaspoon horseradish sauce, or 1 teaspoon mustard, or 1 tablespoon mayonnaise. Alternatively, add thin slices of tomato and pitted black olives and spread with cream cheese.

Smoked Salmon (Lox) and Cream Cheese Sandwich. Lay thin slices of lox over mild cream cheese on rye bread, dark pumpernickel, or bagels.

Tuna Fish or Salmon Sandwich. Mix 1/4 cup (60 ml.) canned flaked tuna or salmon with 2 tablespoons mayonnaise.

You may also add 1/2 hard-boiled egg, chopped, 1 tablespoon finely chopped celery or green pepper, and a squeeze of lemon juice.

Sardine Sandwich. Lay sardines whole on the bread topped with thin slices of hard-boiled egg and a little mayonnaise, or mash them with a little grated onion and lemon juice.

Onion Sandwich. Cut thin slices of onion and salt them until softened and mild. Spread with mayonnaise.

Cheese Sandwich. Mix 1 1/2 cups (355 ml.) shredded Cheddar or Swiss cheese with a teaspoon of pickle relish or chutney and 1/2 cup (120 ml.) mayonnaise. Spread onto the bread and top with shredded lettuce.

Cottage Cheese Sandwich. Mix 1 cup (240 ml.) cottage cheese with 3 tablespoons each of chopped pitted olives, chopped gherkin, chopped onion, and chopped red, green, or yellow pepper. Add 1 tablespoon chopped parsley and season to taste with salt and pepper.

Health Sandwich. Enough for two.

In a bowl mix 1/4 cup (60 ml.) each of grated carrots, bean sprouts, shredded lettuce, shredded white cabbage, shredded radish, and chopped tomatoes. Add 2 tablespoons raisins and 2 tablespoons walnuts or pecans and dress with the juice of half an orange and half a lemon. Pack between slices of whole grain bread.

Reuben Sandwich. Use pumpernickel or sour rye bread. Lay 1 slice of Swiss or Gruyère cheese on a slice of corned beef and heap 3 tablespoons sauerkraut on top. Spread with 1 1/2 tablespoons Russian dressing and cover with another slice of corned beef or a thin slice of chicken or turkey breast. Toast the sandwich, wrap quickly in foil, and keep warm in an insulated bag or box.

Club Sandwich. This many-layered sandwich is now popular in cafés and bars all over the world. Some like to serve it as a triple decker with 3 slices of toast, but it is perhaps more successfully eaten with only 2.

For a picnic it is good to bring all the ingredients, cut into slices and seasoned with salt and pepper where necessary, in separate boxes to be assembled by everyone for themselves on the spot. Toast many slices of bread, and butter them in advance.

This is how you make a club sandwich: Spread one slice of buttered toast with a little mayonnaise, then place on it a crisp lettuce leaf, 3 or 4 thin slices of cooked chicken or turkey breast, 3 slices of tomato, 3 slices of bacon, fried crisp and drained on a paper towel, with a few dabs of mayonnaise in between each layer, and cover with a second slice of toast. Cut in quarters diagonally and serve with olives and pickles. In France this usually comes on a bed of mustard and cress.

Hero, Submarine, Hoagie, or Grinder. This is best made on the spot with Italian or French bread loaves cut into individual 6-in. (15-cm.) pieces. Bring all the ingredients presliced or shredded and assemble to taste at the picnic.

Split the bread lengthwise, butter, and, if you like, spread with mayonnaise and mustard. Fill with overlapping slices of Cheddar, Swiss, fontina, and provolone cheese and a choice of the following meats: salami, capocollo, mortadella, bologna, or ham. Cover with sliced tomatoes, thin onion rings, pickle slices, ribbons of baked or raw green or red peppers, pitted olives, and shredded lettuce. Let everyone choose what he or she likes.

Meatball Hero.   *(Enough for 4)*

1 1/8 lb. (1/2 kg.) ground beef	2 tablespoons light vegetable oil
1/2 cup (125 ml.) dried	1 onion, finely chopped
bread crumbs	3/4 cup (180 ml.) tomato paste
1 clove garlic, crushed	2 1/2 cups (590 ml.) canned
2 tablespoons finely	peeled tomatoes
chopped parsley	Two 12-in. (30-cm.) loaves
1 tablespoon finely chopped basil	French bread
1 lightly beaten egg	1/2 cup (125 ml.) grated Parmesan
Salt and pepper	

Combine the beef, bread crumbs, garlic, herbs, egg, salt, and pepper. Work well with your hands and roll into small 1 1/2-in. (4-cm.) balls. Heat the oil in a saucepan, add the onion, and fry, stirring, for about 2 minutes. Add the meatballs and brown them all over, then stir in the tomato paste and pour in the peeled tomatoes. Season with salt and pepper and cook, covered, for about 30 minutes. Split the bread lengthwise, arrange meatballs cut in half along the length, and cover with sauce. Sprinkle with Parmesan cheese and press the top half of bread on top.

Muffuletta. This Italian sandwich from New Orleans is made with a round Italian loaf, about 10 in. (25 cm.) wide, packed so full that it becomes about 3 in. (8 cm.) high. It is large enough for two.

   Mix about 1/4 cup (60 ml.) each chopped stuffed green olives, chopped black Greek olives, and chopped Italian pickles. Dress with a mixture of 6 tablespoons olive oil, 1 tablespoon vinegar, 1 or 2 crushed garlic cloves, 1 tablespoon finely chopped parsley, 1 teaspoon oregano, salt, and pepper.

   Cut the loaf across right through and pour the dressing over each half to moisten the bread well. Pile layers of thinly sliced Italian salami, chopped Italian salad, thinly sliced provolone cheese, and Italian ham on the bottom half, and cover with the top half.

Poor Boy. This New Orleans–style sandwich can be made with anything from hamburgers and garlicky fried potatoes to fish and crabmeat, but the standard roast beef sandwich is the best version. The rich gravy that soaks through the bread is the best part.

   If you can make this on the spot and warm the bread up in foil over a fire it will be all the better; otherwise it will still be good.

   Cut a very fresh (warmed if possible) French loaf in half. Spread the bottom with 1/2 cup (125 ml.) mayonnaise, pile on 1 cup shredded lettuce, and lay 6 thin overlapping slices of roast beef on top. Pour 1/2 cup (125 ml.) meat gravy over them and top with 1 or 2 thin slices of tomato. Cover with the top half of the bread.

M. F. K. Fisher's Thoughts on Sandwiches

They can be indescribably bad. They can also, as any practical person knows, be the true opposite, given the right ingredients and the right time and place. Picnics can be right. So can a warm living room, and so can a small cold French railroad station at dawn, if one reaches down in the steamy gassy air toward a little buffet wagon trundling along the quay, and brings up a sandwich made of a fresh long roll with ham dangling out of it and good butter to hold it together.

Our family has combined the last two elements of protected hearthside and touristic nostalgia to invent a Railroad Sandwich which, we feel with smug modesty, is perfection. The recipe would be almost scandalous to print in proper form, involving as it does certain elements of live human flesh, but I can sketch a commendable outline, I hope. For one Railroad Sandwich, always referred to by its full name with some reverence, buy a loaf of the best procurable "French" bread at least eighteen inches long to serve perhaps six people. Have on hand at least a half pound of sweet butter, not too cold to spread, and an equally generous pound or so of the highest quality of sliced boiled ham. A pot of mustard of the Dijon type is indicated to add an optional fillip. Slice the loaf from end to end in two solid pieces, and then carefully remove all you can of the inner crumbs. *All!* Spread the two hollow shells generously with butter, and with judicious smears of mustard if desired. Lay upon the lower half of the loaf plenty of ham slices, overlapping thickly. Tuck them in a little at the edges, but not too neatly: a fringe is picturesque to some people, and pleasantly reminiscent; to my family it is essential. Put the two halves firmly together, and wrap them loosely in plastic or foil or wax paper, and then a clean towel. Then, and this is the Secret Ingredient, call upon a serene onlooker (a broad or at least positive beam adds to the quick results, and here I do not refer to a facial grimace but to what in other dialects is called a behind-*derrière*-bum-ass-seat-etc.) to sit gently but firmly upon this loaf for *at least* twenty minutes. One of the best of our sitters over some twenty years of assistance was Bonnie Prince Charlie Newton, built like a blade of grass during those useful and far-gone years, but with a curiously potent electricity between his little beam and the loaf, almost like infrared cookery. He could make the noble sandwich flat without squirming on it, and melt the butter and marry it to the mustard and the crisp shattered crusts, better than anybody. Even without this charmer, though, a Railroad can be a fine thing, cut upon rescue into thick oblique slices and given the esoteric ingredients: first a long loaf of French bread, then . . . then. . . .

Of course it is usually possible to fake edible sandwiches from supermarket supplies, especially if one can count on animal hunger to dull perception of the cheating, but there is nothing like good bread, to begin with. It should be of firm texture, and at least a day out of the oven in the presliced stuff we are growing used to. The filling should be of good quality, and should be spread or laid right to the sides of the foundation, and even spill over a little if feasible, rather than lie lumpishly in the middle. Sometimes sandwiches are good made with mayonnaise instead of butter, with chicken for instance . . . and here I mean real mayonnaise, although I have often settled for the boughten kind in jars, and some people insist they prefer it. Common sense is called for, always: lettuce will wilt and be slippery if it waits too long, and many people despise it with bread; jam will make everything stained and soggy unless it is curbed by ample butter spread evenly on both slices. . . .

French Bread

The long crisp bread, cut in four then split through lengthways, buttered generously, and filled even more generously with pâté, rillettes, saucisson, ham, or cheese, has long been popular.

Here are some alternatives recently brought from across the Channel.

For a fishy mixture combine the contents of a can of sardines (bones removed) and a small can of tuna with half their weight in butter. Add 3 teaspoons anchovy paste, a good squeeze of lemon or 2 tablespoons wine vinegar, 2 tablespoons finely chopped onion, and 2 tablespoons finely chopped parsley. Work it all to a paste. You can also add 2 mashed hard-boiled egg yolks or a few chopped pickled gherkins.

Another fishy mixture is finely shredded crab with a little chopped anchovy and capers, all bound together with a light mayonnaise.

Pan Bagnat

More an hors d'œuvre–stuffed loaf than a salad sandwich, it is from the Provençal coast of the Mediterranean and as common there as the game of boules.

Usually made in a baguette (a long French loaf), it is equally good in a round flat country loaf or in small individual bread rolls. Prepare at least 2 hours before but preferably the day before.

2 baguettes or 6 rolls	1 large Spanish onion or 1 small
2/3 cup (150 ml.) olive oil	bunch spring onions
4 tablespoons wine vinegar	2 green peppers
Salt and pepper	1/2 cup (125 g./4 oz.) pitted
1 clove garlic, pressed (optional)	black olives
1 1/8 lb. (1/2 kg.) tomatoes	1 3/4-oz. (45-g.) can anchovy fillets

Cut the loaves or rolls in half across. Generously sprinkle the inside of each with a vinaigrette of olive oil and vinegar seasoned with salt, pepper, and garlic. Cut the tomatoes, onion, and peppers into thin slices. Lay on the bottom halves of the bread. Garnish with olives and anchovy fillets and cover with the top halves of the bread. Press well together and wrap tightly in aluminum foil. Leave in a cool place with a weight on top long enough for the juices and oils to be well absorbed. To serve, cut into slices (if using a round loaf, cut in wedges like a cake).

Danish Open Sandwiches

These are a good idea, as you can assemble them on the spot to everyone's individual taste. They should be beautiful to look at with very little bread and plenty of filling. Take a selection of sliced cold meats in a box, fill another with crisp fresh lettuce and raw vegetables, all washed and clean, and another with seafood and salted or pickled fish. You may also want cheeses, hard-boiled eggs, relishes, and sauces. Bring salt and pepper, mustard, lemons, mayonnaise, and pickles. Arrange the components carefully, starting with a thin flat base.

Pita

I am bound to have an affection for the flat hollow bread of my childhood. But now everyone has discovered its versatility—not least the children.

Cut in half, pita bread makes the two perfect pockets which are the traditional holders of shish kebab and the now ubiquitous donner: meats grilled on skewers or on a spit, with their toppings of mixed salad. In fact they can and do hold almost anything. In the Middle East, most things sold on the street, from meatballs to whole beans, salads, and pickles, are dropped in the pouches by vendors.

A friend who gives a picnic on Primrose Hill for at least fifty people every year stacks piles of cut pita before a dizzy array of salads and beans, cheeses, eggs, and canned and pickled fish. Everyone fills their own pitas and comes back for more.

It is the ideal picnic bread which does away with cutlery and plates. Warm it up, if you can, just before you need it; it is not nearly so good cold. If it is dry moisten with water, wrap in aluminum foil, and leave for a moment in the oven or over a gentle fire.

Fill with whatever you like. In Egypt they pour in "ful medames" (small brown beans), adding a hard-boiled egg cut up into pieces. In Israel with falafel—fried rissoles of mashed chickpeas topped with salad and tahina (see p. 86)—it is the national meal in the hand. My children fill pita with tuna and olives and slices of tomato, cucumber, and onion sprinkled with a dressing.

Indians, Arabs, and Italians all make flat pies of bread dough baked together with a variety of traditional stuffings. It is simple enough to make these fillings and to slip them into a ready-made pita through a slit on the side or by cutting it in half. Bring them filled to the picnic and warm them up on a gentle fire, preferably wrapped in foil.

An Indian mashed potato filling. Fry half a chopped onion in a little butter and mix with 2 boiled mashed potatoes. Add a few chopped coriander leaves or a little parsley, a good squeeze of lemon juice, 1/4 teaspoon paprika, a pinch of cayenne and of ground ginger, 1 teaspoon crushed coriander, fennel, or aniseed, and 1/2 teaspoon garam masala (see p. 191). Salt to taste and stir well.

An Indian cauliflower filling. Boil a small cauliflower until it is very tender; boil separately a handful of green peas until they are really soft. Drain. Chop the cauliflower fine and lightly crush the peas. Mix together and add your favorite aromatics: some finely chopped herbs, salt and pepper, cayenne or ground chilies if you like it hot, and a teaspoon of cumin, coriander, or garam masala.

Lahma bi ajeen, an Arab minced meat filling. Soften 1 1/8 lb. (1/2 kg.) finely chopped onions in a little oil. Add 2/3 lb. (3/4 kg.) lean minced beef, and fry, stirring, until it has changed color. Add 1 lb. 12 oz. (800 g.) of canned peeled tomatoes, drained and mashed, 1 small can tomato purée, 1 teaspoon sugar, 1 teaspoon allspice, the juice of half a lemon, a small bunch of parsley (finely chopped), salt to taste, a pinch of cayenne pepper, and Worcestershire sauce.

Eggplant filling. Put a layer of thin, fried eggplant slices over a layer of thin slices of a good melting cheese, such as Gruyère or Cheddar. Sprinkle with black pepper and a touch of grated nutmeg.

Pizza-type fillings. Press into the pouch of bread combinations of tomatoes (sliced fresh ones or mashed canned ones), slices of mozzarella or other good melting cheeses, pitted olives, anchovy fillets, thin salami slices, seafood, or strips of cooked ham. The result is close to the stuffed pizzas from the region of Calabria which contain the filling inside a covered bread dough pie. They are good cold, but even better hot. You can wrap each in foil, heat in a moderate oven until the cheese melts, and pack in a hot box. Otherwise make a fire on the spot and warm them up in the foil.

VEGETABLE
AND OTHER DIPS

With the advent of the food processor many people have been tempted to mash things to a paste and to convert them into mousses and molds with the addition of beaten egg whites or gelatin.

A few vegetables that have recently become fashionable as dips at cocktail parties have been puréed for centuries by chopping and pounding because the treatment really suited them. These creams make an admirable first course and are ideal to dip into with pieces of bread or a cracker while waiting for the rest of the meal to cook on the fire. There are also recipes for Tapenade and Olivade on page 145.

Bruce Aidells' Creole Herbed Cheese *(for more than 6)*

Serve this with vegetable crudités, crackers, or bread.

1 small red bell pepper, finely chopped	1/2 teaspoon cayenne pepper
1 small green bell pepper, finely chopped	1/4 teaspoon sage
	1/4 teaspoon thyme
1 rib celery, finely chopped	1 teaspoon coarsely ground
4 green onions, finely chopped	black pepper
2 tablespoons butter	1 teaspoon Hungarian paprika
1 tablespoon tomato paste	1/2 cup (120 ml.) chopped parsley
2 cloves garlic	Salt and pepper to taste
1 1/8 lb. (1/2 kg.) cream cheese	

Sweat the peppers, celery, and green onions in butter and let cool. Purée the vegetable mixture in a food processor with tomato paste and garlic and add cream cheese, spices, parsley, salt, and pepper to the paste. Allow to cool.

Guacamole / Avocado Cream

In Mexico, where the fruit originates, there are innumerable versions of this hors d'œuvre, which also makes a good sauce for chicken, boiled meats, and fish.

Peel and mash 2 large ripe avocados. Add 1 or 2 finely chopped green chilies, the juice of 1/2 or 1 whole lime or lemon, salt and freshly ground pepper to taste, and a pinch of sugar.

Variation: You may leave it as it is or add a peeled, seeded, and chopped tomato, a few finely chopped spring onions, a small grated onion or a clove of garlic, crushed, and a small handful of finely chopped fresh coriander leaves (the Mexicans' favorite herb). Beat in a few drops of olive oil.

For some reason it is widely thought that leaving the pit of the avocado in the cream will prevent it from tarnishing; I believe that lemon juice does this better.

Cover the bowl if you will not be eating it straight away.

Eggplant Purée

This is the "poor man's caviar" of the Middle East, an appellation it well deserves.

3 large eggplants	Juice of 1 lemon or more
3–4 tablespoons olive oil	Salt and pepper to taste

GARNISH (optional)

Onion, finely chopped	Fresh mint leaves, chopped
Parsley, chopped	

Grill the eggplants until their skin is black and blisters. As soon as you can handle them, peel off the skins, squeeze out some of the juices, and mash the pulp with a fork. Season with plenty of olive oil, lemon juice, salt, and pepper. Use a blender or a food processor to make a smooth cream. Garnish with a little finely chopped onion and plenty of chopped parsley and fresh mint leaves.

Variations: A good alternative to this basic appetizer is to add plenty of yogurt and a touch of pressed garlic. You may also add 2 tomatoes, peeled and chopped.

Bean Purées from the Middle East

Each country of the Islamic world has a favorite bean to make those sharply seasoned creams which are the invariable accompaniment to grilled meats and indeed to most things. Chickpeas are the base of hummus, which has been adopted as the national dish of Israel. All types of beans and lentils can be used. They must be soaked, drained, simmered in fresh water (salt being added when they are already tender), and cooked until very soft. They are then pounded to a pulp or put through a blender or food processor with enough of their cooking water to make a thick cream.

After that the fun begins, for it is one of those foods that is made by repeated tasting and adding. Some ingredients are constant: plenty of olive oil, lemon juice, garlic, salt, and pepper, though quantities vary. Spices depend on the region, the usual ones being ground cumin, coriander, and cayenne (put in a lot of this pepper if you like it fiery).

Garnish with chopped parsley or coriander leaves and a dribble of olive oil.

Serve with pita bread.

A very popular combination is a mixture of chickpea purée and tahina (see p. 86).

Boiled Carrot Salad Dip

This is a fiery Moroccan salad. Make it with old carrots, which taste better. Add the flavorings gradually, to taste. The color is beautiful. Serve as a dip with bread or bits of raw vegetables.

1 1/8 lb. (1/2 kg.) carrots	3 tablespoons wine vinegar
Salt and pepper	4 tablespoons olive oil
1/2–1 teaspoon harissa or	2 cloves garlic, pressed
1 teaspoon paprika	1/4–1/2 teaspoon ground ginger
A good pinch of cayenne pepper	A few green or black olives to garnish
1–2 teaspoons cumin	

Peel the carrots and boil in salted water until very soft. Drain and mash with a fork in a bowl and stir in the rest of the ingredients (except olives), or better still turn to a smooth purée in a blender.

Serve cold garnished with a few olives.

Variation: Alternative additional flavorings are 2 tablespoons honey and 1 teaspoon cinnamon.

Taramasalata

This is not the traditional recipe for the Greek fish roe salad, but I prefer it to the original and it fares better on a hot day.

1/4 mild Spanish onion
1/2 lb. (225 g.) smoked cod roe
Juice of 1 lemon

1/2 lb. (225 g.) cream cheese
  or ricotta

Put the onion through a blender or food processor. Add the cod roe, washed
but not skinned—the skin accentuates the color of the dip and does not harm
the texture—add lemon juice, and blend to a smooth paste. Add cream cheese
or ricotta and blend for a few seconds only until properly mixed. (If left too
long, the cream becomes too liquid.)

Mousse de Caviare

1 1/2 oz. (40 g.) unsalted butter
4 oz. (115 g.) red caviar (lumpfish roe
  will do)
2/3 cup (160 ml.) sour cream

4 teaspoons lemon juice
Black pepper
Salt
2 egg whites

Melt the butter over a double boiler and blend it with the caviar, sour cream,
lemon juice, and pepper. Put in the refrigerator for an hour. Salt the egg
whites and beat them until very stiff. Add lightly to the caviar mixture and
put back in the refrigerator.

Variations: Instead of 4 teaspoons lemon juice, use 2 teaspoons each of lemon
juice and vodka; or 1 tablespoon lemon juice and 1 teaspoon aquavit; or use
some white bread soaked in milk instead of the egg whites (or nothing at all,
if you are happy with the volume as it is).

PÂTÉS, TERRINES, GALANTINES, MOUSSES, AND CHOPPED LIVERS

Terrines, pâtés, galantines, and rillettes are part of our dreams of French
parties de plaisir. Monet and Manet, Watteau, Tissot and Renoir, and Fer-
nand Léger have depicted them with good bread and plenty of wine on white
tablecloths spread on the grass beneath leafy trees.

Meat mixtures blended to smoothness or chopped to coarseness, delicately spiced and flavored with wines and spirits, have always been French
picnic favorites. They are much easier to make than they seem, and there are

endless possibilities involving a variety of meats, chicken, and game. Here are a few recipes, but for those who wish to expand further their knowledge of the art of charcuterie there is no better guide than Jane Grigson's *The Art of Making Sausages, Pâtés, and Other Charcuterie*.

Terrine de Campagne   *(for more than 6)*

1 1/8 lb. (1/2 kg.) fat belly of pork, medium ground or chopped

1 1/8 lb. (1/2 kg.) lean veal, medium ground or chopped

1 1/8 lb. (1/2 kg.) pig, beef, or calf's liver, trimmed of sinews and skin and finely ground or chopped

2 oz. (60 g.) pork back fat or fat bacon, chopped

1/2–1 tablespoon salt

1/2 teaspoon pepper or 6 peppercorns, crushed

1/2 teaspoon thyme

1/2 teaspoon allspice

1/2 teaspoon nutmeg

1–2 cloves garlic, pressed

5 tablespoons Cognac

3 tablespoons white wine

2 large eggs

6 juniper berries (optional)

To line the terrine: slices of pork fat or fat bacon or caul fat

Mix all raw meats and the other ingredients very thoroughly. Cook a little bit of the mixture and then taste for salt and other seasonings, remembering that when a pâté is cold, the flavors will be muted.

Line the bottom and sides of a terrine (large enough to hold them or about 6-cup capacity) with strips of pork fat, bacon, or caul fat, leaving aside a few for the top, and fill with the meat mixture. Cover with the remaining strips of fat. Place the terrine in a baking tray filled with water and bake uncovered in a preheated 320°F (160°C) oven for 1 1/2 hours or until the pâté begins to shrink away from the sides of the dish and the surrounding liquid has no more trace of pink. (The inside should be pink and moist—not gray and dry.) Take it out of the oven and let it cool. To make it compact and easier to cut it should be weighted down. Cover the top with foil or greaseproof paper, top with a flat piece of something that fits inside the terrine, and place a heavy weight on top. Put in the refrigerator with the weight. The pâté is best eaten after 3 days, but if you want to keep it for more than a week, cover the cold terrine with a good layer of melted pork or pour aspic (p. 87) over it. It will keep the pâté moist.

If you want to serve the terrine unmolded, put it in a bowl of hot water to loosen the bottom and run a knife around the sides of the dish, then turn upside down onto a platter. If it doesn't come out dip the bottom of the terrine in hot water for a few seconds. To serve cut into thick slices.

Variations: You may use minced duck, chicken, rabbit, or hare instead of veal. Or you may add to the mixture diced pieces of these meats or cooked ham or tongue.

Rabbit Pâté   *(for more than 6)*

3–4-lb. (1 1/2–2-kg.) rabbit, with liver
2 lb. (1 kg.) chicken livers
1/2 cup (120 ml.) brandy
1 cup (235 ml.) Madeira
2 shallots, chopped

2 tablespoons kosher salt
2 teaspoons black pepper
1 teaspoon thyme
1 teaspoon quatre épice

THE STOCK

1 carrot
1 whole onion plus 1 cup chopped or
   diced onions
2 ribs celery
4 tablespoons (60 g.) butter
1 1/2 lb. (675 g.) garlic sausage
1/2 lb. (225 g.) slab bacon
1/2 lb. (225 g.) chicken giblets
1/2 lb. (225 g.) salt pork
1 1/8 lb. (1/2 kg.) pork or bacon rind,
   boiled until soft
2 eggs

1 1/8 lb. (1/2 kg.) smoked ham, cut in
   1/2-in. (1 1/4-cm.) dice
1 teaspoon savory
1 tablespoon crushed juniper berries
1 teaspoon sage
To line the terrine: caul fat, bacon, or
   sliced fatback
1 cup (250 ml.) shelled pistachios
Thyme
Sage
Savory
Cornichons

Remove all the meat from the rabbit and cut the fillet meat into strips. Marinate the strips, rabbit liver, and half the chicken livers in 2 tablespoons of the brandy, 1/4 cup of the Madeira, and shallots. Add a pinch of the salt, pepper, thyme, and quatre épice. Cover and set aside for at least a couple of hours.

Meanwhile, make a stock by covering the rabbit bones with cold water. Bring to a boil and remove the scum. Add the carrot, whole onion, and celery and simmer for 1 hour or longer. Remove the bones and vegetables, and reduce the liquid to 1/2 cup. In a small skillet, sauté the chopped onions in the butter until soft.

Using a fine grind on the meat grinder or a food processor, grind the remaining rabbit meat, sausage, slab bacon, giblets, salt pork, pork or bacon rind, sautéed onions, and the rest of the chicken livers.

In a large bowl combine well the ground meat mixture, the stock, eggs, diced ham, spices, and the remaining brandy and Madeira. Line a 6-cup loaf pan or terrine with the sliced fat, reserving enough to cover the top. Place half the ground meat mixture in the terrine. Now place the marinated whole livers down the center and on either side lay in the strips of rabbit fillet. Pour over all of this the marinade. Sprinkle in the pistachios and cover with the remaining meat mixture. Seal the terrine with the fat, and sprinkle with thyme, sage, and savory. Wrap the mold in foil and place in a pan with water halfway up the sides.

Bake in a 350°F (180°C) preheated oven for 2 1/2 to 3 hours or until the pâté registers 160°F (70°C) on a meat thermometer.

Cool overnight. Slice and serve with cornichons.

Sweetbread Terrine   *(for more than 6)*

This is quite a delicacy. Make it two days ahead.

1 1/2 calf's sweetbreads	4 tablespoons white wine
1/2 medium onion, finely chopped	2 eggs
2 tablespoons butter	1/2 teaspoon cinnamon
Salt and white pepper	1/4 teaspoon ground ginger
To line the terrine: thin slices of lard	1/4 teaspoon allspice
or fat bacon or caul	2 bay leaves
1 1/8 lb. (1/2 kg.) veal, minced	1/2 teaspoon thyme
1/2 lb. (1/4 kg.) lean pork, minced	1 cup (250 ml.) aspic
3/4 lb. (3/8 kg.) pork fat, minced	(p. 87), melted
2 tablespoons Cognac	

Soak the sweetbreads in cold water for 2 hours, changing the water twice, then bring them to the boil in fresh water in a saucepan and simmer 2 minutes. Drain and rinse with cold water (this is to keep them firm). Pull off the rubbery sinews. Now press between two trays covered by a clean cloth, put a weight on top, and leave them for several hours. This gets rid of the undesirable pink liquid which gives them a rubbery texture.

Fry the onion in the butter until softened, add the sweetbreads, season with salt and pepper, and cook gently for 10 minutes, turning them over once. Line a round terrine entirely with the lard or bacon slices or caul, letting these hang out over the edges.

For the forcemeat stuffing, put the two meats and fat through a processor or have them minced fine. Work well together and add Cognac, wine, eggs, spices, and salt and pepper.

Spread layers of stuffing and sweetbreads in the terrine, starting and ending with the meat stuffing. Press down. Bring the lard or bacon slices or caul to rest over the meat. Lay the bay leaves on top and sprinkle with thyme. Cover with foil, put in a tray filled with water, and bake in a 325°F (165°C) oven for 1 hour, then reduce the heat to 300°F (150°C) and bake for 2 hours longer. Remove from the oven and pour the aspic into the terrine. Let it cool, then refrigerate.

Terrine aux Légumes

This light vegetable terrine, which can be cooked a day in advance and served cold, is one of the popular dishes taught by American Linda Gassenheimer at her London cooking school.

2 lb. (1 kg.) fresh spinach or frozen
    chopped spinach
2 tablespoons butter
2 eggs
1 tablespoon cream

1/2 cup (120 ml.) diced carrots,
    parboiled for 10 minutes
1/2 cup (120 ml.) elbow macaroni,
    cooked al dente and well drained

THE BÉCHAMEL SAUCE

3 cups (3/4 liter) milk infused with 2
    parsley stalks
2–3 peppercorns
1 bay leaf
Small slice of onion

1 blade mace
2 tablespoons (30 g.) butter
3 tablespoons (21 g.) flour
Salt and pepper
Nutmeg

Wash and trim the spinach and place in a pot with about 1/4 cup (60 ml.) water. Cook until tender and drain thoroughly. Chop in a food processor or pass through a food mill. Place the butter in the pan and return the chopped spinach to the pan to dry it out.

Prepare the béchamel: Gently simmer the milk with the parsley stalks, peppercorns, bay leaf, onion, and mace. In a separate pan melt the butter and remove from the heat. Blend in the flour to give a slack roux. Pour the strained tepid milk into the roux all at once. Stir over the heat until the sauce is thick and glossy. Cook a few minutes to cook the flour. Add salt and pepper and nutmeg to taste.

Beat the eggs and cream into the sauce. Taste for seasoning. Add more salt, pepper, and nutmeg if necessary. Mix in the spinach, carrots, and cooked macaroni and pour into a buttered terrine. Stand in a bain marie filled with boiling water. Poach in this way in a 325°F (165°C) oven for 50 to 60 minutes or until firm to the touch.

To serve, let stand until cool; cover and refrigerate. Slice from the terrine. Or if you prefer, slip a knife around the edge of the terrine and unmold and slice.

Hint: If unmolding the terrine, butter the terrine and place a piece of grease-proof or waxed paper in the bottom and butter the paper. This will help it to unmold more easily.

Chicken Galantine   *(for more than 6)*

This is really more a sausage than a galantine. The boning is easier and does not have to be perfect. Raisins or sultanas give it an unusual flavor.

1 large roasting chicken	Salt and pepper

THE FORCEMEAT STUFFING

3/4 lb. (3/8 kg.) lean veal, finely minced	1/2 teaspoon allspice
3/4 lb. (3/8 kg.) lean pork, finely minced	4 tablespoons Cognac
1/2 lb. (1/4 kg.) pork fat, finely minced	2 eggs
1/4 lb. (125 g.) ham, coarsely diced	2 tablespoons raisins or sultanas
1 1/2 teaspoons salt	3 tablespoons pistachios, very
Pepper	coarsely chopped

THE BROTH

1 carrot, cut into pieces	1/4 teaspoon thyme
1 onion, cut into pieces	4 cloves
1 rib celery, sliced	Salt and pepper
A few parsley stalks	3/4 cup (180 ml.) Madeira
2 bay leaves	

Cut off the chicken wings, pull out the wishbone, and, placing the chicken on its breast, cut down the backbone. Then, following the carcass with a sharp knife, cut the meat away from the bone. Cut the joint at the shoulder, then on top and around the breastbone and down on the other side. Remove the carcass. Cut around the thighbones and pull them away from the meat. Remove the meat from the wings. With this, and any bits scraped off the carcass, line the skin where there is no meat. Season with salt and pepper.

Make the stuffing. Put the meats through a food processor or work well with your hands until well blended and a smooth paste. Work in the rest of the stuffing ingredients.

Place the open chicken on a wet cheesecloth, skin side down, spread the forcemeat evenly on top, and bring the sides of the chicken together over it. Then pull the skin from both ends (top and bottom) over to enclose the stuffing. Roll up, wrapping the chicken into a tight sausagelike bundle in the cheesecloth. Tie the ends and center firmly with string. Put in a large saucepan with the broth ingredients and the chicken carcass. Bring to the boil, remove any scum, and simmer for 2 hours, adding water when necessary. Let the chicken cool in the broth, then lift it out, unwrap it, and put it in a long earthenware mold. (It is usually pressed down overnight by a weight at this stage, but this step can be eliminated.) Strain the cold stock to remove the fat, then boil it down to reduce it to about 1 1/2 cups (355 ml.) of good jelly. Pour it over the chicken and refrigerate.

To serve, cut into 1/2-in. (1 1/2-cm.) slices and garnish with the chopped-up jelly.

Cold Beef, Ham, and Prawn Sausage   (for more than 6)

This "carne fiambre"—cold beef, ham, and prawn (or shrimp) sausage—of the Dominican Republic is from Elisabeth Lambert Ortiz's *The Complete Book of Caribbean Cooking*. This is a traditional dish for a *día del campo* (picnic) or for an outdoor Sunday buffet luncheon. It is served with pickled cucumbers, pimiento-stuffed olives, and lettuce and tomatoes with an oil and vinegar dressing.

1 1/8 lb. (1/2 kg.) lean ground beef
4 oz. (115 g.) lean, boneless ham,
   coarsely chopped
1/2 lb. (225 g.) large raw prawns or
   shrimp, shelled, deveined, and
   coarsely chopped
1 medium onion, coarsely chopped
1 clove garlic, coarsely chopped
1 fresh hot red or green pepper,
   seeded and chopped

Salt and freshly ground pepper
2 eggs
Saltine crackers
1/3 cup (80 ml.) tiny frozen
   peas, defrosted
1 egg, well beaten, for coating
1 onion, sliced
Bay leaf

Put the ground beef, ham, prawns, onion, garlic, and hot pepper through the finest blade of a meat grinder. Or, chop everything as fine as possible and combine. Season to taste with salt and pepper. Add the 2 eggs, one at a time, mixing thoroughly. Coarsely crumble enough crackers to make about 1 1/2 cups (450 g.), then crush with a rolling pin. Beat the crackers, 1/2 cup (150 g.) at a time, into the meat mixture with a wooden spoon, until the texture is smooth. It should not be sloppy, but firm enough to hold its shape. Use only the amount of cracker crumbs necessary. Last of all, fold in the peas as gently as possible. Shape the mixture into a roll about 10 in. (25 cm.) long and about 3 in. (8 cm.) in diameter.

Cover a piece of waxed paper generously with more cracker crumbs. Roll the sausage in the crumbs so that it is thickly coated all over. Roll it in the beaten egg, then roll it again in more cracker crumbs to coat thickly. Center the sausage on a double thickness of cheesecloth. Wrap the cheesecloth lengthwise over the sausage to enclose it completely. Tie the ends securely with kitchen string. In the old days, the sausage would have been sewn into a kitchen cloth, but cheesecloth does just as well.

Place the sausage in a heavy, covered casserole large enough to hold it comfortably. Add the sliced onion and the bay leaf, and enough water to cover the sausage by about 2 in. (5 cm.). Bring to the boil, reduce the heat to a simmer, cover, and cook for about an hour, or until the sausage is firm to the touch. Lift out of the casserole by the cheesecloth ends and allow to cool. Remove the cheesecloth and place the sausage on a large platter. The cracker crumbs and beaten egg will have formed an attractive outside coating. Cut into 1/2-in. (1 1/2-cm.) slices to serve.

Saucisson en Brioche

Linda Gassenheimer, who teaches cooking in London, gave this recipe.

1 French sausage in one long piece about 8 in. (20 cm.) long and 2 1/2 in. (6 1/2 cm.) in diameter	1/2 teaspoon sugar
	3 1/4 cups (420 g.) flour
	1/4 teaspoon salt
	5 tablespoons (75 g.) sugar
1/2 oz. (15 g.) fresh yeast	4 whole eggs
2 tablespoons warm water	4 1/2 oz. (130 g.) butter, softened

If the sausage is the type you cook, then do this and cool it before using. Activate the yeast by adding the warm water (blood heat, tepid) plus 1/2 teaspoon sugar to it. Place in a warm spot. It is ready when it is frothy, like the head on a glass of beer.

Place the flour, salt, and 5 tablespoons sugar in a bowl and make a hole in the center. Place the eggs in the center and lightly beat to break them. Add the activated yeast to the eggs and mix. Draw in the flour and beat for 5

minutes to aerate the mixture and make the dough uniform. Beat the softened butter into the mixture; this will take about 10 minutes. Put in the refrigerator for 2 hours. Take out and beat for another 5 minutes. Rest, covered, in the refrigerator overnight. Take out and beat for 10 minutes.

Grease a large bread pan and half fill it with dough. Cut the sausage to fit lengthwise in it. Cover the sausage with the remaining dough and set to rise about 3 hours or until double in size. Place in a preheated oven at 400°F (205°C) and bake about 30 minutes. It is done when a knife inserted comes out clean.

To serve, slice as for bread.

Jambon Persillé   *(for more than 6)*

This is best packed in a cold box on a hot day, as the jelly might not hold.

3 1/3-lb. (1 1/2-kg.) piece of ham	8 peppercorns
1 calf's foot or 2 pig's feet	4 shallots, chopped
1 bottle dry white wine or strong	Bunch of parsley, very finely chopped
dry cider	1 tablespoon white wine vinegar
A few celery leaves	
A few sprigs of herbs (tarragon,	
thyme, chervil, bay leaf)	

Soak the ham in cold water for a few hours to remove some of the excess salt. Blanch and drain it. Clean the calf's foot or pig's feet and blanch them for a few minutes in a large pan to remove the scum. Pour the water out and put the ham in. Add the wine or cider and enough water to cover. Add celery leaves, herbs (not the parsley), peppercorns, and shallots; then simmer gently, covered, for 2 to 3 hours. Remove the ham when it is very tender and flakes easily. Discard the calf's foot or pig's feet and reduce the stock further if necessary, until it coagulates on a cold surface. Cut the ham into little pieces or flake it, then crush it, and put it in a bowl. Strain the gelatinous stock through a fine sieve or muslin. Let it cool and remove the fat, then add the parsley and vinegar and taste to correct the seasoning. Stir well. Pour over the ham in the bowl. Let it set in the refrigerator. Either serve from the bowl or turn it out onto a plate and cut it into slices.

Ham Mousse

1 1/2 lb. (675 g.) ham	2 tablespoons flour
1 carrot, sliced	2 1/4 cups (500 ml.) part stock, part
1 onion, chopped	cider, or white wine
Celery leaves	1/3 lb. (100 g.) Gruyère
Parsley stalks	cheese, grated
Pepper	3 eggs, separated
2 tablespoons butter	A pinch of nutmeg

Poach the ham in enough water to cover, with carrot, onion, some celery leaves, a few parsley stalks, and some pepper until it is tender—about 1 hour. There is usually no need to add salt, especially if the ham is smoked. Lift out from the pan and cut up into pieces. Chop it fine or use a food processor.

In another pan, melt the butter, add the flour, and stir it in well. Gradually add the stock and wine or cider, in equal parts, stirring all the time until the sauce thickens. Add the cheese, ham, egg yolks, and a pinch of nutmeg and stir well.

Beat the egg whites until stiff and fold them into the sauce. Butter a bowl deep enough for the mousse to rise and pour the mixture in. Put in a low 300°F (150°C) oven for an hour.

Carry it in its bowl to the picnic.

Chicken Mousse

1 plump chicken	A few sprigs of tarragon or parsley,
2/3 cup (150 ml.) heavy cream,	finely chopped
beaten stiff	A pinch of cinnamon or nutmeg

Salt and pepper
A squeeze of lemon juice and a little
    grated zest

3 eggs, separated
2 tablespoons Cognac or port
    (optional)

Skin, bone, and grind or finely chop the chicken. Put it in a bowl with the cream, herbs, spices, salt, pepper, and lemon juice and zest to taste. Add the egg yolks and stir well. You may add a little Cognac or some port.

Beat the egg whites until stiff and fold in gently. Pour into a well-buttered oven dish or mold with enough room for the mousse to rise. Bake in a 300°F (150°C) oven for 1 hour.

Bruce Aidells' Chopped Liver

1 1/8 lb. (1/2 kg.) onions, thickly sliced
1 cup (250 ml.) chicken schmaltz (i.e.,
    chicken fat)
1 1/8 lb. (1/2 kg.) fresh chicken livers
    (do not use frozen)

1/2 cup (125 ml.) gribbines
    (cracklings remaining from the
    rendered chicken fat) (optional)
Salt and pepper

Cook the onions slowly in 1/2 cup schmaltz until light brown. Sauté the chicken livers in 1/2 cup (150 ml.) schmaltz on a high heat quickly so that the livers are still pink on the inside. Let the onions and livers cool and chop with the gribbines with a fine blade on a meat grinder. Season with salt and pepper to taste. Refrigerate.

Chicken Liver Mousse

This makes an elegant first course served with thin toast.

1/2 lb. (225 g.) chicken livers
1/4 lb. (115 g.) butter
Pinch of thyme or mixed herbs
Salt and pepper

1 clove garlic, pressed
3 tablespoons brandy or Madeira
Melted butter

Clean the livers, removing bile bag and filaments. Sauté briefly in 2 tablespoons of sizzling butter until they just turn color. Add a sprinkling of herbs, salt, pepper, and garlic, and cook for about 5 minutes longer. While they are still pink inside, remove from the fire. Blend to a smooth paste in a blender or food processor with the rest of the butter and the brandy or Madeira. Put into a pot and seal with a layer of melted butter.

Variations: Make a lovely cream by mixing the liver paste with 2/3 cup (150 ml.) heavy cream, stiffly beaten, instead of the remaining butter.

Port is a good alternative to brandy, and a faint touch of allspice or nutmeg is also good.

EGGS

Hard-boiled Eggs

At a time when women limited their walks to a stroll around the shrubbery, a little governess strode alone and unprotected up the slopes of Snowdon. Nelly Weeton confessed in her diary in 1809 (published by Edward Hall in 1936) to a "lovely impulse of delight" and a craving for wild solitary places which drove her to brave the terrors of tramps and drovers.

She sometimes even hid from other walkers and climbers "purposely that they might not distinguish my dress or features, lest seeing me at any other time, they should know where they had seen me; and I should dread the being pointed at in the road or the street as—'That is the lady I saw ascending Snowdon alone!'" She noted: "I put my maps, memorandum book, three boiled eggs and a crust of bread into a work bag, and thus equipped, sallied forth."

This time-honored food is not to everybody's taste, but there are ways of making hard-boiled eggs most agreeable.

In the Middle East, eggs are sometimes simmered for at least 6 hours or overnight until they become "hamine," that is, with a pale creamy yolk. A light brown color is given to the whites by adding onion skins or coffee grounds to the water. Pour in a little oil so as to have a thin film floating on the surface to prevent the water from evaporating.

For extra joy at a picnic color your eggs with special dyes and polish the shells with a lightly oiled cloth. Or shell them and simmer them unshelled for a few minutes in water with a pinch of turmeric or Indian food-coloring powders. This too is a Middle Eastern festive habit.

Chinese tea eggs (cha yeh tan), with their delicate cracked-china look, give an elegant touch to a picnic. They also have a fine taste. Boil 6 eggs in water for 10 minutes. Remove and very gently crack the shells with the back of a spoon. Return them to the pan. Cover with fresh water, adding 1/2 teaspoon aniseed, 2 tablespoons soy sauce, 2 tablespoons tea (preferably orange pekoe), and 1 tablespoon salt. Simmer on the lowest possible flame for 1 1/2 hours, adding water so that the eggs remain submerged. Leave to cool and soak in the cooking water for 5 to 8 hours. Shell carefully.

Hard-boiled eggs need not be eaten with salt and pepper alone. They are delicious sprinkled with spices and herbs. A lemon juice and oil dressing suits them too. Either sprinkle on as you eat or dip into a bowl containing dressings and seasonings. My father taught me to cut up the egg on the plate and smother it with a mixture of olive oil, lemon juice, a little crushed garlic, a pinch of allspice, and cumin. He says it is the way of Aleppo in Syria. An Iraqi way is to mix sliced hard-boiled eggs with mango pickle. They make a meal of these accompanied by fried eggplant slices and a salad of tomatoes and spring onions.

If you have not got far to go, eggs are always good with homemade mayonnaise (see pp. 81–2) and capers. But if it is likely to spoil in hot weather make the Greek garlic sauce skorthalia (see p. 84) or a nut sauce (see p. 85).

Deviled Eggs

Hard-boil enough eggs to have one per person. Shell them carefully, cut them in half lengthwise, and remove the yolks.

Mash the yolks with mayonnaise, lemon juice, salt, and pepper, adding, if you like, a little mustard, Worcestershire sauce, curry powder, or cayenne. You may also add little bits of things such as any of the following: capers, caviar, chopped anchovy, nuts, pickles, peppers, celery, olives, ham, chicken, and shrimp or chopped herbs such as parsley and chives or spring onion. Stuff the yolk mixture into the whites and stick the halves back together.

Creole Stuffed Eggs

Boil 12 eggs until hard. Cut in half, mix the yolks with an equal volume of Creole Herbed Cheese (p. 30), and pipe into the egg whites.

Bruce Aidells' Eggs Stuffed with Smoked Salmon

1/4 lb. (115 g.) smoked salmon
1/4 lb. (115 g.) cream cheese
12 hard-boiled eggs, shelled
    and halved

1 tablespoon lemon juice
Salt and pepper

In a food processor cream together the salmon, cheese, and egg yolks. Add the lemon juice, salt, and pepper. Pipe into egg whites.

Omelets

One thing that Spaniards, Italians, and Arabs have in common is the thick omelets heavy with meat and vegetables and all kinds of foods. They are the Spanish tortillas, the Italian frittatas, and Arab *ajjas*, and I have traced their ancestry to the Persian *kuku*. Quite unlike light French omelets, which are quickly cooked over high heat, these are cooked slowly over low heat in a heavy-bottomed frying pan until firmly set. They must also be cooked on both sides, either turned over with a spatula if small, or turned over on a plate then slipped back into the pan or pushed under the grill to brown the top.

They are as good cold as they are hot.

Of the vast range of Middle Eastern omelets here are two made with herbs and one with vegetables. Meat ones are on pages 172–3.

An Arab Ajja

1 large onion, chopped
2 leeks, well washed and
    finely chopped
1–2 tablespoons vegetable oil
6 eggs

A large bunch of parsley,
    finely chopped
Salt and pepper to taste
1 1/2 tablespoons butter

Fry the onion and leeks in a little oil until golden. Beat the eggs until yolks and whites are blended, then stir in the onions, leeks, parsley, salt, and pepper. Melt butter in a large frying pan until it foams, then pour in the egg and vegetable mixture and cook very slowly until set; then turn and cook the other side.

An Iranian Kuku

6 eggs
Large bunches each of parsley, fresh
   coriander, and chives, washed,
   dried, and finely chopped

Salt and pepper to taste
1 tablespoon currants or sultanas
A few walnuts, coarsely chopped
1 1/2 tablespoons butter

Beat the eggs in a large bowl with a fork. Add the herbs, salt, pepper, currants or sultanas, and walnuts. Stir well and pour onto hot, foaming butter in a large, thick-bottomed frying pan. Cook gently until set. Then turn over to cook or brown under the grill.

Ajja Khodar Meshakel / An Arab Mixed Vegetable Omelet

1 large onion
3 tablespoons hot oil
2 cloves garlic, pressed
2 leeks, washed and finely sliced
3 zucchini, washed, ends removed and
   sliced medium thick
1/4 lb. (115 g.) fresh or frozen
   broad beans

2 tomatoes, peeled, seeded,
   and chopped
Salt and pepper
1/4 teaspoon nutmeg
2 tablespoons finely chopped parsley
7 eggs
1 1/2 tablespoons butter or oil

Add the onion to the hot oil and cook, stirring, until soft and transparent. Then add the garlic and vegetables. Cook, stirring, until soft, adding a little water when too dry. Season to taste with salt and pepper and the nutmeg. Then stir in the parsley. In a large bowl beat the eggs with a fork until blended. Stir in the cooked vegetables.

   . Put the butter or oil into a 10-in. (25-cm.) omelet pan and roll it over the bottom and sides of the pan. When hot, pour in the egg mixture and cook gently until the bottom of the omelet is set and the top is still creamy. Place the omelet pan under a hot broiler for a minute or two until the top of the omelet is dry. Turn out onto a large plate. Allow to cool. Cut in wedges like a cake.

Tortilla de Patatas / Spanish Potato Omelet

This basic omelet can be varied endlessly to suit the taste of every region of Spain. Try adding cooked chicken, bacon, ham, chorizos (spicy sausages), cut

into small pieces, and cooked vegetables such as spinach, green beans, asparagus, and tomatoes. A little chopped parsley, fresh coriander leaves, or mint
is sometimes used, and a good pinch of chili or cayenne will give the omelet
a Mexican flavor.

5 tablespoons olive oil	Salt and pepper
3 potatoes, peeled and diced	6 eggs
3 onions, chopped	

Heat the olive oil in a heavy frying pan. Add the potatoes and onions and sauté
gently. Add salt and pepper and continue to cook over a low heat until the
vegetables are cooked (about 20 minutes), stirring occasionally. Beat the eggs
in a bowl. Lift the vegetables out of the pan, leaving the oil behind. Add them
to the eggs and stir well. Keep the oil hot in the frying pan and pour in
the egg and vegetable mixture. Lower the heat and press the potatoes and
onions down. Cook until the eggs have set firmly. Now either turn the omelet over on a plate and slip it back into the pan upside down to cook the
other side, or put the frying pan under the grill until the top is firm and
slightly brown.

Frittata

An Italian omelet with the flavor of fresh basil and Parmesan, pecorino, or
mozzarella is spooned by the ladleful into hot oil and cooked gently, pancake-
like, on both sides. Make a stack to hand out with a salad as a light main
course.

Beat the eggs lightly with a fork until yolks and whites are just blended.
Add salt and pepper and a good amount of grated cheese if it is a mild one,
less if it is sharp (Gruyère may also be used). If you do not have fresh basil,
add another herb.

Melt a little butter or oil in a large, heavy-bottomed frying pan. When
it begins to foam but before it becomes colored, pour in the egg mixture by
the ladleful and turn the heat down as low as possible. When the eggs are
firmly set turn the omelet over to cook the other side or finish the top under
the grill.

A variety of fillings may be added to the egg mixture: thinly sliced cooked
artichoke hearts or cooked asparagus cut into small pieces, sautéed onions with
peeled and chopped tomatoes, thinly sliced fried or boiled zucchini, and

chopped ham or diced bacon. My children's favorite frittata is made firm and solid by beating in 2 medium mashed potatoes for 6 eggs.

We sometimes pour all the mixture together into the pan and cook it for 15 minutes on a low flame before putting it under the broiler.

SAVORY TARTS AND PIES

Nearly all societies have made a habit of taking pies on their travels and picnics. With their moist fillings and dry crust they are the ideal transportable food.

A thirteenth-century Arab traveler and scholar, Abd al Latif al Baghdadi, describes a singular Egyptian pie "fit to be put before kings and wealthy persons when they go hunting far from home or take part in pleasures in far off places . . . easy to transport, difficult to break, pleasing to the sight, satisfying to the taste, and keeps hot a very long time" (quoted in Zand and Videan's *The Eastern Key*).

This is how he describes Raghif Alsiniyyeh:

They knead it with 5 1/2 rotles of sesame oil in the same way as they make the bread called khoschcnan. They divide the whole into two parts, spreading one of the two parts in a round shape of a raghif (cake) in a copper plate made for this purpose of about 4 spans in diameter, and which has strong handles. After that they arrange on the dough three roasted lambs stuffed with chopped meats fried in sesame oil, crushed pistachios, various hot and aromatic spices like pepper, ginger, cloves, lentisk, coriander, caraway, cardamom, nuts and others. They sprinkle rose water, in which they have infused musk, over all. After that they put on the lambs and in the spaces left, a score of fowls, as many pullets, and fifty small birds, some roasted and stuffed with eggs, others stuffed with meat, others fried in the juice of sour grapes or lemon or some other similar liquor. They put above them pastry, and little boxes filled, some with the meat, some with sugar and sweet-meats. If one would add one lamb more, cut into morsels, it would not be out of place, and one could also add fried cheese.

When the whole is arranged in the form of a dome they again sprinkle rose water in which musk has been infused, or wood of aloes. They cover it again with the other part of the dough, to which they begin to give the shape of a broad cake. They are careful to join the two cakes of dough, as one makes pastry, so that no vapour escapes. After that they put the whole near the top of the oven until the pastry is solid and begins a degree of cooking. Then they lower the dish in the oven little by little, holding it by the handles, and leave it until the crust is well cooked and takes on a rose red colour. When it is at this point it is taken out and wiped with a sponge, and again sprinkled with rose and musk water, and then brought out to be eaten.

Although Moroccans still prepare giant pigeon pies *(bstila)* on special occasions, the Middle East today prefers smaller pies, of which there are an enormous variety in all shapes and sizes and diversity of pastry and filling.

The great old English pies which contained a stag or a lamb or a stuffed kid surrounded by dozens of goslings have also fallen into oblivion along with the heavy oat and chestnut tarts, but the smaller ones are still traditional English picnic fare. Lately, easy transport and the trend toward lighter food have made the French-style open-faced tarts and flans the most popular. A good way to carry them is in their own pan or tin, covered with a large foil or other cover held together securely with masking tape. If the pan has a removable bottom, tape it to the sides and wrap in a plastic bag or foil.

The range of tarts is wide, with most as good cold as they are hot or warm. The choice alone is difficult.

Shortcrust Pastry for Tarts and Quiches

Everyone has a favorite crust. I use the following as a base for most of my savory tarts. It fills a 12-in. (30-cm.) tart tin.

1/4 lb. (115 g.) unsalted butter	1/2 teaspoon salt
1 3/4 cups (250 g.) flour (all-purpose or a mixture of white and whole wheat)	1 egg
	3–4 tablespoons water

GLAZE

1 egg white (for shell)
1 egg yolk (for top crust)

In a large bowl work and rub the butter into the flour, sifted with the salt. Add the egg and just enough water by the tablespoonful for the dough to stick together. Do not work it any further, and let it rest in a cool place for an hour.

Roll out the dough on a floured board with a floured rolling pin. Lift it gently by wrapping it over the rolling pin and let it drop and settle into a pie pan or tart tin which does not need to be buttered. Trim the edges with a knife.

Partially bake the pastry shell before filling: prick with a fork in several places; put a piece of buttered foil or waxed paper over the dough and weight it down with dry beans to prevent it from puffing up.

Bake in a preheated 400°F (205°C) oven for 20 minutes. Then remove beans and paper, brush the inside of the shell with egg white to glaze it and prevent it from becoming soggy with the filling, and bake 5 minutes longer.

Use the same pastry as the lid for a pie. Brush with egg yolk for a warm brown glaze.

An Eggplant Tart

1 2/3 lb. (3/4 kg.) eggplant
Salt
A little vegetable oil
1 partially baked shortcrust pastry shell
    (preceding recipe)
14-oz. (400-g.) can peeled tomatoes

Pepper
A few fresh basil leaves, finely
    chopped, or 1 teaspoon
    dried basil
A sprig of parsley, finely chopped
3 eggs

Slice the eggplant. Sprinkle with salt and let the juice disgorge for about an hour. Rinse and squeeze dry a few at a time. Fry in hot oil, turning over once, until soft and nicely browned. Drain on absorbent paper. Spread over the pie shell.

Mash the tomatoes with a fork. Add pepper, basil, and parsley and beat in the eggs. Pour over the eggplant and bake for 20–30 minutes in a 400°F (205°C) oven.

A Zucchini Tart

1 2/3 lb. (3/4 kg.) zucchini
3 eggs
3/8 cup (200 ml.) heavy cream (or a
    mixture with light cream)

Salt and pepper to taste
1 partially baked shortcrust pastry
    shell (p. 50)

Trim, wash, and slice the zucchini very thin. Beat the eggs, add the cream, and season with salt and pepper. Cover the pie shell with the zucchini and pour the cream and egg mixture over them. Bake in a 325°F (165°C) oven for 30 to 40 minutes. The zucchini will still be crisp.

Another Zucchini Tart

1 large onion
4–5 tablespoons oil
1 2/3 lb. (3/4 kg.) zucchini,
    thinly sliced
Pepper

A pinch of nutmeg
1 partially baked shortcrust pastry
    shell (p. 50)
1/2 lb. (225 g.) aged Cheddar,
    coarsely grated

Fry the onion in oil in a large pan until it is golden. Add the zucchini and fry, turning them constantly, until they are soft. Season with pepper and nutmeg (no need of salt, but you may like some). Spread this all over the pie shell and sprinkle on the cheese. Put it in a 400°F (205°C) oven for 20 to 30 minutes.

A Ratatouille Tart

This is one of my favorites which I make differently every time.

Make a ratatouille as described on page 100. Fill a well-browned, fully baked pastry shell (see pp. 50–1) with it. Sprinkle generously with grated Gruyère, mozzarella, or matured Cheddar. Put in a hot oven until the cheese has melted.

Pissaladière

This specialty of Nice owes much to neighboring Italy. It is like an onion pizza, but although it is traditionally made with bread dough, it is equally happy in a pastry shell.

THE FILLING

2 1/4 lb. (1 kg.) onions, chopped
1/2 cup (120 ml.) olive oil
12 anchovy fillets

2 tomatoes
20 pitted black olives
Salt and pepper

Cook the onions in the olive oil on low heat for about 30 minutes or longer until soft, but do not let them brown.

If you want to make the crust with bread dough, use a fistful of pizza or French bread dough, punched down after its first rising, and roll the dough into a large thin round and put it into an oiled tin or use a partially baked pastry shell (see p. 50). Spread the onions all over. Place the anchovies in a star and in between the rays place slices of tomatoes and black olives, or make a crisscross pattern with the anchovies. Sprinkle with salt and pepper and a little oil and put in a 400°F (205°C) oven for 20 minutes. Then turn the heat down to 300°F (150°C) for another 20 minutes if you are using the bread dough.

Variation: Add 3 cloves of garlic, chopped, and 4 skinned and chopped tomatoes to the softened onions and cook further with the seasonings.

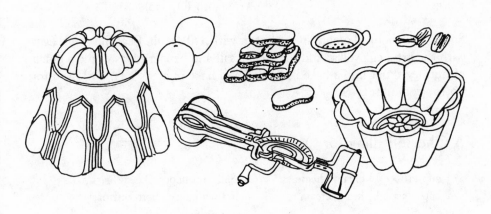

Quiche

Quiche Lorraine

Everyone knows this famous bacon tart with a cream and egg custard, but here it is as a reminder.

6 slices of bacon
1 partially baked shortcrust pastry
    shell (p. 50)
6 large eggs

2 cups (1/2 liter) heavy cream
Salt and pepper
A pinch of nutmeg

Lightly cook the bacon and cut into pieces. Drain and arrange on the pastry shell. Beat the eggs and stir in the cream. Season with salt and pepper and a pinch of nutmeg and pour over the bacon in the pastry shell. Cook in a 300°F (150°C) oven until filling sets—about 30 minutes.

Quiche with Onions

My own favorite comes from Alsace and is made as the one above with the following filling:

2 1/2 lb. (1 1/4 kg.) onions,
    finely chopped
3 tablespoons butter
Salt and pepper
2 eggs

3 egg yolks
7/8 cup (200 ml.) heavy cream
A pinch of nutmeg
A baked shortcrust pastry
    shell (p. 50)

Soften the chopped onions in the butter with a little salt. Beat the whole eggs with the extra egg yolks. Add the cream, salt and pepper to taste, and a pinch of nutmeg. Pour into a baked pie shell and bake in a 325°F (170°C) oven for 30 to 40 minutes.

A Cheese Filling for Quiche

2/3 cup (160 ml.) cream cheese
2/3 cup (150 ml.) heavy cream
1 egg
3 egg yolks

Salt and pepper
1 fully baked shortcrust pastry
    shell (p. 50)

Beat the cream cheese with the cream, egg, and 3 egg yolks. Season to taste with salt and pepper, fill the pastry shell, and bake for about 30 minutes in a 400°F (205°C) oven.

You may vary this by substituting grated Gruyère or Roquefort for the cream cheese.

Jane Grigson's Kipper Flan

Short pastry made with 1 1/4 cups
    (175 g.) flour
1 fat kipper (9 oz./250 g.)

1 cup (200 ml.) heavy cream or 1/2
    cup (100 ml.) each heavy and
    light cream

| 3 eggs | Salt and pepper |
| 1 tablespoon French or German mustard | Juice of half a lemon |

Line an 8 1/2-in. (21-cm.) tart tin with a removable base with the pastry. Prick all over and bake blind for 5 minutes until set but not browned. Meanwhile jug the kipper (pour boiling water over it, allow to soak 5 minutes, and drain). Remove bones and skin and arrange pieces on the pastry case. Beat together the cream and eggs; add the mustard gradually to your taste. Season. Pour over the kippers and bake at 350°F (180°C) for 30 to 40 minutes, until the filling is golden brown and puffed up. Now quickly squeeze half a lemon over the flan.

Leek Pie

1 2/3 lb. (3/4 kg.) leeks	1 1/4 cups (300 ml.) light cream
3 tablespoons butter	Salt and pepper
5 slices lean bacon	A pinch of nutmeg
2 eggs	1 egg yolk

Carefully trim and wash the leeks. Chop them small and soften in the butter, stirring until just tender. Lightly fry the bacon in its own fat in another pan and cut it into small pieces.

Beat the eggs, stir in the cream and seasonings, and pour over the leeks and bacon.

Pour into a pie pan and cover with a thinly rolled shortcrust (p. 50). Brush the pastry lid with beaten egg yolk and bake at 300°F (150°C) for 30 minutes or until set and the crust brown.

Jane Grigson's Raised Pie   *(for more than 6)*

The most traditional of English picnic fare.

Make either a hot water dough, or shortcrust pastry, with 1 1/8 lb. (1/2 kg.) of flour, and other ingredients in proportion. Line a cake tin with a removable base, about 6 1/4 in. (16 cm.) in diameter, with three-quarters of the dough. Put the rest aside, for the lid.

Cube 2 1/4 lb. (1 kg.) boned meat—either shoulder of pork, or pie veal, or chicken cut from the bone. Mix it with 9 oz. (250 g.) cubed gammon or ham or bacon (essential for flavor and a nice pinkish color).

Add a finely chopped onion, salt, pepper, parsley, 1 teaspoon thyme, and 1 teaspoon anchovy essence.

If you want to embellish the pork filling, prepare 3 peeled, cored, sliced eating apples to layer in with the meat. An extra spicing of cinnamon, nutmeg, and allspice is also a good idea.

If you want to embellish the veal filling, hard-boil 4 eggs and shell them. Make the pie in a large loaf tin rather than a cake tin, and put the eggs in a line down the middle, so that they are completely encased in meat.

When you fill the pastry, mound up the meat inside to support the lid nicely. Lay on the last of the pastry, pinching the edges together. Decorate the top and make a central hole. Brush over with beaten egg. Bake 30 minutes at 400°F (205°C) then lower the heat to 325°F (160°C), for 1 1/2 hours. Protect the lid, if it becomes brown too soon, with a piece of foil or butter paper.

As the pie cooks, make a jellied stock. For this put all the bones from the pie meat into a large pan, plus a pig's trotter or veal knuckle bone if you want a really firm set for the jelly. Not essential, but desirable. Add an onion, carrot, herb bouquet, and water to cover generously. Boil for 2 hours, strain off and reduce by boiling to half a pint. Cool and chill, to be sure of the set. Gelatin should not be necessary.

Cool the pie in its tin for an hour, then remove it. When it is cold, melt the jellied stock so that it is runny but not hot, and pour it into the pie through the center hole, using a funnel. Leave until next day. It can be transported in the tin in which it was cooked. Take plenty of salads, lettuce, tomatoes, watercress, celery.

Meat Pie with an Arab Flavor

This filling usually goes on top of a pizza-type dough rolled very thin. For taking out it is best to cover it with any type of pastry such as shortcrust (see p. 50) or puff (the commercial one will do).

1 1/8 lb. (1/2 kg.) onions, finely chopped	1 small (2-oz./60-g.) can tomato paste
Oil	1 teaspoon sugar
1 1/2 lb. (675 g.) lean lamb or beef, ground	3/4 teaspoon ground allspice
	1–2 tablespoons lemon juice
1 1/8 lb. (1/2 kg.) fresh tomatoes, peeled and chopped, or a 14-oz. (400-g.) can peeled tomatoes	Salt and pepper
	3 tablespoons finely chopped parsley (optional)
	A pinch of cayenne pepper (optional)

Soften the onions in a little warm oil until they are transparent and have lost their water, taking care not to let them color. Mix the meat, tomatoes, and tomato paste in a large bowl. If you are using fresh tomatoes, get rid of as much of their juice and seeds as possible, and crush them to a pulp. If you are using a can of tomatoes, drain them well. Add sugar, allspice, and lemon juice, and season to taste with salt and pepper. Drain the onions of oil and add them to the meat mixture. Knead well by hand. Some people like to add a good bunch of finely chopped parsley and a little cayenne pepper as well.

Flatten into a pie tin or baking tray and cover with pastry. Bake in a 325°F (165°C) oven for about 45 minutes or longer, until the meat is done and the crust brown.

Another Ground Meat Filling from the Middle East

1 large onion, chopped
2 tablespoons oil
1 1/8 lb. (1/2 kg.) ground beef
Salt and pepper
1/2 teaspoon cinnamon

1/2 teaspoon allspice
2–3 tablespoons water
1 tablespoon raisins or sultanas
2 tablespoons chopped walnuts

Fry the onion in the oil until golden. Add the beef, crush it with a fork, and stir well. Add salt and pepper, cinnamon, and allspice and cook until the meat changes color. Moisten with the water and add the raisins or sultanas and the chopped walnuts.

Chicken Pie of Moroccan Inspiration

A deep-dish pie that can be made in a round deep pie dish or a rectangular baking dish. The alternate filling uses a cooked chicken and is of French more than Moroccan inspiration.

PASTRY

Prepare some shortcrust with about
   1 2/3 cups (225 g.) flour and

half this amount of
butter (p. 50)

THE FILLING

1 large chicken
1 1/8 lb. (1/2 kg.) onions, grated
A good bunch of parsley, finely chopped
1/2 teaspoon each of cinnamon,
   allspice, and ground ginger

Salt and pepper to taste
8 eggs
3/4 cup (115 g.) blanched almonds
Cinnamon
Powdered sugar

Boil the chicken with the onions, parsley, spices, salt, and pepper. Remove the chicken when the flesh is tender enough to fall off the bones. Reduce the stock to 1 cup (1/4 liter). Add the eggs, lightly beaten with a fork, and cook on a very low flame, stirring constantly until creamy. Fry the blanched almonds in a little oil or toast them under the grill until just golden. Chop or break them into coarse pieces with a pestle and mortar.

Bone the chicken and cut into pieces. Stir into the egg mixture. Fill a deep pie dish or rectangular casserole. Roll out the pastry and lay over the top of the filling. Bake in a 325°F (165°C) oven for 30 minutes or until the pastry is cooked and brown. Sprinkle with cinnamon and powdered sugar when it comes out of the oven.

For a Filling Using Cooked Chicken

ALTERNATE FILLING

1 large onion, chopped	9 oz. (250 g.) mushrooms, sliced
2 tablespoons oil or butter	

SAUCE

1 1/4 cups (300 ml.) milk	2 eggs
5 tablespoons butter	1 large cooked chicken
5 tablespoons flour	A few sprigs of parsley, finely chopped

Soften the onion in the oil or butter. Add the mushrooms and cook for a minute or two. Make a stiff béchamel sauce: Season and warm the milk. In another pan melt the butter. Add the flour, stir until well blended, and cook gently a minute or two. Add the milk a little at a time, removing the pan from the heat with each addition, then returning and beating vigorously as sauce thickens. Continue until sauce is smooth and creamy. Let it cool and stir in the 2 eggs. Skin and bone the cooked chicken and cut it into small pieces. Mix everything together, adding finely chopped parsley.

Phylo Pies with Paper-Thin Pastry

All countries that have been under Ottoman rule make all manner of pies with a flour and water dough worked to a soft elasticity and stretched to paper thinness. It is sold here in Greek and Middle Eastern shops as phylo in 1 1/8-lb. (1/2-kg.) packets of 24 sheets measuring around 12 by 18 in. (30 by 46 cm.). It makes a convenient wrapping for any sort of filling. Each country has its favorite traditional shapes, from large round pies and rolls to triangles, cigars, nests, and coils. The least fiddly and simplest to make and the easiest to keep hot on an outing are the long rolls common in Greece. Made in individual portions, they are easy to hand out.

The secret of handling phylo is not to leave it exposed to air for long, as it will dry out and break easily. Keep it well covered in its plastic wrap. While you work, have all the cut pieces neatly piled. Cover them with a damp cloth if you have to leave them for more than a few minutes.

The meat and chicken fillings given on page 57 can be used for phylo pies, but a Greek one is especially appropriate.

On Easter Sunday and Monday on the Greek islands picnics and family gatherings are held everywhere: in the mountains and by the sea or in yards under the shade of grape vines. Lambs are roasted on the spit and wine flows freely. After Mass the village priest stands holding the Cross at the door for everyone to kiss and people hold hands in a large circle which symbolizes the renewal of friendship. Long wooden trestle tables are set out in the churchyard and spread with crisp white tablecloths. Each family brings its own food and wine and passes some of it around. Pies are popular fare. After lunch seesaws and swings are put out for the children, there is backgammon and dancing, and jokes are exchanged.

Spanakopita Filled with Spinach and Cheese

Bread dough is sometimes used instead of phylo. Although feta cheese is used in Greece, cottage cheese will do very well.

2 1/4 lb. (1 kg.) fresh spinach, or
    1 1/8 lb. (1/2 kg.) frozen
1 large onion, chopped
3–4 tablespoons olive oil
1/2 lb. (225 g.) feta or cottage cheese

Pepper (salt only with
    cottage cheese)
A grating of nutmeg
Melted butter

Wash the spinach, remove large stems, drain, and coarsely chop.

Fry the onion in the olive oil until golden. Add the spinach and cook in its own juice, stirring until it is just tender. Add the cheese and seasonings —hardly any salt is needed if you are using feta.

To make rolls, put 2 sheets of phylo together, brushing each with melted butter. Put a good line of filling along one of the longer edges and roll up, folding the two ends into the roll as you go. One roll is usually enough for two people. Lay rolls on a greased baking tray and put in a preheated moderate 350°F (180°C) oven for about 45 minutes or until they are crisp and golden.

Cheese filling for Spanakopita

1/2 lb. (225 g.) cottage cheese	Pepper
1/2 lb. (225 g.) feta cheese, mashed, or aged Cheddar, grated	A few sprigs of parsley or mint, finely chopped
2 eggs	

Mix together the cottage cheese with the mashed feta or Cheddar cheese and the eggs. Add the pepper and chopped parsley or mint.

To make an individual pie wrap up 2 or 3 tablespoons of filling in one sheet of phylo which has been brushed with melted butter, making sure that the packet is leakproof. A rectangular or square shape is simplest. Put in a 350°F (180°C) oven for 30 to 45 minutes until nicely colored.

COLD MEATS
AND POULTRY

With all the miseries brought by the rigors of the English climate, it is not surprising that indoor picnics have sometimes been the most successful, as this one, described by William Hickey in his *Memoirs* (edited by Peter Quennell, 1960), seems to have been.

The coronation of His present Majesty [George III] being fixed for the month of September, my father determined that all his family should be present at the ceremony. He therefore engaged one of the nunneries, as they are called, in Westminster Abbey, for which he paid fifty guineas. They are situated at the head of the great columns that support the roof, and command an admirable view of the whole interior of the building. Upon this occasion they were divided off by wooden partitions, each having a separate entrance with lock and key to the door, with ease holding a dozen persons. Provisions, consisting of cold fowls, ham, tongues, different meat pies, wines, and liquors of various sorts were sent to the apartment the day before, and two servants were allowed to attend. Our party consisted of my father, mother, brother

Joseph, sister Mary, myself, Mr and Miss Isaacs, Miss Thomas, her brother (all Irish), my uncle and aunt Boulton, and their eldest daughter. . . .

It was past seven in the morning before we reached the Abbey, which having once entered, we proceeded to our box without further impediment, Dr Markham having given us tickets which allowed our passing by a private staircase, and avoiding the immense crowd that was within. We found a hot and comfortable breakfast ready, which I enjoyed, and proved highly refreshing to us all; after which some of our party determined to take a nap in their chairs, whilst I, who was well acquainted with every creek and corner of the Abbey, amused myself running about the long gallery until noon, when notice having been given that the procession had begun to move, I resumed my seat.

Exactly at one they entered the Abbey, and we had a capital view of the whole ceremony. Their Majesties (the King having previously married), being crowned, the Archbishop of Canterbury mounted the pulpit to deliver the sermon; and, as many thousands were out of the possibility of hearing a single syllable, they took that opportunity to eat their meal when the general clattering of knives, forks, plates, and glasses that ensued, produced a most ridiculous effect, and a universal burst of laughter followed. The sermon being concluded, the anthem was sung by a numerous band of the first performers in the kingdom, and certainly was the finest thing I had ever heard.

Great Roasts

Nothing can be simpler to take out than a roast prepared the day before. Cooked (not overcooked) in a way that retains its flavor and moisture, it is as good cold as hot. Let the meat stand and cool down gradually. Either take a very sharp carving knife and a chopping board to slice it on the spot or thinly slice it beforehand and carefully wrap the reassembled roast so that it does not dry out.

Tastefully presented with vegetable garnishes a simple meat platter can look very grand.

Arrange slices around a large serving platter, with cold vegetables or a salad in the center, or garnish with olives, pickled cucumber, and radishes. To accompany a fine-flavored meat serve a good cold sauce or a fruity chutney (see p. 310) and a loaf of bread. If you can heat it up, serve a garlic or anchovy one. A variety of sauces good with beef, pork, lamb, and veal are given on pages 88–9.

Flavoring the Roast

You may like to try some embellishments of flavor which become more pronounced when cold.

Beef. A coating of mustard and oil suits it very well. Pieces of anchovy may be pushed into a few incisions made with a sharp pointed knife.

Lamb. Make a few incisions with a sharp knife into a leg or shoulder and press into them slivers from 2 or more cloves of garlic, squeezing a mint leaf in with them. Or you can make a paste with a mixture of crushed garlic and rosemary, thyme, or marjoram and press it into the cuts.

Lamb also goes particularly well with sharp fruits. Push some dried apricots which have been previously soaked or some sour cherries into the meat in the same way.

A Moroccan way is to press a mixture of salt, pepper, cinnamon, and grated onion under the skin. Sometimes fresh grated ginger and chopped coriander leaves are added. Another is to rub the meat with a mixture of paprika, cumin, crushed cloves of garlic, salt, and pepper. The meat is overcooked very slowly until it can be pulled off easily with the fingers.

Pork. Various dried fruits give pork a delicious flavor and texture. Use dried figs, raisins, and prunes alone or together. Soak them in water (Cognac makes it very special) and press them whole, chopped, or mashed into deep incisions, with salt and pepper, crushed or slivered garlic, and chopped herbs such as parsley and thyme.

Sami Zubaida, who cooks pork very well, sometimes inserts juniper berries or thin slivers of fresh ginger and star aniseed in his large joints.

Veal should be larded for roasting, as it tends to be dry. Press a little dried thyme and grated lemon rind into the flesh through incisions; for a bit of fantasy raisins or sultanas can be pushed in behind them.

All meats are improved by steeping in a wine or cider marinade, but for most of us that is an extravagance.

You may like to have a roast boned by the butcher. In that case lay the meat skin side down, remove excess layers of fat, and spread with a fruity sauce (see pp. 88–9) or a garlic and herb mixture before you roll it up and tie or skewer it for roasting.

For a tasty Italian note insert slices of cheese such as Gruyère or feta in the pockets of the roll.

Cold Tongue

Buy a salted smoked or pickled tongue (it is not usually too salted, but if it is, leave it to soak for an hour in two changes of cold water). Wash and put in a large pan. Cover with cold water, bring to the boil, and skim well. Add a few vegetables—carrot, celery stalks, onion, turnip, all cut up; parsley stalks, a bay leaf, and a few peppercorns. Simmer for about 3 hours until the bones come away easily. Cool in the liquid. It is easier to skin the tongue while still a bit warm. Trim away some of the root, removing the bones. Press into a round dish or tin and cover with its own liquid. Cover well with foil and press it down with a weight. Leave overnight. Cut it up just before serving and serve with Cumberland Sauce (see p. 89).

Meat Salads

With meat salads you can feed many people relatively cheaply and at the same time produce an admirable party dish. The meat is best slowly boiled until tender (see p. 132), but you may also use a leftover roast.

Cut in small pieces into a bowl. Add chopped spring onions and plenty of parsley, a few capers if you like, and thin slices of pickled cucumber. Season generously with a vinaigrette (p. 79).

For a meal in itself, toss in some boiled new potatoes, cut into slices, quartered hard-boiled eggs, a few olives, radishes, whatever you like.

Jellied Meats

Moist boiled meats served in their own jelly, or one made with a calf's or pig's foot, are a delicious alternative to roasts. Use lean boneless cuts. Cook the day before and slice ready for serving into a box with the jelly poured over it. Keep as cool as possible.

Jellied Pork

Cover a roast such as a loin of pork with wine or water. Put in a pig's foot, which has been well cleaned and blanched for 10 minutes to get rid of the scum. Add salt and pepper, a sprig of parsley, and 2 bay leaves. Simmer until the meat is tender. Discard the skin and bones from the foot and leave the meat to cool in the stock. Then chill. To serve, scrape the fat from the top, slice the meat, chop the jellied stock fine, and arrange it around the meat.

Jellied Veal   *(for more than 6)*

3 1/2–4 1/2 lb. (1 1/2–2 kg.)
　　boneless rolled veal roast, from
　　leg, loin, or shoulder
2 tablespoons oil
1 calf's foot
Wine or water
Salt and pepper
2 bay leaves

A sprig of parsley
A little thyme
2 cloves garlic, finely chopped
2 anchovy fillets (optional)
A slice of lemon
2 chopped onions
2 chopped carrots

Turn the veal in the oil in a heavy casserole until it is lightly colored. Add a well-scrubbed calf's foot which has been cut in half and blanched in boiling water for 10 minutes to remove the scum. Cover with wine (Madeira or a little Cognac for a grand occasion) or water. Add the rest of the listed ingredients.

Cook slowly for 3 hours until the meat is very tender, adding water if necessary. Take out the meat, slice, and arrange it in a bowl or mold. Remove the skin and bones from the foot, add the bits of meat to the bowl, and pour over the strained stock. Chill in the refrigerator.

In Egypt we used to flavor the meat with lemon (half to a whole one), a teaspoon of turmeric, which gave it a golden color, and 2 crushed cloves of garlic. We used no wine.

Jellied Beef / Bœuf à la Mode en Gelée Rolled Roast
(for more than 6)

3 1/2–4 1/2 lb. (1 1/2–2 kg.) rolled
　　roast of beef, fat removed
Oil
Half or whole bottle of red or dry
　　white wine
2 tablespoons brandy
A dozen or more small pearl onions
4 carrots, sliced

2 cloves garlic, chopped
2 bay leaves
1 teaspoon thyme
A few parsley stalks
Salt and pepper
6 cloves
2 calf's feet

Brown the beef in a little oil in a large, heavy casserole. Add the wine, brandy, and enough water to cover the beef. Add vegetables, herbs, salt, pepper, and cloves.

In another pan, bring to a boil the 2 well-scrubbed calf's feet and simmer for 10 minutes to remove the scum. Then drain and put near the meat in the saucepan.

Cook at a very slow simmer for 3 to 4 hours until the meat is very tender, adding water to keep it covered. Remove the calf's feet and parsley stalks. Slice the meat into a plastic box for carrying to the picnic, pour the sauce over it, and chill. When it has set, scrape off the fat which has formed at the top with a spoon and clean off what is left with a paper towel.

To serve, turn out and garnish with parsley, watercress, or young lettuce leaves. The meat is kept tender and moist by the jellied stock.

Lamb Cooked in Foil—a Greek idea

If you have an insulated container (see p. 371) for meat, there is no better meal than the Greek lamb cooked with cheese. Season individual portions of lean meat (such as a good thick slice from the leg) with salt and pepper and wrap up with a slice of feta or kefalotiri cheese in oiled aluminum foil, closing the packets tightly. Cook gently in a medium oven for at least an hour, until the meat is very tender. Put the packets, as they are, straight into the insulated container.

My brother brought back an exquisite version of this dish, made with vine leaves, from a recent visit to Athens. I have tried it with leaves from my neighbor's garden and matured Cheddar. If you do not have access to fresh leaves you may use those in brine, which need soaking in many changes of water to remove the excess salt. Simply poach fresh ones for about a minute, until they change color and become limp. Line the foil with leaves to cover the meat and cheese.

Variation: An alternative flavoring comes with a sprinkling of dried or fresh chopped mint and, if you like, a touch of crushed garlic.

If you do not have an insulated container you can always heat up the packets over a fire at the picnic.

Meatballs with Nuts and Raisins

However humble the status of meatballs, they are the perfect food to hand out when the company is large. These are rather special and very tasty.

2 1/4 lb. (1 kg.) minced lean lamb,
    beef, or veal, or a mixture
    of these
1 large onion, grated
2 eggs, lightly beaten
2 tablespoons raisins or sultanas
    moistened in a little water
A handful of walnuts,
    coarsely chopped

A small bunch of parsley,
    finely chopped
Salt and pepper to taste
1 teaspoon each of ground cinnamon
    and allspice
Oil

Put all the above ingredients (except oil) into a large bowl. Knead well with your hands to achieve a smooth texture which holds well together. Roll into balls the size of a walnut. Fry gently in a little oil, shaking the frying pan and turning them until they are colored all over and cooked through. You will need to do them in batches. Drain on absorbent paper. Pack them hot or cold.

French Pork Fricadelles

1 1/8 lb. (1/2 kg.) pork, minced
1 large potato, boiled and mashed
2 cloves garlic, crushed
2 tablespoons finely chopped parsley
3 tablespoons grated Parmesan

2 eggs, lightly beaten
Salt and pepper to taste
Flour
Oil

Combine the above ingredients (except flour and oil) and knead into a smooth paste. Shape into flat round cakes, dip in flour, and gently fry in oil until brown, turning over once. Drain on paper towels before packing hot or cold.

Coppiette

Islam may be responsible for the pine nuts and raisins in these Roman-style rissoles.

2 1/4 lb. (1 kg.) lean beef, minced
3 slices ham, finely chopped
2 cloves garlic, crushed
A few sprigs of parsley, finely chopped
A sprinkling of marjoram
A grating of nutmeg
2 eggs, lightly beaten
2 thin slices bread, crusts removed,
    soaked in milk and squeezed dry

2 tablespoons sultanas
2 tablespoons pine nuts (they may be
    lightly fried first)
4 tablespoons grated Parmesan
Salt and pepper to taste
Fine bread crumbs
Oil

Mix and knead the above ingredients (except crumbs and oil) in a large bowl. Shape into cakes or balls, roll in bread crumbs, and deep-fry in oil until crisp and golden brown, turning over once. Drain on absorbent paper. Eat hot or cold.

Meat Loaf

Most countries have a version of the meat loaf, an all-time picnic favorite, but Italy has the greatest variety. One that came early into my life was an Italian polpetone made by our Yugoslav nanny, Maria. It is nicer cold than hot.

1 1/2 lb. (700 g.) beef or veal, minced
2 slices white bread, crusts removed
1 onion, finely chopped or grated
1 egg, lightly beaten
1 bunch of parsley, finely chopped

1 teaspoon ground allspice, or a pinch
    each of cinnamon and nutmeg
Salt and pepper
3 hard-boiled eggs, shelled
Flour

Work the minced meat to a smooth paste with your hands or pound it with a pestle and mortar. Soak the bread in water and squeeze dry; add the onion, egg, parsley, spices, and seasoning. Roll the hard-boiled eggs in a little flour so that the meat sticks better to them. Either divide the meat mixture in three and pat some around each egg individually or make one long roll with the eggs embedded in it in a row. Pat into a solid compact loaf or loaves and wrap in well-oiled sheets of foil. Bake for 45 to 60 minutes in a 350°F (180°C) oven. Open the wrapping for the last 10 minutes to let the meat color.

In the meantime make a tomato sauce:

1 onion, chopped	1 cup (1/4 liter) water
2 tablespoons oil	1 bay leaf
2 cloves garlic, pressed	A few celery stalks
1 6-oz. can tomato paste	Salt and pepper

Fry the onion in the oil. When it is brown, add the remaining ingredients. Simmer gently for at least 20 minutes.

Let the meat cool down before cutting it into thick slices or it will break. Use a sharp knife very carefully. Put the slices together again in a box and cover with sauce. This is best done the day before serving.

Variations: Italians like to add grated Parmesan (about 3 tablespoons) and 2 or 3 slices of chopped ham, and they may simmer the rolls in wine.

A Middle Eastern version is made with a handful of fried pine nuts and a few sultanas worked in with the meat.

A Polpetone from Italy

Like the previous one, this loaf may be stuffed with hard-boiled eggs, but it is simpler and just as good without. You can always serve the eggs separately with it.

1 1/2 lb. (700 g.) minced veal	2 1/2 oz. (75 g.) Gruyère, grated
1 large onion, finely chopped	Salt and pepper
1 1/8 lb. (1/2 kg.) fresh spinach cooked in its own juice or 1/2 lb. (225 g.) frozen, thawed, and finely chopped	2 eggs
	2 slices of bread, crusts removed, soaked and squeezed dry

Mix all the ingredients together, working them to a paste with your hands. Press into a buttered terrine and cook in a 325°F (165°C) oven for 1 hour.

Variation: Add 2 big handfuls of cooked rice to the mixture (as well as the bread).

Cold Chicken

For chicken to be good cold it is especially important for it to have been cooked in a way that preserves its moistness. Cooking it in foil, in its own juice, is a particularly simple method.

Place the cleaned chicken on a large sheet of aluminum foil. Rub the bird with butter or oil, and wrap it up with the aromatics of your choice into a well-sealed parcel. I put an onion in the cavity and sprinkle the bird liberally with lemon juice, crushed garlic, fresh tarragon when I have it, otherwise parsley or coriander leaves, sometimes rosemary from my garden, and salt and pepper.

Cook the bird at a high temperature, 425°F (220°C), for 1 hour. Open the wrapping for the last 10 minutes if you like it brown. Close it again to take on your picnic.

Variation: Otherwise, braised or boiled chicken is better than chicken roasted without the foil, which is too dry. Simmer gently in water to cover with an onion stuck with cloves, a carrot, 2 bay leaves, a sprig of parsley, celery leaves, salt, and pepper for an hour or until the juices are no longer pink. Let the chicken cool in its own stock.

You will find sauces to go with cold chicken on pages 80–2, 85–6, 88–9, 310.

Chicken (and Other Poultry) Salads

Salads will make a chicken go further; here are some suggestions to be made up with a chicken poached in a flavorsome stock.

Remove skin and bones and cut the meat into strips. Toss in a vinaigrette (see p. 79) or one which has been mixed with fresh or sour cream.

Or dress with a light mayonnaise (see p. 82), to which may be added coarsely ground walnuts, almonds, or hazelnuts. Garnish before serving with sliced or quartered hard-boiled eggs and some chopped parsley. You may like to arrange the salad on a bed of young romaine lettuce leaves.

Another excellent salad is chicken mixed with a small handful of toasted split almonds and coarsely chopped walnuts, a small bunch of grapes, seeds removed, 2 finely sliced apples, dipped in lemon juice, and a bunch of cress. Dress with fresh cream whipped with salt and pepper to taste, and flavored if you like with a touch of crushed garlic.

The following four turkey and chicken salad recipes were given to me by Bruce Aidells, chef, cookery teacher, and demonstrator in Berkeley, California.

Mexican Turkey or Chicken Salad with Lime, Chili, and Fresh Coriander

2 lb. (1 kg.) poached chicken breasts or white turkey, sliced in thin shreds
1 small head green cabbage, finely shredded
1/2 teaspoon chili powder
3 limes
4 tablespoons fruity olive oil

1 teaspoon chopped garlic
1/2 teaspoon salt
1 cooked carrot in 1/2-in. (1 1/2-cm.) dice
1 bunch fresh coriander, coarsely chopped
8 cherry tomatoes, halved

Combine all ingredients except about 3 tablespoons of the coriander and the cherry tomatoes. Toss well, place in a bowl, and garnish with the remaining coriander and cherry tomatoes.

Turkey Salad Olivier

2 lb. (1 kg.) diced cooked turkey meat
1 kosher dill pickle in 1/4-in. (3/4-cm.) dice
4 tablespoons minced spring onion
1 1/8 lb. (1/2 kg.) boiled new potatoes in 1/2-in. (1 1/2-cm.) dice
1/2 cup (120 ml.) sour cream

1/2 cup (120 ml.) homemade mayonnaise (p. 81)
1 1/2 teaspoons dried dill weed or 1 tablespoon fresh dill
1 tomato
1 hard-boiled egg
6 black olives

Combine turkey, pickle, onion, and potatoes with sour cream and mayonnaise and mix well with 1 teaspoon dill. Mound on a platter or shallow bowl and garnish with tomato, egg, and olives. Sprinkle with remaining dill.

Chicken or Turkey Salad Niçoise

2 lb. (1 kg.) shredded cooked chicken
    or turkey
1 1/8 lb. (1/2 kg.) boiled potatoes in
    3/4-in. (2-cm.) chunks
1 1/8 lb. (1/2 kg.) zucchini, blanched,
    in 3/4-in. (2-cm.) chunks
1 1/8 lb. (1/2 kg.) cooked green beans
1 cup (1/4 liter) vinaigrette with
    garlic (p. 79)

2 tomatoes, cut into wedges
2 tablespoons capers
4 anchovy fillets
1/2 cup (120 ml.) Kalamata olives
4 hard-boiled eggs, cut into wedges
1 whole pimento, cut into strips

Combine the chicken or turkey, potatoes, zucchini, and green beans and toss in 3/4 cup (180 ml.) of the vinaigrette. Mound on a platter or shallow bowl and garnish with tomatoes, capers, anchovy, olives, eggs, and pimento. Pass the remaining vinaigrette in a bowl.

Turkey Salad Véronique

1/2 cup (120 ml.) homemade
    mayonnaise (p. 81)
1 1/2 cups (355 ml.) sour cream
2 tablespoons lemon juice
2 tablespoons Dijon mustard
4 cups (900 g.) cooked long-grain rice
4 cups (900 g.) diced white
    turkey meat

2 cups (465 g.) green grapes
1 bunch spring onions, chopped
1 tablespoon chopped fresh chervil or
    tarragon (do not use dried)
4 tablespoons white wine
1 cup (155 g.) roasted sliced almonds

Mix together the mayonnaise, sour cream, lemon juice, and mustard. Combine all the other ingredients except half of the almonds, and toss in the dressing. Garnish with the remaining almonds.

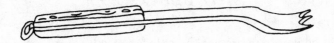

Pigeons (or Squab) with Dates

Of Moroccan inspiration.

6 pigeons, cleaned and washed
3 onions, finely chopped
1–2 cloves garlic, crushed
3 tablespoons oil
Salt and pepper

3/4 teaspoon ground ginger
1 teaspoon cinnamon
1 2/3 lb. (3/4 kg.) fresh dates, pitted
1/4 cup (60 g.) sesame seeds

Put all the ingredients except the dates and sesame seeds in a pot and half cover with water. Simmer 30 minutes, turning the birds over once, then add the dates and cook a further 10 minutes. Put in a serving bowl and sprinkle with sesame seeds. You may eat this cold.

Quails with Grapes

Also Moroccan. Although usually eaten hot, this is also good cold.

6 quails
3 tablespoons oil
1/2 teaspoon ground ginger
Salt and pepper

1 1/8 lb. (1/2 kg.) fresh large white
     grapes, peeled and seeded
A squeeze of lemon juice

Clean, singe, and wash the quails. Brown briskly in oil on all sides in a large pot for about 6 minutes. Season with ginger, salt, and pepper, add grapes and lemon juice, and cook gently for another 10 minutes until the quails are done and the grapes softened. Allow to cool.

COLD FISH
AND SEAFOOD

Salmon and salmon trout are not the only fish that are good eaten cold. Sea bass, cod, haddock, halibut, turbot—indeed most seafood makes excellent cold dishes.

It is not often practical to take a large fish whole on a picnic; the answer is to skin and cut it into pieces when it is already cooked, for it is best cooked whole.

Poached Fish

Poach a whole fish in a stock made by simmering water (with an equal quantity of dry white wine or cider if you like) for 30 minutes with a carrot, an onion, 2 stalks of celery, all chopped, a few parsley stalks, 2 bay leaves, a sprinkling of thyme, salt and a few peppercorns, and a tablespoon of vinegar or a squeeze of lemon. Let it become warm before you put in your fish, then slowly bring it to a simmer again. The timing depends on the size of the fish; cook until the flesh is translucent. It is best to undercook, for the fish continues to cook in the broth off the fire.

Baked Fish

It is better still to bake your fish in foil with a moistening of oil or white wine and seasonings. In this way, flavor and texture are at their very best. Do not overcook. Allow 10 minutes per inch of thickness measured at the thickest point of the fish, and bake in a hot oven.

All the fish needs is a good sauce, many of which are given in the section on sauces (see pp. 81–6).

Fish and Seafood Salads

Not many people realize the pleasure and attractiveness of a salad made from the produce of the sea. It is one of the best and simplest first courses to offer.

Any firm flaking fish can be used alone or together with any of the following: cooked crab, shrimp, scallops, mussels. Cook the fish as directed in the preceding recipes and dress generously with a vinaigrette and plenty of finely chopped fresh herbs and spring onions.

Variations: A light mayonnaise with whipped cream or sour cream, or the creams alone with fresh herbs, can be used instead of the vinaigrette.

My favorite salad is a version of this one, mixed with fluffy rice. The combination of fish, white rice, and greenery is as pleasing to the eye as to the palate. I like it just as it is, but it is also pleasant combined with finely chopped raw vegetables such as tomatoes, olives, peppers, cucumber, and celery.

For the rice: Use long-grain rice, basmati or patna, soaked in boiling water and salt first to remove the starchy dust which may cause it to become sticky, then rinsed in cold running water. Cook in any way you like. My way is to boil the rice in plenty of salted boiling water for only 4 minutes until it is still a little hard. Drain in a sieve and put back into the same pan with a few tablespoons of a light oil. Return it to the heat with the lid on for it to continue to cook in its own steam.

An Unusual Dressing for Shrimp

For 1/2 lb. (225 g.) shrimp, mix the juice of half a lemon, 1 teaspoon anchovy paste, 2 tablespoons water, 2 tablespoons olive oil, and 1/2 teaspoon of English mustard. Toss cooked, peeled shrimp in this and serve on a plate with a border of radish and cucumber slices.

Fish Terrine

This is another dish like the fish mousse on page 146 which is made easy by the use of a food processor.

You may use salmon for the forcemeat, alternating with layers of fillet of sole or trout; or a cheaper fish such as whiting for the forcemeat between slices of salmon. The fillets remain slightly undercooked, very much to my taste, but you may prefer to poach them first.

THE FORCEMEAT

1 1/8 lb. (1/2 kg.) fish, skin and
  bones removed
1/4 lb. (125 g.) butter
1/4 lb. (125 g.) white bread, crusts
  removed, soaked in milk
3 eggs
Salt and pepper

A pinch of spices (mace, nutmeg,
  or allspice)
A small bunch of herbs (tarragon,
  chervil, or parsley), finely chopped
Juice of half a lemon
1 clove garlic, crushed

Chop and pound the fish and add the butter and bread. Purée in a food processor or blender with the rest of the ingredients above.

THE TERRINE

1 1/8 lb. (1/2 kg.) salmon, sole, or trout   Salt and pepper

Remove skin and bones from the fish and cut into 3/8-in. (1-cm.) slices. Spread a layer of forcemeat at the bottom of a buttered terrine. Cover with a layer of salmon slices seasoned with salt and pepper and continue alternating layers, finishing with a layer of forcemeat. Cover with a buttered greaseproof paper and the lid and put in a pan of water in a 400°F (205°C) oven for 45 to 60 minutes, until the top feels springy.

To keep a long time, cover when it is done with a layer of melted clarified butter. Otherwise make a jellied broth with fish cuttings and bones. Reduce and flavor if you like with dry white wine. Stiffen if necessary with gelatin (see Aspic, p. 87). When it has cooled, pour over the terrine by degrees as much as the contents will absorb. This gives the terrine a fine texture. Cool overnight in the refrigerator.

Variation: For an alternative presentation, cover the terrine with a firm pie crust (see p. 50). Decorate with pastry leaves and make a hole for the jelly. Serve with a cucumber salad.

Linda Gassenheimer's
Salmon and Cucumber Pâté in Aspic

It may be unmolded and served on a platter or it may be sliced from the terrine as for a meat terrine.

THE COURT BOUILLON

1 1/4 cups (295 ml.) fish stock
1 1/4 cups (295 ml.) white wine
1 small carrot, sliced
1 small onion, sliced

1 bay leaf
Parsley stalks
Branch of thyme

THE ASPIC

1 1/8 lb. (1/2 kg.) salmon fillet (salmon
    trout may be used)
1 cucumber, cut into thick julienne
2 hard-boiled eggs, coarsely chopped
2 tablespoons chopped parsley
2 teaspoons chopped tarragon
1 tablespoon chopped chervil
    (if available)

4-oz. (115-g.) can pimentos, sliced
    in julienne
2 tablespoons drained
    green peppercorns
1 envelope gelatin dissolved in 2
    tablespoons white wine, Madeira,
    or Marsala

Simmer all of the ingredients for the court bouillon for about 30 minutes. Poach the salmon in the bouillon for about 2 to 3 minutes. Remove the salmon and discard any bones that remain. Pat dry with paper towel and cut into thick julienne strips.

To prepare the aspic, strain and clarify the court bouillon and add enough white wine, Madeira, or Marsala to make up 2 1/2 cups (590 ml.) of liquor. Sprinkle in gelatin (this is more than is usually necessary—calculated for use in hot weather). Bring to near boiling point, whisking all the time to dissolve the gelatin. Let it cool.

Place the terrine in a bowl or pan of cold water and ice. It will be easier to work over the ice water. Spoon a 1/4-inch layer of the cooled aspic over the bottom of the pan. Spoon in another thin layer of aspic and wait for it to start to set. Sprinkle in the cucumber, eggs, fresh herbs, pimentos, and peppercorns in a thin layer. Then spoon more aspic over the mixture. Continue in this manner in alternating layers. With each layer wait until the aspic is nearly setting before adding more ingredients. In this manner the terrine will be filled with all of the ingredients floating evenly throughout. The last layer should be one of aspic. Refrigerate to set.

A Kipper Mousse

Take along fresh whole wheat bread or toast to serve with this mousse.

4 fat kippers	7/8 cup (200 ml.) heavy cream
1 tablespoon gelatin	4–5 tablespoons sherry or the juice of
A pinch of cayenne pepper	1 lemon (optional)

Poach the kippers in boiling water for 5 minutes. Keep 7/8 cup (200 ml.) of the liquid and dissolve the gelatin in it. Refrigerate. Bone the kippers and leave them to cool. Put them in an electric blender with the slightly cooled jelly. Add the cayenne, cream, and sherry or lemon juice. Blend until smooth and pour into a wetted mold. Leave to set.

Smoked Mackerel Pâté

Other smoked fish may be used, such as whiting. Trout is expensive but particularly good. Kippers have to be immersed for a few minutes in boiling water. Have thin toast or brown bread and lemon wedges to serve with this.

2 fleshy moist smoked mackerel
2/3 cup (150 ml.) sour cream
5 1/2 oz. (150 g.) cream cheese or
    cottage cheese

Salt and pepper
Juice of half a lemon

Remove skin and bones from fish and flake into a blender. Add sour cream and cheese (sieved if the cottage variety) and blend until smooth. Season to taste with salt and pepper and lemon juice. You may need to do the blending in batches. Press into a pot. I once covered the pâté with a layer of Gooseberry Sauce (see p. 88) with magnificent results.

Lake Pontchartrain Crabmeat

A recipe from eastern Louisiana, where backfin lump crabmeat is often served chilled with a slightly tart, creamy sauce. In regions where fresh lump crabmeat is unavailable, you may substitute fresh frozen crabmeat by defrosting it as quickly as possible and draining before patting the meat dry in a paper towel.

1 1/8 lb. (1/2 kg.) crabmeat
1 1/4 cups (295 ml.) mayonnaise
1/4 cup (60 ml.) heavy sour cream
1 lemon

3 tomatoes, cut in wedges
1 small green pepper, seeded
    and diced
1 small cucumber, peeled and diced

Flake crabmeat with a fork. Combine mayonnaise with sour cream and squeeze in about 2 tablespoons of lemon juice, then blend just enough to mix well. Add crabmeat and vegetables and toss to distribute ingredients evenly.

Fried Fish

Cold fried fish often appears in old continental cookbooks as "à la juive." This is how it is prepared here with any of the following: haddock, cod, hake, plaice, or sole. Depending on the fish, it may be filleted or cut into thick steaks. Wash and drain the fish and season with salt and pepper. Dip in beaten egg yolk and then into fine matzo meal. Fry in deep hot oil, turning over once until both sides are a golden brown. Drain on absorbent paper. (My mother-in-law reverses the process. She covers the fish in bread crumbs first and then dips in lightly beaten egg.)

    Serve with lemon wedges.

Goujons

Little fried strips of fish (mock gudgeon) fried the day before make a lovely communal dish piled onto a plate garnished with parsley and with a bowl of sauce such as Aïoli (see p. 83) to dip into.

It is best to use sole, but plaice and other flatfish are also good. Cut into strips and dry on paper towels. If you are going to serve right away it is enough to dip in flour or in egg and bread crumbs. If the fish is going to wait for several hours or a day, it will stay firm and crisp if you dip in a light batter made in the following way. Mix 7/8 cup (125 g.) flour, 1 tablespoon oil, an egg yolk, and 2/3 cup (150 ml.) water, beating well. Leave for an hour, then fold in the stiffly beaten egg white. Deep-fry in very hot oil, keeping each piece of fish separate until crisp and golden. Drain on absorbent paper and keep covered in the refrigerator.

Fish Fritters

In the countries around the Mediterranean they like to use salt cod, desalted and freshened, but any kind of fish may be used, fresh or smoked. Fritters take time to shape and to fry, but they are lovely when they are done, and easy to hand out. You can keep them hot in an insulated box, but they are also good cold. Where necessary soak or poach the fish first. Skin, bone, and flake, then chop, mince, or shred as finely as possible.

For the binding: a stiff béchamel sauce or soaked bread is sometimes used, but
mashed potato gives a much better texture.

FOR 1 1/8 LB. (1/2 KG.) OF FISH USE:

1 1/8 lb. (1/2 kg.) potatoes	A little parsley, finely chopped
2 lightly beaten eggs	1–2 scallions, finely chopped
1 clove garlic, minced	Salt and pepper

Boil the potatoes in water or milk, mash thoroughly, and add to the fish with the eggs, garlic, parsley, scallions, salt, and pepper.

Knead well together and shape into small flat round cakes. Roll in flour and fry in hot oil until golden.

For a crisper shell dip in beaten egg, then in bread crumbs, before frying.

Variation: Add 2 or 3 tablespoons of grated Parmesan or another sharp cheese.

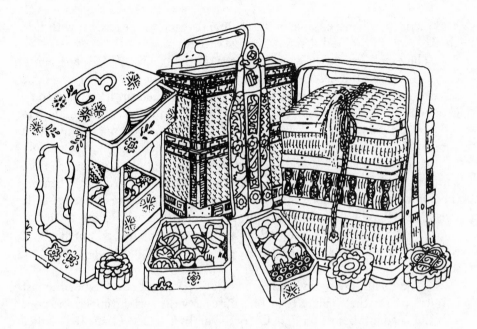

COLD SAUCES
AND RELISHES

Since moist foods are not generally considered the right kind to carry, serve, or eat out, a good sauce or dressing or a tasty relish is doubly appreciated.

Most people become adventurous when it is a matter of enlivening cold meats, and cold saucery is one area where the exotic is acceptable. France may be the land of sauces, but Britain has a greater repertoire of cold ones. And though Escoffier immortalized them with names such as Cambridge, Cumberland, Gloucester, and Yorkshire, the flavors of vinegar with sugar, fruits, and spices bear tribute to early influences from the Far and Near East dating from the Crusades and the spice trade as well as the colonial heritage.

Vinaigrette

The classic French dressing, a mixture of oil, wine vinegar, salt, and pepper, to which fresh green herbs and parsley are often added, mustard occasionally, and garlic by those who like it, plays a very important part in the world of cold foods. It is indispensable with salads and vegetables, excellent with fish, chicken, and meat, and it merits special attention.

The excellence of the sauce depends on the quality of the ingredients. Good olive oil is the best, but peanut oil, sunflower oil, and other vegetable oils will also do. Walnut oil is particularly delicious, especially if you have some chopped walnuts in the salad. The usual proportion of vinegar to oil is 1 to 3, but you may vary it to your own taste. Use the proportion 1 to 4 with a lighter oil such as sunflower oil. Lemon juice or cider vinegar may be substituted for wine vinegar. Add salt and freshly ground black pepper to taste and beat vigorously until well blended. (There is a purist notion that beating them into the vinegar alone first will allow the salt to dissolve better.) A little mustard, preferably Dijon, stirred into the vinegar before beating in the oil is good for the stronger-tasting salads such as endive, chicory, arugula, and watercress. Stir in fresh chopped herbs—parsley, chives, and basil—just before serving.

Some salads, especially fresh green leaves, are best seasoned at the last minute, so carry the vinaigrette in a separate jar with a well-fitting lid and pour over the salad just before serving. Carry the herbs in a little plastic bag. Other salads, such as those made with cooked vegetables, are best when they have been allowed to absorb their dressing and should be mixed some hours in advance.

With capers and gherkins. Excellent with chicken, beef, veal, fish, and vegetables is a vinaigrette to which have been added capers, pickled cucumbers, spring onions, and a variety of green herbs such as parsley, chives, chervil, and watercress, finely chopped.

With cream or sour cream. I very often mix equal quantities of cream or sour cream and vinaigrette with most attractive results.

Another unusually good cream sauce for fish, hard-boiled eggs, and vegetables such as leeks is made this way: Beat an egg yolk with about 4 to 6 tablespoons of cream in a bowl until well blended, then add about 2/3 cup (150 ml.) vinaigrette very slowly, beating vigorously as you would a mayonnaise. You may add a little lemon juice to taste, and stir in some fresh green herbs.

With mustard. I was recently served a creamy sauce with the texture of mayonnaise but which contained no eggs, only mustard, oil, and seasonings. It was poured over crisp young leeks and slices of barely cooked Jerusalem artichokes. Beat 3 tablespoons French mustard in a bowl with 3 tablespoons boiling water. Now add olive oil a little at a time, beating constantly with a whisk. Add 1/3 to 2/3 cup (75 to 150 ml.) to make a thick sauce. Season to taste with salt and pepper and some lemon juice. Add parsley or fresh chopped green herbs just before serving.

Mint and Herb Sauces

For the traditional English sauce for lamb, wash, dry, and chop very finely, blend, or pound a handful of fresh mint leaves. Bring to the boil 6 tablespoons wine vinegar with 3 tablespoons water and 2 tablespoons powdered sugar. Throw in the mint and remove from the heat.

Variations: Do the same with minced chervil, chives, marjoram, basil, and rosemary, all of which are good with cold meats.

A less orthodox but delicious mint sauce is made with red currant jelly and orange juice added to taste.

All of these keep well in bottles.

Mayonnaise

Until the reign of Henry IV this sauce had no name in France. It was simply called "cold sauce." According to Pierre Lacam, the duke of Mayenne was eating a cold chicken dressed with it while Henry's troops were advancing. He refused to leave the table until he had finished and lost the battle of Argues. The sauce was mockingly named "mayennaise" as a result of this episode. Carême transformed it to "maynonaise," and later the French Academy accepted it as mayonnaise.

A hot day will do it no good. So unless it can be kept cool it is best not to have it at all or to have a good commercial variety instead.

The mystique which surrounded the making of mayonnaise in the days when only a wooden spoon and a bowl were used still clings. Now that it takes only minutes with an electric beater (or blender or food processor—see below), it often separates in the making, but it can be easily saved.

3 egg yolks

1 tablespoon wine vinegar or

2 tablespoons lemon juice

1/2–1 teaspoon salt

A pinch of white pepper

1 cup (1/4 liter) olive oil

Beat the egg yolks by themselves for at least a minute until they become thick and sticky. Add the vinegar or lemon juice and the salt and pepper, and beat for half a minute longer. Pour the oil from a measuring cup drop by drop, beating all the time until the sauce thickens (which it begins to do by the time a third of the oil has been used). Continue to beat, adding the oil in a thin trickle and making sure that it is being absorbed, until the mayonnaise is a very heavy cream. If it separates it can be saved by starting again with a new yolk and beating the spoiled sauce into it by the spoonful at first, then very slowly. If the sauce is to be kept for a few days, 1 to 2 tablespoons of boiling water beaten in at the end will prevent curdling.

Food processor mayonnaise is better made with 1 whole egg and 2 yolks. Put the eggs in the processor bowl and continue as above. It will take only a minute.

Blender mayonnaise: Use 3 whole eggs and proceed as above.

A stiff mayonnaise is obtained by mixing with about half the quantity of melted aspic jelly (see p. 87). For a fluffy texture, whip the mixture as it begins to set.

For a light mayonnaise, whip in a little fresh cream, sour cream, or yogurt.

For a green version, add as much as you like of finely chopped fresh herbs: chives, chervil, parsley, tarragon, watercress—coriander leaves too. Blanch the herbs if you mean to keep the sauce for several days. Squeeze them dry, chop fine, and add them to the mayonnaise.

For a red one, add tomato purée.

For an anchovy flavor that goes well with cold fish, mousses, and terrines, wash 3 to 4 anchovy fillets. Chop and pound them to a purée. Add 1 tablespoon capers, 2 tablespoons pickled gherkins, and 2 tablespoons parsley, all finely chopped. Beat the mixture into the mayonnaise. These quantities are for 1 cup (1/4 liter) of sauce. You may use anchovy paste instead of fillets. Other fishy flavors are obtained by beating in shrimp or lobster eggs or any type of caviar which you happen to have.

For a thick Greek version, add a few tablespoons of ground almonds and a mashed boiled potato or slices of bread, crusts removed, soaked in water and squeezed dry.

For a curry mayonnaise, good with chicken and shellfish, add curry powder to taste, about 1 teaspoon for 1 cup (1/4 liter) and, if you like, a pinch of powdered ginger. Stir in 1 tablespoon raisins that have been allowed to swell in water and 1 tablespoon slivered almonds or a little fruity chutney.

For all of these you may prefer to use a mixture of olive oil with a lighter one such as sunflower.

Russian Dressing

2 cups (1/2 liter) mayonnaise
1 tablespoon Dijon mustard
2 tablespoons finely chopped onion

1 tablespoon Worcestershire sauce
2 tablespoons inexpensive caviar

Blend the ingredients well together.

Thousand Island Dressing

1/2 cup (120 ml.) salad oil
Juice of half an orange
Juice of half a lemon
1 teaspoon paprika
1 tablespoon finely chopped onion

1 tablespoon Worcestershire sauce
1 tablespoon Dijon mustard
1 tablespoon finely chopped parsley
Salt

Blend the ingredients thoroughly.

Massachusetts Thousand Island Cream Dressing

1/2 cup (120 ml.) mayonnaise made
  with tarragon vinegar
2 tablespoons finely chopped pimentos
2 tablespoons finely chopped
  green olives
2 tablespoons finely chopped green
  pepper

1 tablespoon finely chopped chives
2 tablespoons tomato ketchup
2 tablespoons chili sauce
1/2 cup (120 ml.) heavy cream,
  whipped
1 hard-boiled egg, finely chopped

Blend mayonnaise with chopped vegetables and stir in ketchup and chili sauce. Fold in stiffly whipped cream. Just before serving add chopped egg.

Aïoli

A garlicky mayonnaise from Provence is an excellent accompaniment for fish and vegetables.

6 cloves garlic
2 egg yolks
Juice of half a lemon or more

1 cup (235 ml.) olive oil
Salt and pepper to taste

Crush the garlic in a mortar or a press. Beat it with the egg yolks. Add the lemon juice and the oil very slowly, beating all the time. Add a few drops of water if it gets too thick to prevent the cream from curdling. If it does curdle, start all over again with a new egg yolk and pour the curdled sauce in a thin stream onto the yolk, beating all the time. Season to taste with salt and pepper.

For a thicker, firmer sauce you may add 1 mashed boiled potato or a slice of white bread, crusts removed, soaked in water or milk and squeezed dry, before you beat in the oil.

Skorthalia

This garlicky sauce from Greece made with bread and no eggs keeps better than mayonnaise. Make it in a blender or use a mortar. Pour it over fish and vegetables.

6–7 slices good white bread
3 large cloves garlic, crushed
Juice of half a lemon or 2 tablespoons
    white wine vinegar

2/3 cup (150 ml.) olive oil
Salt and pepper

Remove the crusts from the bread. Soak in water, then squeeze. Put in the blender with the garlic and the lemon juice or vinegar. Gradually add the olive oil to achieve a smooth thick cream, then stir in water (2/3 cup/150 ml.) to thin the sauce. Add salt and pepper to taste and blend well.

Other Sauces for Fish

A type of mayonnaise based on hard-boiled rather than raw egg yolks that keeps better on a hot day.

Put 2 hard-boiled yolks in a blender with 2/3 cup (150 ml.) olive oil and the juice of half a lemon or a tablespoon or two of vinegar. Add salt and pepper to taste. The sauce should be the consistency of mayonnaise. A crushed clove of garlic, 2 to 4 pounded anchovy fillets, and a good bunch of finely chopped parsley will give you a traditional Italian *salsa verde* (see p. 133).

You may alternatively add a teaspoon of mustard and a pinch of cayenne pepper for what Escoffier called a *"Sauce Cambridge."*

Half an onion, finely chopped, or 2 finely minced spring onions and a few finely chopped pickled cucumbers or capers turns it into a *sauce tartare.*

A small but strong fresh pimento, well pounded, will make it fiery.

Nut Sauces

A whole range of sauces based on a variety of nuts, ground to a paste and highly seasoned, originates in the Middle East. Usually named tarator, they are equally good for meats, chicken, fish, and boiled or raw vegetables. They are simple—a matter of mixing and tasting—and cannot fail.

Each country makes use of its indigenous nuts, so versions depend on local trees.

Tarator with Pine Nuts

The favorite accompaniment to fish in Lebanon is the most exquisite as well as the most expensive, for nowhere are pine nuts cheap. However, people cheat and put in more bread and fewer nuts. It can be made in a blender. Otherwise pound it to a paste in a mortar.

2 slices white bread
12 oz. (350 g.) pine nuts
2 cloves garlic, crushed

Salt and white pepper to taste
Juice of 1 or more lemons

Remove the crusts of the bread, soak in water, then squeeze dry. Add the pine nuts, crushed garlic, salt, white pepper, lemon juice, and enough water to make 1 cup (235 ml.) of liquid. Blend to a very smooth cream.

Turkish Khiyar Tereturu

Present this with cucumber, cauliflower, or another such salad with a dribbling of olive oil poured over it.

1–2 slices white bread
1/2 lb. (225 g.) fresh walnuts or
    blanched almonds
1–2 cloves garlic, crushed

4 tablespoons wine vinegar or the
    juice of 1 or more lemons
Salt and pepper

Remove the crusts from the bread, soak in water, then squeeze dry. Grind the walnuts or blanched almonds in a blender. Add the bread, crushed garlic, wine vinegar or lemon juice, and salt and pepper to taste, and blend, adding enough water to bring it to the consistency of a light cream.

A Light Tahina

Nothing brings the Arab flavor to a dish more than the pale sauce based on the oily pulp of mashed sesame seeds which you can buy in a jar in Greek and Middle Eastern shops. As good with fish as it is with any salad, many people pour this on meatballs and chicken.

2/3 cup (150 ml.) or more lemon juice	2 cloves garlic, crushed Salt and pepper
1 cup (235 ml.) tahina	About 1/2 cup (120 ml.) water

Gradually add the lemon juice to the tahina, beating vigorously. Add the crushed garlic, salt, pepper, and enough water for a light cream. You may put all this through the blender.

Fresh Cream Sauce

Fresh heavy cream makes one of the most delicious sauces for cold fish. Bring 1 cup (1/4 liter) heavy cream to the boil with a good bunch of chopped fresh herbs, mixed if you like, and chosen from tarragon, parsley, chervil, chives, watercress, and coriander leaves. Season to taste with salt and pepper and simmer for 7 to 8 minutes. You may also like to add a crushed clove of garlic and a squeeze of lemon. Chill, then whisk until it is thick and smooth. The French, who like this with watercress, call it a mousseline.

Mustard and cream sauce. Stir 2 teaspoons good Dijon mustard into about 7/8 cup (200 ml.) fresh cream with the juice of a medium lemon and salt and pepper to taste.

Horseradish Sauces

How you make this old English sauce is purely a matter of taste.

Grate as much fresh horseradish as you like into some whipped heavy cream. About 2 heaped tablespoons should be enough for 2/3 cup (150 ml.) cream.

You may also stir in a pinch of powdered sugar, a few drops of wine vinegar, a sprinkling of salt and pepper, and a touch of mustard.

Variation: Sour cream is a delicious alternative to fresh cream.

Here are Jane Grigson's directions for Escoffier's version (from *Good Things*).

1/2 cup (50 g.) shelled walnuts	1 tablespoon white bread crumbs
1/2 cup (50 g.) grated horseradish	2/3 cup (150 ml.) heavy cream
A pinch of salt	1 teaspoon wine vinegar or
1 teaspoon sugar	lemon juice

Pour boiling water over the walnuts and leave them for a moment or two. You will then be able to remove their fine skins (which can add a bitter taste to this sauce). Chop the nuts finely, then mix with the rest of the ingredients. Add the vinegar or lemon juice gradually—the whole teaspoon may not be to your taste, or you may like to add a little more.

Good for salmon and trout as well as for cold beef.

Cream Cheese

For many years now people have been serving cream cheese dips with drinks. Few realize what an excellent accompanying sauce for cold meats, eggs, and fish they are. Use a light, full-fat cream cheese such as the French fromage blanc. Whip it well, adding yogurt, cream, or a little olive oil if it is too thick. Flavor with fresh chopped herbs such as mint, basil, chives, tarragon. Add crushed garlic or very finely chopped onion. If you cannot find fromage blanc, a good alternative is to blend equal quantities of cottage cheese and yogurt.

Make it sharp with lemon juice or beat in a little tomato paste to give it color. Grated raw cucumber, salted and drained of its juices for half an hour, finely chopped bits of pickled cucumber, fennel, celery, and capers, all or one, are pleasant additions.

My own favorite is simply cream cheese mixed with oil, garlic, and basil when it is available.

Aspic

Although aspic plays an important part in cold buffet food, in glazing and holding decorations of bits of cucumber, tomato, egg, truffle, and tongue in place with a coating of shining jelly, this function is of no interest in this book; it does not stand up very well to warm weather, and we are concerned with simple presentation rather than decoration. Moderate use may be made of jellied stock to contain and hold food together in a mold provided that it is carried in a cool container.

Aspic is particularly unpleasant when not properly made. The best is made with jellies obtained from boiling knuckle of veal, calf's or pig's feet, clarifying the stock, and reducing it. Much simpler for the limited use we are putting it to is one made with gelatin and a well-flavored stock in the following way:

2 cups (450 ml.) water	A sprig of thyme
2/3 cup (150 ml.) white wine	Lemon juice
1/2 onion, chopped	Salt and pepper
1 carrot, chopped	3/8 cup (100 ml.) sherry, Marsala,
A few celery ribs, chopped	or Madeira
A few parsley stalks	1 oz. (25 g.) powdered gelatin

Simmer the water and white wine with the vegetables and the herbs, a squeeze of lemon, and salt and pepper for 30 minutes until the liquor is well flavored. Strain and let it cool a little. Add sherry, Marsala, or Madeira and sprinkle in the gelatin. Bring it to the boiling point, whisking all the time to dissolve the gelatin. This will set firm on cooling. It may be mixed with mayonnaise for a firm sauce.

Fruit Purées

These excellent summer companions to cold meat, chicken, and fish, simply cooked with no embellishments, are refreshingly acid in the springtime and sweeter later in the summer. They may otherwise be lightly sweetened and exotically flavored with wines and spirits, spices and vinegars.

Gooseberry sauce was introduced to me by Jane Grigson. It is not only a May-time companion for mackerel. You can serve the early acid green fruit with roast duck, pork, ham, goose, or lamb. As the sauce is to be eaten cold, I make it with no butter. Top and tail the gooseberries. Put them in a heavy pan. Moisten with a few tablespoons of water, port, or leftover white wine (a Muscat is excellent) and let them soften very slowly until they are easily mashed with a fork. If too acid, add a sprinkling of sugar; if too sweet, add a squeeze of lemon or orange juice. Also try the juice of fresh ginger pressed in a garlic press. A few drops are enough.

For an apricot purée for lamb, chicken, and duck, simmer dried apricots with water to cover until they are easily mashed. Put through a blender or mash with a fork. You may add a squeeze of lemon juice if the fruits are not sharp enough (they vary greatly) and a pinch of cinnamon or allspice.

For a prune purée, simmer prunes in red wine or port until they are soft. Remove the pits and put the fruit with the liquor through a blender. This is also good mixed with chopped walnuts. Serve with pork, turkey, chicken, or beef and try it also with fish. You may also flavor with cinnamon or nutmeg.

For a cranberry sauce for meat and fowl, simmer 1 1/8 lb. (1/2 kg.) cranberries in 1 cup (1/4 liter) orange juice with 1/2 lb. (225 g.) sugar and lemon juice to taste.

A cherry sauce can be made with canned or bottled pitted black cherries. Simmer in a pan with 3 to 4 tablespoons wine vinegar for 1/2 lb. (225 g.) cherries to reduce the liquor and soften the fruit. Mash with a fork.

Cumberland Sauce

The best English sauce for cold meats depends on good red currant jelly, which is not always easy to find. It is useful to make a small stock in late summer when jars are plentiful in the shops. The sauce keeps for weeks in a jar in the refrigerator.

Here is Michael Smith's recipe in *Fine English Cookery.*

3 oranges	2 teaspoons dry mustard
3 lemons	1 small onion, very finely chopped
1 1/8 lb. (1/2 kg.) good red	A little salt
currant jelly	Tip of a teaspoon powdered mace
2/3 cup (150 ml.) ruby port	1 sherry glass cider vinegar

Using a potato peeler, remove the rind from all 6 pieces of fruit. Care must be taken that no white pith is taken off with the rind, as this is the bitter part of the citrus fruits.

Collect the strips of rind together into manageable piles, and with a very sharp, thin-spined knife shred the rind as finely as you possibly can. Try to shred it as fine as a pin, for this will ensure that your sauce is good looking and elegant.

Put the shredded peel into a pan and pour over enough water to cover it. Bring the contents of the pan to the boil and immediately pour into a strainer. Cool the peel under running cold water for a minute or so, then put on one side.

Squeeze and strain the juice of 2 of the oranges and 2 of the lemons. Bring this to the boil with all the remaining ingredients and simmer for 15 minutes over a low heat, stirring to ensure that the jelly melts evenly and doesn't catch.

Add the shredded rind and boil for a further 5 to 10 minutes until the sauce starts to thicken. Cool then refrigerate until the sauce is fully thickened. Serve chilled and do not strain.

A Peppery Relish

I shall never forget the spoonful of relish offered by a Yemenite family camping on the banks of the Sea of Galilee. I thought I would never be able to taste anything again, so powerful were the peppers with which it was made. Tears running down my cheeks, and gasping for breath, I heard that the other ingredients were onions, vinegar, spices, raisins, and sugar.

Here is a similar recipe which will not make you cry. Made with sweet peppers, it is an adaptation of Escoffier's "piments pour viandes froides" by Elizabeth David in *Spices, Salt and Aromatics in the English Kitchen.*

You need 2 large, fat, fleshy, sweet and ripe red peppers (about 1 1/8 lb./1/2 kg. gross weight), 1/2 lb. (225 g.) of mild Spanish onions, 1 1/8 lb. (1/2 kg.) of ripe tomatoes, 1 clove of garlic, 4 1/2 oz. (125 g.) of raisins, half a teaspoonful each of salt, powdered ginger (or grated dried ginger root), and mixed spices such as allspice, mace and nutmeg, 1/2 lb. (225 g.) white sugar, 4 tablespoons of olive oil, and 2/3 cup (150 ml.) of fine wine vinegar.

Melt the finely chopped onions in the olive oil, add the chopped peppers (well washed, all core and seeds removed), salt and spices, and after 10 minutes the peeled and chopped tomatoes and the raisins, garlic and sugar; lastly the vinegar. Cook extremely slowly, covered, for at least one hour and a quarter.

Good with cold meats; keeps a few weeks in a jar.

VEGETABLES, SALADS, COLD RICE AND PASTA DISHES

There is no more pleasant way to celebrate the summer months than with the season's fresh vegetables and those from abroad to add variety. Have them raw or lightly cooked and still crisp, to preserve their natural taste and appearance. No picnic should be without vegetables, and the more there are the better, especially when they are in the form of a salad. Even Brillat-Savarin, who had not much time for vegetables, made an exception for salad which "freshens without enfeebling and fortifies without irritating."

Crudités / Raw and Cooked Vegetables in a Vinaigrette Dressing

The French have a most alluring way of serving up all manner of raw and cooked vegetables as an hors d'œuvre, each vegetable arriving singly in its own dish or in an assortment arranged on a large plate. It makes a regal side dish.

Prepare a selection of these fresh salads with an eye on harmony of taste, color, and texture, with a fruit or two as a pleasant surprise. Dress them in advance and carry each vegetable in a separate plastic bag ready to arrange when it is time to eat.

Radishes. Clean and wash in cold water. Serve alone with bread and butter and salt, or as part of an arrangement.

Cucumbers. Peel and slice very thin or cut in longish thin sticks. Salt generously and leave in a strainer to allow the juices to drain away for at least an hour before serving. If the cucumber is still salty, rinse with a little cold water. Dress with a vinaigrette. You may replace the vinegar with lemon juice and add a few tablespoons of fresh cream or sour cream. Sprinkle with fresh chopped chives, chervil, and tarragon, whichever is available. Or make a cream dressing without oil: beat 3 parts light cream with 1 part lemon juice, adding salt and pepper to taste.

Tomatoes. Wash and cut into slices (do not peel). Toss in a vinaigrette dressing. Sprinkle with finely chopped or grated onion or some chopped spring onion, parsley, and when available basil and tarragon. Some people like to add a little crushed garlic.

Marinated mushrooms. Wash well. Trim off a thin slice from the earth-covered ends. Leave them raw or blanch them first for a minute in lemon-acidulated salted water. Marinate for at least an hour in a vinaigrette with a few finely chopped spring onions or a little crushed garlic, plenty of finely chopped parsley, a little thyme, and a crumbled bay leaf. You may like to use lemon juice instead of vinegar.

Carrots. Old carrots are tastiest. Scrape off the skin and grate. Stir in a vinaigrette made with lemon juice instead of vinegar and add a little sugar to taste, usually about a teaspoon for 3 medium carrots. Add finely chopped fresh parsley and any fresh herbs available: chives, chervil, tarragon, or feathery fennel leaves. Dried mint crumbled onto the carrots gives them an especially fresh taste.

Red or white cabbage. Slice very thin or grate and season with a sharp vinaigrette. You may also sprinkle with salt and leave to lose water and soften in a strainer for up to 4 hours before dressing.

Cauliflower. I like cauliflower raw, the flowerets thinly sliced and macerated in a vinaigrette for at least an hour before serving.

   Another way is to break into flowerets and boil them in salted water for a few minutes until only slightly tender but not too soft. Dress with a vinaigrette and chopped herbs or with 2 tablespoons fresh cream, beaten well, 1 tablespoon Dijon mustard and 1 tablespoon finely chopped fresh tarragon, chervil, or chives. Mayonnaise also makes a good dressing. Sprinkle if you like with slivered or chopped almonds.

Avocado. Peel and cut in half to remove the stone. Slice and dress with a vinaigrette or fresh cream beaten with lemon juice, salt, and freshly ground black pepper.

Fennel. Remove the outer leaves. Cut into thick slices and dress with oil, lemon, salt, and pepper.

Green or red peppers. Turn under the grill or over a flame until the skin becomes blistered and charred. Peel or rub off the skin. Core and seed and slice the soft mellowed flesh into fairly wide ribbons. Dress with a well-flavored vinaigrette. Sprinkle with chopped parsley and a little crushed garlic if you like.

You may like to serve this pepper salad mixed with tomatoes or with anchovy fillets.

Celeriac. Peel, wash, and shred the raw celeriac for "céleri-rave rémoulade." Cover with water and a little lemon juice to prevent discoloration. Blanch for 2 minutes in well-salted boiling water and drain well. Mix with mayonnaise or fresh cream flavored with a little lemon juice and Dijon mustard (1 tablespoon for 7/8 cup/200 ml. cream).

In Provence grated celeriac is fried in oil with chopped onions and a little garlic until it is just colored. It is served cold with a vinegar, salt, and pepper dressing, mixed with chopped anchovy, black olives, capers, and a sprinkling of chopped parsley.

Beets. Boil them in their skins until just tender. Peel while still hot and dress with a vinaigrette made with lemon juice and a generous amount of sugar to taste. You may also add a good squeeze of orange juice. Or dress with fresh cream beaten with a touch of Dijon mustard, a little lemon juice, salt, and pepper.

Asparagus. Pour over them a well-flavored vinaigrette with a little finely chopped gherkin or blanched toasted almonds. Alternatively use 1 tablespoon vinegar and 4 tablespoons fresh cream.

Celery. Separate the sticks so as to wash off the earth lodged deep between them and serve with salt.

Jerusalem artichokes. Peel and boil in salted water until barely tender. Drain, slice, and dress with a mustardy vinaigrette, plenty of chopped parsley, and a little crushed garlic.

Vinegared Vegetables. You can turn raw vegetables into instant pickles. Use carrots, turnips, cauliflower, celery, and cucumber, all cut into thin sticks, slices, or flowerets. Sprinkle generously with salt and let the juices run out for an hour. Pat dry. Then moisten with just enough wine vinegar to cover and leave for a further hour before serving.

Sweet-and-sour eggplant. Dice. Salt and leave to stand until they lose their juice. Fry in a pan in olive or light vegetable oil with a little crushed garlic. When they are cooked and lightly colored, add 1 tablespoon sugar and 2 tablespoons wine vinegar. Cook for a further 5 minutes. Allow to cool.

Green beans. Break the ends off the beans with your fingers and pull off any tough thread that surrounds them. Wash, plunge into salted boiling water, and boil vigorously until just tender. Drain and season while still hot with a vinaigrette sauce and chopped parsley. You may also like to sprinkle with a little finely chopped Spanish onion. This is good with canned flaked tuna or strips of herring.

Pears. Peel and slice some firm pears—I prefer Conference in England, Bosc in the U.S. Season with sugar, lemon, and chopped fresh mint.

Melon. Remove the rind and cut the melon into cubes. Serve as it is or dress with a vinaigrette or with port.

Grapefruit. Peel the skin with a sharp knife, removing all the pith. Cut into slices, then into pieces. Sprinkle with sugar and a few drops of sherry.

Oranges. Peel the skin off with a sharp knife and remove all the pith. Cut the fruits into thin slices and sprinkle with cinnamon just before serving. This is also excellent mixed with a large bunch of watercress and dressed in a vinaigrette sauce.

Lettuce or Green Leaf Salads

Whether you use soft round lettuce, Boston, Bibb, romaine, chicory or endive, buckwheat, escarole, corn salad, red leaf, or raddicchio, season it at the last minute, just before serving, with a vinaigrette. Add Dijon mustard if you like for the stronger-tasting leaves and sprinkle with parsley or fresh chives, chervil, or tarragon, all very finely chopped. Watercress, peppergrass, dandelion, nasturtium, or wild mustard will make the salad very special.

Variations: Add cress and walnuts just out of their shells. Diced Gruyère or grated Roquefort may be thrown in, or sliced apples or oranges. Other additions which find favor these days are sliced hard-boiled eggs, raw mushrooms, bits of celery, spring onion, green pepper, pears, chopped anchovy, and capers.

My own favorite additions are fried croutons with garlic and fried bacon pieces.

Coleslaw

Shred a small head of cabbage, removing the hard core. Dress with vinaigrette or vinaigrette with cream or sour cream (pp. 79, 80) or mayonnaise (p. 81) or the fresh cream sauce (p. 86) to which it is good to add 1 tablespoon sugar and 2 tablespoons vinegar. You may like to add a teaspoon of caraway, celery, mustard, or dill seed, or a mixture of these. The cabbage will soften as it should in about 2 hours.

A carrot, a green pepper, a small onion, a sharp apple, or 2 ribs of celery, chopped or coarsely grated, are common and very good embellishments to this popular salad.

Marian Harland's Cabbage Salad

1 small cabbage	1 tablespoon sugar
1 cup (235 ml.) vinegar	Salt and pepper
1 tablespoon butter	2 tablespoons sour cream

Shred cabbage. Put vinegar, butter, and sugar in a saucepan and bring to a boil; pour over cabbage and set aside to cool. Stir in a little salt and pepper and, just before serving, toss with the sour cream.

Waldorf Salad

Put 2 tart apples and 1 sweet apple, all cored and diced or thinly sliced, 1 head of celery, diced or thinly sliced, and 1/2 cup (80 g.) chopped walnuts or pecans in a bowl and toss with 3/4 cup (180 ml.) mayonnaise.

New England Summer Salad

1 head lettuce
2 teaspoons minced mustard leaves
1/2 cup (120 ml.) chopped watercress
4 radishes, sliced

1 small cucumber, sliced
3 hard-boiled eggs, chopped
Fennel or nasturtium blossoms

THE DRESSING

2 teaspoons sugar
1 scant teaspoon salt
Freshly ground pepper
1 teaspoon prepared mustard

1/2 cup (120 ml.) vinegar
3 tablespoons salad oil
1 clove garlic

Wash greens and pat dry. Combine dressing ingredients, reserving garlic to rub interior of salad bowl. Add prepared greens, radishes, cucumber, and eggs, and toss everything with the dressing. If fresh fennel is available, garnish salad with finely chopped tops; or scatter nasturtium blossoms over salad.

Moroccan Grated Carrot Salad

1 orange
1 1/8 lb. (1/2 kg.) carrots,
   coarsely grated
Juice of 2 oranges
Juice of 1 lemon
3–4 oz. (85–115 g.) raisins or sultanas
1–2 tablespoons honey

5 tablespoons olive oil
2 tablespoons orange blossom or
   rose water
1/2 teaspoon ground ginger
1 teaspoon cinnamon
Salt and pepper
1 bunch coriander leaves, chopped

Mix all the ingredients together in a bowl.

Variation: Carrot and Orange Salad—also Moroccan. Peel and cut the one orange into small pieces and mix with the grated carrot. Dress in a mixture of the juice of 2 oranges and a lemon, honey, olive oil, orange blossom or rose water and the seasonings. Stir in a bunch of chopped coriander leaves. This, too, originates in Morocco; it is very refreshing to serve with a hot spicy dish.

Turnip and Orange Salad

This salad is from Tunisia.
    Wash 1 1/8 lb. (1/2 kg.) young turnips and slice them very thin. Macer-

ate for an hour in a mixture of 3 tablespoons olive oil, the juice of a bitter Seville orange or a grapefruit or a mixture of orange and lemon juice (it needs to be sharp) with a crushed clove of garlic, salt, and pepper. A pinch of cayenne is optional.

Serve as it is with a few sprigs of parsley, or add a chopped-up orange.

Greek Salad with Cheese

My favorite meal on the island of Skopelos was a salad made of crisp romaine lettuce cut into pieces, with strips of green pepper, 3 or 4 quartered tomatoes, a few onion rings, 12 black Kalamata olives, and the white crumbly feta cheese, about 4 oz. (115 g.), cut into cubes. Toss this in a dressing of olive oil and lemon juice with a little salt and some freshly ground black pepper just before serving.

I have also eaten this same salad with a sprinkling of chopped dill or fennel leaves, a few capers, and chopped gherkin.

A French version is made with very thin slices of Gruyère and some toasted croutons rubbed with garlic thrown in.

Italian Pepper and Fontina Cheese Salad

Cut 3 peppers into thin strips, removing the core and seeds. Broil until the skins blacken, then peel and slice them. Put them in a bowl with 4 oz. (115 g.) sliced fontina and toss in 2 tablespoons olive oil mixed with 1 teaspoon Dijon mustard, 2 to 3 tablespoons cream, and salt and pepper to taste.

Salade Niçoise

Some mixed salads are a meal in themselves.

There are not one or two or three versions of salade Niçoise—but dozens, depending on what is available. The constants are tuna, anchovy fillets, hard-boiled eggs, tomatoes, and black olives. Suit yourself with the other vegetables, but here is one good version. Add more of one thing if you have less of another.

BASIC INGREDIENTS

4–6 tasty ripe tomatoes, quartered, or 8 small cherry ones
3 hard-boiled eggs
7-oz. (200-g.) can tuna

6–10 anchovy fillets
12 fat black olives
1/2 mild red onion, sliced into thin rings

OPTIONAL ADDITIONS

Up to 1 1/8 lb. (1/2 kg.) green beans, cooked briefly

A small handful of cooked dried haricot beans

1 pepper, sliced into rings

3 sliced cooked artichoke hearts

1 crisp romaine lettuce heart, separated

6 large radishes, sliced

1 sour cucumber pickle, sliced

The salad may be dressed before setting out with a vinaigrette made with plenty of good olive oil, chopped basil or parsley, a little crushed garlic, and a few capers.

Present it on a bed of young lettuce leaves.

Couronne Marinière

Bread in a salad is not uncommon, usually in the form of croutons, little toasted or fried cubes. In this simple country dish from the south of France it forms a soft moist bed.

Slice good farmhouse bread and remove the crust. Lay at the bottom of a serving dish. Moisten with a sprinkling of water, or vinaigrette dressing, but not enough to become too soggy. Cover with a layer of tomatoes which have been softened in boiling water, peeled and mashed with a fork, and seasoned with a little crushed garlic, chopped basil, oregano, salt, and pepper. Lay on top as many anchovy fillets as you like.

Bean Salads and Lentils

Beans are nourishing and sustaining picnic fare, but they must be properly cooked and dressed.

If you can find fresh ones just wash and boil vigorously in salted water until tender, and season.

All types of dried beans can be used: white haricot beans, red kidney beans, black-eyed peas, navy beans, flageolets, butter beans, as well as chickpeas and large lentils. Soak in water to cover overnight, drain, and bring to the boil in fresh unsalted water. Simmer slowly and add salt only when they start to become tender. When you can crush them between your fingers, after 30 to 90 minutes, depending on the variety, drain and place in a bowl. Season while still warm with a vinaigrette or with an olive oil and lemon juice dressing, adding fresh herbs such as chervil, marjoram, basil, parsley, and scallions chopped very fine.

Variations: Peeled and chopped tomatoes and finely chopped Spanish or Italian onions may be added, as well as black olives and quartered hard-boiled eggs. A little crushed garlic and cayenne may be stirred into the dressing. Some people like to sweeten the beans with a little sugar.

Or flavor with crushed garlic and plenty of powdered cumin.

Potato Salads

Everyone has a different recipe for the most common salad used to "fill up" on a hungry picnic.

I like one made with marinated herring fillets and dessert apples.

Cook waxy new potatoes in their skins in salted boiling water. Peel and slice them into a bowl. Dress while still hot with a vinaigrette sauce into which have been stirred some Dijon mustard and a good amount of finely chopped Spanish onion or spring onions, parsley or chervil. Add as many marinated herring fillets as you like and thinly sliced eating apples which have been dipped in water acidulated with a little lemon to prevent them from darkening.

For a classic American potato salad combine diced cooked new potatoes with coarsely chopped hard-boiled eggs, finely chopped celery, and, if you like, a little finely chopped onion and some sweet pickle relish. Let the potatoes soak up a little vinaigrette dressing, then bind with plenty of mayonnaise, thinned if you like with sour cream or yogurt.

Other good alternatives are made with one or a few of the following: quartered hard-boiled eggs, sliced artichoke hearts, green beans, fennel and celery, small quartered tomatoes, pickled gherkin slices, watercress, bits of shrimp, shellfish, tongue, or ham.

You may like to use lemon juice instead of vinegar or a mayonnaise dressing instead of the vinaigrette and garnish with watercress.

The Japanese have an attractive way of sprinkling a potato and shrimp salad with blanched and seasoned chrysanthemum petals.

Mushrooms à la Grecque

The Greek method of cooking vegetables in oil is one of the most delicious for vegetables that are to be eaten cold. Almost all vegetables, except perhaps peas, are suitable. They keep very well, for weeks even, covered and refrigerated.

Mushrooms treated in this manner are the most popular and now habitually carried by the hors d'œuvre cart in hotels and restaurants throughout the world.

Use small button mushrooms. Wash them and cut off a thin slice from the end of the stem. Leave them whole if they are small; otherwise cut them in quarters.

3 tablespoons olive oil	A sprig of thyme
3 tablespoons lemon juice	A small bunch of parsley,
1/3 cup (80 ml.) white wine or water	finely chopped
1–2 cloves of garlic, pressed	Salt and pepper
1 bay leaf	1/2 lb. (250 g.) mushrooms

Bring to boil all ingredients except mushrooms. Throw in the mushrooms, and cook, stirring constantly, for 5 minutes. Taste and adjust the seasoning if necessary. Refrigerate and carry to picnic in its sauce.

Variation: For a different flavor, try a little bit of rosemary, a few celery leaves, and a couple of cloves.

Ratatouille

This Provençal dish, better cold than hot, may be served as an hors d'œuvre, a salad, or a filling for an open tart (see p. 51).

2 large eggplants	5 zucchini
Salt	Pepper
1/3 cup (100 ml.) olive oil	Fresh herbs, finely chopped, such as
2 Spanish onions, thickly sliced	parsley, basil, oregano,
2 cloves garlic, pressed	or marjoram
2 green peppers	2–3 tablespoons lemon juice
5 tomatoes	or vinegar

Cut the eggplant into cubes. Sprinkle liberally with salt and allow the juices to drain in a colander for about 30 minutes. Heat the olive oil in a large pan. Fry the onions until they are soft and slightly golden. Add the pressed garlic and stir. Rinse and squeeze the juices out of the eggplant. Add to the pan along with the peppers, seeded and cut into small strips. Stir, and when they begin to color, add the tomatoes, peeled and cubed, and the zucchini, washed and trimmed and cut into thick slices. Season with salt and pepper. Cover the pan and stew the vegetables in their own juices on a very low flame for 30 to 45 minutes. Stir in a good amount of the chopped herbs and cook for a few minutes longer. Add lemon juice or vinegar.

Eggplant in a Sweet-and-Sour Sauce

My favorite alternative to cold ratatouille comes from Italy. The refreshing sweet-and-sour taste suits cold dishes so much better than hot ones.

2 lb. (1 kg.) eggplant
Salt
Olive oil
1 large Spanish onion, coarsely
    chopped
3 cloves garlic, crushed

14-oz. (395-g.) can peeled tomatoes
Pepper
1 tablespoon sugar
3 tablespoons wine vinegar
1 good bunch parsley, finely chopped

Wash and cube the eggplant. Sprinkle with salt and leave for about an hour in a colander for the juices to drain away. Rinse and squeeze the water out with your hand, a few cubes at a time. Cover the bottom of a pan with olive oil. Sauté the eggplant until colored. Do as many as will cover the pan at a time and drain on absorbent paper.

    In a large, heavy-bottomed saucepan, fry the onion in 2 tablespoons olive oil, stirring occasionally. When it is lightly colored add the garlic, and when this begins to color add the peeled tomatoes. Cut them up or mash them with a wooden spoon. Add a good amount of pepper, the sugar, and vinegar, and cook for 10 minutes over moderate heat. Add the eggplant and cook for 10 minutes more, adding salt to taste (remember that the eggplant have already been salted). Add parsley a few minutes before the end of cooking time. Serve cold.

Little Onions à la Grecque

1/3 cup (80 ml.) olive oil
1/3 cup (80 ml.) wine vinegar
1/3 cup (80 ml.) dry white wine
1 bay leaf
A sprinkling of thyme, tarragon,
    oregano, or basil

2 cloves garlic, pressed
2 teaspoons sugar
1 1/8 lb. (1/2 kg.) small
    pickling onions

Put all ingredients in a large pan. Add water to cover them. Bring to boil and simmer gently until onions are tender but still firm (about 10 to 15 minutes).

Sweet-and-Sour Onions

1 1/8 lb. (1/2 kg.) pearl onions
5 tablespoons olive oil
2–3 tablespoons wine vinegar
2 teaspoons sugar
Salt and pepper

A sprinkling of mint, thyme, tarragon,
     basil, or parsley
2 cloves garlic, pressed
White wine or water

Sauté the onions in the oil, shaking the pan occasionally until they are golden. Add the rest of the above ingredients, covering with the white wine or water. Simmer gently until the onions are tender but still firm.

Moroccan Onions

Add a handful of sultanas or raisins and 1 or 2 tablespoons of tomato purée to 1 1/8 lb. (1/2 kg.) pickling onions as they cook slowly in 5 tablespoons oil. Add water to cover when they are colored and cook gently until tender.

Labnieh / Rice and Yogurt Salad with Fresh Broad Beans

2 cups (1/2 liter) plain yogurt
1 tablespoon dried mint
2 cloves garlic, minced
Salt and pepper to taste

1 1/8 lb. (1/2 kg.) long-grain
     rice, cooked
1/4 lb. (115 g.) cooked fresh
     broad beans

Beat the yogurt in a bowl with the mint, garlic, salt, and pepper. Mix in the rice and broad beans. Serve at room temperature.

Rice Salad

Rice makes an excellent salad, but it must not be mushy. Cook it so that each grain is separate from the others and still has a little bite (p. 74). Toss while still hot with a dressing heavier in olive oil than vinegar or lemon juice, and salt and pepper to taste. Add plenty of finely chopped fresh herbs: parsley, basil, tarragon, chives, whatever you like.

To this basic salad a variety of finely chopped vegetables may be added —asparagus, cauliflower, green beans, carrots, all barely cooked, pickled gherkins, and juicy black olives. Each region around the Mediterranean seems to have its own special version.

An Andalusian one has tomatoes, peppers, and spring onions or mild red onions with parsley.

In the Poitevin they add plenty of mushrooms slightly cooked in salted water with tomatoes and onions.

Dried fruits make a good alternative to vegetables. While still hot add a good amount of moist raisins or sultanas; chopped up, dried and soaked apricots; and toasted almonds or pine nuts. To the dressing add a sprinkling of allspice or a little nutmeg and cinnamon.

Another good way to eat cold rice is with great pourings of yogurt or sour cream or a mixture of both.

Pasta Salads

Italians find it hard to spend the day without their own homemade pasta. The answer, when it is too difficult to bring primus and pans away from the kitchen, is the cold "holiday" version. It is as tasty and unusual as it is simple and inexpensive.

For pasta salad: boil pasta until barely tender to the bite. Drain and pass under the cold water tap. Put in a bowl with a vinaigrette dressing. Add some fresh basil, coarsely chopped, or if this is not available, some parsley, and a little crushed garlic.

I like it as it is, but you may prefer to add a few tomatoes cut into thick wedges and a mild sweet onion cut into thin rings or a few chopped spring onions.

You can use any type of pasta for this salad, such as: fettucine, tagliatelle, linguine, bucatini, conchiglie, fusilli, penne, ziti, garganelli, orecchiette.

Cold Pasta with Fried Zucchini

Encountered in Sicily.

1 1/8 lb. (1/2 kg.) small zucchini
5 tablespoons olive oil
1–2 cloves garlic, finely chopped

A few mint leaves, finely chopped
Salt and pepper
1 1/8 lb. (1/2 kg.) spaghetti

Cut the zucchini along their length into very thin slices and fry in hot oil with the garlic and mint, adding salt and pepper to taste. Boil the spaghetti in salted water until done al dente and drain quickly. Mix with the zucchini in a salad bowl and add salt and pepper to taste.

Variation: Add 2 tablespoons toasted almonds.

Rigatoni Salad in "Carretiera Sauce"

Also from Sicily.

1 1/8 lb. (1/2 kg.) tomatoes, cubed,
  seeds removed
2 cloves garlic, chopped
1 strong chili pepper, chopped
5 basil leaves, chopped
4 tablespoons olive oil

Salt and pepper
1 1/8 lb. (1/2 kg.) rigatoni (or
  mezzani, ziti, or peune)
Grated pecorino cheese to
  taste (optional)

Put everything except the pasta and cheese in a bowl, adding salt and pepper to taste, and leave for at least 2 hours for the flavors to infuse. Boil the pasta in salted water and drain when cooked al dente. Stir it into the bowl and add pecorino cheese when it has cooled.

Sicilian Pasta Salad

We found a different version in each village.

1 1/8 lb. (1/2 kg.) spaghetti or
  spaghettini
Salt
1 clove garlic, finely sliced

3 anchovy fillets, finely chopped
1 yellow sweet pepper, finely chopped
1 tablespoon capers

3 1/2 oz. (100 g.) tuna in oil
3 1/2 oz. (100 g.) caciocavallo cheese,
    cut into thin strips

3 oz. (85 g.) mozzarella cheese, diced
Pepper
4 tablespoons olive oil

Cook the pasta in vigorously boiling salted water and drain when it is only just done (al dente). Put in a bowl with the rest of the ingredients and stir well.

Variations: You may add all types of pickled fish and shellfish.

Tuna Macaroni Salad

An American version.

1 2/3 cups (385 ml.) cooked
    elbow macaroni
1 cup (235 ml.) chopped cabbage
1/4 cup (60 ml.) chopped sweet pickle

1 tablespoon minced onion
7-oz. (200-g.) can tuna, drained
3/4 cup (180 g.) mayonnaise or
    salad dressing

Combine all ingredients at least 1 hour before serving time, tossing thoroughly.

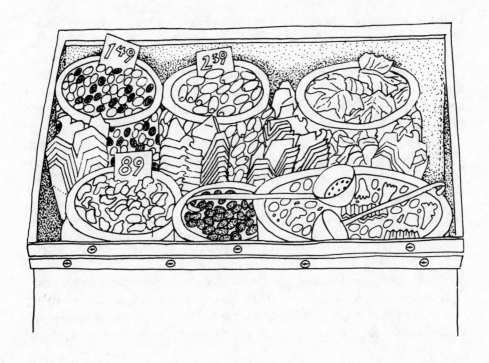

Cold Oriental Noodles

Cold noodles are served in China and Japan as a summer appetizer. This dish derives its inspiration from both. Its special quality lies in the delicate blend of flavorings, sour and hot, sweet and salty, which come into play in the dressing. If it is packed with vegetables and bits of meat or fish it becomes a meal in itself. No harm comes if it is done well in advance.

13 oz. (375 g.) yellow or
   white noodles
2 tablespoons peanut or sesame oil
8 oz. (225 g.) snow peas, tails and
   strings removed
8 oz. (225 g.) bean sprouts
8 oz. (225 g.) frozen shelled shrimp
3 1/2 oz. (100 g.) ham, diced
1 green, yellow, or red pepper, diced
6 spring onions, finely chopped
1 1/2 tablespoons sesame sauce
   or tahina

4–5 tablespoons soy sauce
2 1/2 teaspoons sugar
3–4 tablespoons rice vinegar
3–4 tablespoons dry sherry
3 tablespoons peanut or sesame oil
Salt
1/2 teaspoon chili (or to taste)
2 cloves garlic, crushed
Juice of two or three 1 in. (2 1/2-cm.)
   pieces of fresh ginger root

Boil the noodles in salted water until just al dente, drain, and rinse quickly in cold water, then toss in the oil to keep them from sticking.

Bring water to boil with salt in a large saucepan. Throw in the snow peas, then a minute or two later when they are done but still crisp, add the bean sprouts. Drain a minute later, as soon as the sprouts are slightly limp. Put in a very large bowl with the shrimp, ham, pepper, and spring onions and add the noodles.

Make up the dressing very carefully by mixing all the remaining ingredients, starting with the lesser quantities and tasting all the time. You can extract the ginger juice by squeezing the cut-up pieces in a garlic press. Pour over the salad and toss well.

Additions: It is also very good to add such things as chopped pickled ginger, canned Chinese mushrooms, baby corn, sliced water chestnuts, a cucumber, unpeeled and cut in thin rounds, and sliced Japanese oranges.

Variation: Another delicious noodle salad is made with shredded omelet. Beat two eggs lightly with 2 teaspoons powdered sugar. Coat a large frying pan with oil and heat it up until it sizzles. Pour the egg in and cook on medium-high heat. Turn over with a spatula when eggs begin to set. Cut into thin shreds.

CHEESE

Fromage, poésie!
Parfum de nos repas,
Que deviendrait la vie
Si l'on ne t'avait pas?

For Monselet, the writer of these lines, cheese was the poetry and perfume of his meals.

In recent years the English-speaking world has come to appreciate cheeses almost as much as the French do. Indeed for many who have adopted the habit of serving a well-chosen selection before the dessert, it has become a preoccupation like wine—one of the good things of life. For them the necessity of a well-assorted cheese board is as evident outdoors as it is indoors.

Colette once confided that if her daughter should ever ask her advice as to what to contribute on a picnic her ready answer would be: "If you provide the dessert they will be content. If you choose the cheeses they will be grateful." In fact Colette blushed with pride when her daughter brought the cheeses as well as the desserts on such an occasion.

Now that many grocers and specialty shops carry a good and large selection of cheese, there is much to choose from. Bring three or four, different in flavor and consistency and whenever possible buy local cheeses matured on the spot. Cheeses that do not sweat or become too runny are preferable on a hot day. As they are susceptible to temperature and air, wrap each one separately in plastic bags and remember to wrap up tightly any leftovers as soon as you have finished. The best way to keep hard cheeses like Cheddar is to wrap them in a kitchen towel rung out in vinegar.

If you carry cheeses in a cold insulated box or bag, take them out at least half an hour before serving, depending on the weather. Bring a simple cheese board or platter to pass around or lay the cheeses on a bed of leaves in a flat basket.

It is worth noting that many people are happier with a piece of cheese followed by fruit than with any sort of dessert and share Brillat-Savarin's feeling that "a last course at dinner, wanting cheese, is like a pretty woman with only one eye." It was he too who described a modest picnic in romantic terms. "Then from his knapsack very calmly and contentedly he takes cold chicken and golden encrusted rolls, packed for him perchance by loving hands, and lays conveniently by the wedge of Gruyère or Roquefort which is to be his whole dessert."

Provide crackers or biscuits and good bread; plain or fancy, white, whole grain, rye, pumpernickel or embellished with walnuts. It may be soft and delicate, coarse and crusty, but it must be freshly baked, otherwise it is best to have one ready in the freezer. Allow 3 to 4 hours for a large loaf to thaw (out of its freezer bag) or rebake it straight from the freezer in a medium oven for 30 to 40 minutes. Cut the bread just before you are ready to serve the cheese and pass it around in a shallow napkin-covered basket or let everyone pull or break it with their hands.

DESSERTS

Fruits of the Season

The young nineteenth-century British curate Francis Kilvert noted in his diary during one of his many long walking expeditions: "my luncheon in my pocket, half-a-dozen biscuits, two apples and a small flask of wine."

Even when it is a banquet there is no doubt that fruit is the happiest conclusion to an outdoor meal. Nothing is more delicious than the fruits of the season when they are at their best. When they are past their prime or have not quite reached it, they can be macerated in fruit juice and spirits, turned into a salad, poached in syrup, or made into fools and purées, jellies and tarts. These are summer desserts that cannot be bettered.

If you take the trouble to peel and cut up the fruit and give each one the treatment that suits it best, be it a sprinkling of sugar, a certain perfume, or a touch of spice, your friends will be grateful. If fruits are to macerate in spirit or fruit juices the longer they do so the better. Leave for a few hours or a whole day in a cool place.

Oranges. Peel with a sharp knife, removing the white pith as well. Cut into thin slices and sprinkle with powdered sugar and a little Cognac or Cointreau. Dust with powdered cinnamon when serving.

Pears. So that they do not darken, squeeze some lemon juice over freshly peeled and cut slices. Sprinkle with powdered sugar and a little Kirsch.

Watermelon. This idea for a watermelon party comes from America. Plug a big one and fill with all the red wine it will hold, setting it aside to mellow and cool for a few hours before sampling. You can make this beautiful by carving a design on the skin with a sharp paring knife.

Melon. Flavor with a sweet dessert wine, port, or sherry. Make a circular incision around the stem, remove the top, and take out the seeds. Sprinkle the inside with 1 or 2 tablespoons of sugar and pour in a wineglass full of the wine. Replace the top and chill.

Peaches make one of the most delicious fruit desserts. Skin and cut into eight pieces, removing the pit. Sprinkle with powdered sugar and a little lemon juice and cover with a sweet wine, a red Bordeaux, or a rosé and leave for an hour or longer.

Served on a bed of vanilla ice cream (if you are not eating just outside the house carry ice cream in an insulated bag or box with a freezer pack) and covered with fresh raspberry purée, they form the dish made famous by the singer Nellie Melba. Alternatively, Jane Grigson suggests using gin and fresh orange juice with peaches. The Italians fill peaches with chopped candied fruits and peel.

Strawberries, which I have gone into at length on page 156, are good with port.

Raspberries are best flavored with Kirsch or Grand Marnier. Both raspberries and strawberries may or may not need a sprinkling of sugar.

Large dessert gooseberries. Top and tail them, sprinkle with sugar, and cover with a white dessert wine—Muscat de Frontignan is the one that suits them best.

Pomegranates. Cut them open and turn out the cluster of seeds, each surrounded by clear sharp pink flesh, into a bowl with a spoon. Sprinkle with sugar and a few drops of rose water or orange blossom and chill.

Blackberries, bilberries, mulberries, loganberries, barberries. Gathered or bought, these must be very ripe. Sprinkle generously with sugar and leave them in the hot sun to give up their juice and soften for as long as possible. Crush them lightly if they require a little help. They need only their own fragrance to enchant, but if you must, no one will stop you from adding a little red wine or Cognac, and bilberries like a mint leaf placed here and there among them.

Bananas and dates are usually indigenous to the same countries. They also go very well together. Put alternate layers of banana slices and peeled and halved pitted fresh dates (or the semidried ones from California) straight into a plastic picnic box. Pour fresh light cream all over and leave for at

least an hour—the longer the better. The fruits will acquire a lovely
creamy stickiness.

Pineapples. The finest dessert fruit grown in tropical lands can make the most
spectacular presentation (see p. 149) but for a picnic the best way to offer
it is simply sliced. Remove the rind with a sharp or serrated knife. Cut
into thick slices, sprinkle with powdered sugar only if it requires it, and
pour a little maraschino over each slice at least an hour before serving.
    You may like to cut the slices into pieces, macerate them in a liqueur
with a little sugar if necessary, and smother with heavy cream whipped
until very thick and flavored with a little sugar and the same liqueur. This
is known as *pineapple Romanoff.*

Mangoes are my favorite fruits and the finest of desserts, so good that they
are best left alone. In Egypt we used to say that they should be eaten

in the bath because their juices stained. It is for this reason perhaps that they were so popular at beaches—to be eaten before plunging into the sea.

Papayas. Cut them open, remove the seeds, and sharpen with a little lime juice.

Mixed Fruit Salads

There are countless different ways of making a fruit salad using single fruits or combinations, depending on what is available. Use any fruits in season, as well as imported ones; for a good combination, contrast flavors, textures, and colors: the acidity of citrus with sweet soft peaches, bananas, and pears, and sometimes with the unexpected hardness of coarsely chopped walnuts or

slivered blanched almonds. Prepare straight into the serving bowl or picnic box.

All the fruits must be ripe and unblemished. Peel them, remove the pith from oranges, hull, top, and tail or simply wash, drain, and dry well. Some, like strawberries, must be washed very quickly without letting them soak in water, as this impairs their flavor. Remove stones and slice or cut larger fruit into small pieces. Leave the berries whole. Squeeze a little lemon juice where necessary to prevent the fruits from browning.

Sprinkle generously with sugar, preferably powdered. It will draw out the natural juices, softening the fruit and providing extra liquid for the dressing, which is usually made with lemon juice or orange juice or a combination of both. If you like, add some sweet liqueur or spirit or wine. Try adding a touch of spice such as cinnamon or ginger or a sprinkling of chopped fresh mint for an unusual flavoring. I often add a tablespoon or two of rose water or orange blossom water instead of alcohol when there are children who do not care for spirits.

Variations: Most delectable are fruits left to macerate in a glass of Cognac or some champagne with a little sugar until they are truly impregnated.

Another good dressing is a syrup made by simmering the juice of 1 lemon and 2 oranges with 1 cup (200 g.) sugar and 7/8 cup (200 ml.) water until it thickens enough to coat a spoon. Add 3 to 4 tablespoons Kirsch, rum, maraschino, Benedictine, or Cointreau.

The salad should be allowed to macerate for at least 2 hours in the refrigerator or cold box, but soft fruits such as strawberries or raspberries are best added only half an hour before or when serving. Carry them separately.

Cream, light or heavy, whipped and flavored if you like with sugar and a little of the spirit used in the salad, may be passed around.

Fresh unsalted cream cheese is a good alternative to cream for fruit salads. Lately my family has become addicted to fruit salad smothered in a light French cream cheese beaten with sugar and folded into stiffly beaten egg whites, which we put in the freezer for an hour. We carry it out in a cold box.

An elegant container for a fruit salad is a melon or watermelon shell. Cut a slice off the top and scoop out the flesh without breaking the rind. Fill the empty shell, put the lid on, and carry in a sealed plastic bag.

Fruit Fools and Ice Creams

Sweetened fruit purées combined with heavy cream are easy to make, and they are one of the delights of summer. Opinion varies as to the proportion of cream and fruit and the amount of sugar, but that of course is a matter of preference.

All kinds of fruits can be made into fools and they can be put into the freezer to become simple and delicious ice creams. Carry them out in an insulated bag or box with cold pack inside.

Gooseberry Fool

This is my favorite fool.

1 1/8 lb. (1/2 kg.) gooseberries
2 tablespoons butter
Sugar

1 1/4 cups (300 ml.) fresh
heavy cream

Cook the gooseberries very slowly in the butter until they soften and change color. Crush them with a fork and add sugar to taste. Whip the cream and stir it into the cooled purée. Pack and chill or freeze before putting in a refrigerated box or bag.

Variations: I like this fool as it is, but you might like it better with a little Muscat wine. Another old flavoring for gooseberry is elderflower. Put a head of flowers in the gooseberry while it is stewing and remove it before mashing the fruit.

Strawberry and Raspberry Fools

These soft fruits make lovely fools if they are very ripe. You may use slightly battered ones going cheap but be careful to throw away any bad ones.

1 1/8 lb. (1/2 kg.) strawberries
   or raspberries
1 1/4 cups (300 ml.) heavy cream

Sugar
2–3 tablespoons Kirsch, port, or
   Madeira (optional)

Hull the fruit, wash very briefly, and drain. Whip the cream in a blender until very firm. Add the fruits and sugar to taste and blend until they are well mashed.

Although to my taste the fool is perfect with no other flavoring, some people like to add 2 or 3 tablespoons of Kirsch, port, or Madeira.

Variation: A custard may be used instead of the cream. Whisk 3 egg yolks in a bowl placed over a pan of boiling water. Add 1 1/4 cups (300 ml.) cream, a little at a time, beating constantly, and continue to stir until the custard has thickened. Let it cool; then fold it into the fruit purée. Put it in the freezer if you want ice cream.

Other fools can be made in the same way with apricots, pineapples, and peaches.

Fruit Mousse

A fool becomes a mousse when it is lightened with a snow of egg white.

Stew 1 1/8 lb. (1/2 kg.) fruit in as little water as possible, until it is soft. Pass through a sieve or put through an electric blender. Sweeten to taste. When cooled, stir in about 2/3 cup (150 ml.) whipped heavy cream and fold in 2 stiffly beaten egg whites. Chill to serve very cold.

Fruit Jellies

One delicious way of taking fruit cream on an outing is to set it with gelatin.

Fruit shapes, molds, dillies, and tivolis were very popular in the nineteenth century, inspired by the voluptuous shapes produced by the chefs who left during the French Revolution. The new techniques of the Industrial Revolution turned out molds of extraordinary shapes. Arrowroot and cornstarch or calf's foot jelly were used to set them. Today powdered gelatin is easier to use and works very well. It is not necessary to turn out the jelly, but if you must have an elegant sculpture, brush the mold well with almond or another light oil before pouring in the mixture.

All kinds of fruits may be used. Strawberries, raspberries, melon, and mangoes are best raw or macerated in spirit; pears, plums, peaches, apricots, and apples are best poached in syrup. Dried fruits should be stewed.

Fruit jellies need not be nursery food. You can flavor them with spirits. Use rum with pineapple and calvados for apple; Kirsch and maraschino are good with most fruits, and you can flavor with spices such as cinnamon and cloves.

Turn to a pulp by passing through a sieve or in a blender or simply mash with a fork.

Dissolve 1 oz. (30 g.) gelatin in 1 cup (1/4 liter) freshly squeezed fruit juice such as orange juice or the poaching syrup (see p. 119) in a bowl placed in a pan of boiling water. Then blend well into 3 cups (3/4 liter) fruit purée. This makes a quantity enough for 10 to 12 people.

Pour into a bowl, or into an oiled mold if you want to turn it out. Refrigerate for at least 4 hours until it sets.

Variations: Try varying the texture by stirring in some pieces of fruit.

Or you can build alternate layers of jellied purée and sponge fingers or ladyfingers soaked in liqueur.

Whipped cream can also be stirred into the jellied fruit purée when it is cool and has begun to set—2/3 to 1 1/4 cups (150 to 300 ml.) cream for 2 cups (1/2 liter) purée.

Cream Cheese Desserts

So much can be done with ordinary cream cheese with very little trouble. Unsalted curd cheese such as ricotta and a variety of cream cheeses can be turned into delicious desserts simply by stirring in some powdered sugar and flavoring. They must be as fresh as possible without a trace of sourness. Some people like to pass them through a sieve or an electric blender, but for me beating with a fork will do. Stir in a little fresh cream if you like, and let everyone decide how they would like to eat it—with honey, as we used to do in Egypt; with sugar and a dusting of cinnamon, as I learned in Greece; or stir in a spirit or liqueur such as rum, or Kirsch, which is a popular Italian way. Or add a squeeze of lemon or orange juice and a bit of zest.

You may lighten the cream cheese by adding a stiffly beaten egg white for each 8 oz. (225 g.). Or you can stiffen it with a teaspoonful of powdered gelatin, thoroughly dissolved in 2 tablespoons of very hot water for the same quantity, and leave to set.

Paskha, a Russian Easter dish, is the inspiration for this.

3 1/2 lb. (1 1/2 kg.) curd or cottage cheese	Sugar
3 eggs	1/2 lb. (225 g.) chopped mixed crystallized fruits
7 oz. (200 g.) unsalted butter, softened	Grated rind of an orange or lemon
2/3 cup (150 ml.) heavy or sour cream	

Drain the curd or cottage cheese in a sieve. Beat in the eggs, butter, cream, and sugar to taste; blend until smooth. Stir in the crystallized chopped fruits and grated rind.

Find a mold with a hole in it. A good idea is to use a clay flowerpot (soak this in water for at least an hour to remove any taste of clay). Line with cheesecloth. Fill with the cheese mixture, pressing it down well. Lift the sides of the cheesecloth over the cheese and press it down hard with a weight. Place on a rack over a bowl or tray and leave to drain overnight in a cool place. Unmold it on a plate only when you are ready to serve. Decorate with bits of crystallized fruit if you want to be grand.

For a romantic picnic, make the following mixture:

2/3 cup (150 ml.) heavy
  cream, whipped

8 oz. (225 g.) cream cheese
2 tablespoons powdered sugar

Fold in a stiffly beaten egg white. Line a heart-shaped container (a basket or pierced metal or china mold) with fine muslin and press the mixture in. Let it drain overnight in a cool place. Turn it out on the picnic and surround it with strawberries. You will feel like a poet.

Mascarpone. This simple Italian country dessert can easily become your family and party favorite.

1/4 cup (75 g.) raisins or sultanas
A little rum or brandy
1 lb. (500 g.) bland cream cheese
1/3 cup (75 g.) powdered sugar or
  to taste

3 large eggs, separated
About 32 ladyfingers

Let the raisins or sultanas swell in rum or brandy in a bowl. Beat the cream cheese and sugar with the egg yolks. Add rum or brandy by the tablespoon, to taste, and beat until a smooth cream. Stir in the raisins or sultanas.

Arrange the ladyfingers side by side at the bottom of a wide shallow bowl. Sprinkle with enough rum or brandy to make them moist but not soggy. Whip the egg whites until stiff and fold gently into the cream cheese mixture. Spread this light fluffy cream over the ladyfingers. Cover and chill.

Mascarpone can be made into an ice cream. Put it straight from the freezer into a cooled cold box. In Italy when it is to be served at home, it is often put straight into individual wineglasses after it is made.

Variations: An excellent variation is made with bitter chocolate shavings, and another with chopped-up crystallized fruit instead of raisins or sultanas. My favorite is with a very fine pulverized coffee. Use 2 tablespoons for 1 1/8 lb. (1/2 kg.) cream cheese.

An Orange Dessert

2 large oranges	1/2 lemon
6 eggs	2 tablespoons brandy or orange liqueur
Juice of 2 more oranges	10 or more spoonfuls sugar to taste

Boil the oranges whole for about an hour until they are very tender. Cut them open and remove the pits, then reduce to a cream in a blender with the eggs, orange juice, lemon, liqueur, and sugar. Pour into an ovenproof dish and bake in a 300° F (150°C) oven for about an hour or until firm. Serve cooled but not chilled.

Fruit Tarts

French open tarts are the most welcome hot-weather pastries, especially when the fruits of the season appear in them. Usually, a sweet pastry is baked blind, then filled with a cream or custard on which a variety of fresh or cooked fruits are arranged.

A fruit purée or a jam such as apricot, diluted in water, or even jelly may be poured over the fruit to give it an appetizing glaze. Apples, peaches, apricots, greengages, plums, cherries, grapes, and strawberries all make excellent tarts. These pastries must be transported with care in their tin or dish and covered with foil secured with tape.

A biscuity pastry shell. For a 12-in. (30-cm.) tart:

1/4 lb. (115 g.) unsalted butter	2 egg yolks
1 3/4 cups (250 g.) flour	2–4 tablespoons water or milk
2 tablespoons powdered sugar	

Work and rub the butter into the sifted flour and sugar. Add the egg yolks and just enough water or milk to bind the soft dough, stirring with a knife and then briefly with your hands.

Cover and leave in a cool place for an hour. Then roll out on a floured board with a floured rolling pin. Lay the dough gently into the tart pan or flan mold and pat it snugly into place, pressing it into any fluted sides. Trim the edges, prick with a fork, and line with paper weighed down with dried beans. Bake in a preheated 400°F (205°C) oven for 15 minutes. Take out of the oven and brush with egg white to seal the crust and prevent

it from becoming soggy. Return to the oven for 5 to 10 minutes longer until it is a light biscuity color. It will become crusty as it cools.

An optional bed for the fruit–crème pâtissière (confectioner's custard):

7/8 cup (175 g.) sugar	1 7/8 cups (450 ml.) milk
5 egg yolks	A vanilla pod or a few drops of
1/2 cup (70 g.) flour	vanilla extract

Beat the sugar into the egg yolks until light and pale, then beat in the flour. Bring the milk to the boil with a vanilla pod (or add a few drops of vanilla extract when it has boiled). Pour onto the egg mixture gradually, beating vigorously until well blended.

Pour into a heavy-bottomed saucepan and bring to the boil, stirring constantly. Simmer for 3 minutes longer, stirring occasionally, so that the cream does not burn at the bottom of the pan. You may like to add

2 1/2 oz. (75 g.) ground almonds or pulverized macaroons and 2 to 3 tablespoons Kirsch, rum, or Cognac. Let it cool before you spread it on the pastry shell.

The fruit filling. The most appreciated are often those with the shortest season —strawberries, raspberries, cherries, and seedless grapes. Rinse them briefly and pack as many as you can over the bed of custard.

Plums, greengages, pears, apples, apricots, gooseberries, cherries, peaches, and tangerines all make lovely tarts. They may be left raw, peeled, halved, and pitted where necessary. But it is usual to poach them for a few minutes only in a light syrup.

For the syrup:

1 1/8 lb./1/2 kg.) sugar	Orange juice or red wine
2 cups (1/2 liter) water	2 tablespoons lemon juice

Simmer the above ingredients until the sugar has melted. Poach the fruit for 5 to 10 minutes, depending on the fruit, until just tender. Drain thoroughly and arrange on the custard. You may slice the peaches, apples, and pears.

A light glaze gives a tart a professional touch. Simply melt a jam or jelly such as apricot, red currant, raspberry, or strawberry with a few tablespoons of water and coat the fruit with this.

A sauce of puréed fresh fruit adds a new dimension of flavor. Purée in a blender very ripe, sweet fruits such as strawberries, raspberries, black currants, or the large sweet gooseberries with a little syrup made by simmering 4 to 5 tablespoons of sugar with 7 tablespoons of water and the juice of half a lemon (enough for 1 1/8 lb./1/2 kg.) fruit. Or you can use any stewed fruit. Put it in the blender with a few tablespoons of the syrup they were cooked in—enough to make a light purée.

Pour over the fruit filling. Take some whipped cream to serve with your tart.

Variation: You may dispense with the custard and use a fruit purée as a bed for the fruit.

Mixed Fruit Crumble or Pie

This is easy to make and carry. Use any of the following, alone or together: pears, apples, plums, greengages, gooseberries, apricots, and cherries.

Wash, peel, and remove pits as required. Cut the fruit in half or slice into a deep oven dish.

Sprinkle with sugar to taste, depending on the sweetness of the fruit. For 2 1/4 lb. (1 kg.) of fruit, 4 to 6 tablespoons may be right. Dot with shavings of butter, about 4 tablespoons (60 g.).

Flavor if you like with a sprinkling of cinnamon and a few cloves or a dusting of powdered ginger, or with a squeeze of lemon juice, or with 2 or 3 tablespoons of a fruit brandy such as calvados, marc, or William pear brandy, or with a little grated orange rind.

If it is the season for quinces, peel and chop one up and mix it in—it gives a delightful perfume.

You may also add a handful of split or slivered blanched almonds or some raisins or sultanas.

To make the crumble, mix 1 2/3 cups (225 g.) flour with 1/3 cup (75 g.) sugar. Rub in 3/4 cup (175 g.) unsalted butter to make a crumbly effect and spread it evenly over the fruit.

A shortcut is a crumb crust. Simply crush or grind or put in a blender, plain, buttery biscuits or dry cake. Work in a little butter, just enough to make the crumbs hold together.

To make a pie, use the pastry given on page 117 instead of the crumble over the fruit. Roll it out and lay over the top of the dish to make a lid. Press down around the edge and make a little hole in the center for the steam to escape. Brush with egg yolk and sprinkle with sugar.

Bake crumble or pie in a 350°F (180°C) oven for at least 45 minutes until nicely browned.

Deep-Dish Apple Pie   *(for more than 6)*

This pie is particularly good to take on a picnic because it has no bottom crust to get soggy. Serve it with Cheddar cheese.

Pastry (p. 117)

6 large, tart apples, cored, peeled, and
   thinly sliced

1 cup (90–140 g.) sugar

1 teaspoon cinnamon

1/4 teaspoon nutmeg

3 tablespoons butter

Roll out the pastry to extend beyond the sides of a 9 by 9 by 2-in. (23 by 23 by 5-cm.) baking dish. Mix the apples with the sugar and spices and dot with butter. Cover with the pastry, folding it over and pressing it against the sides of the dish. Crimp the edges and make a few slits in the center so that the steam can escape. Bake in a preheated 450°F (230°C) oven for 15 minutes, then reduce the heat to 350°F (180°C) and bake another 30 to 40 minutes.

Pecan Pie

Serve this pie tepid; it may be garnished with whipped cream flavored with sugar and bourbon or vanilla if you like.

1/3 cup (100 g.) butter	1 cup (225 g.) chopped pecans
1/2 cup (100 g.) dark brown sugar	1 tablespoon flour
3 eggs	1 recipe shortcrust pastry (p. 50)
1/4 teaspoon salt	16–20 pecan halves
1 cup (1/4 liter) dark corn syrup	

Cream butter and add brown sugar slowly, beating constantly until all is absorbed and mixture is fluffy. Add eggs, one by one, beating continuously, then add salt and corn syrup. Toss chopped pecans in flour, then fold them into filling. Line a 9-in. (23-cm.) pie tin with dough and hold down pastry by placing another tin on top, or line with foil filled with beans; bake in a preheated 425°F (220°C) for 10 minutes. Remove from oven, remove extra tin or foil, and prick bottom of crust with fork. Pour in filling. Lower heat to 350°F (180°C) and bake for 35 minutes, or until pie is firm. Decorate top by making border of pecan halves and bake for 5 minutes more.

Cakes and Cookies

The rich, dry, solid type of cake recommended for travelers in all the old cookbooks is best left for the very long journey when it will have to last for days. A fragile one like meringue would crumble at the first jolt. The ideal cake for a picnic or a short journey is a fresh, moist one that you can serve as a dessert and then again for tea and which you can finish in the car on the way home. You do not want cream or butter fillings which can melt or spoil, and you do not need trimmings—only really good ingredients and simplicity.

And of course the easiest thing to do is to make cookies and sweetmeats in advance and to pack them in a box to pass around.

Fresh Fruit Cake *(for more than 6)*

This is a delicious and refreshing pound cake made with one or a number of mixed fruits.

1 1/2–2 1/4 lb. (675 g.–1 kg.) fruit such as apricots, plums, greengages, cherries, gooseberries, apples, peaches, pears, and dates
1/2 lb. (225 g.) unsalted butter

1 1/2 cups (300 g.) sugar
5 eggs
2 cups (280 g.) sifted all-purpose flour
1/2 teaspoon salt

Preheat the oven to 325°F (165°C). Wash or peel, top and tail, core or pit the fruit as necessary and cut into largish pieces. Cream the butter, add the sugar, then the eggs one at a time, beating well to a pale, light cream. Stir in the flour and salt and mix well. Pour into a buttered and floured 9-in. (23-cm.) cake pan. Lay the fruit on top and press lightly into the cake mixture (do not bury it in entirely). Bake for 1 1/2 to 1 3/4 hours. Cool in the pan for 5 minutes before turning out onto a rack.

Orange and Almond Cake *(serves 6–10)*

This is a very moist cake that is good as a dessert.

2 large oranges
6 eggs
1/2 lb. (225 g.) ground almonds

1/2 lb. (225 g.) sugar
1 teaspoon baking powder

Wash and boil the oranges (unpeeled) in a little water for nearly 2 hours (or 30 minutes in a pressure cooker). Let them cool, then cut them open and remove the pits. Turn the oranges into pulp by rubbing them through a sieve or by putting them in an electric blender or food processor. Beat the eggs in a large bowl. Add all the other ingredients, mix thoroughly, and pour into a buttered and floured cake tin with a removable base if possible. Bake in a preheated moderately hot oven (400° F/205°C) for about an hour, then have a look at it—this type of cake will not go any flatter if the oven door is opened. If it is still very wet, leave it in the oven for a little longer. Cool in the tin before turning out.

Carrot Cake *(serves 6–10)*

1/3 cup (100 g.) unsalted
    butter, softened
1 1/3 cups (245 g.) brown sugar
4 eggs
1 teaspoon cinnamon
1/2 teaspoon allspice
Zest of 1 orange
2 cups (245 g.) finely grated
    raw carrots

1 cup coarsely chopped hazelnuts
2 teaspoons baking powder
1 teaspoon baking soda
1/2 teaspoon salt
2 1/2 cups (350 g.) sifted
    all-purpose flour

Preheat the oven to 350°F (180°C).

Beat the butter and sugar together, then beat the eggs in, one at a time, to a pale light cream. Add the spices and orange zest and stir in the carrots and nuts. Mix the baking powder, baking soda, and salt into the flour, then fold gradually, a tablespoon at a time, into the first mixture. Turn into a buttered and floured 8- or 9-in. (20- or 23-cm.) cake pan and bake for an hour or until a skewer comes out clean. Let it cool in the pan for a few minutes, then loosen the sides with a knife and turn out on a rack.

Apricot Cake *(serves 6–10)*

1/2 lb. (225 g.) dried apricots
    (preferably a sharp variety)
1/4 lb. (115 g.) hazelnuts (preferably
    with their skins)

1 cup (190 g.) sugar
6 eggs

Preheat the oven to 325°F (165°C).

Put the apricots in a saucepan with 2/3 cup (150 ml.) water and simmer a few minutes until they soften. Grind or chop the hazelnuts fine but not so fine that they are a mush. Blend the slightly cooled apricots to a paste and mix them in a bowl with the nuts and sugar. Separate the eggs and add the yolks to the mixture. Beat the whites stiff and fold into the mixture. Stirring 3 or 4 tablespoons in first makes it easier to fold in the rest. Pour the mixture into a buttered and floured 9-in. (23-cm.) cake tin and bake for 1 hour. Cool in the pan before turning out.

Banana and Walnut Bread *(serves 6–10)*

1/3 cup (100 g.) unsalted butter
3/4 cup (175 g.) sugar
2 large eggs
3 large bananas, mashed
2/3 cup (150 ml.) sour cream
1/2 cup (75 g.) coarsely
    chopped walnuts

2 tablespoons rum
1 teaspoon baking soda
1/2 teaspoon salt
1 1/2 cups (210 g.) sifted
    all-purpose flour
1 teaspoon cinnamon

Preheat the oven to 350°F (180°C). Beat the butter and sugar together, then beat in the eggs. Add the bananas, sour cream, walnuts, and rum. Mix the baking soda and salt into the flour and gradually fold into the first mixture, a tablespoonful at a time. Pour in a lightly buttered and floured 8- or 9-in. (20- or 23-cm.) cake pan and bake for about 45 minutes or until a skewer comes out clean. Cool in the pan for 10 minutes before loosening the sides with a knife and turning out onto a rack.

Chocolate Cake *(serves 6–10)*

9 oz. (250 g.) bitter or
    plain chocolate
2 tablespoons milk

1/4 lb. (115 g.) ground almonds
6 tablespoons sugar
6 eggs, separated

Melt the chocolate with the milk in the top of the double boiler over boiling water. Mix the melted chocolate with the ground almonds, sugar, and egg yolks, and beat well. Fold in the stiffly beaten egg whites and pour into a buttered and floured cake tin, preferably one with a removable base. Bake in a preheated 375°F (190°C) oven for about 1 hour.

Coconut Cake *(serves 6–10)*

1 1/4 cups (300 ml.) milk
1 cup (235 ml.) dried,
    shredded coconut

1–1 1/2 cups (200–300 g.) sugar
4 oz. (115 g.) ground almonds
4 large eggs

Scald the milk and pour it over the coconut. Leave for 30 minutes, stirring occasionally, then drain off the milk which has not been absorbed—unless you like a very moist cake, in which case keep all the milk. Stir in the sugar and ground almonds. Separate the eggs and add the yolks. Beat the whites stiff, then fold them gently into the mixture. Pour into a buttered and floured 8-in. (20-cm.) cake pan and bake in a 300°F (150°C) preheated oven for 1 1/4 hours.

A Quick and Good Cheese Cake   *(serves 6–10)*

This is not very sweet, and you may like to increase the sugar. I like this cake simple, but you may prefer to add raisins or sultanas or chopped candied citrus peels in the cheese mixture.

5 plain, buttery biscuits	3 eggs
2 tablespoons butter, softened	Zest of 1 lemon
1 1/8 lb. (1/2 kg.) curd cheese	1 tablespoon lemon juice
2/3 cup (150 ml.) sour cream	
1/3 cup (75 g.) powdered sugar (or more)	

Preheat the oven to 350°F (180°C). Break the biscuits into crumbs with your hands and work in the butter. Spread evenly over the bottom of a buttered 8-in. (20-cm.) baking pan or flan ring. Beat the curd cheese, add the sour cream and the sugar, and beat in the eggs one by one. Add the lemon zest and juice and ladle the mixture over the crumbs, being careful to disturb them as little as possible (if you pour it in, the crumbs will disperse). Bake for 45 minutes. Let it cool.

Brownies

1/4 lb. (115 g.) butter	1 teaspoon vanilla extract
2 oz. (114 g.) unsweetened chocolate	1/2 cup (70 g.) flour
1 cup (225 g.) sugar	A pinch of salt
2 slightly beaten eggs	1/2 cup (115 g.) chopped walnuts

Melt butter with chocolate in top part of a double boiler, over hot water, and mix well. Sift sugar and stir in eggs, then fold in the chocolate mixture and the vanilla. Stir in flour a little at a time, then salt. Finally stir in walnuts. Pour this batter into a greased 8-in. (20-cm.-)square pan. Bake in a preheated 325°F (165°C) oven for about 30 minutes; don't bake too long, for brownies should be slightly moist and chewy and never dry. When cool, cut into 16 squares.

Date Drops

Chop and pound to a paste or put through a food processor an equal quantity of pitted, dried dates (of the moist variety) and shelled walnuts. Roll into small balls and turn to cover in powdered sugar.

Stuffed Dates

This is an old Middle Eastern sweetmeat that keeps for weeks.

6 oz. (180 g.) ground almonds
1/3 cup (75 g.) powdered sugar
3–4 tablespoons rose water or orange
    blossom water

1/8 lb. (1/2 kg.) dried dates (the
    slightly moist California ones
    are good)

Mix the ground almonds and sugar in a bowl. Add just enough rose or orange blossom water to bind them into a firm paste. Put in less than you seem to require, for once you start kneading with your hands the oil from the almonds will act as an extra bind. You can always add more as required. Make a slit on one side of each date with a sharp knife and pull out the pit. Press in a small lump of ground almond paste and close the date slightly so as to reveal the filling well.

DRINKS

One tries to simplify things outdoors, and I am quite happy to wash down pies and cold meats, vegetables and desserts, with one wine only. But for the dedicated drinkers who believe like Brillat-Savarin that "the palate becomes cloyed and after three or four glasses, it is but a deadened sensation that even the best wine provokes," it is right to offer two. Have a light refreshing white, commended by Savarin as "less affected by movement and heat and more pleasantly exhilarating," which you can carry chilled in a refrigerated box or keep cool in the river, and a hearty stout red wine that cannot be unduly harmed by the journey, or a rosé, which is said to be particularly delicious by the sea.

Serve straightforward and relatively inexpensive wines. They will taste better on a picnic, while the fine aged ones are too delicate for rough outdoor handling and will be overpowered by all the competing perfumes of nature.

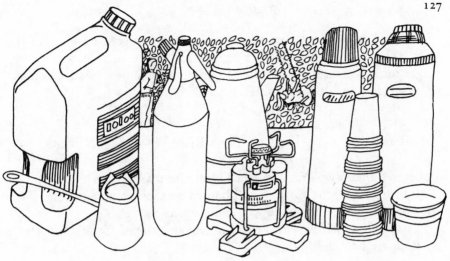

If you are not having wine, take along some good beer and good cider. And, of course, there is nothing as grand as a champagne picnic.

Provide all the nonalcoholic drinks that you can in hot weather. You cannot beat freshly pressed citrus fruit and homemade lemonade for their sharp clarity. It is fun to serve them with bits of fruit and plenty of ice.

My own summer favorites are fruit cups and punches, which quench the thirst, provide a little stimulant, and are most agreeable without being expensive. Mix them up beforehand and pour them in chilled flasks or bottles, leaving the soda to add just before serving. Keep them in a cold box along with lots of ice cubes.

And don't forget the coffee and tea.

Kir

This makes a cool and elegant apéritif to welcome guests as they arrive for a party on the terrace. Mix it individually in the glass. Stir 1 tablespoon of cassis, the black currant liqueur, or black currant or raspberry syrup into a glass of chilled white wine.

Sangría

There are endless recipes for this Hispanic citrus drink, which conjures up for me orgies of grilled sardines and roast pork, windswept beaches and Portuguese voices. Children love it too.

Pour 2 bottles of red wine into a large jug. Add an orange and a lemon, thinly sliced, and 1 or 2 tablespoons of sugar. Leave to macerate in the refrigerator for 2 hours. When ready to serve, put in a handful of ice cubes and as much or as little soda water as you like.

Instant Borscht with Beet or Tomato Juice—Yogurt Drink

I discovered these two drinks in Israel at my Aunt Germaine's.

Beat together equal quantities of bottled beet juice and sour cream and season to taste with salt and pepper and a squeeze of lemon.

Tomato juice and yogurt are just as happily coupled. Season to taste. Both are best chilled.

A Yogurt Drink

This is an everyday drink in India and the Middle East. Beat equal quantities of yogurt and water with a good sprinkling of crushed dried mint, and season to taste with salt and pepper. Chill and pour into a cold thermos.

Sour cream may be used instead of yogurt.

Sweet-and-Sour Syrup

A most refreshing drink that comes from Iran. Boil 2 cups (1/2 liter) water with 2 1/4 lb. (1 kg.) sugar and 1 cup (1/4 liter) red wine vinegar until the syrup is thick enough to lightly coat a spoon. Drop a small bunch of mint in and let it cool. Dilute in ice-cold water in a thermos or, better still, do so on the spot directly into the glasses.

Tea

To make tea, bring fresh cold water to a rolling boil. Heat the teapot with some of the boiling water, then empty it out. Measure out 1 rounded teaspoon tea per cup into the pot, pour boiling water in, and allow to steep for 3 minutes. Strain tea into a warmed thermos as soon as it is made and please carry milk and sugar separately.

Iced tea is as refreshing on a hot day as hot tea is heart-warming on a cold one. Strain and chill before pouring into a cooled thermos.

Apart from lemon there are many flavorings that marry well the tangy taste of tea when it is cold. Mint is a traditional one. Add a few leaves of spearmint when you brew. Vanilla also goes particularly well—a discovery I made in the Seychelles where both leaves and pod grow and where the vanilla is ground and packed together with the tea. Put a pod in the pot. It can serve again and again.

You may like to try spices such as a stick of cinnamon or a few cloves, to be strained off when the tea goes into the thermos, and allow people to sweeten with honey in the glass as you serve.

Rose petals give tea a special fragrance; otherwise add a drop of rose water or orange blossom essence. This is what we were given to drink as children in Egypt to make us sleep. It was very soothing.

If you are going to drop some ice cubes into the thermos, make the tea a little stronger than you would normally, to allow for the dilution.

Coffee, Hot or Iced

Make good coffee and strain into a warmed thermos. It keeps very well this way. For an iced drink make it extra strong, not too long in advance. Strain into a jug, cover to preserve as much of the aroma as possible, and chill before pouring into a cooled flask. Add a few ice cubes.

You may add sugar and cream or milk. Or you may like to try a few spices such as cinnamon, nutmeg, or a few cloves or a cardamom pod. Sweeten with honey and add a strip or two of pared lemon zest if you like.

Best of all, especially in cold weather, is to lace with spirit: Cognac, rum, whiskey—all are excellent.

EATING IN THE GARDEN,
ON THE TERRACE,
OR IN THE BACKYARD

Herodotus tells in his *Book III* of an expedition, planned by Cambyses, the son of Cyrus, and King of the Persians, to see a reputed table in the open air which had been mentioned by Homer. In the *Odyssey* the god Poseidon had gone to Ethiopia, "in the hope of burnt offerings, bulls and rams, by hundreds:

and there he sat feasting merrily." In the *Iliad*, it was Zeus who "went yesterday to Oceanus, to the blameless Ethiopians for a feast, and all the gods followed with him."

The expedition was a failure because of the stark natural conditions in that part of Africa. This is how Herodotus tells the story:

> Cambyses planned an expedition . . . to send spies first of all into the
> land of the Ethiopians, in the first place to see the so-called table of
> the sun that was said to be established amongst these Ethiopians, to
> find out whether there really was such a thing; besides this they were
> to look into other matters, carrying for appearance's sake presents to
> the King. Now the table of the sun was said to be something like this:
> There is a meadow in the outskirts of the town filled with the cooked
> flesh of all kinds of quadrupeds; the various magistrates of the city make
> a practice of placing the meat here every night; in the daytime anyone
> who chooses is at liberty to go thither and feast. The natives say that
> the ground itself, from time to time produces all these things. This is
> the account of the so-called table of the sun.

A table in the sun has always been an object of fascination. When it is in the garden, on the terrace, or in the backyard, one has easy access to the kitchen, and if there is any likelihood of rain one can usually transfer the party indoors. It is nice to bring everything out at once and to allow guests to help themselves and to take part in the cooking. Of course all the recipes for food prepared in advance or cooked on the spot are suitable for the garden table.

Boiled Meats and Vegetables

In *The Raw and the Cooked* the French anthropologist Claude Lévi-Strauss finds that societies have generally placed boiled meats lower than roast ones in the hierarchy of foods. However, opinion on the gastronomic value of boiled foods has varied over the years. An eighteenth-century encyclopedia noted that boiled meat was "one of the most succulent and nourishing foods available to man." Brillat-Savarin, of a later generation, prejudiced against *le bouilli*, wrote that the truth was beginning to penetrate about the "meat without its juice." "Bouilli is no longer served by the self respecting host," he said; "it has been replaced by a roast fillet, a turbot or a matelote." It was to be used for making broth, then left to the servants' hall.

Others have been lyrical in its praise. The epicurean hero Dodin-Bouf-fant, in Marcel Rouff's *The Passionate Epicure,* dared to serve it to the Prince

of Eurasia and a group of gastronomes. That "fearsome boiled beef, scorned, reviled, insulting to the Prince and to all gastronomy," placed imposingly on an immensely long dish, produced a magical and total change of heart. This is how Marcel Rouff describes the dish:

> The rather thick slices, their velvety quality guessed at by every lip, rested languidly upon a pillow made of a wide slice of sausage, coarsely chopped, in which the finest veal escorted pork, chopped herbs, thyme, chervil. This delicate triumph of pork-butchery was itself supported by ample cuts from the breast and wing fillets of farm chickens, boiled in their own juice with a shin of veal, rubbed with mint and wild thyme. And, to prop up this triple and magnificent accumulation, behind the white flesh of the fowls (fed exclusively upon bread and milk), was the stout, robust support of a generous layer of fresh goose liver simply cooked in Chambertin.

These days boiled meats are justly appreciated. They certainly deserve the cliché of culinary literature, the word "succulent."

Bollito Misto / Boiled Meats   *(makes a very large quantity)*

Bollito misto is the great family Sunday lunch of the Piedmont in northern Italy. When the variety of meats is considerable and the accompanying sauces attractive it becomes a feast for special occasions.

The following ingredients are for well over 20. You will need a very large pot in which all of them can be added at intervals, depending on the time they take to cook, or you can divide them between two saucepans. To scale down, omit one or more of the meats.

Serve with *salsa verde* and *salsa rosa* (see following recipes), a green piquant sauce and a red one, both of which are highly individual sauces in which components and proportions are mixed to taste. Other sauces such as horseradish (p. 86) may be added.

3 carrots, cut into pieces	Salt and pepper
2 onions stuck with 6 cloves	1 calf's or 2 pig's feet, cleaned
4 tomatoes, peeled	and blanched
1 bunch celery leaves	1 ox tongue or 2 veal tongues
1 bunch parsley stalks	1 cotechino sausage
4 bay leaves	2 1/4 lb. (1 kg.) brisket of beef
2 sprigs of thyme	2 1/4 lb. (1 kg.) brisket of veal

1 boned calf's head (without the brains) (optional)

1 chicken or small turkey

Half fill a very large pot with water and put in the vegetables, herbs, salt, and pepper. Bring to the boil and add the calf's or pig's feet, tongue, sausage, and beef. Remove the scum as soon as it appears and simmer gently for an hour. Lift out the tongue, and when it is cool enough to handle, cut off any fat and gristle. Slit the skin at the top and peel it off, then drop it back into the simmering pot. Add the veal and the optional calf's head and simmer a further 1 1/2 hours, then add the chicken or turkey and simmer for an hour longer or until the bird is done. Add water to keep the meats covered throughout and adjust the seasoning. All the meats should be very tender. Keep them in their broth until it is time to serve. Cut the meat at your picnic table or slice it onto a very large and deep serving dish. Moisten with broth or it will dry out, and cover with plastic wrap.

Each meat will have a special delicious savor lent it by the other meats.

It is good to accompany bollito misto with an assortment of boiled vegetables such as carrots, leeks, cabbage, new potatoes, and boiled white haricot beans.

Salsa Verde Piedmontese

1/4 cup (60 ml.) finely chopped anchovy fillets

1/4 cup (60 ml.) drained and finely chopped capers

1/4 cup (60 ml.) drained and finely chopped gherkins (optional)

1 onion, finely chopped

4 cloves garlic, crushed

1 large bunch parsley or basil, finely chopped

2–4 tablespoons vinegar or lemon juice

1 tablespoon strong mustard (optional)

1 red pepper, finely chopped (optional)

Olive oil

Put all the ingredients except the oil in a large bowl, mix well with a wooden spoon, and beat in oil—about 2 cups (1/2 liter)—enough for a light sauce. All this can be done very well in a blender.

Variations: A thicker version of this sauce is made by adding 2 slices of white bread, crusts removed, soaked in milk and squeezed dry. Another is with 4 mashed hard-boiled egg yolks. Put either one in at the beginning before you add the oil.

Salsa Rosa Cruda

This is a relish of raw vegetables.

2 lb. (1 kg.) very ripe tomatoes, peeled
    and finely chopped
1 red onion, grated
1–2 cloves garlic, crushed
3–4 red peppers, seeded, broiled,
    and peeled, or steamed and
    finely chopped

1–2 small hot peppers, finely
    chopped (optional)
Salt and pepper
1/2 cup (120 ml.) or more
    olive oil

Mix all the ingredients well together.

Elisabeth Lambert Ortiz's Fiambre Potosino
(Cold Meats in the Style of San Luis Potosí)

So many houses in Mexico still have large gardens, the weather is totally predictable and Sunday is the day when the family gathers for comida, the large midday meal. It is a perfect occasion for a picnic, but not for us. My mother-in-law hated picnics of any kind. I never found out why. She would simply purse her lips and decline to discuss the matter. And on the day we would have had the picnic it invariably rained, great gouts of water streaming out of an angry sky, and though she would look meaningfully upward she never said "I told you so." I was therefore particularly gratified when relatives on the other side of the family invited us to stay, and we had a lovely Northern picnic, Fiambre Potosino, cold meats in the style of San Luis Potosí, a state in the north of Mexico. No one present was actually from San Luis and our picnic took place in the grounds of a small rancho (farm) in Querétaro, also in Mexico's north, that a cousin was running. On another occasion there we had a barbacoa, a whole lamb cooked in an earth oven lined with agave leaves, the plant from which tequila is made. Barbacoa can't be reproduced everywhere, but Fiambre Potosino can.

    Elizabeth Borton de Treviño, the American writer who lives in Mexico, told me that years ago as a young woman she attended a great Fiambre given by the Governor of the state. Behind each two guests at the long tables, set in the open air, sat a young girl in the local costume, full skirt, peasant blouse, rebozo (coloured woollen stole) with dark hair in ribboned plaits, patting out tortillas and cooking them on a little charcoal brazier at her side. The tortillas were put into little napkin-lined woven straw baskets which ensured that guests got them fresh and hot in a never ending supply. It was a very grand affair.

Traditionally guests sit at a long table covered with a white cloth, with the whole Fiambre in great platters on the table, so little extra service is needed. One helps oneself. Of course the meal can be served as an outdoor buffet, or at small tables set in the garden, or anywhere one chooses. It is a most flexible feast and is very jolly. Since everything can be prepared ahead of time it is practical as well.

(for more than 6)

MEATS

2 1/4 lb. (1 kg.) boneless pork loin
 or shoulder
2 veal tongues, about 1 2/3 lb. (3/4
 kg.) each, or 1 ox tongue, about
 3 1/2 lb. (1 1/2 kg.)

1 plump chicken
3 pig's feet, halved
Salt

MARINADE

1 1/2 cups (450 ml.) olive oil
1/2 cup (150 ml.) wine vinegar,
 preferably white
Salt
Freshly ground pepper

2 teaspoons Dijon mustard
1 clove garlic, crushed
1 tablespoon drained, chopped capers
1/4 cup (5 g.) finely chopped parsley

GARNISH

1 small head romaine lettuce, shredded
3 large tomatoes, sliced
3 large avocados, peeled and sliced
5 canned chipotle chilies, stuffed with
 cottage cheese or pickled jalapeño
 or serrano or large chilies

Radishes
Black olives
1 white onion, finely chopped

Cook each of the meats separately, covered, in simmering salted water. Allow about 2 hours for the pork and the veal tongue, 1 hour for the chicken, and 3 hours or longer for the pig's feet. Cool each of the meats in its own stock. When cool enough to handle lift out the tongues, peel, and remove any bones or gristle. Slice. Slice the pork. Bone the chicken and cut into pieces. Bone and cut up the pig's feet. Place all the meats in a large bowl.

Mix all the ingredients of the marinade together. Pour half the marinade over the meat, mixing lightly but well. Allow to stand at room temperature for 2 hours, or longer. Reserve the remaining vinaigrette.

To serve, make a bed of lettuce on one or more platters. Arrange the meats on top. Garnish the edge of the platter with the tomatoes, avocados, chilies, radishes, black olives, and sprinkle the tomatoes with the chopped onion. Serve the remaining vinaigrette in a sauceboat.

Serve with hot tortillas in napkin-lined, covered, small straw baskets, or with quartered crisp-fried tortillas, or tortillas del norte (flour tortillas) or with tamales blancos (unfilled tamales) or with crisp rolls and butter.

Fondue Bourguignonne

This convivial dish, where guests dip cubes of tender meat into boiling oil, is not really practical for more than 6. You need long-handled forks and the special deep metal pot which narrows at the top to prevent the oil from spattering. Use a table heater or a small barbecue. Serve with a basket of sliced French bread, and a good salad.

Cut fillet of beef into 1-in. (2 1/2-cm.) cubes, allowing 1/3 to 1/2 lb. (150 to 225 g.) of meat per person. Have ready an assortment of condiments —salt, pepper, lemon wedges, and three or four sauces—horseradish (see p. 86), curried, green, or garlicky mayonnaise (see p. 83), a fruity chutney (see p. 310), a peppery relish (see p. 90) will all do very well.

Everyone must look after his own piece of meat: impale it on the end of the fork, put it in the very hot oil, and leave it in until it is done to his liking, then dip it into one of the sauces arranged on each plate.

Chinese Hot-Pot

This do-it-yourself meal can be a marvelous communal event. The array of thinly sliced raw ingredients in small individual saucer-size dishes, to be cooked in a bubbling broth by the guests themselves at the table, plus a variety of dips and mixes, makes a splendid spread.

Use a traditional charcoal-burning firepot with a funnel through the middle or a flat-bottomed, fondue-type cooker which burns alcohol or Sterno. Provide long fondue forks, mesh scoops, or slotted spoons as well as individual plates, bowls, and chopsticks.

There are many regional Chinese recipes for hot-pot; they vary mainly in the choice of meats and seafood. We give here a list used in different parts from north to south to choose from. You may have only one in a large quantity or the whole lot in small portions.

Prepare in advance 4 cups (1 liter) of chicken, meat, or vegetable broth.

For 6 to 8 people have about 5 lb. (2 1/4 kg.) meat and seafood chosen from the following, and 2 to 3 lb. (1 to 1 1/2 kg.) vegetables:

Tender beef (rump or fillet) steak, sliced thin
Leg of lamb, sliced thin
Leg of pork, sliced thin
2 chicken or duck breasts, sliced thin
Chicken or duck livers
Fillet of fish (halibut or sole)
Shrimp, shelled, cleaned, and deveined
Squid, cleaned, head and backbone removed, and sliced thin

1 Chinese cabbage, shredded (the core removed)
1 lb. (1/2 kg.) spinach, washed and stems removed
4 squares fresh bean curd, cut into bite-size pieces
1/2 lb. (1/4 kg.) transparent cellophane noodles
1/4 lb. (115 g.) dried mushrooms (soaked in water)

FOR THE SAUCE, COMBINE IN A BOWL

1 cup (235 ml.) dark soy sauce
1/2 cup (120 ml.) thin soy sauce

1 cup (235 ml.) red wine vinegar
1 tablespoon sugar

OTHER CONDIMENTS, EACH IN SEPARATE BOWLS

6–8 eggs, one for each guest
1/2 cup (120 ml.) sherry
1/4 cup (60 ml.) crushed garlic

1/4 cup (60 ml.) grated ginger root
1/4 cup (60 ml.) Chinese chili sauce
1/4 cup (60 ml.) hoisin sauce

Let the broth come to the boil indoors while you mix the sauce and the guests each beat a raw egg into their bowls. Pour the broth into the hot-pot at the table and let it boil vigorously before you put in about a quarter of the vegetables, noodles, and bean curd. Let guests plunge their chosen morsels of meat or seafood into the broth for a few seconds (pork takes a minute or two) and retrieve them together with some vegetables, bean curd, and noodles with chopsticks, forks, or mesh scoops. The usual procedure is to dip this in raw egg, then in sauce and condiments, before eating.

Continue with the rest of the vegetables, meat, and fish until they are finished, then ladle the remaining much-enriched broth in the bowls over the eggs to be eaten like a soup with a little sauce mixed in.

Variation: Although it is not really traditional, it is very good to add more vegetables such as snow peas and bean sprouts, cauliflower cut into flowerets, and thinly sliced cucumber and zucchini.

A Japanese-Style Fondue

Have chicken livers or oysters wrapped in bacon and vegetables such as small mushrooms, pieces of green pepper, and onion with the meat. Give guests fondue forks or chopsticks and let them sauté their food in a mixture of oil and butter rather than deep-fry. Give each person a small bowl of soy sauce for dipping. Add a little vinegar or lemon juice (1 tablespoon for 3 to 4 tablespoons of soy), a touch of sugar, and a squeeze of ginger obtained by pressing a fresh raw piece in a garlic press—all to taste.

Cheese Fondue

Very simple for a small party of 4 to 6 people is the Swiss dish of cheese melted in wine into which everyone dips cubes of bread. If you do not have the traditional dish, use a small casserole or heavy-bottomed pan over a table stove or alcohol or Sterno burner, or any sort of small flame or hot plate. Rub the inside of the pot with a cut clove of garlic. Pour in 1 3/8 cups (450 ml.) dry white wine and put over medium heat. When it is warm add about 1 1/2 lb. (700 g.) cheese, grated or cut into small pieces. Use Gruyère, Emmenthal, or Vacherin or a mixture of these. You can also combine them with Cheddar. Stir gently with a wooden spoon until the cheese melts into a light creamy sauce. Add freshly ground black pepper, a pinch of grated nutmeg, and 3 to 4 tablespoons Kirsch (or whiskey, gin, or vodka). Bring the pan to the table and let it bubble slowly over very low heat.

Cut up some French bread into squarish pieces, leaving the crust on. Everyone must spear the cubes with forks (long-handled ones if possible) and dip them into the mixture, stirring right down to the bottom of the cheese until it is all finished. Serve with a plate of raw vegetables or a good salad.

Cappon Magro / A Genoese Fish Salad

Although the name implies a fasting dish, it is as grand as the type of fish you use and as colorful and gaudy as you wish to make it.

Boil until just tender a variety of vegetables: salsify, cauliflower, green beans, carrots, zucchini, artichoke hearts. Toss them in a vinaigrette and arrange on a large serving dish on a bed of hard dry biscuits or use slices of bread dried out in the oven. Rub bread if you like with a clove of garlic, and moisten with vinaigrette or a little vinegar diluted with water.

Surround with an assortment of cooked fish and shellfish. The success of the dish depends on the choice of fish and vegetables. For a grand party use shrimp, even lobster, and scallops or mussels with a large firm fish. For a modest affair use cheaper fish and place in the center instead of around the vegetables. The secret is to almost undercook the fish (poach or bake in foil) so that it is firm and flakes well. Remove all skin and bones and dress generously with a vinaigrette made with lemon juice rather than vinegar.

Pour over the following green sauce:

1 large bunch parsley, finely chopped	6 anchovy fillets
2 cloves garlic, crushed	6 tablespoons wine vinegar
1/2 onion, chopped	2/3 cup (150 ml.) olive oil
1 large boiled potato	Salt and pepper
4–5 chopped gherkins	

Combine ingredients in a blender and blend to a smooth light cream, adding more oil if necessary. You may add 1 or 2 tablespoons capers, a hard-boiled egg yolk, or a few pitted green olives.

Garnish the dish further with any of these: radishes, olives, anchovies, quartered tomatoes, hard-boiled eggs, small lettuce leaves, and pickles.

A Feast of Vegetables, Boiled and Raw

An assortment of vegetables of the season is a perfect and simple solution for a summer day. Italians like to serve what they can raw; the French prefer them just slightly cooked. Make the selection a feast for the eye and choose from the following: celery separated into sticks, carrots peeled and cut into quarters, cauliflower separated into large flowerets and blanched for 2 minutes in salted water if you must, young lettuce leaves, radishes, green and red peppers cut into strips, spring onions, fennel cut into thick slices, little turnips, zucchini, mushrooms, endives—all must be very young and tender. Trim and wash them before cutting them up.

There are two sauces which will make a feast out of these vegetables.

Bagna Cauda ("hot bath" in the Italian Piedmont). It is a hot anchovy and garlic sauce for the whole company to dip into. Heat some butter and oil very gently—the proportions are variable but can be 1/2 lb. (225 g.) butter with 3 tablespoons of olive oil—in a shallow earthenware or heavy-bottomed pan with 6 crushed cloves of garlic. When the butter is sizzling and the garlic has not yet turned brown, take the pan off the heat and add 8 anchovies which have been pounded in a mortar. (You may use an equivalent amount of anchovy paste instead.) Stir with a wooden spoon. Return the pan to a low heat and continue cooking, stirring until the anchovies have dissolved into a paste. Add black pepper.

Bring the pan to the table and keep hot over a small spirit stove or a candle or in the ashes of a burnt-out fire. Let everyone pick vegetables with a fork and dip them in. Heavy cream may be used, about 2/3 cup (150 ml.), instead of butter. Have some good bread cut in thick slices and some young red wine for this cheerful ceremony.

A garlicky aïoli (see p. 83) brings the flavor of Provence to the table. In the south of France they would also have some boiled green beans, waxy new potatoes, asparagus, and artichoke hearts. Serve any of these with hard-boiled eggs, cut in half, and some good pieces of poached fish, if you want to make a complete meal of it.

Eat with your eyes closed, and a deep blue sky and a sun-drenched wall will appear!

Crêpes

The happiest moments of my boarding school days in Paris were those spent in the Latin Quarter, with my brothers and Egyptian contemporaries. We were regular clients at a crêperie where we would have a complete meal of crêpes, usually starting with a ham and cheese or a chicken filling and ending with a sweet one with honey or Cointreau, all washed down with good strong cider.

Crêpes have remained a favorite food for me, and my children love to be offered a variety of fillings to be rolled up on demand.

The batter recipe I use came from my first cookbook, a 1955 edition of *Tante Marie's French Kitchen.*

2 cups (1/2 liter) milk	1 teaspoon salt
1 1/4 cups (300 ml.) water	1 tablespoon salad oil
2 cups (280 g.) flour	1 tablespoon brandy (optional for
2 eggs	sweet crêpes)

Add the milk and water to the flour gradually, beating constantly so that the batter becomes very smooth. Add eggs, salt, oil, and brandy. Beat the batter until smooth and set aside to rest for an hour or two. Heat a large frying pan and grease very slightly. Pour a large spoonful of the batter into the frying pan and move around until its entire surface is covered. Both the batter and the resulting crêpe should be thin. When it is brown, turn with a large spatula and cook a moment on the other side. Continue this process until all the batter is used. Pile the crêpes on a large piece of foil and wrap them up to keep them warm in the oven until ready to serve. You may make them in advance and keep them in the refrigerator or freezer, but let them thaw slowly for 2 to 3 hours.

At the table have a frying pan over a small burner of any kind. Keep it well oiled. Put each pancake in, cover with a few tablespoons of filling, and cook for 2 minutes, long enough for the ingredients to become really hot. Roll up and serve.

Serving crêpes in this manner is justified only if you have a variety of fillings to offer. Here are some suggestions:

Ham and cheese. Grate 1/2 lb. (225 g.) cheese (mozzarella, Gruyère, Cheddar —anything that melts well) and cut 4 slices of ham into small pieces. Sprinkle all over the pancake. (This is how we had it in France.) For a grander version, beat 1 cup (1/4 liter) heavy cream with 2 egg yolks, add cayenne pepper and nutmeg, and stir in the ham and cheese.

A Neapolitan filling of tomatoes and cheese. Peel and chop 1 1/8 lb. (1/2 kg.) tomatoes. Soften in 2 tablespoons olive oil with very little salt, black pepper, and a few basil leaves, finely chopped. Mash with a fork and stir in 3 oz. (85 g.) thickly grated Parmesan. You may like to add 2 anchovy fillets, finely chopped, or a tablespoon of anchovy paste.

Spinach and cheese. This is an Italian filling for pancakes called crespolini. Mix 1/2 lb. (225 g.) chopped and cooked spinach (you may use frozen), 1/2 lb. (225 g.) cottage or curd cheese, 2 eggs, 2 tablespoons grated Parmesan, and 1/4 lb. (115 g.) chicken livers, lightly cooked in butter and finely chopped. Season with black pepper and very little salt.

Chicken filling. This will serve a whole party. Boil a chicken until it is very tender (see p. 69). Skin and bone it and cut the meat into small pieces. You may add 1/2 lb. (225 g.) mushrooms sliced and lightly cooked in butter.

Prepare a béchamel sauce: Melt 3 tablespoons butter in a pan and add 3 tablespoons flour. Pour in 1 cup (1/4 liter) of the chicken stock, stirring constantly until the sauce thickens. Add salt and pepper and a touch of nutmeg. Stir in 1 cup (1/4 liter) cream and 3 egg yolks, and heat, stirring, until the sauce thickens—it must not boil. Add a squeeze of lemon juice or 2 tablespoons Cognac. Stir in the chicken pieces.

Bring hot to the table and roll up a few tablespoonfuls in a hot pancake.

Seafood. Use freshly cooked crab, mussels, or shrimp moistened with whipped cream, seasoned with salt and pepper, and sprinkled with finely chopped parsley.

Seafood in a sauce from Provence. Cook a chopped onion in 2 tablespoons olive oil until it is golden. Add a clove of garlic, crushed, and when it colors add a medium can (14 oz./400 g.) peeled tomatoes. Mash them with a fork. Season with salt and pepper and fresh or dry herbs such as basil, parsley, or thyme. Simmer for 10 minutes, add the seafood, and cook through.

A Russian filling. Caviar, chopped herring, or smoked salmon mixed with sour cream and finely chopped onion is a typical filling for Russian blinis and is excellent cold, spread on a hot pancake.

Sweet Crêpes

For a dessert, heated pancakes may be served with lemon and sugar or spread with jam such as raspberry, apricot, or strawberry, or with honey. Or you may like to try one of these fillings.

Sugar and liqueur. Use Cointreau, Kümmel, Kirsch, Curaçao, or Cognac. Sprinkle generously over the pancakes. You may even heat a little alcohol in a tablespoon and set it alight and pour it over the rolled-up pancakes in the pan. Another way is to beat the flavoring or alcohol into some softened butter with the sugar and spread it all over the pancakes.

Crêpes du couvent are filled with a purée of cooked and sweetened pears.

Crêpes normandes are made with apples, peeled, cored, cut up, and sautéed in unsalted butter with sugar to taste and a squeeze of lemon juice. Fold in some whipped cream and, if you like, a touch of calvados. You may also add some apricot jam and some slivered almonds.

Cheese with orange or lemon. A good filling which is popular in Israel for blintzes is cream or curd cheese flavored with grated orange or lemon rind and the juice of these fruits. Stir in sugar to taste.

Two family favorites. Into stiffly beaten cream stir a good quantity of strawberries, chopped and sprinkled with sugar and Kirsch, or chestnuts in syrup, also chopped with some of their syrup. Both are truly regal.

A WEDDING PARTY

There is something unforgettable about a wedding celebrated in the open, even if it is under the shelter of a marquee. Emma Rouault's wedding to Charles in *Madame Bovary* was celebrated in a cart shed. Here is Gustave Flaubert's description:

> The table had been laid under the wagon shed. It was laden with four sirloins, six fricassées of chicken, veal in the casserole, three legs of mutton, and, as a centre-piece, a handsome roast sucking-pig flanked with meat balls cooked in sorrel. Decanters of brandy stood at each corner, and bottles of sweet cider were frothing round their corks. The glasses had all been filled to the brim with wine in advance. Great dishes of yellow cream, which quivered whenever the table was shaken, bore on their smooth surfaces the initials of the newly-married couple

picked out in hundreds and thousands. A pastry cook from Yvetot had been employed to provide the tarts and sweet stuffs. Being new to the district, he had excelled himself, and appeared in person when the sweet stage was reached, bearing aloft an elaborate confection which drew cries of admiration. The base was formed of a cube of blue paste-board representing a temple with a portico, colonnades and stat-uettes of white plaster with stars of gold paper. Above this was a castle made of Savoy cake, surrounded by tiny battlements of angelica, al-monds, raisins and oranges cut into quarters. Finally, at the very top which depicted a green meadow complete with rocks, lakes composed of jam and little boats made of nut shells, was a small Cupid balancing himself on a chocolate swing, the two uprights of which were topped with natural rosebuds by way of finials.

Eating went on until evening. When guests were tired of sitting, they wandered about in the yards or played a shove ha'penny in the barn, after which they returned to the table. When the feast was nearing its end, some of them fell asleep and snored, though they woke up again when coffee appeared.

With relatively little money, some organization, and a good shopping list, a few extra borrowed pans and a little help from children and friends, one person can easily cater for a wedding party of 40 to 50 people in two days. And the result can be far more interesting, delicious, and elegant than any caterer can provide.

A cold buffet is the most practical way of entertaining, with everything put on the table for people to serve themselves and return to their own tables set around the garden. Presentation and color are important, for it must be a feast for the eye as well.

As people arrive, serve champagne, but also have on hand an alternative for those who would prefer a longer, more refreshing drink.

Champagne Cup. Just before serving, mix 3 bottles of chilled champagne, 1 1/2 bottles of chilled soda water or white grape juice, 2/3 cup (150 ml.) orange liqueur, and 1 1/2 lb. (675 g.) or more ripe raspberries or strawberries.

Citrus Cup. To 3 bottles of chilled champagne and 1 1/2 bottles of soda water, add 3 oranges and a pineapple cut into small pieces, 2 lemons, thinly sliced, 1/2 cup (100 g.) sugar, and 3 sprigs of fresh mint. You may add 2/3 cup (150 ml.) frozen orange concentrate.

Appetizers to Serve with Champagne

Canapés may be served on rounds of shortcrust, puff, or flaky pastry, baked until golden, or on crackers or biscuits or slices of brioche. Bread, fresh or toasted, makes the simplest base. Use any very good bread. Slice it thin and cut it into bite-size pieces. To toast, dry pieces out thoroughly on a rack in the lowest oven temperature until they are a delicate brown. Brush with melted butter as they come out, let them cool, and spread the filling just before serving in order to keep them crisp.

All the sandwich fillings given on p. 153 will make suitable canapés. However, I am especially fond of spreading them thickly with olivade and tapenade, two cream dips offered in Provence with pastis.

Olivade. The restaurant in the Vaucluse which puts this specialty of Marseilles on every table while you read the menu would not give me the recipe. This improvisation is from memory.

Chop and pound or put in a blender or processor 1 1/8 lb. (1/2 kg.) pitted fleshy black Mediterranean-type olives. Add 3/4 lb. (340 g.) cottage cheese—more if the olives are very salty—and about 4 tablespoons brandy. Mash and blend to a smooth paste.

Tapenade. Everyone has his own way of making this cream, which derives its name from the capers that go into it. They are called *tapéno* in Provençal.

Blend 1 1/8 lb. (1/2 kg.) pitted black olives with a 4-oz. (115-g.) can anchovy fillets and a 7-oz. (200-g.) can tuna in oil, 1/2 cup (115 g.) capers, and 4 crushed cloves of garlic. Add pepper, 2/3 cup (150 ml.) Cognac, and enough olive oil to achieve a smooth paste.

This mixture goes well with hard-boiled eggs. Chop 2 finely and sprinkle over the paste.

Smoked salmon cigarettes. Cut thin slices of smoked salmon into 1 1/2-in. (4-cm.) strips. Season some curd cheese or a bland cream cheese, such as Philadelphia, with a good squeeze of lemon juice and a little pepper. Put a tablespoonful along one edge of the strip and wrap the smoked salmon around it. Lightly dip the ends of the rolls in black lumpfish roe (use Limfjord) so that it picks some up.

Stuffed mushrooms. Wash and remove caps and dip them in lemon juice. Stuff them with cream cheese beaten with a little crushed garlic, finely chopped fresh herbs such as parsley, chives, or tarragon, and salt and pepper.

Little stuffed tomatoes. Cut the tops off 24 small cherry tomatoes. Hollow out, keeping the centers for something else. Sprinkle inside with vinaigrette and stuff with the following mixture: 3 oz. (85 g.) tuna (or more, depending on the size of the tomatoes), 2 hard-boiled eggs chopped, a handful of capers, a few tablespoons of finely chopped fresh herbs (parsley, chives, spring onions), and salt and pepper. Moisten the mixture with 2 tablespoons mayonnaise flavored with anchovy paste.

Fish Mousse

A fish mousse is far cheaper and to my taste more delicious than the classic cold salmon, and you can also decorate it, if you like, with all the trimmings beloved by Escoffier—small pieces of cucumber, anchovy fillets, capers, tomato slices. For me tarragon leaves plastered simply around it are enough. Chervil or flat parsley will also do.

Formerly an arduous task for the ordinary cook, the making of a mousse is now as easy as anything for one who possesses a food processor. Tomato gives this one a pale salmon color. The quantities should fill three ring molds and serve 25 people.

Serve with a green mayonnaise (see p. 82) or another light sauce for fish.

3 1/2 lb. (1 1/2 kg.) fish (I use a mixture of haddock, halibut, and cod)
8 egg whites
5-oz. (140-g.) can tomato purée
Salt and pepper to taste
A good pinch of nutmeg or 1 teaspoon allspice
A pinch of cayenne pepper
3 cloves garlic, pressed

A good bunch fresh herbs (parsley, tarragon, chervil, chives, watercress)
Juice of 1 lemon or 4 tablespoons Cognac
1 3/8 cups (450 ml.) light and heavy cream, mixed
1 1/8 lb. (1/2 kg.) shrimp or fillets of fish (sole, salmon, or salmon trout), cut into strips

Remove the skin and bones and put the raw fish (not the shrimp or fillets) in an electric blender or processor with the egg whites, or chop and pound it and beat in the whites, until it is a smooth mixture. Add the tomato purée, salt, pepper, nutmeg or allspice, cayenne, garlic, herbs, and lemon juice or

Cognac. Mix well. Leave in the refrigerator for 1 to 2 hours. Beat the cream until stiff and add to the fish mixture, stirring it in until well blended. Pour a little into 3 ring molds lined with well-oiled or buttered foil, alternating with layers of fillets of fish or shrimp, and starting and finishing with the fish mixture. Cover with foil. Put in a tray of water in a preheated 400°F (205°C) oven for 30 to 50 minutes, until the mousse has shrunk slightly away from the sides and the top feels springy.

If you want to keep the mousses for more than a day in the refrigerator, pour about 2/3 cup (150 ml.) aspic jelly (see p. 87) mixed with chopped herbs over them after they have cooled. Turn out when you are ready to serve and peel off the foil carefully.

Circassian Chicken

My friend Belinda Bather finds that this is one of the most popular dishes at the parties she caters for. She brought back the recipe from Turkey, where she lived for ten years. For about 40 people multiply it by 5 and prepare it the day before. An attractive way of presenting this is spooned in portions on young romaine lettuce leaves.

1 large chicken	2–3 slices white or whole wheat bread,
1 onion	dried out in oven
A few parsley stalks	4 cloves garlic, crushed (optional)
A few celery leaves	2 tablespoons paprika
A sprig of tarragon	2–3 tablespoons walnut or other
Salt and pepper	light oil
8 oz. (225 g.) walnuts	

Gently boil the chicken in water with the onion, parsley, celery leaves, tarragon, salt, and pepper for almost an hour until chicken is tender but not yet falling apart.

Put the walnuts (make sure they do not taste rancid, as they sometimes do) through a blender and grind them very fine. Put separately in the blender the dried-out bread. Mix together in a saucepan and moisten with enough of the above chicken broth to make a porridgelike consistency. (Belinda sometimes adds garlic at this stage.) Add salt and 1/2 to 1 tablespoon paprika and simmer over gentle heat for a few minutes until mixture thickens.

Skin and bone the chicken. Cut it into thin strips or pull it into shreds with your fingers. Mix two-thirds of the sauce with the shredded chicken, arrange on a large serving dish, and pour the rest of the sauce over it. Dribble on the oil into which you have stirred a tablespoon of paprika.

Vitello Tonnato

This Italian picnic favorite may be cooked a day or two before, but the sauce is best prepared on the day. To serve 40 multiply the quantities by 5.

2 1/4 to 3 1/2-lb. (1–1 1/2-kg.) boned leg of veal	1 1/4 cups (300 ml.) olive oil
1/2 bottle white wine (optional)	Juice of 1 or 2 lemons
1 carrot	7 oz. (200 g.) canned tuna fish, flaked
1 rib celery, sliced	5 anchovy fillets, chopped
1 onion, chopped	Salt and pepper
1 bay leaf	Capers
A sprig of parsley	Pickles, thinly sliced
2 egg yolks	Chopped parsley

Put the veal with the wine, carrot, celery, onion, bay leaf, and parsley sprig in a pot. Cover with water. For the sauce, make a mayonnaise (see p. 81) with the egg yolks, olive oil, and lemon juice. Blend the tuna fish, anchovy fillets, and a little veal stock—just enough for a creamy consistency. Fold this into the mayonnaise and season to taste with salt and pepper.

Cut the meat into thin slices, spoon over the sauce, and garnish with a few capers or thin slices of pickles and parsley.

Zucchini with Raisins and Pine Nuts

From Sicily, a taste of the Arab world. Make 4 or 5 times this quantity for 40 people.

1 large onion	3 tablespoons wine vinegar
2/3 cup (150 ml.) olive oil	Salt and pepper to taste
2 cloves garlic, pressed	3 tablespoons pine nuts or 1/4 lb.
2 1/4 lb. (1 kg.) zucchini, thinly sliced	(115 g.) slivered almonds
3 tablespoons raisins or sultanas	

Fry the onion in the olive oil until it is golden. Add the garlic and stir. Add the zucchini and lightly fry, stirring occasionally. Add raisins, vinegar, salt, and pepper, and cook gently for 10 minutes. Fry the pine nuts (or almonds) in a separate pan until colored. Add to the zucchini a few minutes before the end of cooking. Almonds are a cheaper but a good alternative.

Peperonata

Make it with red peppers or a mixture of red, green, and yellow to give color to the table.

3 large onions, sliced	2 1/4 lb. (1 kg.) tomatoes, skinned
1/2 cup (120 ml.) olive oil	and chopped
4 cloves garlic, pressed	Salt and pepper to taste
10 large peppers, seeded and cut into	A bunch of parsley, finely chopped
thin strips	

Fry the onions in oil in a very large pan until just golden. Add the garlic and peppers and cook very gently, stirring all the time, until they soften. Add the tomatoes, salt, pepper, and parsley. Cover and cook until the vegetables are soft.

A Green Salad

Prepare several bowls of lettuce with sprigs of cress and a sprinkling of fresh herbs—parsley, chives, or chervil, finely chopped—ready to be dressed with a vinaigrette at the last minute.

A Spectacular Fruit Salad

An elegant way of presenting a salad of the fruits in season is in the half shells of small melons and pineapples. For 40 people have at least 20 of either or 10 of each. Cut in half to serve as cups. Scoop out the whole of the inside, discarding seeds and hard inner cores. Chop up melon and pineapple and mix with strawberries and raspberries and, if you like, sliced bananas, mangoes, or fresh figs cut into pieces. You can also have grapes or cherries. Add sugar to taste and flavor with a liqueur. Pile the fruit mixture into the shells.

Peaches and Cream

This way of serving peaches is a delightful alternative to the fruit salad. You may add a vanilla pod to the syrup for extra flavor, and equal quantities of port and water can be used instead of the red wine.

6 peaches   1/2 lb. (225 g.) strawberries, chopped
2 1/2 cups (600 ml.) red wine   1/2 lb. (225 g.) raspberries
1 lb. (500 g.) sugar
1 1/4 cups (300 ml.) sweetened
    cream, whipped

Peel and halve the peaches. Make a syrup by boiling the red wine with sugar
and poach the peaches until just tender. Drain and cool before filling with the
whipped cream and strawberries, and pour over a raspberry purée made by
blending the raspberries with a little of the reduced syrup.

Almond Fingers to Serve with Coffee

You will find the paper-thin dough called phylo in Greek grocers or bakers.
A 1-lb. (450-g.) packet of 24 sheets will give you 96 little pastries if the sheets
are all good. It keeps for 3 days in the refrigerator.

1/2 lb. (225 g.) ground almonds   3/4 cup (200 g.) unsalted butter
2/3 cup (125 g.) granulated sugar   1 lb. (450 g.) phylo dough
2–3 tablespoons rose or orange   Powdered sugar
    blossom water

Mix the ground almonds with the granulated sugar and moisten with 2 or 3
tablespoons of rose or orange blossom water. Melt the butter, cut the sheets
of phylo into four rectangles, and pile them together, so they do not dry up,
as soon as you have opened the packet.

Brush each rectangle with melted butter and put a heaped teaspoonful
of filling at one end. Roll up into a cigar shape, folding the longer sides slightly
over the filling when you have rolled it halfway.

Place on a buttered baking tray and brush very lightly with melted butter
(at this stage you can put the pastries, covered, in the freezer for several
weeks). Bake in a preheated 350°F (180°C) oven for about 20 minutes or until
lightly golden. When they are cold sprinkle with powdered sugar. They will
keep for several days in a tin.

ENGLISH
TEA ON THE LAWN

An illustration in a Cairo schoolbook of my childhood showed a daintily set tea table on a well-mown lawn. Tea caddy, silver teapot, cream and milk jugs, sugar bowl, slop basin with silver strainer, and fine bone china service were laid out on a light Chantilly lace cloth. They symbolized the mystique of Englishness. The text, as I remember it, may well have originated from *Lady Sysonby's Cook Book* (1935), in which she says:

> A tea table without a big cake in the country in England would look very bare and penurious. The ideal tea table should include some sort of hot buttered toast or scone, one or two sorts of sandwiches, a plate of small light cakes, and our friend the luncheon cake.
> Add a pot of jam or honey, and a plate of brown and white bread and butter—which I implore my readers not to cut too thin—and every eye will sparkle, and all those wishing to follow the fashionable craze of slimming will groan in despair.

A note follows that this little foreword was written before the days of austerity.

Tea drinking came into fashion in England in the middle of the eighteenth century as an outdoor activity. On Sunday afternoon Londoners flocked to tea gardens situated in open country on the fringes of the city to take tea and bread and butter and to be entertained with illuminations, firework displays, concerts, and promenades. The Vauxhall, the Ranelagh, Cuper's, and Marylebone Gardens were very large parks with shrubs, flowers, pools, fountains, and statues. There were arbors covered with creepers and set into the hedges for the tea drinkers. And if it rained, people could shelter under the rotunda and continue to enjoy the concerts. By the beginning of the nineteenth century their popularity had waned. But the habit of drinking tea in the afternoon had become a national institution honored and observed by the middle classes and the aristocracy. Though it has now somewhat fallen into disuse, to be served tea in the garden is still one of the joys of England.

About Tea

In the past it was usual to offer a choice of China and Indian tea, and two pots were prepared. It is still very pleasant to be given the choice. Almost all teas that you can buy are already blended, but you can improve on them by adding a specially fragrant one, or you can create your own blends by trying and tasting.

Indian teas, generally thick, rich, and heavy, full-bodied with a good color and fragrance, may be served with milk or lemon, and they may also be mixed with China teas.

Delicately fragrant, China tea is sometimes scented with dried flowers. Jasmine petals are left in the blend, but larger petals of gardenia, orange blossom, and roses are removed when the tea has absorbed their scent. Not everyone likes Lapsang Suchong with its smoky flavor and tarry tang. Earl Grey is a varying blend which sometimes also includes Darjeeling. Its fragrant flowery aroma derives from the oil extracted from the zest of bergamot fruit. Most people prefer to have China tea without milk or sugar and rather weak.

Iced tea is a lovely drink to serve on a hot day. Make tea extra strong, strain, stir in sugar or honey and citrus juice if you like (lemon, lime, or orange) —all to taste. You may pour it hot into long glasses filled with ice or cool it first, covered, in the refrigerator. Garnish with thin slices of lemon, lime, or orange. For other flavorings see page 129.

Sandwiches

English tea sandwiches are dainty affairs. They should be cut very thin with a sharp knife, trimmed of crust or not, and cut in half or in four. Day-old bread, white or whole wheat, makes cutting easier. Butter lightly and fill generously. To keep them any length of time before serving, wrap in a damp cloth, plastic bag, or aluminum foil, and keep in a cool place.

An anchovy filling that keeps. Chop or pound anchovy fillets and beat in about twice the amount of butter. A little finely chopped parsley or minced black olives or capers may be added as well as chopped hard-boiled eggs.

Cucumber. Peel the cucumber, slice very thin, sprinkle with salt, and allow the juices to be drawn out for at least an hour. Dry on paper towels if you like, lay on buttered bread with a squeeze of lemon and a little freshly ground pepper, and cover. Alternatively, spread the cucumber slices with thick heavy or sour cream or with mayonnaise mixed with finely chopped parsley or chives.

Tomato. Scald tomatoes, peel, and remove the seeds. Chop or mash the pulp with a fork, adding a little salt and pepper, and if you wish a sprinkling of oil and vinegar. You may like to sprinkle a little Worcestershire sauce, or a light powdering of cayenne pepper and sugar, on top.

Sardine. Bone and mash canned sardines with salt and pepper and lemon juice. Or beat in cream cheese or a mixture of cottage cheese and sour cream until you have the desired consistency. Garnish with chopped parsley or watercress.

Mushroom. Slice raw mushrooms onto buttered brown bread. Season with salt and pepper and lemon juice. Alternatively, you may sauté in a little butter, drain, and moisten with cream.

Ham. A good old-fashioned way is to shred or chop it. Season the butter lightly with salt and pepper and mustard and garnish with a lettuce leaf.

Cress. Wash and dry before pulling the leaves off stems. Cut small with scissors and season lightly with salt and pepper, olive oil, and vinegar or simply bind with mayonnaise.

Cheese and watercress. Mix together grated Cheddar and half the quantity of butter and moisten with sour cream. Stir in some watercress, washed and cut small with scissors.

Chicken. Boil the chicken and shred or chop it. Moisten with cream or mayonnaise, season with salt and pepper, and garnish with lettuce or watercress.

Egg. Mash hard-boiled eggs with mayonnaise or with butter, salt, pepper, a squeeze of lemon, and if you like some finely chopped spring onions or chopped pickles.

Rolls

Thin slices of bread and butter, spread with a filling and rolled up tight, make an elegant tea-table feature. Slice the rolls with a very sharp knife or leave them whole. Shrimp, smoked salmon (with cream cheese and brown bread), and asparagus make excellent fillings. Serve with lettuce and watercress.

Sweet Sandwiches

As children in Egypt we were amazed to see our English school friends mashing bananas with heavy cream and putting them into a sandwich topped with a very thin layer of strawberry jam. Other sweet concoctions with local exotic ingredients were a layer of honey sprinkled with chopped raisins, dates, and walnuts, a paste of ground almonds or brown tahina with honey, or honey covered with the heavy cream made from rich buffalo milk. Mashed halva is another delightful tea-time legacy of colonial days.

Mrs. Leyel's Sandwiches

Mrs. Leyel, who believed that there was "as much art in preparing sandwiches as in preparing a French menu," devoted much space to them in *The Gentle Art of Cookery*. Her secret was to use plenty of butter and to grate, shred, or chop all meats rather than leave them in slices. Here are some of her combinations:

Chicken and chopped almonds with cream seasoned with salt and pepper and paprika.

Chicken and ham with mayonnaise covered with slices of cucumber.

Salmon mashed with butter, or moistened with cream, seasoned with salt, pepper, and Worcestershire sauce, covered with cucumber slices dipped in French dressing and finely chopped parsley.

Pounded shrimp and mayonnaise sprinkled with salt, pepper, and lemon juice.

Cheese pounded to a paste with butter, seasoned with a touch of tarragon vinegar and prepared mustard.

Chopped olives and cream cheese.

Chopped hard-boiled eggs mixed with mango chutney, 1 teaspoonful for each egg, and some watercress.

Cooked, flaked smoked haddock mixed with cream and finely chopped parsley, seasoned with salt and cayenne.

They will easily make a substantial high tea.

Cinnamon Toast

Cinnamon toast is something special. Cut the bread into fairly thick slices and toast one side only. Butter the untoasted side liberally and sprinkle each piece with ground cinnamon and brown sugar. Brown under the broiler and rush to the table in the garden. Cut into fingers if you like.

Apple Sponge Cake

I have eaten this refreshing sponge cake in my friend Barbara Maher's garden, which conveniently backs onto mine. It is one of many delicious recipes I have sampled while she has been compiling her book on cakes.

Most fruits, apart from citrus, are suitable for this recipe: pears, rhubarb, gooseberries, grapes, plums, and strawberries are delicious.

1 cup (140 g.) all-purpose flour	Zest of 1 lemon
6 eggs, separated	3/4 cup (150 g.) melted cooled butter
3/4 cup (150 g.) powdered sugar	3/4–1 lb. (340–450 g.) firm apples

Prepare a Genoese sponge mixture: sift the flour two or three times, whisk the egg whites to form stiff snowy peaks, beat in half the sugar, and gently fold in the rest, using a large metal spoon, taking care not to lose any air. Lightly fork the egg yolks in a separate bowl and fold them and the lemon zest into the egg whites. Next carefully fold in the sifted flour and finally the melted butter. Pour just less than half the mixture into a greased, floured, and sugared 10-in. (25-cm.) springform or Savarin mold. Place in a preheated 350°F (180°C) oven for about 10 minutes to set the mixture; this prevents the fruit from sinking to the bottom. Peel, core, and slice the apples (not too thin or they harden as they cook). The quantity can vary depending on the depth of the tin you use. Take the set cake from the oven and gently lay the apples all over. There is no need to sugar them, as the mixture is already sweet enough. Cover with the remainder of the Genoese mixture and return to the oven. Bake for a further 45 minutes, or until it has browned well, shrunk from the sides of the tin, and a skewer comes out dry when plunged into the center. (Bear in mind that the more fruit there is the longer it will take to cook.)

Date and Nut Cake   *(for more than 6)*

My mother discovered this cake in South America and calls it *torta de datiles y nueces.* It is very rich and moist.

8 oz. (225 g.) dried pitted dates	6 eggs
1 teaspoon baking soda	1/2 teaspoon salt
2 1/2 cups (350 g.) self-rising flour	1 tablespoon cinnamon
3/4 cup (180 ml.) milk	6 oz. (180 g.) walnuts,
1 cup (225 g.) butter	coarsely chopped
1 cup (200 g.) sugar	

Chop the dates coarsely and put them in a bowl. Add soda and dredge with flour. Cover with boiling hot milk and let the mixture cool, stirring occasionally.

Cream the butter and sugar well, beat in the eggs one by one, then stir in the rest of the flour gradually with the salt. Add the cinnamon, the date and milk mixture, and the walnuts. Turn into a buttered and floured 9-in. (23-cm.) cake tin or two smaller ones and bake in a preheated 375°F (190°C) oven for about an hour (45 minutes if you are using small tins).

Strawberry Teas

A popular summer entertainment in the early nineteenth century was for guests to pick strawberries for themselves. Jane Austen describes a party collecting around the strawberry beds in *Emma:*

> . . . and Mrs. Elton in all her apparatus of happiness, her large bonnet, her basket, was very ready to lead her way in gathering, accepting, or talking. Strawberries, and only strawberries, could now be thought or spoken of. "The best fruit in England—everybody's favourite—always wholesome. These the finest beds and finest sorts. Delightful to gather for one's self—the only way of really enjoying them. Morning decidedly the best time—never tired—every sort good—hautboy infinitely superior—no comparison—the others hardly eatable—hautboys very scarce

—Chili preferred—white wood finest flavour of all—price of strawberries in London—abundance about Bristol—Maple Grove—cultivations—beds when to be renewed—gardeners thinking exactly different —no general rule—gardeners never to be put out of their way—delicious fruit—only too rich to be eaten much of—inferior to cherries. Currants more refreshing—only objection to gathering strawberries the stooping—glaring sun—tired to death—could bear it no longer—must go and sit in the shade." Such, for half an hour, was the conversation.

Few things are as welcome as strawberries and cream at tea time, especially if they are home grown.

Hull and wash the strawberries briefly. Drain well. Serve in bowls, whole or cut in half if very large. Pass around the sugar and a bowl of cream, whipped if you like. You may perfume the cream with maraschino or vanilla.

Variations: First half fill a bowl with cream. Whip it lightly, then drop in as many strawberries as it will hold, stirring gently. Leave to stand and chill for an hour. The cream will be a delicate pale pink. Dredge with sugar before serving.

An attractive alternative is to serve berries sprinkled with sugar and covered with a raspberry purée. Put fresh raspberries through a blender with a syrup of wine and sugar, or just mash the raspberries with sugar and a little cream, moistening if you like with a sprinkling of wine.

If the flavor of the strawberries is not of the finest, let them soak up a liqueur or spirit or orange juice with sugar to taste. For 2 1/4 lb. (1 kg.) of fruit, add 3 tablespoons each of rum and Cointreau or a little Kirsch or Grand Marnier. With orange juice, use as much as you like, flavor with the grated rind of an orange, and add a few tablespoons of port. Chill, covered, for at least an hour. Not too long before serving whip up 1 1/4 cups (300 ml.) heavy cream until stiff, add 2 tablespoons of powdered sugar, or more to taste, and flavor with 3 tablespoons of the liqueur which has been used in the marinade. Mix with the strawberries, folding gently until every fruit is well coated.

ENGLISH PICNICS

In England picnics for their own sake came into fashion late, at the same time as the mountains, the lakes, and the wilderness. Georgina Battiscombe has collected what she calls a gallimaufrey of these in her book *English Picnics*. Influenced by Jean Jacques Rousseau's cult of nature and by the Romantic poets, singing the virtues of the simple life and extolling the beauties of nature, the English, like the French of the early nineteenth century, responded to the Romantic Movement with a newfound passion for their native land, especially its wild and picturesque scenery, and with a sudden taste for alfresco meals.

Before that, the prevailing distaste for nature in her wilder aspects was one reason for the paucity of English picnics. Mountains and moors had been places of interest and not of beauty. Walkers and travelers to remote areas never seemed impressed by the scenery when they wrote of their adventures and even less about the food they ate, unless it was in the warm safety of an inn and the usual roast beef, potatoes, and potted trout. They ate where they could, preferably indoors, and when outdoors it was usually with disgruntled horror and remembered as cold soggy food endured in the rain in such terms as "My bread being as wet as my feet."

In the first decade of the nineteenth century the curious-sounding name "picnic," spelled Pic Nic or Pick Nick, was given to a meal out-of-doors. Its origins are still not clear, but the oddly matched syllables had first been used for a variety of things, all different, but all equally fashionable. In 1802 the name was given to a hat and to a collection of poems and stories. A Picnic Club was formed for the private performance of theatricals, charades, and music. Though described by one of its members as a "harmless and inoffensive society of persons of fashion," its activities were generally regarded as slightly despicable and faintly improper. From a hodgepodge of anything, a picnic came to mean a party to which all the guests contributed a share of the provisions.

In the *Times* of London of March 18, 1802, a contributor wrote that a picnic supper "consists of a variety of dishes. The subscribers to the entertainment have the bill of fare presented to them with a number against each dish. The lot which he draws obliges him to furnish the dish marked against it, which he either takes with him in his carriage or sends by a servant."

By then, outdoor parties were all the rage and everyone had his version of the ideal picnic. Surtees described it in *Plain and Ringlets* (1860) as "one of those good, useful, indefinite sort of entertainments that may be turned to account in a variety of ways," and he went on to say: "We hold that a picnic is not a picnic where there are well arranged tables and footmen to wait. It is merely an uncomfortable out of doors dinner. A picnic should entail a little of the trouble and enterprise of life, gathering sticks, lighting the fire, boiling the pot, buying or stealing potatoes."

Trollope thought otherwise. In *Can You Forgive Her?* (1864) he says: "There are servants to wait, there is champagne, there is dancing, and instead of a ruined priory, an old upturned boat to be converted into a dining room."

An anonymous writer devoted more than a page of Chambers's *Journal* of June 6, 1857, to picnicking:

A picnic should be composed principally of young men and young women; but two or three old male folks may be admitted, if *very* good-humoured; a few pleasant children; and one—only one, dear old lady: to her let the whole commissariat department be intrusted by the entire assembly beforehand; and give her the utmost powers of a dicta-tress; for so shall nothing we want be left at home. It is not "fun" to find one's self without mint-sauce to his cold lamb; no one who is properly constituted, enjoys lobster without fresh butter, and when you are fond of salad, it is not cheerful to find the bottle of dressing, which was intrusted to young Master Brown, has broken in his filthy pocket: these things all occur, unless we have our (one) dear old lady. Who else would have seen to that hamper of glass being packed with such consummate judgment? Who else would have brought the plate—I confess I dislike steel forks—in her own private bag? Who else could have so piled tart upon tart without a crack or cranny for the rich red juice to well through? Who else has the art of preserving Devonshire cream in a can? Observe her little bottle of cayenne pepper! Mark each individual cruet as it gleams forth from its separate receptacle! Look at the salt box! Look at the corkscrew! Bless her dear old heart! She has forgotten nothing. However humble the meal, let it be complete: and it can't be complete without its (one) dear old lady.

He records his experiences and his views:

I have sat at rich men's feasts, which were partaken of in the open air, whereat powdered footmen have waited upon us decorously, and a bishop said grace; where everyone had a cushion to sit upon, and a napkin folded upon his plate: but I scarcely call that picnicking. And I have taken my repast—brown bread, and eggs and onions, with a flask of the most ordinary wine—outside Disentis, in the valley of the Gri-sons, and ate it upon the hillside by myself, because the town, and the inn, and the people, all smelt so execrably; but I don't consider that a picnic either. I have been one of a party of three hundred, whose various contributions to the common stock have been decided three weeks before the day of meeting, at a lottery, wherein mustard, and bread and pepper were the prizes. Where there were two military bands to dance to, under a thousand Chinese lanterns; where champagne corks went off like platoon-firing; and where it took half an American lake to ice the wine. And I have joined mighty pleasure-companies of the people, where everybody kept his food in his pocket-handkerchief; and having cut it up with clasp-knives, and devoured it, seized every-body else's hands, and ran down grassy hills at speed; but these things, too, I consider foreign to the picnic, which seems, somehow, to signify something snug and well-selected, and quite at variance with monster-meetings of any sort.

Picnics became so fashionable in the nineteenth century that they were satirized in fiction. Surtees described the usual "picnic march": ". . . the promoters with their newly caught conquests first, the half-caught couples second, the mere nibblers third and then what the racing reporters call 'the ruck.' "

In Jane Austen's *Emma*, Mrs. Elton describes the party she is hoping to organize at Mr. Knightley's:

> . . . quite a simple thing. I shall wear a large bonnet, and bring one of my little baskets hanging on my arm. Here, probably this basket with pink riband. Nothing can be more simple you see. . . . There is to be no form or parade—a sort of gipsy party. We are to walk about your gardens, and gather the strawberries ourselves, and sit under trees; and whatever else you may like to provide, it is to be all out of doors, a table spread in the shade, you know. Everything as natural and simple as possible. Is not that your idea?

But Mr. Knightley would not allow his guests to be subjected to the "lurking horrors" of an outdoor meal:

> My idea of the simple and the natural will be to have the table spread in the dining room. The nature and the simplicity of the gentlemen and ladies, with their servants and furniture, I think is best observed by meals within doors. When you are tired of eating strawberries in the garden, there shall be cold meat in the house.

While the English became the most passionate picnickers in the world, instructions for preparing food to take out and for equipping picnic baskets proliferated. The following comes from a *Girl's Own Paper* of 1880, quoted in Dorothy Hartley's *Food in England:*

> Fitted baskets are only suitable for a small party, of three or four persons, for whom one pie and one sweet would be sufficient. For a picnic party, it is better to divide the loads, and if enough guests attend, there would be plenty for all without anyone being unduly overloaded.
>
> A few hints on packing the hampers.
>
> Put the tablecloth and knives and forks on the *top* of the first basket to be unpacked. Cabbage leaves pack well around cool dishes, and contrast well with the pure white of the table napkins. Cold meat dishes

should be carried in the tins, in which they are set. Butter should be moulded, into balls, and parsley taken to garnish it after being set out.

A cold shoulder of lamb is an excellent joint for a picnic, accompanied by a bottle of mint sauce.

It is perhaps better to take the ham ready sliced.

Meat pies, and pigeon, and veal and ham pies are standard for a picnic.

In all pies, the gravy within should be strong enough to form a jelly when cold.

Lobster; the meat picked out and carried in the shell, with mayonnaise and salad packed separately, (it is thought expensively perhaps?) but fish dishes, such as eel moulded in jelly, are cool.

Cold roast ducks are sure to be popular, and cold dressed green peas not to be despised with them. We have known people take cold new potatoes, but did not consider them a success.

A well made salad every one will enjoy, and a cucumber is indispensable! The picnic would not be a picnic if it were absent.

Mrs. Hilda Leyel's recipes are in the best tradition of English picnic fare, inspired as they are from across the Channel. My only criticism is her fondness for gelatin and bread crumbs. Enraptured by a picnic near Itchenor, she put together a collection of enchanting recipes. They were published in *Picnics for Motorists* in 1936. Here are two of them:

Mousse of Haddock

Remove the flesh of one or more smoked haddocks; pick out the skin and bone; chop it finely. Season with cayenne and chopped parsley, and mix it with a little butter and several tablespoonfuls of cream. Stir over a gentle heat till thoroughly hot; add a few drops of lemon juice. Remove from the fire and add the whipped whites of three eggs and put into a wetted mold.

Ham Loaves

Cook some potatoes in their skins and mash half a pound of the potatoes with half a pound of grated lean ham and a quarter of a pound of bread crumbs.

Add plenty of pepper and salt, the thin rind of half a lemon, an ounce of butter and two lightly beaten eggs and some grated nutmeg and chopped parsley.

Make into small loaves. Brush them over with beaten egg and bake.

REVIVAL WEEK

Edna Lewis remembers Revival Week in Virginia in *The Taste of Country Cooking:*

Anticipation of Revival Week began with the first spring planting. Revival was like a prize held out during the long, hot summer days when work stretched from the morning's first light until late evening.

Our Revival Week always began on the second Sunday in August. Memories of slavery lingered with us still, and Revival was in a way a kind of Thanksgiving. There was real rejoicing: The fruits of our hard labor were now our own, we were free to come and go, and to gather together for this week of reunion and celebration.

At the beginning of August, the first harvest was usually over. The work horses and stock were driven to the large community pasture to graze peaceably for the rest of the summer. Only the milking cows and riding horses remained behind. With the field work finished, my father and the other men in the community were able to spend time getting things in order around the house in preparation for Revival Week. The first chore was to lay in a supply of wood for all the extra cooking that would be taking place. Any needed repairs on the summer kitchen were made, the main room was freshly wallpapered, the fireplace and chimney whitewashed. Whitewash also brightened up the outside trim, the fence posts, and even the trunks of the trees that grew around the house.

Although I didn't think about it at the time, I wonder how my mother made it each year to Revival Sunday, with so much to do and without ever varying from the calm and quiet manner that was her nature. Until the field work, which she loved, was over, she had no time to begin her own important preparations for Revival Week. And so, during the week leading up to second Sunday, as well as doing her regular household chores and caring for her brood of chickens, guinea hens, turkeys, and ducks, and her own vegetable garden, she would cut out and sew new dresses of white muslin for the six of us and our two adopted cousins as well as for herself, usually finishing the last buttonholes and sashes late Saturday night in between the cooking that she would have begun for the next day's noontime dinner at the church.

For my brothers and sisters and me, this was a week full of excitement, with friends and relatives arriving each day from distant cities —Washington, Philadelphia, New York. There were new cousins to play with and we could count on at least one trip into town in the buggy or in the back of the farm wagon to buy staples my mother would be needing, such as vanilla, spices, and sugar. Our own farm and garden yielded all of the flour, butter, lard, meat, vegetables, and fruits that we could use.

My mother never started her cooking until late on the eve of Revival Sunday. By this time she would have everything gathered in and laid out that she would need, and, I guess, a carefully planned schedule laid out in her mind as well. When we were bathed and turned into bed, no pies or cakes had yet been made. But when we came hurrying down on Sunday morning, the long, rectangular dining-room table would be covered with cakes ready to be iced and pie dishes lined with pastry dough to be filled and baked. While we counted them and excitedly discussed our special favorites and how many slices of each we could eat, my mother was out in back feeding her fowl. When she came in she would make us breakfast, standing at the stove with her everyday calm. Then she would help us dress, tie on our ribbons, and send us to sit on the porch until noontime with firm warning to sit quietly so that our new clothes would not get mussed. It would seem a very long morning.

Mother would return to the kitchen to continue her cooking. Because she liked to arrive at the church with the food piping hot, my father would attend the morning service alone and then come back for us as soon as it was over. We would be so excited as we climbed into the surrey. I remember how very special I felt in my new dress which helped me overcome the discomfort of having to wear shoes for the first time since March when school had let out. After we were all squeezed in, my father would load on the carefully packed baskets of food. The savory aroma of fried chicken, so warm and close, always pricked our appetites and long before we reached the church, which was only two miles distant, we would be squirming impatiently, though silently.

The churchyard would be filled with people as we drove up; I felt as though everyone was looking at us. My father would drive straight up to one of the long tables that were stretched out in a line under the huge, shady oak trees alongside the church. My mother would spread out a white linen tablecloth before setting out the baked ham, the half-dozen or more chickens she had fried, a large baking pan of her light, delicate corn pudding, a casserole of sweet potatoes, fresh green beans flavored with crisp bits of pork, and biscuits that had been baked at the last minute and were still warm. The main dishes were surrounded with smaller dishes of pickled watermelon rind, beets and cucumbers and spiced peaches. The dozen or so apple and sweet potato pies she had made were stacked in tiers of three, and the caramel and jelly layer cakes placed next to them. Plates, forks, and white damask napkins and gallon jars of lemonade and iced tea were the last things to be unpacked.

All along the sixty-foot length of tables, neighbors were busy in the same way setting out their own specialties. There were roasts and casseroles, cole slaw and potato salads, lemon meringue, custard, and Tyler pies, chocolate and coconut layer, lemon cream, and pound cakes.

When all the food had been placed on the tables, an unspoken signal would ripple down the line and we would all stand quietly while the minister spoke a grace of thanksgiving. We always liked him, for he knew to keep it short. When the solemn words ended, neighbor would turn to neighbor and warm handshakes, hugs, and affectionate welcomes would be exchanged.

And then at last everyone would come forth and be served, guests and friends first, children last. Second Sunday always seemed to have been a perfect day, with everyone looking their best, eating and chatting. My mother and the other ladies were eager to see that all of the guests were served, and there was always a special plate for a special friend. We usually stood behind our table admiring all the sights. There would be two more days of feasting during the week besides a round of visiting and entertaining in every home in Freetown. The festivities ended for us on Friday, when the visitors stopped by to thank us and say good-bye, promising to return next summer.

Here are Edna Lewis's Boiled Virginia Ham and Sweet Potato Pie.

Boiled Virginia Ham

It is said that pigs were brought to Virginia from England during the 1600s, and the meat developed soon became one of the most popular meats in the cookery of the region. Perhaps it is the acorns, peach pits, peanuts, corn, and maybe some truffles found in the oak forest of Virginia, plus the smoked hickory cure taught by the Virginian Indians, that has given the Virginia ham the delicious flavor for which it is famous.

A Virginia ham is one "raised and cured in Virginia." The best are local-cured. The next best is Gwaltney. For those not familiar with cooking Virginia ham: It must first be washed and scrubbed with a stiff brush to remove the moldy covering that usually coats the ham. Preferably soak overnight in water to cover, then discard the soaking water. Cook in enough cold water to fully cover. If the ham is being cooked without soaking, the water should be changed midway through cooking. Discard first cooking water and start over with fresh hot water to cover. Bring the ham to a near simmer, then adjust the burner to hold the cooking to what we always called a mull—just a quiet bubble. Never let boil; as the meat cooks through the heat will have to be adjusted to keep it below the boil. Keep the water above the ham by adding hot water as it is cooked away. Cook for at least 6 hours, at which time the bone begins to protrude at the top of the ham. Test the ham for tenderness by piercing with an ice pick or a skewer. If the ham seems too hard, leave to cool in the cooking liquid for 2 hours.

Remove to a rack to drain and set for 15 minutes. Slice with a sharp, wide-bladed knife. It is easier to slice with the skin on while still warm. Trim some of the skin off the slices and some fat—but not all; ham fat is flavorsome and goes well with the lean in a boiled dinner.

Sweet Potato Pie   *(for more than 6)*

3 cups (420 g.) plus 2 tablespoons
    sifted flour
1 cup (225 g.) chilled, home-rendered
    sweet lard
Salt
1/2 cup (120 ml.) cold water
2 cups (1/2 liter) mashed and sieved
    sweet potatoes
1 cup (200 g.) sugar

1/2 teaspoon cinnamon
1/2 teaspoon fresh grated nutmeg
3 small or medium eggs, separated
2 teaspoons vanilla extract
2/3 cup (170 g.) butter, melted over
    hot water
1 2/3 cups (385 g.) milk,
    at room temperature

In a mixing bowl blend well together with a pastry blender the 3 cups of flour, lard, and a scant teaspoon of salt. When well blended, add cold water and mix together by hand. This is a very short dough, and the water has to be incorporated by hand. After blending the water in, shape the dough into a ball. Sprinkle the dough with 2 tablespoons flour to make it easier to handle.

Divide the dough into pieces for the number of pies to be made (two 10-in./25-cm. or three 7-in./18-cm. pies). Leave to rest for 10 to 15 minutes. It is best to roll the dough out after resting. It is easier to handle while soft. After rolling the dough out, place it in the pie pans, trim, cover, and set in the refrigerator or freezer until needed. Remove and fill while chilled.

In a mixing bowl combine the sweet potatoes, sugar, spices, 1/2 teaspoon salt, beaten yolks, vanilla, and melted butter. Mix thoroughly. Add in the milk and stir well. Beat the whites of eggs to the frothy stage and stir them into the batter. Pour the batter into the pastry-lined pie pans. Bake in a 350°F (180°C) oven for 40 to 45 minutes.

A MIDDLE EASTERN AFFAIR

Some of my happiest childhood memories are of picnics in Egypt. My favorite was on the dunes of Agami in Alexandria. It was timed to coincide with the arrival of migrating quails on the beaches. The birds fell exhausted, to be caught in large nets and collected in baskets. They were cleaned and marinated in a rich cumin and coriander sauce and grilled on the beach over small fires. Fresh Arab bread was bought from the vendors who sang their wares on the beaches and played odds and even for a handful of pistachios or peanuts. The hollow rounds of bread were cut in half, opened out, and placed under the birds to catch their flavorsome juices; then the quails were gathered in them to be eaten as a sandwich, soft bones and all. Watermelons and pieces of coconut and sweet nutty pastries, bought from the vendors, ended the meal.

Another popular picnic spot was near a small dam we called simply "le barrage." We would bring large quantities of ful medames (Egyptian brown beans) in giant saucepans, on top of which were embedded shelled eggs that had been boiled gently for many hours with onion skins until they became light brown and their yolks creamy. A large box lined with foil held a salad of coarsely chopped tomatoes, cucumbers, romaine lettuce, spring onions with parsley, and fresh coriander leaves.

The beans were warmed up over a Primus stove while we unrolled our rugs and settled down in expectation of the "gala-gala," a magician who invariably produced baby chicks out of metal cups and eggs out of noses. We filled pouches of bread with the beans and sprinkled them with olive oil and a squeeze of lemon. Some people liked to add a crushed clove of garlic. We placed an egg cut in four in each portion, pressed down the beans, and topped them with salad. A basket of fruit was followed by a variety of pastries filled with pistachio nuts, almonds, walnuts, and dates, scented lightly with rose water and orange blossom water.

In an area which harbors many of nomadic ancestry and over which the sun shines constantly, eating out is a way of life. There are even official occasions for picnics.

Among these are the *mulids*, when people flock to the principal scenes of religious festivals, public gardens, shrines, tombs of saints, and burial grounds. Thousands gather sometimes for days and nights, sleeping under tents. Dervishes perform and itinerant entertainers recite ancient romances of unrequited love and *crime passionnel*. Conjurers no longer astonish with their age-old tricks, but people watch enthralled. They laugh at the buffoons and admire the acrobat's skill with the same pleasure that children have in listening to the same bedtime stories for years, noticing every little addition and new twist to the plot. Stick dancers, white robes flowing and turbans swaying, simulate a fight. Food is prepared for the whole period of the festival. It can be supplemented from the numerous stalls, erected with the swings and whirligigs, which sell falafels, kebabs, pastries, and sweetmeats and stay open all night, lit up by lanterns. When the festival is over and the tents and stalls are taken down, cracked egg shells, dyed red or yellow to bring joy and happiness, limp lettuce leaves, and discarded empty melon seeds carpet the areas of activity.

The most important of the national picnics in Egypt is not a religious occasion. It is Shem en Nesseem, which celebrates the arrival of spring. Town dwellers go out in the country or in boats, generally northward, eating out in the fields or on the riverbank, smelling the air, which is thought to be particularly beneficial on that day.

But no one waits for an official occasion.

In the Levant a picnic is not for the silent enjoyment of nature. You are too busy and too merry to notice the sea, the mountain, or the riverbank. The rule is the larger the group the better the picnic. The more for backgammon and cards. The more there are to tell jokes, the wealthier the gossip. The more there are who will sing and dance and the more dishes to choose from.

Few occasions can satisfy at the same time the convivial Arab spirit, the pleasure of being entertained, and the legendary hospitality as a picnic does. You are generous host and joyous guest at the same time, and the ultimate aim, to please, is developed to the point of an art in the contents of the picnic basket.

What one eats, as an enthusiast put it, is "anything without a sauce, that is easily transportable, that can be eaten cold, or that is not too difficult to heat up." And that does not leave very much out, for the open-air gourmets will stop at nothing, armed with giant pans and Primus stoves, to bring their food for a picnic.

Relatives, friends, and neighbors are invited to join a party. Each family announces what it will contribute—usually its own favorite, one that it is hoped will be appreciated above all others, supplemented by a last-minute surprise dish. There must be enough to serve at least one portion to each person present. Generosity must be boundless: honor is at stake. Even those who live frugally will surpass themselves in preparing a variety of delicacies.

When I was a child in Egypt, there were traditional specialties fondly taken on certain outings; seaside favorites and desert favorites, those taken on festivals, and very simple foods for casual, spontaneous affairs.

For a large party, the variety of dishes was often absolutely stunning. Set out on a tablecloth or the traditional rug specially woven for outdoor reveling, plates jostled for space. Numerous pies were invariably represented: sanbusak, half-moon shaped shortcrust filled with spicy meat or sharp cheese; fila (the Greek phylo), the paper-thin dough wrapped into little packets around fillings of spinach or cheese or fried minced meat with pine nuts; and the Shephardi specialty pasteles, the small pot-shaped pies filled with *khandrajo,* similar to a ratatouille. Kibbeh was always a favorite, its outer shell of soft lamb worked with cracked wheat holding the traditional fried minced meat with onions and pine nuts delicately seasoned with cinnamon. Regional versions such as one with raisins or an easier one of layers smoothed flat in a tray sometimes replaced it. Rice-stuffed vine leaves were almost always offered. Other vegetables commonly stuffed were tomatoes, zucchini, small eggplants, onions, and peppers. For eating cold, ground meat was not included in the stuffing, but the rice was generously partnered with chopped tomatoes, onion, crushed garlic, a great deal of parsley, and occasionally other herbs such as fresh coriander leaves and mint. Much appreciated, though common, was a meat loaf—*blehat lahma*—holding a variety of surprises such as hard-boiled eggs and apricots, differing according to the family that produced it. Cold chicken was juicy from being cooked sofrito in a pan with oil and a little water, sharply lemony with a taste of garlic and cardamom, and beautifully yellow with turmeric. Otherwise cooked chicken was minced, mixed with veal and pistachio nuts, and patted into balls or shaped as a loaf and cooked again. Fish usually made an appearance as *blehat samak,* finger-shaped rissoles of minced fish flavored with cumin and coriander. Occasionally it was elaborately stuffed.

Salads, a variety of them, simple and unpretentious or rich and exotic, were always present. Vegetables either raw or cooked, cracked wheat and pulses, and even cheese were usually dressed with olive oil and lemon juice rich in chopped onions.

Another dish always encountered was *ajja*—an omelet in the style of the Spanish ones, thick with vegetables or minced meat and excellent cold, accompanied by a bowl of yogurt.

And for the sweet-toothed (as most of us were), there were always pastries to follow the fruit. Baklava, layers of crisp fila filled with chopped pistachios; konafa with the appearance of shredded wheat, also filled with a choice of nuts; basbousa of semolina with coconut, all soused with a slightly lemony sugar syrup perfumed with orange blossom water. For those who did not like sticky fingers, afters were *ma'amoul,* tartlets filled with date paste, or *assabih bi loz,* almond fingers, or the numerous petits fours made with almond paste or caramelized nuts, dried apricots, and dates.

Everything was carefully prepared and well set out in a manner pleasing to the eye. Parsley was sprinkled over or laid in a bunch next to a dish. Colorful pickles, some pink from beets, and olives were placed in small plates and spread out evenly among the bigger ones. Portions were cut diagonally; cayenne pepper was mixed with oil and dribbled on tahina, the popular sesame meal dip, in a crisscross pattern.

"The more one loves, the more one offers and the more one eats"—an Arab proverb assures us that food equals the affection.

The recipes mentioned above and others suitable for picnics are given in *A Book of Middle Eastern Food*. I have included here different versions of special outdoor favorites with a few new recipes.

Share the preparation if you are going with a crowd; otherwise choose one or two of the main dishes to serve with a bowl of yogurt or tahina (see p. 86) and a large salad made of lettuce, cucumber, and tomatoes all chopped up (not too small). Pack it in a plastic bag, ready to be dressed just before you eat. Follow with fruit.

Blehat Samak / Fish Rissoles

2 1/4 lb. (1 kg.) cod and haddock or a
    mixture of any other fish
Five 4-in. (10-cm.) slices whole
    wheat bread
4 medium eggs

2 cloves garlic, crushed
2 teaspoons cumin
Salt and pepper
Oil

Poach the fish for 5 minutes, drain, and flake. Soak the bread, crusts removed, in water, squeeze dry, and crumble. In a large bowl combine the flaked fish, bread, and eggs. Add the crushed garlic and cumin, and season to taste with salt and pepper. Mix well and knead until a smooth paste. Shape the mixture into 1-in. (2 1/2-cm.) balls. Sauté in hot oil until brown, then drain on absorbent paper.

Qras Samak / An Arab Fish Cake with Burghul

Serve this cold with salad and tahina (p. 86).

1/2 lb. (225 g.) fine or medium
    burghul (cracked wheat)

1 1/8 lb. (1/2 kg.) raw minced fish
    such as cod, haddock, or halibut

1 small onion, grated or
    finely chopped
Juice of half a lemon
Salt and pepper

1 good bunch fresh coriander or
    parsley, finely chopped
Oil for shallow frying

Wash the burghul and let it soak in cold water for 15 minutes, then drain it. Either pound all the ingredients (except oil) to a soft paste in a mortar or knead vigorously with your hands. A food processor makes the operation of chopping, mincing, and reducing everything to a doughlike paste very quick and simple. Take smallish lumps, shape into flat cakes, and fry in about 3/4 in. (2 cm.) of hot oil, turning over once until lightly browned on both sides.

Brains Moroccan Style

2 calf's brains or 4 lamb's brains
Salt
Vinegar
3 cloves garlic, crushed
3 tablespoons oil
1 medium (14-oz./400-g.) can
    peeled tomatoes
1 small bunch parsley, finely chopped

1 small bunch fresh coriander,
    finely chopped
1 teaspoon paprika
A pinch of cayenne pepper
    (or to taste)
1 teaspoon cumin
Juice of 1 lemon

Soak the brains in salted water acidulated with a little vinegar for 1 hour. Remove the thin outer membranes and wash under cold running water. Drain well and cut them in 2 or 4. Fry the garlic in the oil in a large pan until the aroma rises. Add the peeled tomatoes and the rest of the ingredients and simmer for a few minutes. Then drop in the brains and cook gently a further 15 minutes.

Sanbusak / Pies Filled with Meat and Pine Nuts

DOUGH

2/3 cup (150 ml.) melted butter
2/3 cup (150 ml.) vegetable oil
2/3 cup (150 ml.) warm water

1 teaspoon salt
About 4 cups (575 g.) flour

In a large bowl combine the butter, oil, water, and salt. Sift into it the flour, stirring well with a fork and then working in with your hands until the dough is a soft ball. Add more flour if necessary and do not handle further.

FILLING

1 large onion, chopped	Salt and pepper
2 tablespoons oil	1 teaspoon allspice
2 tablespoons (25 g.) pine nuts	1/2 teaspoon cinnamon
1 1/8 lb. (1/2 kg.) ground lean lamb	
or beef	

Prepare the filling by frying the chopped onion in the oil until soft and golden. Add the pine nuts and fry until slightly colored. Add the lamb or beef and fry until it has lost its pink color. Add salt and pepper to taste, allspice, and cinnamon, moisten with water, and cook a little longer. Drain in a strainer to remove excess fat.

Either roll the dough out thin on a floured pastry board and cut into rounds about 3 in. (8 cm.) in diameter with a pastry cutter, or take walnut-size lumps and flatten them out as thin as possible between the palms of your hands.

Put a heaped teaspoonful of filling in the center of each round and fold the dough to cover it, making a half-moon shape. Seal by tightly pinching the edges together. Make the traditional festoon-type edge by pinching and folding over at close intervals all along. Arrange on baking sheets, which need not be greased. Brush lightly with beaten egg and bake in a preheated 350°F (180°C) oven, for about 45 minutes, until they are a pale golden color.

This quantity makes more than 30 pastries.

Variation: Cheese-filled sanbusak are as popular as the meat ones. Grate 1 1/8 lb. (1/2 kg.) sharp cheese or a mixture of cheeses including a little Parmesan. Add pepper and stir in 2 beaten eggs.

Meat Ajja / An Omelet

This is an Iraqi recipe from Sami Zubaida's family.

Finely chop a large onion and a large potato. Fry 1/4 lb. (115 g.) lean ground beef in a little oil and stir well until it has changed color. Add a small bunch of parsley, finely chopped, and remove from the heat. Lightly beat 6 eggs and stir in the meat, potato, and onion. Add salt and pepper to taste and a teaspoon each of cumin and coriander and stir until well blended.

Pour a spoonful at a time into hot oil in a frying pan. Turn as soon as the bottom has set firmly and cook the other side. These are easily stacked in a plastic box.

Kukuye Gusht

No one is as good as Iranians are at making omelets. They call them *kuku* and often bake them in a slow oven for more than 45 minutes instead of using a frying pan. Here is an Iranian meat and vegetable omelet.

1 large onion, chopped

1 leek, finely chopped, or a few spring
    onions, chopped

Oil

1 1/8 lb. (1/2 kg.) ground beef

1/4 lb. (115 g.) chopped spinach
    (frozen will do)

A sprig of parsley, finely chopped

Salt and pepper

1 teaspoon cinnamon or allspice

6 lightly beaten eggs

About 2 tablespoons butter

Fry the onion with the chopped leek or spring onions in a little oil until they are soft. Add the beef and fry until it has changed color. Add the chopped spinach, parsley, salt, pepper, and cinnamon or allspice. Stir well and then combine with the lightly beaten eggs in a bowl. Pour the mixture into bubbling hot butter in a large frying pan and cook slowly over a gentle heat for about 15 minutes; then turn the omelet over or put it for a minute or so under the broiler to brown the top. Eat cold.

Kibbeh Naye

This unusual and refreshing raw lamb and cracked wheat paste will be popular with those who are fond of steak tartare. It is one of those dishes that require more than half an hour of mincing and pounding unless you have a food processor, in which case it takes a few effortless minutes. It must be kept cool until it is ready to eat.

My Aunt Latifa used to roll the mixture into small thin fingers and serve them on a bed of lettuce leaves. On a picnic it is easier to spoon 1 or 2 tablespoons into crisp young lettuce leaves, arranging them attractively on a serving dish, or to flatten the kibbeh on a large plate. Decorate with mint leaves, finely chopped spring onions, radishes, and tomato slices, and sprinkle generously with lemon juice and olive oil. Serve with a bowl of young romaine leaves or pita bread to use as a scoop.

8 oz. (225 g.) burghul (cracked wheat)	1/2 teaspoon allspice
1 leg or shoulder of lamb	1 teaspoon cumin
2 large onions, grated or	A pinch of cayenne pepper
finely chopped	2 tablespoons tomato purée
Salt and pepper	

Soak the burghul in cold water for about 10 minutes. Cut away all the skin, fat, and tendons from the leg or shoulder of lamb and cut the meat into small pieces. Drain the burghul in a very fine sieve, and squeeze out the excess water. Mix all these together in a blender, starting with the meat. You will have to do it in batches. Add the salt, pepper, allspice, cumin, cayenne, and tomato purée (to keep the color of the meat red). The mixture might need one or two ice cubes to achieve the texture of a smooth paste.

Bazargan

This old recipe from Aleppo in Syria was rediscovered by my parents in Los Angeles. Unlike tabbouleh, it can be made days ahead and kept in the freezer.

1 1/8 lb. (1/2 kg.) burghul (cracked wheat)	1/4 cup (5 g.) finely chopped parsley
2 large onions, grated or finely chopped	1/2 cup (115 g.) walnuts, coarsely chopped
2/3 cup (150 ml.) olive oil (you may use sunflower oil)	3 tablespoons concentrated sour pomegranate juice or juice of
8 oz. (225 g.) tomato purée	2 lemons
2 tablespoons oregano	2 teaspoons cumin

2 teaspoons ground coriander	Salt and pepper to taste
1 teaspoon allspice	Cayenne pepper to taste

Soak and wash the burghul in fresh cold water for 10 to 15 minutes. Drain well through a fine sieve. Soften the onions in oil but do not brown.

Mix all the ingredients very thoroughly with a fork in a large bowl. Leave for a few hours, preferably overnight, in the refrigerator, for the burghul to absorb all the flavors and to become tender.

Tabbouleh / Cracked Wheat Salad

This Lebanese salad, which now has an international reputation, is refreshing on a summer's day with its abundance of chopped parsley and its lemon and minty flavor. It is the traditional accompaniment to *kibbeh naye*. In the mountain villages of Lebanon freshly picked sharp vine leaves are passed around to scoop up the salad. In towns the pale crisp leaves from the heart of romaine lettuce are provided.

5 oz. (140 g.) burghul	6–8 tablespoons olive oil
5 oz. (140 g.) spring onions or mild Spanish onions, finely chopped	Juice of 1 1/2 or more lemons
3 tomatoes, chopped	Salt and pepper to taste
5 oz. (140 g.) parsley, finely chopped	Vine leaves, lightly poached, or fresh romaine lettuce leaves
A few sprigs of fresh mint, finely chopped, or 2 tablespoons dried mint	

Soak the burghul in cold water for 10 minutes. (There is much controversy about this time.) Drain well and put in a large bowl with all the other ingredients (except leaves). Prepare at least an hour before serving to allow the wheat to absorb the dressing and become plump and tender.

Serve in individual plates lined with vine leaves or lettuce leaves. Place a bowl of firm young lettuce leaves on the table to use as scoops for the salad.

Stuffed Vegetables

A tray of mixed stuffed vegetables cooked in oil is ordinarily brought on outings, as well as rolled vine leaves prepared with the season's new crop. Firmer and less fragile vegetables are best for obvious reasons. A sweet-and-sour flavor is particularly good for these vegetables when they are to be eaten cold the day after they have been cooked.

Stuffed Onions

Peel 2 large Spanish onions. With a sharp knife, make a cut from top to bottom through to the center on one side of each onion. Throw into boiling water and cook until the onions are soft and start to open so that the layers can be detached. Drain and cool slightly before separating the layers carefully.

THE FILLING

3/4 cup (180 g.) rice, washed
　　and drained
3 tomatoes, peeled, seeded, and
　　finely chopped
1 small bunch parsley, finely chopped
2 tablespoons raisins or sultanas
2 tablespoons pine nuts (optional)
Salt and pepper

1/2 teaspoon cinnamon
1/4 teaspoon allspice
2 teaspoons fresh mint, or 1 teaspoon
　　dried (optional)
2–3 tablespoons wine vinegar or 1
　　tablespoon tamarind paste
1 tablespoon sugar
5 tablespoons olive oil

Mix the rice with the tomatoes, parsley, raisins or sultanas, and pine nuts. Season to taste with salt and pepper, cinnamon, allspice, and mint. Put a tablespoon in each separated hollow onion layer and roll up tightly into an oval-like ball. (If the onions are very large, the outer layers are also too large, and are best cut in half before rolling up with the filling.)

　　Put a little oil in a large heavy-bottomed pan, then a layer of discarded onion pieces (or lettuce leaves), so that the vegetables do not get burned, and pack them closely in layers over this. Cover with water mixed with the wine vinegar or tamarind paste (obtained from Indian shops), sugar, and olive oil.

　　Cover the pan and simmer gently for about 60 minutes until onion and filling are done, adding water if necessary. Let cool before turning out.

Stuffed Zucchini

In *A Book of Middle Eastern Food* I gave a recipe for stuffed zucchini cooked in apricot sauce. Here I have put the apricots in with the filling so that they are less messy to hold in the hand.

　　Choose 2 1/4 lb. (1 kg.) medium-size zucchini. Slice off the stem. Using a narrow apple corer, make a hole at the stem end and scoop out the pulp by twisting it around, being careful not to break the skin. The other end must remain closed.

Do not throw away the pulp that comes out in thin long fingers. Boil and dress with a vinaigrette to serve like mock asparagus.

THE FILLING

3/4 cup (180 g.) rice, washed
  and drained
1 large onion
3 tomatoes, peeled, seeded, and
  finely chopped
A small bunch parsley, finely chopped
1/2 lb. (225 g.) dried apricots, finely
  chopped

Salt and pepper
1 teaspoon cinnamon
A pinch of allspice
Juice of 1 lemon
2–3 cloves garlic, crushed
1 teaspoon dried crushed mint

Mix the rice, onion, tomatoes, parsley, and apricots. Season with plenty of salt, pepper, cinnamon, and allspice. Mix well. Fill each zucchini three-quarters full only, to allow the rice to swell. Lay a few thin slices of tomatoes (or lettuce leaves) at the bottom of a wide heavy pan so that the vegetables do not stick or burn. Pack them side by side tightly in layers over this. Cover with water mixed with the lemon juice, crushed garlic, and mint. Simmer very gently, covered, for about an hour or until the zucchini are tender and the filling cooked, adding a little water if necessary.

Stuffed Leeks

Buy 3 of the fattest leeks you can find. Trim and cut off the hard green ends. With a sharp knife carefully make a slit through to the center, and no further, of each leek. Separate the leaves. Throw into boiling salted water and poach until softened. Cut a slice off the root end to free the layers from each other.

THE FILLING

3/4 cup (180 g.) rice, washed
  and drained
3 tomatoes, peeled and chopped
1 large onion, finely chopped
A small bunch parsley,
  finely chopped
Salt and pepper

1 teaspoon cinnamon
A good pinch of allspice
2 teaspoons tamarind paste (from
  Indian shops) or
  2 tablespoons vinegar
1 tablespoon sugar
1/2 cup (120 ml.) olive oil

Mix the rice, tomatoes, onion, and parsley. Add salt, pepper, cinnamon, and allspice. Put a little of the filling along the edge of each leek leaf but not up to the end. Roll up tightly like a cigarette (the narrower, center leaves need to be put together overlapping). Put some discarded leaves at the bottom of a large pan and arrange the leeks side by side on top. Cover with water to which you have added the tamarind or vinegar, sugar, and olive oil. Cover the pan and cook over a very low heat for about 1 hour, adding water as it becomes absorbed, until the leeks and filling are tender.

Lemon Chicken

3 tablespoons oil
1 teaspoon turmeric
2 cloves garlic, crushed
1 cardamom pod, crushed

Juice of 1 lemon
1/2 cup (120 ml.) water
1 chicken, about 3 lb. (1 1/2 kg.)
Salt and pepper

In a large heavy saucepan, heat the oil with the turmeric, garlic, cardamom pod, lemon juice, and water. Put the chicken in the pan, add salt and pepper, and cook very slowly over low heat. Turn the chicken often, adding a little water to keep it moist and to have enough sauce at the end of the cooking when the chicken is tender (about 1 hour). Cut into pieces and remove the skin and some of the larger bones. Arrange in a plastic box and pour the sauce over it.

Lahma bil Karaz / Meatballs with Cherries

2 1/4 lb. (1 kg.) ground lean lamb or
    veal
Salt and pepper
1/2 teaspoon grated nutmeg
1/2 teaspoon ground cloves
1/2 teaspoon ground cinnamon

Oil
1 1/8 lb. (1/2 kg.) sour or morello
    cherries, pitted
Sugar and/or lemon juice
Rounds of Arab bread or slices of
    white bread

Knead the meat with your hand to achieve a smooth, pasty texture. Season with the salt, pepper, and spices, and knead again. Form marble-size balls with the mixture and fry them gently in oil, shaking the pan to color them all over.

Fresh, pitted sour black cherries should be used for this dish if possible. If these are not available, use canned cherries or black cherry jam. Stew the fresh cherries in a large pan with very little water, adding sugar and/or lemon juice to taste according to the sweetness or acidity of the fruit. If using canned fruit or jam, add only lemon, as they will be sweet enough already. Add the sautéed meatballs and simmer gently until cooked through, crushing the cherries with a fork when they become soft enough. Let the sugar in the sauce become caramelized a little, but add more water if this happens before the meatballs are cooked and the fruit is soft.

Serve on pita bread, soft side up. If this is not available, cut thinnish slices of white bread, remove the crusts, and arrange the slices on a large serving dish. Cover each slice with several meatballs and some cherry sauce. This traditional way of serving makes it an easy food to pick up at a picnic.

Salq bi Loubia / Spinach with Black-Eyed Beans

1/4 lb. (100 g.) black-eyed beans	1 large onion
Salt	4 tablespoons olive oil
1 1/8 lb. (500 g.) fresh spinach or 1/2	Pepper
lb. (225 g.) frozen leaf spinach	

Simmer the black-eyed beans in water for about 20 minutes or until they are tender, adding salt to taste when they have begun to soften. They do not usually need soaking and fall apart quite quickly if they are overcooked.

Wash the fresh spinach, removing the thick stems, and drain well. Frozen spinach must be completely thawed and all the water squeezed out of it.

Fry the onion in the olive oil until soft and transparent. Add the spinach and continue to fry, stirring constantly, until well cooked. Add salt and pepper to taste, and stir the drained beans into the spinach to warm through. Now let cool before serving.

Bamia / Sweet-and-Sour Okra

A slight sweet-and-sour flavor is particularly good with cold dishes.

1 1/8 lb. (500 g.) small young okra	2 tablespoons sugar
2 tablespoons oil	Juice of 1 small lemon

Cut off the stem ends and wash the okra. Heat oil in a heavy pan. Add the okra and sauté gently for about 5 minutes. Turn each pod over, then stir in sugar and lemon juice. Add a little water to half-cover the okra.

Simmer, covered, for about 20 minutes or longer, adding a little water occasionally if necessary, and cook until tender. Let it cool.

Lentil and Tomato Salad

1/2 lb. (250 g.) large brown lentils	Salt and pepper
1 large onion, chopped	1 small bunch parsley, finely chopped
4 tablespoons olive oil	2–3 tablespoons vinegar
3 tomatoes, peeled and cut into pieces	

Soak the lentils in water for a few hours. Fry the onion in oil until lightly colored. Add the tomatoes and sauté for a minute. Add the drained lentils, cover with water, and simmer gently for about 30 minutes until they are tender, adding water as required, then season with salt and pepper, add parsley and vinegar, and cook until the lentils are done and the liquid absorbed.

Taste and adjust the seasoning when it is cool. You may need to add a little more olive oil if you like.

Loubia bi Zeit / Green Beans in Olive Oil

1 1/2 lb. (675 g.) green beans	4–5 tablespoons olive oil
1 large onion, coarsely chopped	Salt and pepper
4 cloves garlic, sliced	4 tomatoes, peeled and sliced

Top and tail, string and wash the beans and cut into 2 or 3 pieces. Fry the onion and garlic gently in olive oil until they begin to color. Add the beans and sauté briefly, stirring constantly. Cover with water, add salt and pepper, and simmer until tender and the water is reduced. Add the tomatoes and stir gently until they have softened. Let it cool.

Variation: Instead of using fresh tomatoes, you may stir 1 or 2 tablespoons tomato purée into the water.

A JAPANESE PICNIC

For centuries, no pastime has been considered more pleasurable and more elegant in Japan than an excursion into the countryside with food and wine and a few companions, where verses are composed, inspired by the ever changing faces of nature. Sensitive to the seasons and the weather and to the products of land and sea, the Japanese people celebrate their deep and ancient love for their hills and waters and the progress of the year from spring to winter with poems and food. They have even made a ritual of gazing at the moon, and celebrate the blooming of chrysanthemums and cherry blossoms. In a booklet written in 1936 for the understanding by the West of Japanese food and ways, Professor Kaneko Tezuka describes "flower-viewing" and "moon-viewing" foods which the Japanese take on large party outings with their families and company colleagues, fellow workers, and employees. The cherry blossom is the national flower, and it is customary to rejoice under the trees when they are in full bloom, and to share the "flower-viewing" food.

"Chrysanthemum-viewing food" is also prepared for an ancient autumnal festival on the ninth day of the ninth month of the lunar calendar. Each family carries a varied and traditional feast in stacks of three or four vermilion or pale green lacquered wooden boxes together with small wooden plates to serve on. Those who treasure ancient refinements carry their sake in gourds slung in heavy red cords with tassels. With a mixture of hedonism and an ingrained love of beauty, days are spent enjoying food and extolling the virtues of the evanescent cherry blossoms, which will fall tomorrow like snow, and the first grasses of spring or the chrysanthemum, which will close up for the night but whose roots will never die.

No one in Japan can remain unmoved in the presence of the moon, which is loved in all its shapes and moods; in the spring, shining hazily on the blossoms, in the summer, cool beside the water, and in the winter, clear and cold on frosty nights. They may gaze for hours at it, retiring only when at last it sinks toward the hills, and recite with emotion:

> *Must the moon disappear*
> *In such haste,*
> *Leaving us still unsatisfied?*
> *Would that the mountain rim might flee*
> *And refuse to receive her.*
> —Oriwara Narihira

But most loved of all is the full moon of the autumn harvest called *meigetsu*, which the nobles of ancient times used to woo at Waka-no-wra and Suma, now famous places for "viewing." On the evening of the fifteenth of the eighth month, families sit out on the veranda, enjoying its autumn calm, praising it effusively, and eating the traditional offerings: the fruits of the season, persimmons and grapes, and vegetables such as taros, green soy beans, and little dumplings made of rice flour symbolizing the round silver moon. For the last day of the year there is also ritual outdoor food. Hot soups and stews are served, cod and buri are grilled, and boiled radish is eaten with sweetened miso and buckwheat.

The delights of the packed lunch box are not only reserved for moments of inspiration and ritual, they are very much part of everyday life. Among the attractions of traveling by train, as Kimiko Magasawa and Camy Condon write in *Eating Cheap in Japan,* are the special lunches for travelers that are sold on platforms and trains and in shops near the main stations. This fashion started ninety years ago and spread throughout the country. Different lines have their own specialties, and many stations are known for a particular kind of food—Yokohama Station for Chinese meatballs, Chiba Station for clams and rice. These lunches, called *eki-ben,* are sold in wooden boxes of various shapes, wrapped in beautiful paper, and tied with string. Etiquette requires that the packaging is kept intact for rewrapping in exactly the same way after eating. The contents are usually cold seasoned rice with bits of cooked fish and vegetables. Similar boxes called *o-bento* are sold on motorways, grilled eel being the most popular meal.

A favorite picnic food for children is *onigiri,* balls of rice containing a pickled plum and a small piece of salted salmon or pink cod fish in the center. One special picnic lunch, *maku no uchi,* originated as a meal to be eaten between the acts of the long kabuki plays and came in a half-moon-shaped lacquered box. Four sections contain small rice rolls sprinkled with black sesame seeds, a piece of grilled fish or shrimp, a slice of egg, a few vegetables, and pickles. As always in Japan the arrangement is particularly beautiful to stimulate the appetite.

Sushi

Everywhere in Japan are the sushi shops serving snacks to take away in little boxes. They contain combinations of fish and seafood, cooked, marinated, or simply raw, on a bed of fragrant rice. Although in Japan these picnic favorites are prepared by skilled professionals, they are an easy and delicious way to start an acquaintance with that simple and elegant cuisine which is so different from that of the rest of the world, having evolved in long periods of isolation. Many Japanese shops have now opened in the United States and in London, selling the necessary ingredients, and very fresh fish is obtainable for sashimi, the sliced raw fish which is the best part of sushi.

Prepare everything in advance, ready to assemble at the last minute. The fish must be kept covered and refrigerated in a cold box, but the rice need not be. Take sake or a dry white wine to serve with the food.

The rice. Learn how to make rice with vinegar dressing and the rest is easy. Use short-grain rice which holds together. This recipe is from *The Complete Book of Japanese Cooking* by Elisabeth Lambert Ortiz with Mitsuko Endo.

1 1/8 lb. (1/2 kg.) rice	4 tablespoons rice vinegar
3-in. (8-cm.) square kombu (kelp)	1 tablespoon sugar
2 1/2 cups (600 ml.) water	2 teaspoons salt

Thoroughly wash the rice in several changes of water until the water runs clear, and drain in a sieve for at least 1 hour. Put into a heavy saucepan with a tightly fitting lid. Clean the seaweed with a damp cloth and cut with kitchen shears into a 1/2-in. (1 1/2-cm.) fringe. Bury the seaweed in the rice. Add the water, cover, and bring to the boil over high heat, removing the seaweed just before the water boils. Otherwise it will flavor the rice too strongly. Reduce the heat to moderate and cook for 5 to 6 minutes, then reduce the heat to very low and cook for 15 minutes. Raise the heat to high for 10 seconds, then let the rice stand off the heat for 10 minutes.

In a small saucepan combine the rice vinegar, sugar, and salt. Heat through, stirring to mix. Turn the rice out into a large, shallow dish, preferably wooden. In Japan a bandai *(sushioke)*, a large round wooden dish, would be used. Pour the vinegar mixture little by little over the rice, mixing it with a *shamoji* (wooden spatula) or a fork, and fanning it vigorously to make it glisten. It is a good idea to have a helper do the fanning, though it can be managed alone. The fanning cools the rice quickly and this is what makes it glisten.

Cover the rice with a cloth until ready to use. It can be left standing at room temperature for several hours before using if necessary.

The fish. Have a selection of very fresh raw fish or shellfish which may include salmon, tuna, bass, bream, red snapper, mackerel, sardines, sole, scallops, flounder, squid, clams, sea urchins—any that can be eaten raw. Shrimp must be cooked for 1 1/2 minutes, conger eel for a little longer, and octopus must be tenderized by bashing and boiling. It is possible to settle for one kind of fish only, but a selection is an opportunity for sampling fish at its very best in its natural state. One lb. (450 g.) of fish will serve 4 people as a main course.

The art lies in filleting, skinning, and cutting the fish in 1/4-in. (3/4-cm.) thick diagonal slices about 1 by 2 in. (2 1/2 by 5 cm.) and arranging it with style on a flat dish or wooden platter with a decorative array of raw vegetables, cut in very thin slices or strips. Carrots, white and red radish, cucumber, onions, spring onions, turnips, and pickled ginger are mostly used as garnish.

The fish, which must be impeccably fresh, can be cut in advance, each type packed separately in little plastic bags and transported in an insulated bag or box containing a cold pack. The rice and the vegetables too can be prepared in advance, ready to be arranged at the picnic where everyone can help themselves.

The dip. Have small bowls of soy sauce and of wasabi (green horseradish powder, which is very powerful and can be obtained from Japanese and Chinese stores) mixed to a paste with a little water. You need only the slightest amount of horseradish for a slice of fish.

For a special soy sauce, mix in to taste a little vinegar (preferably rice vinegar) and a pinch of sugar.

To serve. In sushi restaurants, Japanese cooks wet their hands with vinegared water to shape the rice into oblong patties about 1 to 2 in. (2 1/2 to 5 cm.) long without it sticking to their fingers. But it is just as good to spread and press the rice onto a large platter and arrange the fish and garnish on top for everyone to pick up morsels and dip them in the horseradish and soy sauce.

Three Salads to Serve with Sushi

Here are three salads and a sauce from Elizabeth Andoh's *At Home with Japanese Cooking.*

Cucumber and Celery in Apple Dressing

Here is a tart and crunchy salad that goes very well with poultry and fish. Serve it on a bed of lettuce leaves, if you like.

1 cucumber, preferably unwaxed	1/2 Red Delicious apple
1 stalk celery	1 1/2–2 tablespoons chilled *amazu,*
Pinch of salt	sweet-and-sour sauce (see below)

Dice the cucumber into 1/4-in. (3/4-cm.) cubes, peeling it first if it is waxed. Slice the celery lengthwise into 3 to 4 strips, then across into 1/4-in. (3/4-cm.) pieces. Lightly salt the vegetables, then prepare the dressing.

Spread a clean, dry, white linen handkerchief or napkin on your cutting board. Peel and core the apple, then grate it onto the spread cloth. Work quickly to prevent discoloration. Lift up the edges of the cloth and let some of the juice drain out before transferring the grated apple to a glass bowl. Add chilled sweet-and-sour sauce to taste and stir to distribute the apple gratings.

Squeeze the salted cucumber and celery pieces lightly and drain off any accumulated liquid. Toss the vegetables in the apple dressing and serve chilled or at room temperature.

Amazu / Sweet-and-Sour Sauce

This is a simple, basic sauce to be used in many recipes. It will keep for weeks refrigerated in a covered glass or ceramic container. *Makes about 1/2 cup (120 ml.).*

1/2 cup (120 ml.) rice vinegar   1/4 teaspoon salt
1/4 cup (60 g.) sugar

Combine the ingredients listed above in a small saucepan. Stirring with a wooden spoon, cook the sauce over low heat until the sugar and salt melt. Allow the sauce to cool to room temperature before using or storing it.

Red and White Salad

In Japan, red and white are the colors of felicity, and dishes combining these are thought to be particularly festive. Here the deep orange tones of the carrot and dried apricot provide the "red," while the snowy *daikon* radish provides the "white." This vegetable and fruit salad is a classic in its native land, commonly served at the New Year. It could easily accompany grilled fish or roasted poultry any time of the year, though. *Makes about 1 cup.*

1/4 teaspoon salt
Generous 2/3 cup (155 g.) *daikon*
    (Japanese white radish), peeled
    and cut into fine julienne strips
Scant 1/4 cup (60 g.) carrot, peeled
    and cut into fine julienne strips

2–3 dried apricots, sliced into fine
    julienne strips
Peel from 1/4 lemon, sliced into fine
    julienne strips
1/3 cup (80 ml.) *amazu,* sweet-and-sour
    sauce (preceding recipe)

Lightly salt the cut raw vegetables, each in its own bowl. Let the vegetables stand for 5 minutes before squeezing out and discarding all accumulated liquid. Combine the slightly wilted radish and carrot and toss in the apricots and lemon peel. Pour the sweet-and-sour sauce over the vegetables and fruit and allow the mixture to marinate for at least 30 minutes or up to 3 days if covered and refrigerated.

To serve, drain the vegetables and fruit of all excess sweet-and-sour sauce. For a particularly attractive presentation hollow out 6 to 8 lemon halves and fill them with the salad. Serve chilled or at room temperature.

Slippery Mushrooms in Sleet Sauce

Here is a dish that combines several tastes and textures that may well be new to you. Slippery, earthy mushrooms float in a sweet-and-sour sauce to which grated radish adds a sharp, crunchy accent. The Japanese like to eat this dish with salt-grilled fish, though it could be served with roasted poultry, too.

3/4 cup (180 g.) canned *naméko* (slippery mushrooms), drained
2 tablespoons soy sauce
1/4 cup (60 g.) peeled, grated *daikon* (Japanese white radish)

1/4–1/3 cup (60–80 ml.) *amazu,* sweet-and-sour sauce (see above)

Blanch the slippery mushrooms in boiling water for about 1 minute and drain them. Pour the soy sauce over the mushrooms and let them marinate for about 10 minutes.

Place the grated radish on a clean kitchen towel, and gather up the edges to enclose the radish in a small bag. Twist and squeeze lightly. Run it under cold water for a few seconds and then squeeze out all liquid again. Empty the contents of the bag into a small bowl. Add sweet-and-sour sauce, a few spoonfuls at a time, until the grated radish is barely suspended in it and takes on the appearance of semimelted snow.

Drain the mushrooms of any excess soy sauce and toss them in the sleet sauce. To serve, mound about 2 tablespoons of the mushrooms in sleet sauce on small individual plates. Serve chilled or at room temperature.

A PICNIC IN THE HIMALAYAS*

This piece by Madhur Jaffrey was first published in *Gourmet* with the recipes that follow. I include it with my warmest thanks.

Summer vacations saw us in the Himalayas. . . . All relatives would meet in Delhi, and half a train would be booked to take us from Delhi to the foothills of the towering mountains. A fleet of cars was hired to

---

*From Madhur Jaffrey's article in *Gourmet.*

transport us from there to six, seven, or eight thousand feet above sea level, where several houses were rented to accommodate us.

Once settled, we were left pretty much to ourselves: The only organized activity was the picnic. For this event preparations were begun several weeks in advance, with rickshaws or palanquins arranged for the old and the infirm and horses for the riders. The ladies of the house, as well as numerous servants, spent many days preparing the food. Baskets of mangoes were ordered from various North Indian cities: *langras* from Varanasi for those who liked their mangoes tart; *dussehris* from Lucknow for those who liked them sweet and smooth; and *chusnis*, small sucking mangoes, for those who preferred not to eat the fruit but rather to suck the juice straight from the skin. Litchis, those succulent fruits with sweet white flesh, were sent from Dehra Dun. Most of the packing, including pots and pans, the kettle to make Darjeeling tea, portable charcoal stoves, charcoal, disposable earthenware cups, cotton rugs, blankets, towels, serving spoons, and plates, was done the night before, and at sunrise, when the mountains were still shrouded in an icy mist, porters, rickshaws, palanquins, and horses were all assembled. First the porters were loaded with baskets of food and sent off with a party of servants. The walkers, led by my middle uncle, who had a passion for hiking, were the next lot. Third were those who rode in the rickshaws and palanquins, and the last group consisted of those on horseback.

The picnic site was carefully chosen weeks in advance—by the same middle uncle, who also acted as majordomo. Sometimes it was a distant mountain peak several ranges away; at other times it was a thunderous waterfall; once it was a mountain stream rushing through a remote gorge. (Ordinary picnic spots, where most mortals went, were never considered good enough.) Our spots were picked not only for their grandeur but for their inaccessibility in terms of distance or the climbing required.

Clad in heavy sweaters, mufflers, and shawls, our large party moved slowly, making numerous stops along the way. If we passed an orchard, a halt would be called and the farmer was asked if, for a certain sum, we might pick plums or apricots. My favorite groves were those of almond trees. I loved the green almonds, slit open and robbed of their tender white flesh.

We would generally arrive at our picnic spot around midday. If it was beside a waterfall or stream, the children were permitted to swim while lunch was unpacked. The mangoes were placed in the stream to cool, fires were lighted to heat certain dishes (and also to warm the children when they emerged from the freezing water), and a large cotton rug was spread on the ground. Arrayed on the rug were meatballs

stuffed with raisins and mint leaves; potatoes cooked with whole fennel and cumin and fenugreek seeds; chopped goat meat cooked with peas; chick-peas tossed with raw onions, ginger, and green chilies; green beans seasoned with cumin seed, garlic, and lemon; chicken with almonds and yogurt; cauliflower flavored with ginger and Chinese parsley; spiced *pooris* (puffy, deep-fried breads); sour carrot pickles; hot green mango pickles; and spiced cucumbers. The meal was eaten to the accompaniment of tales of adventure and hilarious stories about our ancestors.

After lunch, the older folk would rest, napping on the rug or leaning against rocks and gossiping, and the children would disappear in various directions, fishing, hunting wild berries, or sliding on beds of pine needles. At about four o'clock we would all reassemble for tea. Served in disposable earthenware cups it was accompanied by *mutthris* (biscuits) and my grandmother's thick, sweet tomato chutney. Then the fires were put out, the rugs and utensils were packed, and the whole party would begin the long trek home.

Delhi Chickpeas

3 onions, minced
1/3 cup (80 ml.) vegetable oil
3 tomatoes, peeled, seeded,
    and chopped
1 tablespoon ground coriander
2 teaspoons ground cumin
1/2 teaspoon turmeric
Three 20-oz. (560-g.) cans chickpeas

2 1/2 tablespoons lemon juice
2 teaspoons garam masala (see note)
1 1/2 teaspoons salt
1 tablespoon peeled and grated fresh
    ginger root
1 small fresh green hot chili pepper,
    seeded and minced

In a large deep skillet sauté the onions in the vegetable oil until they are golden. Add the tomatoes, and cook the mixture, stirring, for 10 minutes, or until all of the liquid has evaporated. Add the coriander, cumin, and turmeric and sauté the mixture for 1 minute.

Drain the chickpeas, reserving 1 cup of the liquid, and add the chickpeas and the reserved liquid to the pan with 1 tablespoon of the lemon juice, garam masala, and salt. Bring the liquid to a boil over moderate heat, stirring, reduce heat to low, and simmer the mixture, covered, for about 10 minutes. Remove the pan from the heat and add 1 1/2 tablespoons lemon juice, ginger root, and chili pepper. Serve the chickpeas hot or at room temperature. *Serves 6 to 8.*

Note: To make garam masala (Indian mixed spice) in a spice grinder pulverize 1 tablespoon cardamom seed, a 2-in. (5-cm.) piece of cinnamon stick, broken into pieces, 1 teaspoon each of cumin, cloves, peppercorns, and 1/4 whole nutmeg. Store the spice in an airtight container. Keeps for 2 to 3 weeks. Makes about 3 tablespoons.

Indian Spiced Green Beans

1 1/2 lb. (675 g.) green beans	1 teaspoon salt
1/3 cup (80 ml.) water	Cayenne pepper to taste
5 garlic cloves, pressed	1/2 teaspoon cumin
1 tablespoon lemon juice	1/3 cup (80 ml.) vegetable oil

Trim the green beans and cut them into 1/4-in. (3/4-cm.) slices. In a small ceramic or glass bowl combine the water, garlic cloves, lemon juice, salt, and cayenne. In a 10-in. (25-cm.) enamel skillet cook the cumin in vegetable oil over moderately high heat for 3 or 4 seconds. Add the beans and sauté them for 1 minute. Stir in the garlic mixture, reduce the heat to low, and cook the beans, covered, stirring occasionally, for 20 minutes, or until they are just tender. Increase the heat to high and cook the beans, uncovered, stirring constantly, until the liquid has evaporated.

Cooking in the Open

COOKING OVER EMBERS

Although barbecuing is the most ancient form of cooking, the recent world-wide enthusiasm for the activity has come from America. In 1955 James Beard wrote that America had become enchanted with outdoor cookery. A great nostalgic yearning for the wood fire cooking of the early settlers had crystallized in the new culinary sport of the charcoal grill, and the excellence of the result rapidly made an outdoor barbecue a fixture in American life. Fireplaces were installed in public grounds for the benefit of picnickers, restaurants mastered the art of cooking on charcoal, and almost everyone with a backyard or a balcony was won over to the charm of cooking meat, fowl, fish, or vegetables over an open fire in the casual atmosphere of the open air.

The enchantment grew and spilled out of the country, starting a fashion that swept throughout the world. Barbecuing everywhere now bears the marks of America with its special equipment and accessories, bottled sauces, jargon, rituals and organization, and the whole casual informal lifestyle where men do the cooking and women the hostessing. But while Americans generally concentrated on hamburgers and steaks as the standard fare, other countries dug into their own culinary roots and revived old charcoal specialties.

Among several theories held about the origin of the word "barbecue" (the French say it is derived from *de la barbe à la queue,* which is the way an animal was spitted, from "beard to tail"), the most likely is *barbacoa,* the name of the wooden frame on which the Spaniards first saw the Mexican Indians smoke-dry their fish and cook their meats. European colonizers, like the Spaniards, adopted the techniques of grilling from the Cherokees and Creeks of the Carolinas and the Gulf Coast, and as their cattle and pigs began to thrive and their ranchos took root in arid Texas, New Mexico, and Arizona and in the fertile valleys of California, the practice of barbecuing spread with added refinements in the form of Spanish sauces with the flavor of garlic, hot peppers, and tomatoes. The fiestas of the Spanish ranchers who moved up to California from Mexico early in the nineteenth century are legendary. At those great gatherings freshly killed beef turned on a huge fire or hung waiting in the shade of a tree while the vaqueros and their ladies danced through the night. Traditional community barbecues, whether festive or electioneering occasions, are part of American history and still attract enormous crowds. Long narrow ditches are dug out and stuffed with slowly burning cordwood. Iron bars and chicken wire stretched across the sunken fires carry the meat, and while it cooks slowly the traditional sauces and accompaniments are set out: homemade bread, baked beans, freshly churned butter, pickles, preserves, and all manner of pies and cakes.

Despite the importance of the barbecue, or perhaps because it remains an integral part of the pioneering heritage, many are apt to get into a rut and to fall back on the standard fare of hamburgers and steaks. It is worth looking abroad to see what other countries have been cooking over charcoal for new ideas.

Cooking over a wood or charcoal fire imparts a unique appetizing smoky flavor to food which no other method can capture, and which has caused it to remain a matter of pleasure throughout the world rather than mere necessity. An old Italian saying claims that "Even an old shoe tastes good if it is cooked over charcoal," and the smell, as anyone who has passed a kebab vendor knows, is most alluring and plays a great part in sharpening the appetite.

Although perfectly simple, there is an art in good grilling and roasting which can be acquired with practice. The secret lies in making a good fire, controlling the heat, and distributing it evenly. The food cooked in this way is so good that all one needs to accompany it is a salad, and fruit to follow.

An Open Wood Fire

If you are building a fire choose a spot sheltered from strong winds. Dig or scrape a small trench around the spot to prevent roots from catching fire and smoldering underground.

Build it between large stones, bricks, or logs, lifted by small stones so as to let the breeze circulate underneath and fan the flames. They will act as a windbreak, prevent the fire from spreading, and also hold the grill. A more easily lit and maintained alternative is to dig a shallow pit 8 to 20 in. (20 to 50 cm.) deep (its depth depends on the size of foods to be cooked) and build the fire in it. Dig it in the direction of the wind so as to allow it to fan the flames. Line it with thin stones if the earth is wet.

Wood takes a long time to burn to a bed of embers, especially if it is large or a little damp, so you must start preparations well over an hour before you would like to eat.

Build your fire gradually, beginning with crumpled paper, dry leaves or bark, pine needles, or acorns in a loose pile. Cover with dry twigs—use dead wood and breakable small wood, then sticks converging at the top to let the air circulate.

Thrust a burning match in the center, then add larger pieces of wood, crossing them so as to let air circulate. Split the wood if it seems wet; the inside will be drier. If the logs are too thick, they will take too long to produce a bed of embers. Cut them into relatively small pieces of uniform size so that they burn down to embers at the same rate. Keep your fire small. It is easier to handle and as effective as a larger one.

Do not leave the fire unattended while it burns, and watch for sparks that might catch a nearby branch or grasses. Start cooking only when the wood is reduced to embers. This usually takes about 30 to 45 minutes.

Small pieces of wood or a large pile of dry twigs which die down to embers in 10 to 15 minutes suffice for steaks and foods which cook so quickly that there is no need for embers that will hold their heat for long.

Alicide Bontou in *Traité de la cuisine bourgeoise bordelaise* describes the old way of cooking entrecôte in Bordeaux: "In times gone by gourmets did not disdain an invitation to go down into the wine cellars and eat an entrecôte with the cellar master and the tonnelier, who had a reputation for preparing it well. They made their fire with hoops of chestnut wood from old barrels and claimed that this gave a particularly good flavor to the meat."

The choice of wood is important. It should of course not be rotten, crumbly, or damp. For a good fire use dry slow-burning hardwoods that give long-lasting coals, such as oak, ash, beech (which burns green), hickory, walnut, and maple. Mesquite is now very popular in America, and pecan is also used. Chestnut, lime, and sycamore also make good fuel. Use soft-woods that burn quickly and are good only for kindling to start a fire. Avoid resinous woods such as pine, which gives a turpentine taste to your food. Elder and elm wood are not much good for burning. Spruce, cedar, and birch are soft but add a distinctive biting flavor. Aromatic woods such as fruitwoods, especially vines, and branches of juniper or bay tree can be added to perfume the fire and give a delicious taste to the food being cooked. Hazelnut is good too, and its thin green branches may be used as a spit or as skewers. For some reason, superstition has branded poplar and aspen as "unlucky" woods.

The first Mogul Emperor Babur (1483–1530) had some advice in his diary regarding the firewood to be found around Kabul. This selection is from Annette Susannah Beveridge's translation (1921):

The snow fall being so heavy in Kabul, it is fortunate that excellent fire-wood is had near by. Given one day to fetch it, wood can be had of the khanjak (mastic), bilut (holm-oak), badamcha (small almond) and gargand. Of these khanjak wood is the best; it burns with flame and nice smell, makes plenty of hot ashes and does well even if sappy. Holm-oak is also first rate fire-wood, blazing less than mastic but, like it, making a hot fire with plenty of hot ashes, and nice smell. It has the peculiarity in burning that when its leafy branches are set alight, they fire up with amazing sound, blazing and crackling from bottom to top. It is good fun to burn it. The wood of the small-almond is the most beautiful and commonly-used, but it does not make a lasting fire. The gargand is quite a slow shrub, thorny, and burning sappy or dry; it is the fuel of the Ghazni people.

A Few Words about Mesquite

Mesquite is currently enjoying an unprecedented vogue for barbecuing in America. The thorny, pod-bearing hardwood shrub, known to the Aztecs as *misquitl,* grows wild and thick in the southwestern United States and northern Mexico. It was popularized with the flavors of the Southwest when regional foods came into fashion and received the accolade of the "New American Cuisine" to the point of being called its signature. Devotees praise its long and hot burning qualities and the delicate smoky flavor it imparts to fish, seafood, meat, and fresh vegetables. It does wonders for strong-tasting foods such as game, wild hog, eggplant, and rockfish, and some have claimed that once a person tastes mesquite he'll never use any other wood again.

Mesquite charcoal is more practical and provides the right heat more quickly. The best is made in the old way: stacked in a mound, then covered with hay and dirt or clay to allow just enough air to burn off the acids and gases, and left to smolder for between 7 days and 3 weeks.

Charcoal Fires

Although it is perfectly sensible to burn wood in a commercial barbecue, charcoal, the fuel commonly used for it, is more manageable and burns quickly and well. Lump charcoal is cheaper and catches fire more rapidly, but it burns faster. The charcoal briquets that are sold in hardware stores and supermarkets provide longer, steadier, more intense heat, although they are more difficult to get started. You can buy them also in tidy, self-starting boxes.

Buying the Barbecue

The barbecue trade has blossomed in recent years, and department stores are ready at the first song of the cuckoo with an ever growing selection at prices to meet every budget and with a vast array of equipment and tools.

If you are ready to invest in a good portable or permanent barbecue there is a wide variety to choose from. New models come out every year, and it is therefore most advisable to visit a store with a large selection before you make your choice. Buy a barbecue that is large enough to accommodate your family, larger still if you entertain.

Our first barbecue, a wedding present, was a very light fire-bowl on wheels which we could easily take out on day excursions. It lasted ten years until rust eventually ended its days. For almost as many years now we have had a hibachi (the Japanese word for fire-box). It is the "triple" version which can provide for a large number of people. Although heavy, the sturdy and simple cast-iron bowl is easily transportable in the trunk of a car and has accompanied us on a boating holiday on the Norfolk Broads. We do not mind its ground-level position, as we like squatting. Its advantage is that the three separate grills can be raised or lowered to fit into various special notches.

Your choice must depend on your needs and lifestyle. For camping and picnics the barbecue must of course be portable—small, folding, or collapsible. Choose a comfortable height if you do not like squatting or bending. A heavy one is all right for the garden, and wheels help to move it around. It must be well-balanced and steady. If it has wheels, there must be proper brakes and wedges to prevent its rolling. The material it is made of must be sturdy and long-lasting and preferably rustproof, such as cast iron, porcelain-enameled steel, or cast aluminum.

The fire-bowl should hold enough charcoal for lengthy cooking. The distance from the grill to the fire must be variable, and there must be adjustable air vents on the side of the bowl to regulate the heat.

Wooden handles are best because they do not conduct heat and thus minimize the danger of burning hands.

A barbecue need not be complicated or expensive. Indeed, you may even make it yourself.

Making a Barbecue

Inspired by the Portuguese, we have used a large clay flowerpot. It is best lined with aluminum foil. Push your finger through this and the bottom hole and lift the pot on two bricks to allow for a draft. Half fill with pebbles and cover these with a good layer of charcoal. Place a grill over the top (chicken wire will do). If you are using large enough skewers these can be laid on the edges of the pot without any risk of falling in.

You may use a biscuit tin or an old metal tray with holes punched around the sides to let in air. If you are cooking for two, a thick foil container will hold a couple of hamburgers or two small skewers. An old wheelbarrow can make a useful mobile barbecue. Punch holes through the bottom and sides and fill with stones and gravel. For a large grill rack improvise with parts from an old discarded oven or refrigerator.

At my hotel in the Seychelles large metal barrels were cut in half lengthwise. They were raised to table height for Creole barbecue nights with girders used to make stands. Coconut fronds made a screen from the sea breeze behind the cooks, who dished out spare ribs, slices of sucking pig, sweet potatoes, giant shrimp, bananas, and strange-looking fish.

You can even build a permanent structure in the garden which can be as simple or as elaborate as you like. Use "overburnt" bricks or fire bricks, which do not crack easily, and build in a spot which normally has enough wind to keep a fire alive but which does not send all the smoke straight into the eating area or through the French windows.

The firepan and grill of an electric or gas cooker will do very well for this simple construction. As they come in different sizes, it is best to build around them.

Useful Accessories

Only a few tools are really indispensable, some are useful, but most are only fun. I have been barbecuing happily for nearly twenty years with only a grill, a spit, and skewers. Fish slices, brushes, and forks have come from my everyday kitchen, but I must admit I have occasionally wished I had some tongs handy.

A spit is required for cooking large roasts, whole chicken, or a very large fish. The best ones are made in heavy chrome-plated steel sturdy enough to hold heavy food. Although a battery-operated electric one turns automatically and allows the meat to cook unattended, turning occasionally by hand is part of the pleasure.

The grill must be rustproof, preferably in chrome-plated steel. The bars must not be too far apart or small morsels will fall through. Hinged double grills and baskets are especially good for holding and turning over meat, and particularly fish, easily. The grill must always be well oiled before you begin to cook or the food will stick.

Skewers. Many types are sold. For kebabs, buy long ones in flattened steel with a sharp point at one end. Their sword shape is said to be derived from the swords of Turkish warriors who used to thread meat on them for cooking on an open fire. It prevents the meat from sliding and twisting around while cooking. Some are also slightly twisted to make slipping even less likely. Two-pronged ones may be used for holding larger pieces. Wooden skewers burn, but you can improvise with thin fresh green branches from which the bark has been stripped.

Tongs for turning food or moving embers must be long-handled and so must *basting spoons* and *brushes* (use bristle, not nylon or plastic) to avoid burning fingers. A long *two-pronged fork* may be handy as well as a spatula for turning over small pieces of food.

Thermometers. Some people like to register the heat of the fire more accurately than by hand. A meat thermometer pushed through the center of the meat will determine whether it is done.

Bellows are seldom necessary in countries where there is a wind, but I do occasionally use a round, woven straw fan.

Aluminum foil is invaluable. Use a heavy-duty one, preferably for wrapping foods to cook or to keep warm, as well as for lining the fire-bowl for extra reflected heat and for keeping it clean. It may also be spread out over the grill and used as a hot plate (with holes pricked in if you like if the food is not too fat).

For cleaning barbecue and equipment use a metal brush with detergent and hot water.

The Charcoal Fire

To build the fire, place dry twigs over a loose pile of crumpled paper. Cover with a pyramid of charcoal and set the paper alight. We sometimes use gas from a cylinder to get the fire going. Otherwise several kinds of fire starters are available. Candle stubs are useful. There are also electric and gas starters and a liquid fuel that you sprinkle over the charcoal and let it soak in before you try to light it. But you must not use gasoline or kerosene; they are dangerous and give a bad smell and a bad taste. Once the pyramid of charcoal has ignited and started to burn evenly, rake it and spread it out over the surface you need for cooking, taking care not to disturb the firebed. It will be ready for cooking when it has reduced to glowing ash-covered embers, usually after about 20 minutes.

A common mistake is to use too much fuel, but you will soon learn to estimate how much you need. For small grills it is enough to cover the area taken up by food, two layers deep.

If you are grilling meat for 3 people you may need no more than 14 briquet lumps. If you are spit-roasting, which takes a long time, you will of course need more—as many as 40 to 45 lumps. Even then you start with a few and add more, as you need them. Keep coals in reserve at the side so that they can warm up before being added, a few at a time. Putting on too many cold pieces at once will lower the temperature and cause a lot of smoke.

To save remaining fuel for another occasion smother it with old ashes or throw it in a metal bucket of water.

A refinement is to put a layer of gravel in the fire-box under the charcoal to aid ventilation. (Grease and ashes can be washed off with liquid detergent and the gravel can be used again.)

The Art of Cooking on Embers

Whether you have an elaborate barbecue or an open fire the principle is the same. Cooking is done over the gentle heat of glowing coals or wood embers and you start to cook only when the fire has burned down and the smoke has gone, and a light powdery gray ash covers the glowing coals. Flames will dry out and scorch the food outside and leave it uncooked inside.

You must find out for yourself what heat you require for different types of food and regulate your fire accordingly. Therein lies the art. The cooking time depends on the thickness and type of food, its distance from the fire and from other foods, the quality of the charcoal, the size of the firebed, and weather conditions.

To regulate the heat you can lower or raise the grill. Otherwise, for a hotter fire, push the coals together, and for a lower heat, rake them apart. Shaking the white ash off the embers makes them hotter, as does more air. If there is a strong wind use windbreaks to shield the fire, and if there is not enough breeze, fan the fire or open vents.

For very slow cooking, such as a large roast, use gentler indirect heat. Do not place the food directly over the fire but a little to the side. Or in the style of the gypsies, make a ring of burning coals around it. Let the meat stand for about 10 minutes before carving.

For grilling you need an even temperature. Test the heat by putting your hand above the coals at the distance where you will place the food. If you cannot leave it longer than 3 seconds it is probably too hot. If you can leave it for almost 4 seconds, it is medium hot, and it is warm if you can leave it for 5 seconds. Move pieces already cooked away from the center of the fire to make way for less cooked pieces from the periphery. Use a little water— squirt it with a syringe if you like—to put out any flare-ups which result from dripping fat.

Trust your own taste and judgment. You can learn only by experience.

Aromatics

If glowing embers give food a splendid taste, aromatics can make it superlative. Branches or sprigs of herbs thrown into the fire, when the food can catch their perfume and retain it, are a special refinement. Dried herbs, which burn too readily and whose perfume is quickly lost, must be used just before the food is ready. Fresh herbs give out a more powerful and long-lasting scent. As their moisture and their oils create a cloud of smoke they must be thrown in a little at a time when the meat or fish is almost done. Delicate herbs such as wild thyme and marjoram can be used generously, strongly perfumed ones, such as rosemary, sparingly.

Vine twigs or prunings give a specially delicate taste. They will burst into a crackling flame at the touch of a match. A few handfuls of these alone will suffice for a quick grill. Dried fennel stalks make a good bed on which to grill fish such as sea bass and red mullet; other dried herbs may be added with the stalks. Damp hickory chips at the last stage give a smoky flavor. Pieces of garlic and orange zest in the fire also give a delightful aroma.

H. D. Renner, in *The Origin of Food Habits*, places gastronomy in culture somewhere between painting and perfumery—as a "visual and nasal" art. The smell of roasting meat together with that of burning fruitwood and dried herbs, as voluptuous as incense in a church, is enough to turn anyone into a budding gastronome.

In many regions it is considered good to flavor meat with the food the animal has grazed on, such as the wild thyme whose small purple flowers made the mutton spicy, the laver weed, seaweed, and salt grasses which gave the marsh lamb a distinct iodine tang, the fruit peels and berries of those fed in the orchard or on the moor, or the mint which kept the young lamb happy in the warm valley.

To Smoke Food

Though smoke generally gives an unpleasant taste to food, the one produced by the damp shavings or sawdust or damp branches of aromatic woods such as oak, alder, hickory, poplar, mesquite, or fruitwood (never resinous woods) imparts a delicious flavor. There are many smokers on the market, and there is one you can improvise on page 357. But it is possible to obtain the special smoky flavor by grilling the food first, then smothering the embers with damp sawdust or shavings or damp branches or leaves or herbs plucked from the countryside. If you cover the food with a biscuit tin or similar container or tarpaulin, the elusive scented smoke will permeate it better.

Marinades

However fragrant the aroma provided by burning herbs, it is a fleeting one. For meats to be truly impregnated with flavors, they must be steeped in a marinade for some time. These aromatic baths, usually a mixture of oil and wine, vinegar, or lemon juice, even cider and beer, with herbs and seasonings, flavor and tenderize meat and also prevent foods from drying out on the grill.

The tougher meats and those whose own flavor is not the very best benefit most from this treatment, particularly the smaller morsels cut up as kebab which retain all the flavorings.

Fish needs it the least and is enhanced more by herbs in the belly. Milk is sometimes used with smoked fish and sour cream with fresh fish. Honey may be added to lemon or vinegar for a sweet-and-sour taste. Vermouth, Cognac, armagnac, whiskey, port, and Madeira—all give a magnificent flavor if the fish is coated with them before being wrapped in foil.

There are several classic marinades and many variations. The whole range of herbs, spices, and peppers as well as garlic and onion, lemon zest, and celery leaves finds a place in one or the other. Their use is often a matter of tradition and culture; the better known combinations such as fish with fennel, rosemary with pork, mint with lamb, and tarragon with chicken are certainly good, but it does not mean that others should not be tried.

The method: Put the meat, chicken, or fish in a deep bowl so that it is covered completely by the marinade. Turn occasionally and leave covered for at least 1 hour or as long as 2 days in a cool place or in the refrigerator. The longer you leave it the tastier and the more tender it will be.

Meat should not be chilled when it is cooked or it will be overdone on the outside and undercooked inside. Take out from the refrigerator 1 or 2 hours before you are ready to cook and drain it well, as dripping oil will cause the fire to flare up and smoke. Moisten with the marinade occasionally, using a brush or spoon, to prevent the food from drying out.

Except with fish, salt is not usually included in the marinade, as it may draw out the juices and dry out the meat. Add it when you are ready to cook or at the end of the cooking.

A glaze may be brushed onto meat or chicken about 15 minutes before the end of cooking time to give the food color and luster. Recently a mixture of clear honey, lemon juice, and soy sauce with a sprinkling of powdered cloves has become popular. It should not be put on too soon, as it will caramelize and burn.

Barbecue Sauces

American barbecue sauces inspired from south of the border are gaining popularity abroad. In 1923 Horace Kephart in his book *Camp Cookery* gave the following instructions for an "old-style" barbecue sauce to baste on meat while it is cooking:

"One pint of vinegar, half a can of tomatoes, two teaspoonfuls of red pepper (chopped pepper-pods are better), a teaspoonful of black pepper, same of salt, two tablespoonfuls of butter. Simmer together till it is completely amalgamated. Have a bit of clean cloth or sponge tied on the end of a stick and keep the meat well basted with the dressing as long as it is on the fire."

Sauces now come extremely varied with a number of ingredients, generally hot and spicy, often sour, and occasionally also sweet. They are usually basted or brushed on toward the end of the cooking (for 15 or 20 minutes) to give color and flavor to the crust.

Here are a few classics which can be varied to taste.

A Basic American Barbecue Sauce

1 onion, finely chopped
2 cloves garlic, crushed
2 tablespoons butter
1–2 teaspoons dry mustard
1–2 tablespoons chili powder
1 cup (235 ml.) ketchup

Juice of 1 lemon
4 tablespoons vinegar
4 tablespoons Worcestershire sauce
1 cup (235 ml.) tomato juice
Salt

Cook the onion and garlic in the butter until soft. Stir in the rest of the ingredients, mix well, and cook for 5 minutes more.

A Hot Mexican Barbecue Sauce

1 onion, finely chopped
1/2 cup (120 ml.) olive oil
1 clove garlic, crushed
1 chili pepper, minced
12-oz. (340-g.) can peeled tomatoes,
    chopped (retain juice)

Salt
2 tablespoons chili powder or cayenne
1/4 cup (60 ml.) vinegar

Fry the onion in 2 tablespoons of oil until lightly colored. Add the garlic and pepper, and when the aroma rises add the tomatoes and their juice. Add the rest of the ingredients and simmer for about 5 minutes.

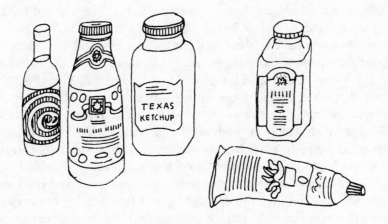

Chicken Barbecue Sauce

1 well beaten egg
1/2 cup (120 ml.) cooking oil
1 cup (235 ml.) cider vinegar

2 teaspoons salt
2 teaspoons sage, crumbled
6–8 drops Tabasco

Combine all ingredients in a jar. Shake well and let stand for several hours before using.

Sweet-and-Sour Barbecue Sauce for Game

1 onion, finely chopped
1 1/2 cups (355 ml.) tomato juice
1/4 cup (60 ml.) wine vinegar
3–4 tablespoons brown sugar

1 1/2 teaspoons chili powder
1 tablespoon dry mustard
1 tablespoon Worcestershire sauce
Salt

Simmer everything together for 5 to 10 minutes.

Variation: Instead of the sugar you may add 1/2 cup (120 ml.) juice from a tropical fruit. This will add a new, exotic flavor.

Basting and Barding—a Protection from Drying

The heat of a fire, far or near, is a harsh form of cooking. Everything except fat meat needs moistening with fat or the result will be dry and hard.

Pure fat, melted butter, or oil (better still a mixture of 1/3 butter and 2/3 oil), or a marinade may serve to baste meat, fish, and vegetables. Use a long-handled spoon to baste a large piece, and where the juices fall into a tray pick up only the fat on top of the gravy. Use a brush for smaller pieces cooked over the fire when drippings are likely to cause flare-ups. If you are in the countryside with wild herbs growing around it is pleasant and attractive to use a few sprigs with which to brush on the fat. Although a little smoke from drippings in the fire is pleasant, too much from a large roast is not. A trough cut out of aluminum foil is a very good idea when using a rotisserie.

It is customary to bard certain lean meats and game and the breast of poultry. Cover with thin strips of bacon or pork fat tied with string. Depending on the size of the meat and the cooking time, much or all of the fat will melt away, lending a distinctive taste to the meat.

In France lacy caul is commonly used instead of strips of fat. Caul fat is a fatty membrane enveloping the intestines. It acts as a self-baster when used as a wrapper. Soak it in lukewarm water for 2 to 3 minutes until it loosens up. Rinse and lay on a dry cloth and carefully open it up. Cut the best parts into rectangles 5 by 7 in. (13 by 18 cm.).

Wrapping in Leaves

Leaves are the most natural protection from the heat of the fire for lean and delicate morsels on the grill. With this wrapping, meat, fish, vegetables, and fruits can be cooked in the ashes and directly over coals.

Papaya, palm, and banana leaves and wetted cornhusks are used in countries where they grow. Banana skins make an excellent moist case, and lettuce and cabbage leaves can also be eaten. Vine leaves, used for a few delicacies and traditionally to wrap up quails and red mullet, lend a distinctive sharp savor.

A fashion adopted in Florida from both the West Indies and Brazil is to wrap any meat in papaya leaves and then either bury it in hot ashes or roast it over coals. The pepsin contained in the leaves softens the meat without affecting its flavor, and tough meat turns out meltingly tender.

A South Sea Island style originating in Tahiti is to wrap all sorts of foods —fruits, root and other vegetables, and grains—in *petakes*, mats woven of fresh palm fronds. These are laid on top of meat in a pit and covered to steam in their juices. The long, slow cooking over hot stones or coals in the pit results in an unequaled richness of flavor, mingling the tastes of meat, fruit, and vegetable.

Cooking en Papillote

Food can be wrapped in damp paper to prevent it from burning or drying out on the fire. Brown paper and newspaper are commonly used, though they do not improve the taste. At the start of the century greased parchment paper became very popular for cooking delicate, quickly cooked foods en papillote. This retained the aroma and juices until the parcel was opened out on the plate.

Foil is more convenient to use and makes it easier to twist edges into a tightly closed seal. The food inside is steamed in its own juice rather than grilled, and though it has none of the characteristic taste of food cooked over coals, it is remarkably successful with vegetables, fish and seafood, chicken breast, and thin slices of veal, which tend to dry out. With it comes the advantage of adding other ingredients or stuffing. It takes a little longer to cook than food put straight onto the fire and only slightly longer than in paper.

Grease the foil so that the food does not stick to it. To make a papillote, cut the paper or foil into a shape large enough to contain the piece comfortably; hearts are traditional, but a circle or a square or rectangle will do equally well. Place the food on one half and fold the other half over it. To fasten the package, hold the edges together and turn them over twice, like a hem, then twist to make an airtight seal. The parcel must be a little baggy to allow for puffing up with the heat.

But you may wrap up the food in any way you like as long as it is properly sealed in.

APPETIZERS AND VEGETABLES OVER THE FIRE

Rather than wait for the meat to be ready, start with tidbits which take a short time on the fire. They are called *amuse gueules* by the French because they are fun. Use a large bed of embers. A wrapping of bacon keeps small things with no fat moist and tender.

A cocktail party in the summer when the days are long and the nights short has added appeal when the appetizers are cooked in the open. Offer a choice of skewered tidbits with dips and other finger foods, both cold and hot. You will find many of these in different sections of the book. Have an attractive selection that will awaken the appetite, substantial enough to fortify the stomach when drinks are being served but not enough to satisfy it; unless the intention is that people should not rush away to a meal.

Shrimp

Only large fleshy shrimp are worth putting on the grill. They are best left unpeeled or, if peeled, left for half an hour in a marinade.

For a garlicky marinade mix olive oil and lemon juice with several cloves of crushed garlic, salt and pepper, and some finely chopped parsley or fresh tarragon. In the Seychelles I discovered a *Creole marinade* of grated ginger with crushed garlic and chili pepper beaten into coconut oil. For other marinades see page 264.

Place in an oiled tightly meshed double grill or thread onto skewers and turn over a gentle fire for about 5 to 6 minutes, basting frequently with the marinade oil or melted butter. Serve with lemon wedges. You can try this with crayfish too.

Garlic Provençal

Put a whole head of garlic in the ashes for 8 to 10 minutes, until it pops and the skin splits. Peel off the skin and sprinkle with a little salt. Eat on crisp bread.

Salted Almonds

Take almonds, blanched or in their skins, sprinkle generously with sea salt, and moisten with water. Put them on a piece of foil placed over the grill. Shake the foil to turn them until they are crisp and begin to color. You may also like to make these hot with paprika or chili pepper.

Stuffed Prunes in Port

Stuff pitted prunes (the California variety will do well) with half a shelled walnut. Soak in a little port and water to cover for 30 minutes until the liquor has been absorbed.

Wrap in a thin slice of bacon and grill until crisp.

Stuffed Olives

Stuff green pitted olives with blanched almonds. Wrap each in a narrow thin slice of bacon and grill until crisp.

Oysters, Scallops, and Mussels

The simplest way of eating shellfish is to place the cleaned and rinsed shells (see p. 339) straight onto a hot grill. When they open they are ready to eat.

Provide salt, pepper, bread, and lemon juice. For a special occasion a sauce can be made by boiling 1/4 to 1/2 cup (60 to 120 ml.) dry white wine with 1 to 2 sprigs fresh herbs—thyme, chervil, parsley, fennel tops—and beating in 1/4 lb. (115 g.) butter off the heat with 2 tablespoons heavy cream, a squeeze of lemon juice, and pepper to taste.

The shellfish may also be removed from their shells and grilled on skewers —with mushrooms in between if you like. Dust with salt and pepper and sprinkle with lemon and oil, then roll in fine bread crumbs (as added protection) before you thread onto skewers and put them on the fire. Baste frequently with oil or melted butter.

Serve on toast with melted butter and lemon wedges.

To make angels on horseback thread oysters, mussels, or small scallops (cut larger ones up) onto skewers, alternating with pieces of bacon, or wrap each one up in a thin piece of bacon before skewering. Grill over a gentle fire, turning twice. Allow 5 minutes for mussels and oysters, 10 minutes for large scallops (5 minutes if cut in two). For other recipes see pages 271, 340.

Grilled Cheese

Cheese slices. Use a hard dry cheese (goat cheese is particularly good, preferably the small whole "crotins"). Put slices (floured if a little moist) on a well-oiled grill not too near the fire. Throw in some herbs, such as rosemary, wild thyme, and sage, which will give a delicate perfume to the cheese. Let it become soft and slightly colored. Another good way that results in a delicious, moist, and flavorsome cheese is to marinate it overnight in olive oil mixed with thyme and a little crushed garlic.

Crème de Gruyère. A French alternative to Welsh rabbit can be prepared in advance and packed in foil ready to put on the fire at the same time as a piece of toast. Mash and mix with a fork 3 Petits Suisses, 2 tablespoons softened butter, and a handful of grated Gruyère. Add a pinch of paprika and one of nutmeg. You might also like to try a sprinkling of dried mint or finely chopped fresh basil. Wrap in a well-oiled piece of foil. Put it on the fire until it melts, and spread on toast while still hot.

Cheese in vine leaves. If you happen to be near a vineyard, cut thick slices of a good melting cheese such as Gruyère, Emmenthal, Bel Paese, Cheddar, or fontina, and wrap each one up in 4 or 5 leaves. Put the packages over a gentle fire until the cheese has melted and absorbed the distinct tang of the leaves. Serve on slices of bread.

Raclette

A Swiss way of melting cheese in front of an open fire derives its name from the French verb *racler,* to scrape. The fromage à raclette, which is made by mountain farmers in the Canton of Valais, can be obtained through the Swiss Centre in England and in the U.S. (Rockefeller Plaza, New York) and in some specialty shops around the world. Evan Jones describes the ceremony of melting and scraping it in *The World of Cheese:*

"Poise half of a Valais cheese on a rock, or brick or a log before the flickering heat of a fierce fire (not glowing embers) and deftly scrape the cheese with a large knife on to heat-resistant plates as it melts into a creamy, bubbly mass."

The pale gold sizzling lava becomes a pièce de résistance accompanied by new potatoes, white onions, and sourish gherkins.

Skewered Chicken Livers

Separate pieces of chicken livers. Season with salt and pepper and a dusting of cinnamon or allspice. Thread onto skewers and turn for about 5 minutes 4 in. (10 cm.) away from the fire, brushing occasionally with melted butter until brown outside but still pink and juicy inside.

Variation: An elegant version is to dribble sherry, port, or armagnac on the cooked livers in the serving dish and to set it alight.

Skewered Bacon and Water Chestnuts

Drain water chestnuts, cut in half, and marinate in port wine for 30 minutes. Cut enough bacon slices into 4 strips to wrap around each piece of water chestnut. Thread several bacon-wrapped water chestnuts onto a skewer. Grill 4 in. (10 cm.) away from the fire, turning the skewers, until the bacon is crisp and brown.

Barbecued Chicken Wings

Remove chicken wing tips and break each wing into two pieces. Marinate 12 wings (24 pieces) for an hour in a mixture of 1/4 cup (60 ml.) olive or vegetable oil, the juice of 1 lemon, 2 crushed cloves garlic, a 1-in. (2 1/2-cm.)

piece of fresh ginger root grated or pressed in a garlic press to extract the juice, salt, and pepper. Put on the grill over a medium fire for 3 to 4 minutes on each side, 4 in. (10 cm.) from the fire.

Variation: For a Japanese flavor, leave the wings in a mixture of 1/4 cup (60 ml.) soy sauce, 1/4 cup (60 ml.) mirin (syrupy rice wine), and 1 to 2 tablespoons sugar.

Sardines Grilled in Vine Leaves

This is fiddly but, if you have the time, well worth trying. It is street food fare in the Middle East, where they also use red mullet and do not bother to remove the backbone.

12 large vine leaves (or 24 small ones)	3 cloves garlic, crushed
12 plump sardines	Salt and pepper
1 bunch parsley, finely chopped	3 tablespoons olive oil
1 bunch coriander, finely chopped	1 lemon

If you use fresh vine leaves, poach them in boiling water for a few seconds until they change color and become limp. If you use leaves in brine, soak them in water for about an hour and change the water twice to remove the salt.

Behead the sardines if you like, cut open the belly and pull out the backbone (it is easily done if you flatten out the fish), clean, and wash. Stuff with a mixture of herbs, garlic, salt, and pepper moistened with olive oil. Roll each fish up in 1 or 2 vine leaves and put over embers about 3 in. (8 cm.) from the fire. Cook 5 minutes on each side. Squeeze a little lemon juice over each and serve hot or cold. Everything is edible, leaves and all.

Sweetbreads

Veal sweetbreads are best for this: they must be very fresh. Soak in cold water for 2 hours, changing it twice. Blanch in water to cover with a teaspoon of vinegar for about 5 minutes, drain, and cool quickly by plunging sweetbreads in cold water. Trim off any skin, cartilage, and tubes without removing the very fine membrane. Break into 1-in. (2 1/2-cm.) pieces, sprinkle with salt and pepper, wrap in thin slices of bacon, and thread onto skewers. Turn on the grill until the bacon is crisp and brown.

Sausages

In America frankfurters or hot dogs, Polish sausage, bratwurst, and white sausage are the familiar ones for the grill, but it is worth experimenting with other kinds (such as Spanish chorizos and Italian sausages, both sweet and hot). A wide variety of good fresh French, Italian, and Continental sausages are made with almost 100 percent meat and with additions such as onions, sweet peppers, pistachios, spinach, truffles, garlic, and spices. French saucisses and saucissons, andouillettes, boudins, and crépinettes are excellent cooked in foil in hot ashes, grilled over glowing embers, or cut up into pieces and skewered, as are Moroccan *mergez* and Italian, German, and Polish varieties.

You may cook the long sausages such as andouillette and boudin whole. Roll up in a coil and pierce right through with a skewer to hold firmly. Prick in a few places only and brush with oil. Place on a grill. These require about 6 minutes on each side while smaller sausages require 2 to 3 minutes only per side.

Arais / Arab Bread Stuffed with Meat

Pita or Arab bread stuffed with spiced ground meat makes a good snack and, if cut up small, a very good appetizer. Serve pita very hot with a piece of lemon and tahina if you like.

6 large pita breads
1 large onion, finely chopped
2 tablespoons oil
1 1/4 lb. (560 g.) lean ground meat—
    veal, beef, or lamb
1 small hot green pepper,
    finely chopped
Salt and pepper

1/2 teaspoon allspice
1 teaspoon cinnamon
2 teaspoons sumak or juice of half
    a lemon
A good pinch of cayenne
1 small bunch parsley, finely chopped
2 tablespoons butter, melted

Cut each pita on one side and open carefully without breaking the bread (warming it up makes it easier).

To make the filling, fry the onion in oil until golden, add the meat, and fry, stirring, until it changes color. Add the pepper, season to taste with salt and pepper, and stir in the spices and parsley. Spread a quarter of the filling into each bread, then press it closed. Brush with melted butter and grill,

turning over once, until both sides are lightly colored. Cut in half and then into wedges.

Variation: You may stir 3 tablespoons fried pine nuts in with the meat.

Bread and Cheese Skewers

In France these brochettes are likely to be made with Port Salut. In Italy, Provatura is used for crostini. St.-Paulin, Gruyère, and Emmenthal may also be used.

Cut good bread into thick slices. Remove crusts and cut into squares. Cut the cheese into slices and then into squares the same size as the bread. Sprinkle with pepper if you like. Thread alternately onto skewers, beginning and ending with bread. Place over dying embers for a few minutes, turning from time to time until the bread is crisp and brown and the cheese has melted.

You may also put small pieces of ham between the cheese and the bread.

Barbecued Vegetables

Any of the vegetables and salads I have described can be taken out to serve at a barbecue, but there is something satisfying about cooking vegetables on the same fire as the rest of the meal. Not least is the richness of flavor they acquire when they are thrown in the ashes or turned over glowing embers.

It is fashionable to thread bits of vegetables such as onions, peppers, and tomatoes with meats on the same skewer. It makes an elegant presentation with refreshing variety, even though they do not all cook at the same rate, and some will be overdone while others will still be only partly cooked. If you are cooking them for their own sake, do them separately in the way which suits them best.

All vegetables can be cooked in foil. Wrap cauliflower, green beans, carrots, peas, onions (cut up into small pieces where necessary) with butter, salt, and pepper in a leakproof packet and leave them for 30 minutes on the grill. Cook them separately or make a mixed bag.

Some well-tried combinations such as ratatouille (see p. 100) are excellent done in foil, and zucchini and eggplant au gratin for which the vegetables are sliced or cubed and the cheese (Cheddar will do) grated.

But this type of cuisine is more for the camper who hankers for indoor favorites. Those who are getting away from the dining room will prefer barbecue specials that they do not make every day.

Cook one or an assortment of vegetables, giving each the time it requires, starting with potatoes, and adding the others in order of their cooking time.

Potatoes

Potatoes can be speared on a spit or laid on the grill, or they can be put straight in the ashes as they are. But it is less messy and much more popular to wrap them, well scrubbed, in foil. They need 1 to 1 1/2 hours on the grill, depending on their size, less among the hot embers.

You may make an incision and slip in half a clove of garlic before you begin to cook.

Serve cut in half with plenty of butter, salt, and coarsely ground black pepper or with heavy cream or sour cream and a sprinkling of chives.

Also good is to use fair-size new potatoes, sliced at 1/4- to 1/2-in. (3/4- to 1 1/2-cm.) intervals (not all the way through) into which are tucked slivers of butter with a bit of chopped herbs such as parsley and chives. Wrap in foil and bake as above.

Another excellent sauce makes it a meal in itself. Mix some grated cheese— Cheddar or Gruyère, for instance—with a little softened butter and some fresh cream. Add black pepper and press the paste into cuts in the hot cooked potato.

Yams and Sweet Potatoes

They acquire a wonderful flavor when cooked in foil like potatoes for about an hour. Serve with butter, salt, and pepper. You may also boil them at home until only partially cooked, then peel them and brown them over the fire.

Onions

Put them, unpeeled, on a spit, over a grill, or in hot ashes. In 25 minutes they will still be crisp. Leave them 45 to 50 minutes if you like them soft. Or you can peel them and cook in foil with a little butter, salt, and pepper.

You may also grill onions cut in thick slices. Brush with oil or melted butter and cook until crisply done.

Turnips

Turnips take about 30 minutes to be done in foil. They are also good cut in slices, brushed with oil, and turned after 5 minutes on the grill, then cooked until tender.

Corn on the Cob

The corniche in Alexandria where we used to promenade by the sea is forever associated with the enticing smell of roasting corncobs. Vendors squatted behind little braziers at regular intervals along the sea front, busily fanning the embers to reinforce the breeze or to pass the time.

If you want to cook them in the Egyptian manner, remove silk and husks and turn over a gentle fire for 15 to 20 minutes until they are well browned with black spots outside and milky tender inside. Serve with salt and coarsely ground black pepper and plenty of butter.

Roast Corn American Style. Corn has always been one of the most important crops of America and part of the history of the country. One of the simplest ways to prepare it was to roast in front of the fire in its husks after the silk had been removed: Pull down the husk, remove the silk, and soak the husks in water so they do not burn. Pull up again, twist closed and put the ears on the grill over hot coals for 20 to 25 minutes, turning them occasionally. Nowadays it makes a popular appearance at picnic barbecues alongside the meat when there are large numbers of people to feed.

At traditional beach corn roasts in America a fire is built in a hole in the sand and kept going until the sand is very hot. Then the coals are removed and the corn, desilked and with the husks twisted together at the top, is put in the hole. Wet sacks are placed on top and covered with sand. The corn is left to steam in its husks for about 20 minutes.

White Radishes

The long white radishes now on the market are delicious grilled. Dip in oil and sprinkle with salt and pepper. Turn over the grill for a few minutes. You will not recognize their taste. If they are large and fat, cut into thick slices.

Peppers

Grill them as they are, turning them until the skin blisters and is slightly blackened. Peel carefully, remove stem and seeds, and cut into strips. The flesh is soft and flavorsome and better than when it is cooked in any other way.

Serve as a salad with a vinaigrette or tomatoes, or simply with olive oil, salt, and cracked peppercorns.

Eggplant

The very best thing you can do with an eggplant is to grill it whole in its skin until it blisters and blackens and becomes limp. Peel or scoop out the flesh, mash with a fork, and season to taste with olive oil, lemon juice, salt, pepper, and, if you like, a touch of crushed garlic. Let it cool before you eat it.

Eggplant cut into thick slices. Salting them and letting the juices drain for at least 30 minutes makes a little difference when eggplant are cooked in this manner. Dip in a mixture of olive oil and a little wine vinegar with a sprinkling of chopped mint and crushed garlic. Drain and cook on the grill for about 15 to 20 minutes, turning over once and brushing frequently with olive oil. If you dip them in flour before cooking it will give you a good crust.

Mushrooms

An old English breakfast, and for that matter evening favorite too, is grilled mushrooms and bacon.

Wash mushrooms and trim their stalks. Coat with oil or melted butter and turn once over a gentle fire, basting again. Cook for 5 to 10 minutes. Large fat ones can take up to 20 minutes. Sprinkle with salt and pepper. Grill the bacon at the same time.

Champignons grillés à la Bourguignonne. Serve with the same butter with which the local snails are stuffed. Prepare this beforehand and bring it in a cool container. Stir a good amount of finely chopped parsley and a little crushed garlic into softened butter. Season with salt and pepper and beat well.

Or you may wrap the mushrooms in foil with the herbed and seasoned butter and put the packet on the grill for about 20 minutes, by which time they will be deliciously steamed.

You may also make a stuffing for the mushrooms by adding some fine bread crumbs to the butter. Cook the caps on both sides. Put some filling in each and let it melt a bit on the grill.

Tomatoes

Grill them whole, turning them on all sides, until they are soft and the skin loose. Peel them and serve, lightly mashed, seasoned with salt and pepper and sprinkled with finely chopped fresh herbs and olive oil or melted butter.

Zucchini

Grill small ones whole, large ones cut into slices and skewered, until tender. They need basting with oil or melted butter. Season with salt and pepper when done (5 to 8 minutes for slices).

BREAD

Several people have told me of experiences in the Sinai desert, by the Red Sea, where a Bedouin offered to cook a fish. He built a fire on some rocks, and while it burned down to embers, he made a dough with some flour and sea water. Then he pulled a fish from a net in the water, pushed a wooden stick through its tail and cheeks, and held it, still wriggling, over the fire between two stones. He brushed some embers away to make room on a fire-blackened stone for the thin flat cake of dough. He turned the fish and bread over once and both were ready at the same time, the fish crisp and brown, the bread puffed out and covered with little black spots.

Unleavened bread is very good, and in many parts of the world it is still the most popular everyday bread. Made with whole wheat, barley, corn, millet, and chickpea flours, it is baked on the hearth, on a griddle or bakestone, or in a frying pan. It is easy and worth trying on a camping trip. Start 30 minutes before you want to eat.

All you need is flour: use a mixture of whole wheat and plain flour, and just enough water—less than 1/2 cup (120 ml.) for a cup of flour—to make it stick together. You may add 1/2 teaspoon salt and 1 or 2 tablespoons oil. Add the water gradually and knead vigorously for 8 minutes or until it is a soft elastic dough, then leave it to rest, covered with a damp cloth, for at least 30 minutes.

Put a sheet of metal or a heavy, cast-iron frying pan over a bed of coals which gives an even heat. Take lumps of dough the size of an egg. Pat into flat cakes with the floured palms of your hands and pull the dough thin. Flour the dough so that it does not stick and lay on the smoking hot sheet or pan. Turn over as soon as bubbles appear (in a minute or so) and let the other side cook for half a minute. Then put the bread straight over the fire on a grill. It will puff up immediately. Turn it over. It will be done when both sides are flecked with black spots (2 to 3 minutes). Brush with melted butter while it is still hot.

Frying Pan Bread

Bradford Angier, in his *Wilderness Cookery,* writes: "About the only cooking odors that even approach the aroma of bread baking outdoors are the sizzling smell of good grilled bacon, coffee bubbling in the heat of a campfire, and fat venison sputtering over hardwood coals."

Here is his recipe for bread made in a skillet. It is the famous bannock of the open places. The basic recipe for one hungry outdoorsman follows. If you want more, increase the ingredients proportionately.

1 cup (140 g.) flour	1/4 teaspoon salt
1 teaspoon baking powder	

Mix these dry, taking all the time you need to do this thoroughly. Have the hands floured and everything ready to go before you add liquid. If you are going to use the traditional frypan, make sure it is warm and greased.

Working quickly from now on, stir in enough cold water to make a firm dough. Shape this, with as little handling as possible, into a cake about an inch thick. If you like crust, leave a doughnutlike hole in the middle. Dust the loaf lightly with flour, so it will handle more easily.

Lay the bannock in the warm frypan. Hold it over the heat until a bottom crust forms, rotating the pan a little so the loaf will shift and not become stuck.

Once the dough has hardened enough to hold together, you can turn the bannock over. This, if you've practiced a bit and have the confidence to flip strongly enough, can be easily accomplished with a slight swing of the arm and snap of the wrist. Or you can use a spatula, supporting the loaf long enough to invert the frypan over it and then turning everything together.

With a campfire, however, it is often easier at this stage just to prop the frypan at a steep angle so that the bannock will get direct heat on top. When crust has formed all around, you may if you wish turn the bannock over and around a few times while it is baking to an appetizing brown.

When is the bannock done? After you've been cooking them awhile, you will be able to tap one and gauge this by the hollowness of the sound. Meanwhile, test by shoving in a straw or sliver. If any dough adheres, the loaf needs more heat. Cooking can be accomplished in about 15 minutes. If you have other duties around camp, twice that time a bit farther from the heat will allow the bannock to cook more evenly.

The same dough can be cooked by baking it on a stick. Horace Kephart in *Camp Cookery* describes it this way:

> *Baking on a Stick.*—Work dough into a ribbon two inches wide. Get a club of sweet green wood (birch, sassafras, maple), about two feet long and three inches thick, peel large end, sharpen the other and stick it into ground, leaning toward fire. When sap simmers wind dough spirally around peeled end. Turn occasionally. Several sticks can be baking at once. Bread for one man's meal can be quickly baked on a peeled stick as thick as a broomstick, holding over fire and turning.

Hush Puppies

The traditional American corn cake is called a hush puppy when it is cooked in a skillet full of hot fat, usually left over from frying the fish. If it is baked in the ashes, the corn breads are known as hoe cakes.

1 10 oz. (285 g.) fine cornmeal	1 egg
1 teaspoon double-acting	1/2 cup (120 ml.) milk
baking powder	Oil for frying
1/2 teaspoon salt	

Mix cornmeal, baking powder, and salt together. Beat the egg with the milk and combine with the rest. Shape into oblong shapes and fry in about 1 in. (2 1/2 cm.) hot oil, turning over once, until brown all over.

Here is a somewhat more fancy skillet bread to complement a meal cooked over a fire:

Skillet Scallion Bread

THE BISCUIT BATTER (OR USE BISQUICK)

2 cups (280 g.) white flour	table salt
1 1/2 teaspoons baking powder	4 tablespoons (60 g.) butter or fresh
1/2 teaspoon baking soda	lard, chilled
1 teaspoon coarse salt or 1/2 teaspoon	3/4 cup (180 ml.) buttermilk

THE FRYING

4 tablespoons (60 g.) butter	5 scallions
1 teaspoon sugar	

Mix all the dry biscuit batter ingredients together thoroughly. Cut the cold butter or lard into small (roughly 1/2-in./1 1/2-cm.) pieces and toss with the dry ingredients. Then with your fingertips (or using a pastry blender or 2 knives) lightly and quickly rub the fat into the flour until the mixture resembles coarse meal; don't overmix. Make a well and pour in the buttermilk, then mix with a fork to make a soft dough. Turn out onto a lightly floured board and knead lightly for 5 or 6 turns. Roll out to 1/2-in. (1 1/2-cm.) thickness and cut the dough into rounds with a floured cookie cutter.

Put half the butter and the teaspoon of sugar in a large skillet, and heat and swirl the butter around. Remove from the heat. Chop the scallions quite fine, using about two-thirds of the green part, and scatter half on the bottom of the skillet.

Place the biscuit rounds on top of the butter-scallion mixture, letting them overlap slightly to fill the whole skillet. Cover and cook over medium-low heat 5 to 6 minutes, until golden on the bottom. Put a large plate on top of the skillet and quickly flip the nest of biscuits over onto it. Melt the remaining butter in the skillet, sprinkle on the remaining scallions, and slip the biscuits back into the skillet, uncooked side down. Cover and cook 5 minutes on this side. Serve immediately.

Skillet-Baked Sesame Seed Cheese Corn Bread

3 tablespoons sesame seeds	3/4 cup (180 ml.) milk
4 tablespoons (60 g.) butter	8 oz. (225 g.) grated Cheddar cheese
1 egg	8 oz. (225 g.) yellow cornmeal

3/4 cup (105 g.) white flour,
      preferably unbleached
1 tablespoon sugar

1 tablespoon baking powder
1 teaspoon coarse salt or 1/2 teaspoon
      table salt

Toast the sesame seeds in a large dry skillet over medium heat, shaking the pan frequently until they are lightly toasted (sometimes they will pop and splutter). Set aside.

Melt the butter slowly in the skillet. Meanwhile beat the egg well, then add the milk, 3 tablespoons of the melted butter, the cheese, and the toasted sesame seeds. Mix the remaining dry ingredients thoroughly and add them to the bowl, stirring enough to blend them well. Pour the batter on top of the remaining tablespoon of melted butter in the skillet. Cover and cook over low heat for 20 minutes until firm on the top. Serve hot directly from the pan in wedges or loosen the edges and slip onto a warm plate.

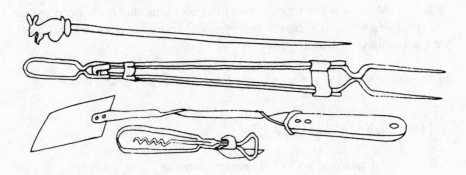

Old-Timers' Flapjacks

One of the most basic outdoor hot meals begins with a frying pan and the ingredients to make a batter. Flapjacks often took the place of bread in covered wagon days in the American West, and under any name—pancakes, griddle cakes, or flapjacks—they remain favorites of many who cook over open fires. Here's an old-time recipe—serve it with maple syrup or honey.

2 cups (1/2 liter) sour milk
8 oz. (225 g.) cornmeal
2 tablespoons flour

1 teaspoon baking soda
1 egg
1/2 teaspoon salt

Mix the sour milk, cornmeal, flour, soda, an egg if available, and the salt. Blend well, adding water if a thinner batter is desired. Ladle spoonfuls onto a lightly greased skillet, and cook over glowing coals, turning once.

Toasted Bread

In both America and England we make so much toast at home but surprisingly little outdoors; yet the best toast is made on the fire. It is a perfect bed for serving many small items of food.

Hold a good thick slice with a toasting fork or grill tongs close to the fire, turning over once so that it is crisp and nicely browned on the outside but still soft inside and able to soak up any juices better.

In Italy bruschetta is the peasant's and hunter's evening meal. Cut a farmhouse loaf into thick slices, place on a grill, and toast both sides to a golden color, but do not let the center dry out. Rub with a peeled and bruised clove of garlic. Sprinkle with salt and freshly ground pepper and a trickle of good olive oil. Eat while hot and crisp.

You may also add a squeeze of lemon and some finely chopped garlic. Try sprinkling with mint, thyme, pennyroyal, or other aromatic herbs. Or eat with a crisply grilled piece of bacon.

In Catalonia they use garlic, oil, and tomato pulp on toasted bread.

A Hot Garlic or Anchovy Loaf

A French loaf wrapped up in foil takes minutes to warm up in the ashes of a barbecue. If it is to be the only hot accompaniment to a cold meat luncheon you can heat it over a small bunch of burning twigs. Flavor the bread with garlic or anchovy before setting out.

Crush 2 cloves of garlic; chop or pound 5 or 6 anchovy fillets. Mash either or both together with about 1/4 lb. (115 g.) unsalted butter. Add coarsely ground pepper. Cut a French loaf into slices but not right through so that the loaf still holds together. Spread the butter between the slices. Close. Wrap in foil and put over a fire or in the ashes for about 15 minutes, turning over once, until crisp and browned.

For an alternative anchovy sauce with oil with which to brush the slices, see page 74, where it is used with shrimp.

SPIT-ROASTING

François Rabelais was much taken with the idea of cooking animals on a spit. This passage is from his satire *Gargantua and Pantagruel:*

Thus as they talked and chatted together, Carpalin said, "And by the belly of St. Quenet, shall we never eat any venison? This salt meat makes me horribly dry. I will go fetch you a quarter of one of those horses which we have burnt, it is well roasted already." As he was rising up to go about it, he perceived under the side of a wood a fair great roe-buck, which was come out of his fort, as I conceive, at the sight of Panurge's fire. Him did he pursue and run after with so much vigor and swiftness, as if it had been a bolt out of a cross-bow, and caught him in a moment; and, whilst he was in his course, he with his hands took in the air four great bustards, seven bitterns, six and twenty grey partridges, two and thirty red-legged ones, sixteen pheasants, nine woodcocks, nineteen herons, two and thirty coushots and ring-doves; and with his feet killed ten or twelve hares and rabbits, which were then at relief, and pretty big withal; eighteen rayles in a knot together, with fifteen young wild boars, two little beavers, and three great foxes. So, striking the kid with his falchion athwart the head, he killed him, and bearing him on his back, he in his return took up his hares, rayles, and young wild boars, and as far off as he could be heard, cried out, and said, "Panurge, my friend, vinegar, vinegar." Then the good Pantagruel, thinking he had fainted, commanded them to provide him with some vinegar. But Panurge knew well that there was some good prey in hands, and forthwith shewed unto noble Pantagruel how he was bearing upon his back a fair roe-buck, and all his girdle bordered with hares. Then immediately did Epistemon make, in the name of the nine muses, nine antique wooden spits. Eusthenes did help to flay, and Panurge placed two great cuirassier saddles in such sort that they served for andirons; and making their prisoner to be their cook, they roasted their venison by the fire wherein the horsemen were burnt. And making great cheer with a good deal of vinegar, the devil a one of them did forbear from his victuals: it was a triumphant and incomparable spectacle, to see how they ravened and devoured. Then said Pantagruel, "Would to God every one of you had two pair of sacring bells hanging at your chin, and that I had at mine the great clocks of Rennes, of Poitiers, of Tours, and of Cambray, to see what a peal they would ring with the wagging of our chaps."

There is something magnificent about roasting a whole animal on the spit. It is spectacular and delicious and an occasion that no one forgets. Though it is an unfamiliar practice in England these days, it was once commonplace to cook all kinds of meat in the fireplace and to bring it straight to the table. The spit rested on iron dogs placed at either side of the hearth, and a fire screen soaked in water allowed the cook-boys to turn the spit without burning themselves. The wrought iron spits had claw-shaped prongs to hold the meat, or holes for tying it on. There were fine spits for stringing birds and others that clasped fish so they did not break. Some cook shops had several cuts of meat turning on four spits placed one above the other. Customers could choose lean or fat pieces, much or little done, and it was cut up for them and served with salt and mustard on the side of the plate. Beer and a roll completed the feast.

Large animals such as castrated bulls were roasted whole in market squares and castle courtyards to celebrate important events. It took from twelve hours to two days for the animal to cook through, and it was often left to passing citizens to turn the spit. Cooking a whole calf still requires a civic event such as a City of London Fair, but suckling pig or baby lamb has become a marvelous way of providing for a large party. For a smaller company a large roast or a bird will do. Young turkeys, game, a month-old goose, or wild or domestic ducks are good on the spit.

Brillat-Savarin claimed that one is born a good roaster, but Escoffier wrote: "Where roasting is concerned, experience is the surest guide as theory, however precise, cannot replace the eye and the sureness which is the result of practice—one becomes a good roaster with a good deal of attention and observation and a little vocation."

The Technique of the Spit

Some barbecues can carry a large piece of meat and even a small animal on the spit, which is usually placed between 4 in. (10 cm.) and 8 in. (20 cm.) from the fire, giving a turning circle of 8 in. (20 cm.) to 16 in. (40 cm.). Depending on the diameter and the type of meat, the distance of the spit from the fire may be adjusted so that the meat is at least 2 in. (5 cm.) away. If it rotates automatically with batteries, it can be left to cook unattended. Push the spit through the center of the roast and adjust holding forks. Test the balance. If the roast is off center, remount.

For roasting fowl such as chicken, duck, and goose, more than one may usually be fixed together on the spit. They should face in opposite directions so as to even out the weight.

An improvised spit. It is easy enough, provided you have the energy, to improvise.

Here are some suggestions.

1. The best support for a spit is iron stakes with notches to raise and lower the roast; otherwise cut two substantial forked green poles. Drive these upright into the ground at each end of the fire to hold a large iron rod (preferably square) or a strong green branch. This must be about 1 1/2 in. (4 cm.) thick and long enough to jut about 1 ft. 4 in. (40 cm.) on either side beyond the supports (stakes) to allow for sagging (especially if the piece is heavy) during cooking. Two people will be needed to turn the spit. A metal spit is more efficient than a wooden one because it conducts heat and allows the inside of the meat to cook at the same time as the outside.

To roast a whole animal push the spit pole right through and let it come out at the base of the neck. Pull out the limbs and hold them together on the spit with skewers or fold them back onto the body. Use a wire or a string to tie them.

For a large piece of meat insert the spit through the center or tie it on. If you leave the bone in, the marrow serves as an inside baster and keeps the meat juicy.

2. You may hold the spit by one support only on one side.

3. One way of cooking meat in the wilds is to have it free-hanging from a branch by a string, over or beside the fire. It turns by itself and does not require much attention. A small roast need be only 7 to 8 in. (18 to 20 cm.) above the embers and turned occasionally as it becomes golden.

Whatever spit you use, it should not be placed over the fire but in front or at the side, so that dribbling fat and juices are not lost in the coals or causing constant flare-ups but caught in a basting pan placed underneath.

The Heat

The heat should be indirect, which means to the side of the meat and not underneath, where dripping juices are likely to cause constant flare-ups. Direct heat will burn the outside before the meat is cooked through. Have a tray underneath to collect the juices for basting. The food should rotate continuously and needs to be basted with the fat that collects in the dripping tray more often than is usual in the oven.

There are different views about procedure, about whether it is best to roast at high heat or low, or some combination of the two, and as to the importance of searing. But the advantage of first sealing and browning at high temperature to form a crust which imprisons the juices and allows the meat to cook further in these juices seems clear.

Place the meat near the fire (1 1/2 to 2 in./4 to 5 cm.) and turn it until it is brown all over and has formed a crust to seal in the juices, then move it farther away for long slow cooking. Bring it close to the fire again for a crisp crackling surface. Meat must be allowed to rest, for this makes it more tender. So it is preferable to time the cooking of a large roast, such as a leg of lamb or a beef roast, to finish at least 15 to 20 minutes before you start to eat. Keep it warm wrapped in foil.

Seasonings and flavorings do not usually penetrate very far inside a large roast, and it is usually necessary to salt and pepper the meat as you carve and serve it.

You may deglaze the pan as you would an oven tray to make a gravy. Remove as much fat as you can with a large spoon. Add a little water or red wine or good vinegar, stir, place the tray over the fire, let the gravy boil up, and reduce.

Small animals such as rabbit or hare and birds such as wild duck and pheasant with a dryish flesh need barding to prevent them from drying out (see p. 206).

For a large animal start the fire 5 to 6 hours before you want to eat; for a smaller one, 1 1/2 hours. It is impossible to give the exact cooking times, as it depends on the size and the tenderness of the meat and the amount of fat in it as well as the intensity of the heat.

Whole Roast Lamb or Mutton   *(for more than 6)*

Every country in the Middle East could claim it as its national dish, and each has its own special way of cooking it. Sometimes baby kid replaces baby lamb.

In the Middle East mint, sweet marjoram, and garlic are all used. Push the herbs with slivers of garlic into incisions made in the meat with a sharp knife.

    The meat requires between 2 1/2 and 4 hours roasting (they like it well done in the Middle East, but you might prefer it slightly pink inside). As it cooks, the smells conjure up the courtyards of traditional Arab houses with turquoise and cobalt blue tiles, *moucharabieh* (wooden lattice) at the windows, and the clusters of multipetaled jasmine with whose perfume they habitually vie. They remind me of the story my grandmother told of her childhood days in Turkey when a beggar holding two thick slices of bread was seen standing outside a pasha's yard, where the servants were roasting a lamb. When they told him to go away, he said: "I am only soaking up the smell."

In Turkey the meat is rubbed with onion juice, salt, and pepper and cooked, wrapped in sheets of paper or foil, until it is half done. Then it is uncovered and basted, often with a bunch of feathers or a cloth tied on the end of a stick, and dipped in the drippings which have been caught in a pan. The meat is served sprinkled with cinnamon.

In Morocco it is usual to have two charcoal fires burning on either side of the animal which is held on its spit about 20 in. (50 cm.) from the ground. The *mechoui,* as it is called, does not need to be turned but is basted often with melted butter and salted water. Each serving is sprinkled individually with cumin and salt.

In France and Italy it is not uncommon in the countryside to cook a whole lamb on the spit. The usual way is to marinate it overnight in a mixture of oil, red or white wine, lemon juice, grated onion, crushed garlic, pepper, rosemary, and thyme.

In England. Fred Carr, for whom Tony Hambro made the spit on page 228, regularly entertains 20 to 30 friends with a young lamb at his house in the country. He buys it frozen at Smithfields, where they sell New Zealand and English lamb weighing 28 to 33 lb. (13 to 15 kg.) throughout the year. (Some specialists who supply Arab restaurants have even smaller ones.)

These are Fred Carr's instructions: Let the lamb thaw for at least 12 hours in its gauze covering. Start preparations very early in the morning if you want to eat at lunchtime. Put the animal, which comes split down the belly, on the spit, which should be less than about 3 ft. (1 meter) from the ground. Tony Hambro drills 2 holes on the metal stake for 2 long sturdy skewers which are pushed through the limbs and hold the animal in position.

Now stuff the lamb with the following (this not only tastes good but makes it look nice): bread crumbs from 1 good loaf of bread, 1 lb. (1/2 kg.) sausage meat, 1 large chopped onion, 1 chopped apple, a handful each of chopped dates and apricots, a few mushrooms, and seasoning. Mix well, put all in the cavity, then sew it up in a neat blanket stitch, using a large needle and twine.

Prepare an oily French dressing with lemon, salt, and pepper and strap a paint brush on the end of a long stick (this will prevent your getting burned when brushing the lamb).

Keep the fire well back from the animal so that it does not get scorched. You need to keep a really good fire going (not just embers) to create proper heat all the time. You will need layers of logs, 3 or 4 high, 2 ft. (60 cm.) long, and 2 in. (5 cm.) in diameter around the animal in 2 semicircles, and you must stake up the fire every 15 to 20 minutes to keep it going.

Turn the spit every so often on the cogwheel and baste regularly. The cooking time will depend on the weather; on a normal summer's day the maximum time for it to be no longer pink but still very juicy is 4 hours. Fred Carr has developed some refinements for even cooking, such as separating the shoulders very slightly from the body by cutting first with a knife, holding them open with a stick, and tying the foreknuckles to the stick.

Sucking Pig

A sucking pig was once a popular delicacy in England, if we are to believe the poet Massinger, who describes a dish served in the City of London in the sixteenth century:

> Three sucking pigs, served up in a dish,
> Took from the sow as soon as she had farrowed,

A fortnight fed with dates and muskadine
That stood my master in twenty marks a piece;
Besides the puddings in their bellies, made
Of I know not what.

These days it is an Iberian specialty with a version in every region. Everywhere in Spain and Portugal it is the great festive dish and the sacrificial offering on saints' days.

To roast a sucking pig takes time, but it is not difficult. You can now obtain a baby pig, one killed when 2 to 6 weeks old and weighing 11 to 15 1/2 lb. (5 to 7 kg.), which will feed up to 20 people. A few butchers prepare and set them ready for the spit and freeze them. Defrost completely, then wash the pig well and rub it with plenty of lemon juice and then oil. Impale it on a spit and cook it about 20 in. (50 cm.) from a gentle fire with a pan underneath to catch the juices. If you can find aromatic wood to burn, such as juniper, all the better. Heat some pork fat on the end of a skewer and as it melts use it and the drippings to baste the pig. Sprinkle with salt and pepper and cook gently, basting occasionally and turning until it is brown all over. It will take between 4 and 5 hours. Wrap the ears in foil so they do not burn; they are considered a delicacy. For an elegant presentation put a stick in the pig's mouth at the start of cooking and replace it with a large red apple when it is done.

In Sardinia, where roast pig is equally popular, it is split in two lengthways and the halves are cooked on either side of the same fire until the skin is crackling—this way it takes less time (about 2 to 2 1/2 hours). It is enveloped in myrtle leaves, which grow on the stony hillsides of the island, and left to absorb their bitter scent before serving.

In America, in North Carolina, pork is the favorite meat for the barbecue. Practically every weekend from September through to March, churches, schools, and civic groups slide handmade posters into store windows to announce a money-raising feast. Whole hogs, shoulders, tenderloin of pork, and spare ribs feed multitudes in events that are famous throughout the South. A whole pig may be stuffed with bread stuffing: Soften a large chopped onion and 4 celery sticks, also chopped, in 1/2 lb. (1/4 kg.) butter. Add 8 cups (3 3/4 kg.) dry bread crumbs and season with salt and pepper.

A marinade. Although it is not strictly necessary, here are some suggestions for those who are operating near the kitchen or roasting in the fireplace: Use only one.

1. Covering the animal with cider overnight gives the pig a very delicate flavor. It is also a good idea to press into a few incisions crushed juniper berries rolled in thyme and coarsely grated pepper. One of my friends inserts slivers of fresh ginger very successfully.

2. Combine 1 1/4 cups (300 ml.) oil, 2/3 cup (150 ml.) wine vinegar, 2 cloves crushed garlic, pepper, and 2 tablespoons or more fennel seeds or a few sprigs of thyme or rosemary.

3. Use a mixture of olive oil and rum.

Soak the pig in one of these and add salt when you are ready to cook.

For those who like a glaze brush with a mixture of honey, ground cloves, and oil during the last 20 minutes of cooking.

In the Italian region of Umbria, stalks and leaves of wild fennel are chopped up with garlic and used as a stuffing.

In Rome sprigs of rosemary are put into the cavity.

Another excellent flavor can be obtained from lemon zest and 2 or 3 cloves of garlic. You may use these flavorings for a roast leg of pork, which is a simpler matter than a whole pig. It requires 2 to 2 1/2 hours of slow cooking.

Sirloin of Beef and Other Prime Cuts

Dust beef lightly with dry mustard, black pepper, and flour to give a crisp crust. Fold the fat end of sirloin under the lean undercut and hold together with string or a skewer.

Best beef does not need slow cooking to make it tender. Start cooking at a high searing heat in front of the fire and keep the heat high if the piece is small or reduce to moderate if it is large. As a rough guide allow about 20 minutes per pound and baste often. If the roast is too lean, tie a thin layer of fat around it. Juiciest when rare, the meat is perfectly tender however briefly it is cooked. Let it rest for 15 to 20 minutes before serving.

Sauces: A good one to serve with this can be made on the spot. Stir 1 tablespoon port with 2 tablespoons red currant jelly and 6 tablespoons gravy collected from the drip tray.

Another one is seasoned whipped cream with fine shavings of horseradish stirred in (see p. 86).

Loin of Veal

Ask the butcher to bone the loin of veal. Marinate for a few hours in a mixture
of equal quantities of oil and dry white wine with a good sprinkling of black
pepper. Roll it up, inserting some sprigs of fresh thyme and rosemary, some
slivers of garlic, and a few anchovy fillets. Secure with string or skewers. As
veal is dry, it is best barded (wrapped and tied in thin strips of fat) to keep
it moist.

Allow about 25 to 30 minutes of moderate heat per pound for it to be
well done and cooked through.

A simple sauce is made by heating up heavy cream with a teaspoon of dry
mustard, salt, and pepper. Add the juices of the pan, skimming off the
fat first.

Shoulder of Lamb with Herbs

Ask the butcher to bone the lamb shoulder for you. Open it, sprinkle with
salt and pepper, and fill with a bunch of fresh herbs such as sweet marjoram,
rosemary, or thyme, a finely chopped onion, and 2 or 3 cloves of garlic,
crushed. Roll up, tie, or skewer and put on the spit. Proceed as indicated in
the roasting techniques (see p. 230), turning slowly in front of the fire and
brushing with oil from time to time. Allow 1 to 1 1/2 hours.

Leg of Lamb *(for more than 6)*

For a French gigot with cream, leave a leg of lamb in the following marinade
for a few hours: 2 cups (1/2 liter) dry white wine with 1 onion, coarsely
chopped, a few sprigs of parsley, some celery leaves, 2 bay leaves, the juice
of 1 lemon, 4 tablespoons oil, 5 peppercorns, and 5 juniper berries.
Turn in front of a moderate fire. (Roasting instructions are on page
230.)
Reduce the marinade in a saucepan over the fire.
Occasionally brush the lamb with oil. When the meat is tender, after
1 1/2 to 2 hours, stir the juices that have dripped from the meat into

the much-reduced marinade. Add a few tablespoons of heavy cream and barely bring to the boil.

Pour a little over each serving.

For a Middle Eastern–flavored roast, mix a few tablespoons of oil with 1 tablespoon paprika, 2 teaspoons cumin, and 2 large cloves garlic, crushed, and push under the skin.

James Beard Favorites

James Beard, the great pioneer of outdoor cookery, has a major responsibility for spreading his own "thrill of the grill" throughout America. He has generously allowed me to feature several favorite recipes from his classic *The Complete Book of Outdoor Cookery,* published in 1955 in collaboration with Helen Evans Brown of California.

The next seven recipes are his, and they follow with my warmest thanks. Others of his *Outdoor Cookery* recipes may be found on pages 243 and 253.

Boned Shoulder of Veal with Anchovies

Have a veal shoulder boned, spread out the meat, brush inside with olive oil, and lay a dozen anchovy fillets across the middle. Roll, tie, spit, and roast slowly, basting with a mixture of olive oil and sweet vermouth in equal parts.

Roast Turkey on the Spit   *(for more than 6)*

The ideal size turkey for roasting seems to be from 15 to 18 lb. (6 3/4 to 8 kg.), eviscerated weight. The turkey may be stuffed or not, as you wish. Truss the turkey, having the legs and wings tied close to the body so that they won't dry out, and making sure that the neck skin is securely fastened at the back with a skewer, and that the cord does not pass over the breast to mar it. A good way is to insert one long or two short skewers through the body at the second joint, and use the ends of the skewer, the ends of the legs and wings, and the tail piece as fastening posts for the twine. The center of gravity of a stuffed turkey is different from that of an unstuffed one, so they are spitted differently. With an unstuffed turkey, insert the point of the spit at the back or spine, just in front of the tail. Have the spit come out about an inch from

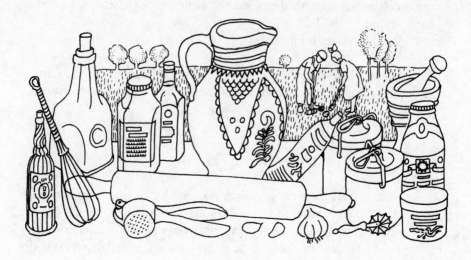

the front end of the breastbone. You'll have to use a hammer or mallet to drive the spit. Now fasten the holding forks securely and balance. If the turkey is stuffed in the body cavity only, the spit is inserted in just about the same way, but if the front cavity is full of stuffing, the point of the spit must emerge farther forward in order to compensate for the added off-center weight. As there is no bone there for the spit to penetrate, the holding forks should be firmly anchored on either side of the wishbone. Until it sets in the cooking, it is difficult to balance a stuffed turkey perfectly, as it can't be stuffed so full that it is rigid. Therefore, the stuffing shifts a little at each turn. Don't worry, however—this won't last long. Baste the turkey or not, as it roasts. We have found that it isn't really necessary, though butter, olive oil, or any baste recommended for chicken may be used.

A turkey of about 14 to 18 lb. (6 1/4 to 8 kg.) eviscerated weight, will take about 3 hours to cook (spit temperature about 250°F/120°C)) and 30 minutes of coasting. (A stuffed turkey will take longer to cook.) We find that if the thermometer, inserted in the thickest part of the breast, reads 175°F (80°C) when coasting starts, it will reach 180°F (80°C) or so, and the turkey will be juicily, perfectly done. Another test is to grasp the end of a drumstick and push it toward the body. If it responds readily, moving without resistance, the bird is done.

Turkey cooked on the spit will be, in most climates, a summer dish, so we see no need to treat it as a holiday meal and have the usual "fixings," unless, of course, you have a charcoal grill in your kitchen. Cranberry sauce is good with it, but so, too, are broiled peaches or pineapple. Creamed onions have an affinity for turkey, but foil-roasted onions have that same quality. Roasted corn is good, as are yams or sweet potatoes, roasted in the ashes. As for stuffing, that might just as well be different, too. Here's one we found delicious:

Turkey Stuffing. Allow about 1 cup (300 g.) stuffing for each pound, dressed weight. For a 15-lb. (6 3/4 kg.) turkey, combine 3 quarts dried or toasted bread crumbs, 3 bunches green onions, chopped and cooked until wilted in 1 cup (225 g.) butter, 1 green pepper, chopped, 1 cup (225 g.) chopped celery, 3 tablespoons tarragon soaked in 1/4 cup (60 ml.) white wine, and the cooked chopped giblets of the turkey. Add enough stock from the giblets barely to moisten, and season to taste with salt and pepper.

Giblet Sauce. If you don't stuff your turkey, you may want some sauce made from the giblets and the drippings. Place a long narrow pan beneath the spit, having it toward the front to catch the drippings. (We have found that two of the old-fashioned 10-cube ice trays, fastened together, are just right.) Cook the heart, neck, wing tips (if you've removed them), and gizzard in salted water to cover. When they are almost done, add the liver. When it is done but still pinkly juicy, chop all the giblets and return to the stock. Take 1/4 cup (60 ml.) of the drippings from your roast, and in it cook 4 or 5 chopped shallots or green onions until wilted. Add 1/4 cup (35 g.) flour, the chopped giblets, and the stock, season with a little soy sauce or Kitchen Bouquet, and add salt and pepper to taste. If desired, some thick cream may be added. Just before serving, stir in a jigger of brandy.

Whole Roasted Liver

Choose a whole calf's or lamb's liver, or a 4- or 5-lb. (2- to 2 1/2-kg.) piece of beef liver. Roll and tie it, stripping it with slices of salt pork or bacon, or have it larded. (If you're feeling fancy, soak the lardoons in Cognac before using.) Spit the liver, and roast it over a moderate fire until the internal temperature is about 150°F (65°C) if you like your liver pink and juicy. This will take from 50 minutes to over an hour. A salad of sliced oranges and sweet onions would be pleasant with this.

Roast Goose

Rub a 12- to 14-lb. (5- to 6-kg.) goose well with salt and some thyme seasoning powder, and rub the inside with a cut half of a lemon. Spit the goose and roast over a medium fire, having a dripping pan placed to catch the fat, which should be saved for baking and other cooking. Pricking the skin with a sharp fork will help the fat to flow. Cook until the leg moves easily in its joint, about 2 1/2 hours. Serve with sauerkraut that has been cooked for 3 hours in red wine and seasoned with a few juniper berries or caraway seeds. Fried potatoes, cooked in some of the goose fat, would be good too. Drink a fine Pinot Noir with this—a memorable meal.

Peking Roast Duck

This recipe, developed by Mabel Stegner for those delectable Long Island ducklings, is quite a production, but more than worth it. Serve it as an appetizer before a Chinese dinner, or with the dinner, but it would be just as sensational if it preceded a meal in any other language. Actually, only the heavenly crisp and flavorsome duck skin is used, so the duckling itself may be saved for other purposes. With it serve the Chinese Doilies (see p. 239)—flat little cakes that are close kin, in fact identical twins, to the Mexican wheat tortilla. The crisp skin is put on a doily, a few shreds of green onion are added, and some of the spicy sauce, then all is rolled together to make as delectable a tidbit as ever passed your lips.

Stuff a Long Island duckling, with paper towels, and allow to stand, uncovered, in the refrigerator for at least 2 days, changing the towels on the second day. Object: dryness. Remove towels and, if possible, put in front of an electric fan for 3 hours. Object: further dryness. Rub the duck inside and outside with Heung New Fun Spices (recipe below), and spit the duck in the usual manner. Have a very hot charcoal fire ready and roast for approximately 1 1/2 hours, or until the skin is a rich mahogany and irresistibly crisp. Slice off the skin with a sharp knife, allowing little or no meat to cling to it. Cut the skin into neat pieces with a sharp knife or scissors, and roll a piece, with some green onion shreds and Red Bean Sauce (recipe below), in the pancakes (doilies). Eat with fingers!

Heung New Fun Spices. Blend together 1 tablespoon each of ground cinnamon and cloves, 1 teaspoon ground black pepper, and 1/2 teaspoon each of ground anise and fennel seeds.

Red Bean Sauce. Put a can of red kidney beans in a blender and mix until smooth. Add 1 tablespoon chili powder, 1 1/2 teaspoons Heung New Fun Spices (preceding recipe) and 1/2 teaspoon salt. In the meantime, cook together 1 cup (235 ml.) plum jam, 1/3 cup (80 ml.) water, and 1 clove garlic, finely minced or pressed. Boil for 5 minutes, stirring. Combine with the bean mixture and cook another 10 minutes.

Chinese Doilies. Cut 1 tablespoon shortening into 2 cups (280 g.) flour that has been sifted with 1 teaspoon salt. Add enough water to make a stiff dough. Knead lightly on a floured board and divide into 24 portions. Roll each piece into a circle as thin as possible, and cook on one side only on a lightly greased griddle, for about 2 minutes. When ready to serve, brush the white sides of the doilies with melted butter, and heat slightly in the oven.

Spitted Breast of Turkey   *(for more than 6)*

This is for those of you who actually prefer the white meat. Purchase a whole breast—it will probably weigh from 5 to 8 lb. (2 1/4 to 3 1/2 kg). Rub well with butter and tie in a compact form, spitting it through the center. Roast over a moderate fire, basting with olive oil and vermouth, or butter and white wine. A 6-lb. (3-kg.) breast will take from 1 1/2 to 2 1/2 hours. Do be careful not to overcook it.

Chicken on the Spit

The chicken must be young and tender. Truss and secure it on the spit. Smear with oil or butter and baste frequently while you turn it beside a good fire for 1 to 1 1/4 hours.

One way of preventing breasts from drying out before the legs are done is to bard them by tying thin strips of fat or bacon over them (see p. 206).

A delicious way of keeping the flesh moist and tender is to stuff butter, beaten with herbs, under the skin. Use tarragon or a mixture of cress, parsley, and chives. Add 2 cloves crushed garlic and season with salt and pepper.

For a sauce, pour a little Madeira in the pan when the chicken is ready and stir in a little cream. Otherwise catch the drippings on slices of bread or toast.

The same technique can be applied to a very young turkey, a baby goose, ducks, and squabs.

Game Birds

Game has always inspired rapturous praise. With the ancients a bird that furnished maybe only a mouthful procured a sort of epicurean ecstasy, and it was said in Rome that the dead may be raised by means of a quail. The Frenchman Vieillot said that the flesh of blackbirds, "so delicate in the time of gathering grapes, acquires at that period a savor which makes it as precious as the quail, but becomes bitter when they feed on the juniper berries, the ivy or other similar fruits." The small birds with slender beaks, called *beccafico* in Italy or fig pecker because in the autumn they attack and eat the figs, were, he said, "In truth, an extract of the juice from the delicious fruits it has fed upon."

Wild pigeon and duck, grouse, young goose, partridge, pheasant, and quail are all excellent cooked over coals. If you have shot them yourself and are camping, they should be hung for 2 to 7 days. The time really depends on personal taste, the size and age of the bird, as well as the weather. Suspend the bird by the middle of the tail feathers. When the body gets loose and full is the time to consider eating. Each person knows when the flesh of a game bird has reached the degree of flavor he likes. If there is no time for hanging, as was the case of a friend who shot a protected bird by mistake on safari in Africa and had to pluck and bury the feathers quickly before roasting it on a hasty barbecue, the flesh is not as gamy but more like poultry.

Pluck the birds, singe if necessary, cut off feet at first joint, wings at the second, and neck close to the body. Draw them carefully, wash the cavities with cold water, and then truss them. You may leave the heads on and pull off the skin from the neck and head and push long beaks into the body on the side.

Most game is not fat and benefits from barding—covering with a thin slice of fat (salt pork, bacon, or pork fat) tied on with a piece of string. This keeps the meat moist and tender and prevents it from drying out. Otherwise baste often with oil or melted butter.

You may flavor birds by stuffing with a small onion, lemon or orange zest, apples or juniper berries, or herbs such as rosemary or sage.

Spit a few birds together side by side, facing opposite directions, and secure them in place with long metal skewers, string, or wire. Turn over a gentle fire for 10 to 40 minutes, depending on their size, basting if necessary. Serve on a thick slice of bread or toast which has caught some of the drippings, with cress and red currant jelly.

It is sometimes simpler to split the birds in half, flatten them, and barbecue them on a hot well-oiled grill, turning over once. In this case they will require much less time. Brush with oil or melted butter or a marinade to keep them from drying out.

The French catch the drippings in a shallow pan and stir in a little wine or port when they are ready to serve, or sprinkle a little Cognac, and flame. Serve on toast with the sauce.

It is common with quail to roast or grill them wrapped in vine leaves. Cover the package further with well-buttered paper or a strip of fat, tied with string or wire.

THE GRILL

This method of cooking briefly, directly over glowing embers, is highly esteemed by gastronomes and gourmets everywhere, but it has not been adopted anywhere as passionately as it has in the countries of Islam. For it is as much part of the gastronomic culture of Muslim India and Muslim Russia as it is of the Arab world, where it is the oldest and still the most common way of cooking meat. Almost everyone, it seems, is a master at searing the meat, judging and controlling the intensity of heat and timing.

Through the influence of its Oriental population barbecuing has lately become fashionable in Israel. During the summer months, families take small barbecues in their cars in the evenings or Saturday lunchtime, and head for the parks or the seafront. Steaks have overtaken kebabs in popularity, as they require less work. I was thrilled to see the small fires dotted about in the darkness while delicious smells wafting in all directions reminded me of Egypt.

A grill (or grid) is the most useful piece of equipment for cooking over a fire, and wire mesh a good enough substitute. If you do not have a grill it is possible to lay meat directly onto the embers.

For perfect grilled meat the cut must be a prime one. It may benefit from a marinade (see p. 203), but often it is sufficient simply to rub it with some oil, salt, and pepper (there is no time for the salt to draw the juices out) just before cooking.

See the chart on page 377 for a rough guide to cooking times. Always be sure to remember that the grill should be well oiled and hot before food is placed on it and that the meat should not be cold. If you are using lean meat brush it with oil or melted butter or the marinade. Use a pastry brush or a small bunch of wild herbs or grasses. Do not baste with a spoon or the dripping fat will cause the fire to flare up. When it is nearly done throw herbs and flavoring into the fire (see p. 202) to give it a perfume.

Foil is a useful companion to the grill for cooking en papillote, which gives excellent results, and one heavy sheet placed on the grill, or two thin layers folded together, have the same effect as cooking in a pan. For small morsels that would fall through the grill, prick the foil with plenty of holes and lay it on the grill.

If you do not have a spit you can turn a large piece on the grill over a low fire for as long as 2 to 3 hours or place, wrapped in foil, in the middle of hot ashes.

If you cook a whole fat piece of meat of uneven thickness on the grill, keep the thin part farther away from the heat than the thick part.

Beef Steaks

Use lean tender meat. The best is well aged and marbled or flecked with white fat. Use porterhouse, sirloin, fillet, or rump steak. Have it cut 1 to 2 in. (2 1/2 to 5 cm.) thick, allowing about 1/2 lb. (225 g.) for a good portion. Trim off excess fat that might drip into the fire and cause flare-ups and unappetizing smoke. Cut small incisions around the steaks, in the skin or gristle, to prevent their curling. Lightly coat with oil and season with coarsely milled black pepper (some people rub the meat with a cut clove of garlic).

Flank steak is a cheaper cut. Remove the outer membrane with a sharp knife and rub with salt and pepper. Put it on an oiled grill 2 in. (5 cm.) from the fire and cook 3 to 4 minutes on each side for rare. Cut thin slices diagonally against the fiber for more tender meat.

A marinade: Although good steak does not really need it, the following will help to tenderize tougher meat and give it a fine flavor: for 6 to 8 steaks mix about 2/3 cup (160 ml.) oil with the juice of 1 lemon, 4 crushed cloves garlic, and some pepper. Soak the meat in it for a few hours. Lay the steaks on a well-oiled grill above glowing hot embers, turn over once, and sprinkle each side with salt when it is well browned.

It is difficult to give cooking times, since we all have different interpretations of what we call rare, medium, and well done, and although we care very much about how it is done our tastes vary widely.

Red meat can be cooked closest to the fire. Those who like it very rare, as the French call *bleu,* simply sear it with fierce heat and that is all. For medium rare and well done, sear first on both sides for a minute on the lowest or the hottest part of the grill and then raise the grill or move the meat away from the hottest part of the fire and complete the cooking until done to the desired degree.

Test the steak by pressing with the finger. If it offers no resistance and remains soft, it is very rare. If it meets with a slightly pliant resistance, it is rare. At this stage a light beading of clear rose-colored blood appears on the upper crust. The juices become clear rather than red when it is medium rare, and when the finger meets a strong resistance it is well done. Finally, make a small cut with a sharp knife: it is the only way to find out if it is done to your taste.

A good way of serving steak is to put it, sizzling hot, on a piece of toast to absorb the juices, with a dab of butter melting over it. For a flavored butter see page 297.

It will be more tender if you let it rest for a minute.

Evan Jones knows a hobo trick for treating a 2-in. (5-cm.) slice of sirloin. He uses it under the broiler, but it will also do for burying the meat straight into the ashes. Cover the meat with a 1 1/2-in. (4-cm.) layer of salt mush (4 parts salt to 1 part water) and leave it to cook for 15 to 20 minutes in the ashes. The white crust protects the meat, sears it, and keeps in its juices.

Boned (or Butterflied) Leg of Lamb

Ask your butcher to bone or butterfly a leg of lamb so that it lies flat. Remove any skin and fat, sprinkle with rosemary, and rub well with oil seasoned with salt, pepper, and crushed garlic. Grill it in the same way as a large steak. Give it fierce heat to begin with on the lowest level and sear 5 to 8 minutes on either side, then raise it to the highest notch and a low heat and cook a further 15 to 20 minutes on each side. It should be brown on the outside but still pink inside.

Alternatively, leave the fat on and cook the fat side first. Cook slowly and do not sear.

Broiled Lamb or Veal Heart

Another recipe from James Beard's *Complete Book of Outdoor Cookery:*

Clean and split a lamb or veal heart, and marinate in 1/4 cup (80 ml.) soy sauce, 2 cloves garlic, finely chopped, 1 teaspoon rosemary or tarragon, 2 tablespoons wine vinegar, 1 teaspoon salt, and 1 teaspoon coarsely ground black pepper, for an hour. Drain, brush with oil, and grill over a rather brisk fire until brown on the outside, but still rare. Serve with rice and a purée of spinach. Less tender hearts, such as pork, may be tenderized this way: 30 minutes before grilling, sprinkle with a teaspoon of unseasoned meat tenderizer, and "fork it in" by jabbing the surface thoroughly with a long-tined fork.

Lamb Chops with Yogurt Sauce

Although to a cattleman a lamb or mutton chop is wool with a handle on, it is considered very good meat in the Middle East.

6 lamb chops	6 tomatoes
Juice of 1 onion	1 1/2 cups (355 ml.) yogurt
3 tablespoons oil	1 tablespoon paprika
Salt and pepper	

Marinate the chops in a mixture of onion juice (made by putting an onion through the blender), oil, salt, and pepper for 1 hour or longer. Cook very quickly 10 to 15 minutes on a hot grill, turning over once until brown outside but still pink and juicy inside. While chops are cooking, heat the tomatoes on the grill until they soften and the peel can be pulled off easily. Beat the yogurt with salt and pepper.

When you are ready to serve, crush a tomato on each plate with a fork, pour a little yogurt over it, and place the meat on top. Dust with paprika.

Hickory-Flavored Pork Shoulder

This recipe was given to me by Evan Jones.

The trick of imitating pit-cooked pork with the authentic Southern flavor as described on page 203 is to use an ordinary barbecue and to smoke with hickory chips that have been soaked in water. Put them on a charcoal fire when the coals are fairly hot.

Meanwhile have a good-size pork shoulder with some fat left on it so there will be drippings onto hickory that ensure savory flavor. Make a basting sauce by mixing 1/2 cup (120 ml.) water, 2 cups (475 ml.) salad oil, 1 cup (225 g.) finely chopped onion, 1 cup (235 ml.) tomato sauce, 1 teaspoon salt, 2 tablespoons Worcestershire sauce, 1/2 cup (120 ml.) vinegar, 1/4 cup (60 g.) brown sugar, and a dash of red pepper; simmer this mixture about an hour. Add a little thyme, basil, rosemary, and grated lemon rind.

When the coals in your grill are gently glowing, put the rack as high above the meat as possible, place the meat on it, and baste with the sauce. Because the aim is to have pork that is delicately soft, barbecuing may take as long as 6 hours, and the meat must be turned frequently with a thorough brushing of sauce each time. Hickory chips must be added from time to time to keep an even heat. When the pork can be cut with a spoon and is glistening with sauce, put it on a table or chopping block and remove all bones, then refrigerate it for an hour or so. Shortly before serving time, remove the congealed fat and chop the meat coarsely with a large heavy knife. Put it in a skillet for reheating and add a little salt and vinegar, to taste.

Loin of Pork

A good way of marinating pork is in brine. Dissolve 1/2 cup (100 g.) sugar and 1/4 cup (50 g.) salt in 2 gallons (3 3/4 liters) of water and add a dozen crushed peppercorns and half a dozen crushed juniper berries with a few sprigs of thyme and marjoram and 6 bay leaves. Leave a boned loin of pork to soak in this bath in the refrigerator for 2 days, making sure that it is entirely covered by weighing it down with a heavy plate.

Take the meat out and let it come to room temperature. Drain and rub well with plenty of olive oil. Cook on a medium fire, turning over often and brushing occasionally with olive oil, for about 30 minutes. The meat should be done, but it will be pink inside because of the treatment in brine. Let it rest for a few minutes before slicing.

Serve with a fruit purée (see p. 88).

Marinated Pork Chops

Although pork chops are excellent simply coated with oil and sprinkled with pepper before grilling, they are even better marinated in a mixture of oil and vinegar with fennel seeds and a little crushed garlic. (See section on marinades, p. 203.) Cook for 7 to 8 minutes on each side.

Other well-tried marinades include oil, wine or cider with grated fresh ginger, sage, wild thyme, juniper berries, sherry, lemon, and grated orange or lemon zest.

As in the following Italian recipe for stuffed veal chops, you may cut through the meat and slip in a thin slice of Gruyère or fontina with a sage leaf. Moisten with oil, sprinkle with pepper, and cook as usual, but a little longer.

Stuffed Veal Chops

An excellent Italian recipe.

Slit each chop horizontally almost to the bone to make a pocket for the filling. Push in thin slices of fontina or Gruyère with some black pepper and a sprinkling of chopped fresh herbs. Rosemary will do well. Lay the chops flat, press the top and bottom together again, and beat the edges hard. Lightly coat with oil and sprinkle with pepper, then cook directly on the grill or wrapped in foil for 15 to 20 minutes.

Variation: Also try stuffing the chops with a combination of ham and cheese.

Escalope of Veal

As the flesh of veal is a little insipid, it benefits from flavoring in a good marinade. The Italians, masters at making the most of this, their favorite meat, like the following rosemary marinade: mix 2 tablespoons vinegar with 3 to 4 tablespoons oil, 1 clove garlic, crushed, a good sprig of rosemary, and some pepper.

You may use scaloppine or cutlets cut thin from the leg. Pound the meat lightly to flatten it. Put on a gentle, medium heat for about 2 minutes, turning over 2 or 3 times. Brush frequently with oil or melted butter, as it does not have much fat to keep it moist.

Alice Waters at Chez Panisse does not use a marinade and serves veal cutlets with mustard butter. For this, soften 6 tablespoons butter and mix well with 2 tablespoons Dijon mustard. Finely chop 1 shallot, a bunch of parsley, and a dozen chives and mix into the butter with coarsely ground pepper to taste.

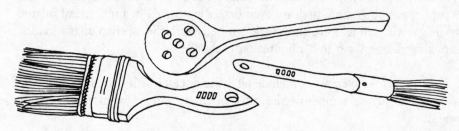

Ralph Hancock's Grilled Veal Recipe

The best grilled veal I have eaten recently was cooked by Ralph Hancock on the windowsill of his Knightsbridge flat. Here is his recipe as he wrote it for me.

Veal chops, preferably big and thick

MARINADE

1 part cooking oil, as light as possible— peanut or sunflower are ideal	Garlic, coarsely chopped and crushed— plenty of this
1 part old leftover wine (almost any kind will do—I prefer an acid, even sour, red wine with a little cheap sherry)	Coarsely ground black pepper and rosemary—lots of these as well. Do not add any salt.

Marinate the chops for about 6 hours. I always remove the bones and fat, simply to save space in the dish. It helps the process if you prick the meat with a fork. Turn a few times during the marinating to make the penetration even.

Grill very quickly on a charcoal grill. Just before you put the meat on, throw a branch of rosemary on to the charcoal and immediately add the meat so that it is impregnated with aromatic smoke. Oil the bars of the grill or the meat will stick. Add salt *after* the meat is done, plus a bit more pepper and a squeeze of lemon if you like.

Cotelettes de Veau en Papillote

Cooking in foil is well suited to veal, which has a tendency to dry out. The preparation may be done at home, and the packets carried out all ready to put on the grill (see p. 207).

Sauté some chopped shallots or spring onions, and add a few sliced mushrooms, fresh herbs such as parsley, thyme, or rosemary, salt, and pepper. Place on a sheet of foil, cover with a seasoned veal chop, and tightly wrap up the package.

Cook the packages over a good fire, turning once. They will take a little longer than meat cooked without foil: 15 to 20 minutes, depending on how thick the meat is.

Venison Steaks

Use young venison, cut from the leg, or cutlets. If it is tough, marinating in oil with red wine and port and crushed juniper berries will tenderize it as well as enhance the flavor. Grill very swiftly on both sides to sear, then more slowly until well done, brushing the steaks occasionally with melted butter, oil, or the marinade. Serve with a pat of butter, dusted with salt and pepper.

Rabbit or Hare

Skin, draw, and joint a young rabbit and cut the body into 3 or 4 pieces. Marinate for 2 hours at least in a mixture of 1 cup (235 ml.) dry white wine or a red wine and 1/2 cup (120 ml.) vinegar with 2 crushed cloves garlic, a sprinkling of thyme and oregano, 2 broken bay leaves, salt, and pepper.

Stud with larding bacon or wrap in thin strips of fat bacon. Put on the grill over medium heat, turning over once for about 20 to 30 minutes until tender but still pink. Or, if you prefer not to use bacon, be sure to brush with oil or melted butter several times while cooking to prevent the meat from drying out.

Sauces: Italian sweet-and-sour sauce is a legacy of ancient Rome. Boil 4 tablespoons sugar in 2/3 cup (160 ml.) red wine vinegar until the syrup thickens.

Alternatively, heat 4 tablespoons wine vinegar, then stir in 3/4 cup (180 ml.) sour cream and a few crushed juniper berries.

Lebanese Kibbeh

One version of this much-loved combination of meat and cracked wheat is cooked over charcoal. It is worth trying, for it is delicious and makes the meat go further when there is a large party to feed. It is easy to make with a food processor; otherwise it needs much mincing, pounding, and kneading. Serve with a salad and yogurt and some pita bread that has been warmed on the fire.

1 1/8 lb. (1/2 kg.) burghul (cracked wheat)	Salt and pepper A bunch of parsley, finely chopped
2 medium onions	2 teaspoons allspice or cinnamon
2 1/4 lb. (1 kg.) finely ground lamb with a good amount of fat (a shoulder is good)	(optional)

Soak the burghul in cold water for about an hour until it is bloated and tender. Drain through a fine sieve and squeeze out excess water. Grate or finely mince the onions. Pound together with the lamb in a mortar and knead vigorously by hand, or turn to a smooth paste in a food processor, a few batches at a time, adding salt and pepper to taste, and the parsley. You may like to add the allspice or cinnamon—it is not orthodox, but many people do. Take egg-size lumps of paste and shape into flat cakes.

Cook over a medium fire until crisp and brown on the outside (about 10 minutes), turning over once. The fat should keep the cakes moist and tender inside.

Variation: In Syria and Lebanon people push a lump of fat into the center of the cakes to lubricate them as it melts during the cooking, or dip them in a pan of sizzling fat just before serving.

Hamburgers

The most popular of all America's outdoor foods is also the most maltreated. After its appearance broiled and bunned at the St. Louis World's Fair in 1904 it rapidly became the favorite international takeout fast food. It is the ideal barbecue meat, but unless treated with care it will turn out dried and tasteless instead of deliciously juicy and flavorsome.

The secret of success is to use good-quality chopped beef, 1 1/2 lb. (675 g.) for 4, with a good amount of fat, lightly and freshly ground (if you can do it yourself in a food processor, all the better), to season it well with salt and freshly ground pepper, and to handle it and shape it as lightly as possible so that it holds together without becoming compact. Make the patties thick enough, 3/4–1 in. (2–2 1/2 cm.) thick is about right; place them on an oiled grill 4 in. (10 cm.) from the fire and cook them quickly so you get a brown crust while the inside remains pink. Cook 4 minutes on each side for rare, 5 minutes for medium, and 6 minutes for well done. If the patties are thinner, cook for a shorter time and brush occasionally with melted butter.

You may also like to add a few refinements such as these: a beaten egg will help to hold the meat together; a small onion, grated or blended, or a little cream or melted butter, will preserve the juiciness and add to the flavor. A small bunch of parsley, finely chopped, is very pleasant. I believe all these things together make a Mexican *chuletas.*

In New Orleans they make their hamburgers hot with a mixture of cayenne, paprika, and chili powder.

For a Cheeseburger: Top with a slice of cheese, Cheddar, Gruyère, or Monterey Jack, and let it melt slightly over the meat.

Serve on hot buttered hamburger rolls or toasted buns accompanied by one or several of the following garnishes: ketchup, mayonnaise, prepared mustard, chili sauce, sweet pickle relish, dill pickle slices, thinly sliced onion rings, slices of tomato, lettuce leaves.

Mixed Grill

There is no need to feel limited to one type of food. Perhaps the best thing to offer at a barbecue party is a selection of meats, each cooked in the way that suits it best. Cut the portions small so that guests can have more than one choice.

Cargolade. In the Roussillon in France a variety of meats is put on the grill with unusual companions: the small snails which feed on the local vines. Try this with any snails that have been purged and cleaned. Put the hole facing toward the sky and leave them on the grill for the last 5 to 6 minutes. The usual meats are lamb and pork chops, both thinly cut, pork sausages and blood sausages, all brushed with olive oil. For the flavor of the Roussillon, make a sauce by crushing a whole head of garlic (each clove peeled) and mashing it to a paste with a pestle and mortar or in a blender. Add salt and pepper, then very gradually add olive oil, beating or blending until the sauce has the consistency of a mayonnaise. This can be done beforehand, for it keeps well. While the meat is cooking, spread on thick slices of country bread to serve with the meats.

Grilled Liver

Calf's, pork's, or lamb's liver is excellent grilled, but it must be wrapped in fat or it will dry out.

Season to taste with salt and pepper and use lacy caul fat (see p. 207) or strips beaten very thin to cover it. Place on a very hot grill. Turn over after 2 to 3 minutes and cook 2 to 3 minutes more until just done and still pink and juicy inside.

Grilled Chicken

It is easier to cook a chicken on the grill than to roast it on a spit, and it takes half the time. Here is how they do it in Italy.

Lay the chicken with the breast down and split it open along the whole backbone. Crack the breastbone and pull the chicken out as flat as you can so that it cooks evenly. Cut the wing and leg joints just enough so as to spread them flat. Turn the chicken over with the inside of the carcass facing you and pound it as flat as you can. In France they call this way of cooking by the provocative name *à la crapaudine,* for its shape is reminiscent of a toad. Make an incision in the thigh so that it cooks more evenly.

Put it in a bowl with a marinade made by mixing the juice of 1 lemon, 5 tablespoons olive oil, some coarsely ground black pepper, 2 or 3 of sprigs of fresh rosemary, 1/2 cup (120 ml.) red wine, and perhaps an ounce of brandy, especially for squab, for at least 2 hours, turning it over once.

Place the oiled grill quite high, 4 to 5 in. (10 to 13 cm.) above the embers. When the fire is ready lay the chicken on it, skin side toward the fire. Grill until the skin has turned golden brown, brushing with oil from time to time. Sprinkle with salt and turn over more than once, leaving it longer on the bone side until the juice coming out of a thigh (when it is pricked with a fork) is no longer pink—usually about 35 to 45 minutes. Small spring chickens and Rock Cornish hens take approximately 30 minutes. Throw herbs or fruitwood twigs into the fire at the last minute for a special aroma. Serve garnished with sprigs of parsley and lemon wedges.

For a delicious Creole flavor: Mix the following marinade: 3 tablespoons olive oil, 2 tablespoons tomato purée, 2 pressed garlic cloves, 1/2 teaspoon ground ginger or a 1 1/2- to 2-in. (4- to 5-cm.) piece fresh ginger root, grated, and a good pinch of cayenne or chili pepper.

A French way for squab: Brush with Dijon mustard, dip in bread crumbs, and grill 5 minutes each side.

In Greece they pour a sauce of beaten yogurt over it.

Jointed or Boned Chicken

Farther east, chicken is usually jointed and sometimes boned. Cooking time over a lower grill is shorter, and in this way legs and drumsticks can be started before the breasts or put where the fire is hottest with the breasts on the periphery. Legs take about 40 minutes, boned breasts 10 to 15 minutes to cook through.

A very popular Middle Eastern marinade is made with olive oil, pepper, and plenty of lemon juice and crushed garlic. Sprinkle with salt when the chicken begins to color. Serve in pita bread heated on the fire.

This marinade comes from the Caucasus: Beat a little paprika, a pinch of cayenne pepper, and 2 to 3 cloves crushed garlic into some olive oil.

For an Indian tandoori recipe see page 288.

Chicken Breasts en Papillote

The best way of cooking boned chicken breasts is in foil (see p. 207). Brush generously with oil or melted butter, season with salt and pepper, and sprinkle with fresh tarragon, parsley, or coriander leaves and a little crushed garlic if you like. They cook in about 20 minutes. Close the foil well so that the juices do not leak out, and turn over once. Turkey breasts or boned turkey meat of any kind will also do very well.

A *stuffing* may be spread on the flattened breasts and wrapped up ahead of time. Here are a few suggestions:

1. Work equal quantities of fine bread crumbs and softened butter to a paste; season with salt and pepper. Add a generous amount of crushed garlic and enough finely chopped parsley to make it very green, and moisten if you like with a teaspoon or more of Cognac.
2. Moisten ground almonds or walnuts with fresh cream and mix with a little crushed garlic, salt, and pepper.
3. To spread chicken liver pâté or mousse is a traditional way in France.
4. Add chopped onions fried until soft with sliced mushrooms and chopped parsley.
5. In Italy a purée of peeled, seeded, and mashed tomatoes, sprinkled with some finely chopped fresh basil or parsley, is very popular. A thin slice of mozzarella is sometimes added.

Quails

Cut the quails open down the back and marinate in oil and lemon juice, salt and pepper, grated onion, and a touch of nutmeg or ginger for an hour or as long as possible. Dip in bread crumbs before putting on the grill for 5 to 6 minutes and turning over once.

You will need 2 quails per person.

Another elegant marinade is a mixture of 1 1/3 cups (325 ml.) dry white or red wine and 1/4 cup oil with a dozen crushed juniper berries and a dozen crushed peppercorns, 3 bay leaves, and 2 crushed cloves garlic. This will marinate 12 quails.

Season with salt and put on the grill over medium heat, breast down, for 2 to 3 minutes, brushing with oil or melted butter.

Toast 12 slices of bread at the same time and serve the quails on these with lemon wedges.

Variation: Cora and Bob Brown give a recipe for stuffed quail in *American Cooks.* Leave quails whole and stuff with dry bread crumbs browned in butter, mixed with chopped pecans, and seasoned with salt and pepper. Turn over the grill and serve on toast.

Grilled Duck Breasts

From James Beard.
Bone the breasts and pound them gently to flatten them a little (to about 1/4 in./3/4 cm. thick). Marinate for several hours in red wine with black pepper, sprigs of thyme or marjoram, and bay leaves.

Put on a medium-hot grill for 6 minutes, turning over once until done but still juicy.

Serve with orange quarters and roasted chestnuts.

Chinese Broiled Duckling

Again, from James Beard.
Allow 1 Long Island duckling for each 2 or 4 persons, depending on the size of the bird and the appetites of the *convives.* Split or quarter the duckling and rub with a mixture made with 2 egg yolks, 1/3 cup (80 ml.) soy sauce, and 1/4 cup (60 ml.) honey. Broil, cut side down, for about 45 to 60 minutes, over a low fire, turning a few times. Toward the end of the cooking, raise the fire in order to crisp the skin.

SKEWER COOKING

Kebabs

Kebabs are the best-known foods of the Middle East. This is not surprising, since they are part of the street food tradition of the region, and tourists who never get a taste of local home cooking invariably come across a kebab vendor.

Even where there is no restaurant tradition to speak of there will always be cafés selling them. There are many varieties. In Greece and Turkey the meat is interspersed with tomatoes, onions, and peppers with a bay leaf here and there. In Egypt, pieces of meat are threaded alternately with minced meatballs. Iranians serve them on a bed of fluffy white rice with a raw egg yolk embedded in the center. In Morocco they are tiny and fiery. Lamb, the favorite meat of the area, is generally used, each country favoring different aromatics.

Use leg or shoulder of lamb. Cut the boned meat into 3/4- to 1-in. (2- to 2 1/2-cm.) cubes (Moroccan brochettes are smaller), trim off any skin and excess fat but do not throw the fat away; it can be used to lubricate the meat. Two lb. (1 kg.) is enough for 5 or 6 skewers. Leave the meat to marinate, covered in a cool place, for at least an hour or overnight—the longer the better.

A marinade: the usual ingredients are oil (I use a light vegetable one) and lemon, onion juice obtained by grating onions or putting them in a blender, and pepper. Other additions which you may like to try are ground cinnamon and allspice or cumin and coriander (1 or 2 teaspoons of each) and a touch of cayenne. Salt is added during cooking.

Just before you are ready to cook, thread the meat onto skewers with a flat wide or twisted blade. A few pieces of fat squeezed between the meat will prevent it from drying out, and a piece of onion or a bay leaf will give it flavor. Sprinkle with salt. Although I am not in favor of

putting vegetables on the skewer with the meat, as their cooking times differ, some people like to. If you do, cut small firm tomatoes into quarters and green peppers into pieces as large as the meat, and thread them alternately.

Cook very quickly over a hot charcoal fire—you do not even have to have a grill; two bricks or stones will do as supports for the skewers. Turn the skewers occasionally, brushing with oil if the meat is lean and has no bits of fat in between, until it is well browned outside but still pink and juicy inside—usually in about 7 to 10 minutes.

Serve with a cucumber and tomato salad with plenty of finely chopped onion and shredded white cabbage and lemon wedges. You may slip everything in half a pita bread which has been warmed up on the fire. The usual accompaniment is tahina (see p. 86).

Souvlakia. For the Greek kebab with pork, use leg or shoulder cut up in the same way, and marinate in a mixture of olive oil, lemon juice, a good sprinkling of wild thyme, oregano or marjoram, pepper, and a few bay leaves. Grill longer and more slowly to cook through (about 15 minutes).

A *gypsy recipe* which originates in Hungary uses fillet of beef. Marinate in oil mixed with a good amount of paprika, a sprinkling of thyme, black pepper, a few broken bay leaves, and strips of lemon zest. Thread the last two on to the skewers in between the meat when you are ready to cook. Sprinkle with salt and place close to the embers for 4 to 5 minutes, turning over once.

Minced or Ground Meat Kebabs

Luleh in Iran, brochettes in Morocco, and kofta in the Arab world and India are not only the cheapest but also the tastiest kebabs because the flavorings are worked into the meat. Though lamb is traditionally used, beef and veal also make good kofta kebabs.

Use fat meat or add some extra fat if it is too lean, to keep them moist and tender. The secret is to work the meat to a smooth paste. Grind it twice or ask your butcher to do so, then work it well, kneading with your hands. In the Middle East people pound it with a pestle and mortar, but for those who have one, a food processor does the job very well starting from cubes of meat.

Here is my own everyday recipe: for 2 1/4 lb. (1 kg.) minced lamb (preferably fat), add 2 medium onions, grated, 1 good bunch of parsley, finely chopped, 1 teaspoon each of cinnamon, cumin, and allspice, salt and pepper to taste.

Work the meat to a paste and leave to rest for an hour. Wet your hands then take a lump and pat it around the skewer in the shape of a sausage 4 to 5 in. (10 to 13 cm.) long, or shorter. Press firmly so as to prevent it from slipping. Turn often over a hot fire for 5 to 8 minutes. Be careful not to overcook, as they dry out rather quickly.

You may find it easier to pat the meat into plump round patties, smaller than the usual hamburger, and to cook them on the grill.

Serve with a tomato and cucumber salad in the usual pita bread if you like, accompanied by tahina sauce (see p. 86) and lemon wedges. Or put on toast with yogurt poured over them. An extravagant garnish is pine nuts browned on foil over the fire.

Variations: To the basic kebab mixture you may add 4 to 5 tablespoons of browned pine nuts, or a handful of chopped pistachios or walnuts and one of moist sultanas. Shape into plump patties and cook on the grill.

My Moroccan friend Fatima Ouazzani makes peppery and spicy brochettes in the following way: for 2 1/4 lb. (1 kg.) minced meat add 2 grated onions, 2 teaspoons cinnamon, 2 teaspoons cumin, salt, 3 teaspoons sweet red pepper (such as paprika), a large pinch of cayenne pepper, a good bunch each of fresh coriander and parsley, a sprig or two of mint, all finely chopped. Work the mixture to a paste, pat into long sausage shapes on skewers, and cook as above. Garnish with sprigs of parsley and lemon wedges.

Chopped Chicken Cakes (from James Beard)

Bone 3 chicken breasts or half a large turkey breast, and put on a chopping board. Using two heavy French knives, one in each hand, chop the meat in small bits. When it is well hashed, add as much cream as it will absorb and still be firm enough to mold. Add salt and pepper, form the meat into one large or several individual cakes, brush well with butter, and broil over charcoal, turning once, until delicately brown. This will take 12 to 14 minutes over a medium fire. Serve with parsley butter or just with a wedge of lemon and a great piece of butter melting on each cake. These cakes, by the way, may be sautéed in butter instead of broiled over coals. The meat may also be chopped with one knife—it will take longer and won't be as spectacular, but it will do the job nicely.

Kidneys on Skewers

There are several ways of cooking kidneys over a fire. In *The Complete Indian Housekeeper and Cook* Mrs. Gardiner and Mrs. Steel have them skinned, cut with a sharp knife from the outside round part with a deep, but not too broad, incision, and filled with chopped herbs. Cook gently until tender, basting occasionally with oil or butter.

Variations: Split kidneys in half and remove cores and fat, or cut them up into pieces. Thread onto skewers alternating with bits of fat, if you have them, and bay leaves. Cook no longer than 10 minutes, about 3 to 4 in. (8 to 10 cm.) from the fire, brushing with oil or melted butter and turning over once at least. Sprinkle with salt and pepper and serve on hot toast with lemon wedges.

You may also skewer the kidney pieces wrapped in a thin slice of bacon to keep them moist.

Moroccan Lamb's Liver Brochettes

Kouah, as they are called, are delicious providing the liver is not allowed to dry out, which it will do if not properly moistened with fat. Cut 2 1/4 lb. (1 kg.) liver into pieces and marinate in oil mixed with 1 teaspoon cumin, 2 teaspoons paprika, a good pinch of cayenne, and salt. Wrap each cube with a thin piece of caul fat or simply thread with alternate pieces of lamb fat. Grill as quickly as possible on a moderate fire until the outside is nice and brown and the inside still pink and juicy.

Sprinkle with wine vinegar and accompany with a salad and bread.

Italian Mixed Grills

For each skewer have a cube of pork, one of boned chicken, and one lamb's liver as well as a small lamb chop. Let them marinate in olive oil with a good sprinkling of fresh rosemary and coarsely ground black pepper. Add 3 or 4 juniper berries if you have them and leave to marinate for a few hours.

Thread the meats onto skewers, alternating them with a small slice of bacon and a sage leaf. Cook over medium heat for 10 to 15 minutes. Sprinkle with salt and serve on a bed of shredded lettuce.

Lombello Arrosto. Cut a fillet of pork into 3/4-in. (2-cm.) slices. Thread onto skewers, alternating with slices of bread cut to the same size and slices of Parma ham. Grill on a medium heat for 12 to 15 minutes until well browned but juicy inside.

Spiedini Misti di Spoleto / Mixed Kebabs from Spoleto

The Middle East is not alone in cooking small morsels of meat on skewers. Italy has a few dishes of this type; one of its best comes from Spoleto.

Pig's liver is often included in this Italian kebab, but it usually gets dry before the other morsels of meat get cooked.

1 1/8 lb. (1/2 kg.) pork cut from the loin	4 juniper berries, crushed
	Pepper
2 chicken breasts, skinned and boned	Salt
6 small lamb chops	1/4 lb. (115 g.) bacon, thinly sliced
6 tablespoons olive oil	1 bunch sage leaves
2 sprigs of rosemary, finely chopped	

Cut the pork and chicken into 6 pieces each and marinate with the lamb in a mixture of olive oil, rosemary, juniper berries, and pepper for at least an hour in a cool place. Sprinkle with salt and thread onto 6 skewers, alternating with the bacon, cut into pieces, and a sage leaf. Place the skewers on an oiled grill over medium heat for about 10 to 15 minutes, turning a few times and brushing with the marinade, until done.

Crocchette di Carne / Italian Meat Croquettes

A specialty of Calabria and Lucania.

1 1/8 lb. (1/2 kg.) meat—veal, pork,
    or lamb—minced
2 slices white bread, crusts removed
Milk
Salt and pepper
2 lightly beaten eggs
2 tablespoons grated pecorina cheese

1 tablespoon cream
1/4 lb. (115 g.) chopped salami
2 sprigs of parsley, finely chopped
1/4 lb. (115 g.) fat salt pork or bacon
6 large slices bread, lightly toasted
Oil

Put the meat in a bowl. Soak the bread in a little milk, then squeeze it dry. Add to the meat with the rest of the ingredients except the fat pork or bacon, the toasted bread, and the oil. When you add salt take into account the saltiness of the cheese. Mix well and knead vigorously into a firm well-blended paste which can hold together on skewers. Take small lumps of meat mixture, roll into balls, and thread onto flat skewers, alternating with thin slices of salt pork and pieces of toast cut into small squares. Place the skewers over a medium fire on an oiled grill and cook gently, turning over once and brushing with oil, for about 8 minutes until nicely browned.

Chicken Pieces on Skewers

Those who have had chicken kebabs in a Middle Eastern restaurant know it either as a splendid dish or as a miserable one, for kebabs can easily become dried out and hard. The main thing is to keep them well oiled and not to overcook. Usually only chicken breasts are used, skinned, boned, and cut into 3/4- to 1-in. (2- to 2 1/2-cm.) pieces. Leave in a marinade for at least an hour, longer if possible. Add salt just before threading on skewers and cook for about 6 to 10 minutes (until cooked) on a medium fire, turning over frequently and brushing with oil or melted butter or the marinade.

Marinades: My favorite is a common enough mixture of olive oil and lemon juice (usually equal quantities), coarsely grated pepper, and a little crushed garlic.

You can use dry white wine and herbs such as tarragon or rosemary or grated lemon zest.

A delicate taste is given in Turkey with onion juice obtained by grating a large onion or putting it through a blender, and adding pepper and cinnamon.

Yogurt tenderizes chicken. Flavor it with the spices of your choice: cardamom seeds removed from their pod, allspice, cinnamon, cumin, coriander. I have given a recipe for tandoori and tikka chicken in the Indian menu, page 288, which uses yogurt as a base.

The most famous chicken kebabs come from Japan. My friend Marion Maitlis brought back this recipe. Marinate bite-size pieces of chicken (2 boned breasts) for 2 in a mixture of 4 tablespoons soy sauce, 4 tablespoons mirin (rice wine) or medium sherry, 2 tablespoons oil, and 2 tablespoons sugar for a few hours. You may vary the balance of flavors by adding a clove of garlic and a piece of ginger, both crushed in a garlic press to extract their juice, and some grated orange or lemon zest. Thread on miniature skewers, alternating with small pieces of green pepper, spring onion, and mushroom (you may add halved chicken livers), and cook for 8 to 10 minutes, turning and brushing frequently with the marinade.

Ground chicken, unlike ground meat, is not part of the butcher's trade, but it is now easy to make at home with a food processor. Grind raw chicken flesh very fine. Mix in a little grated onion and finely chopped parsley and season with salt and pepper and a sprinkling of cinnamon. Work well and press into a sausage shape on skewers or pat into little flat cakes. Brush with oil or melted butter and cook briefly over medium heat, turning over once and basting frequently. Serve with lemon wedges. Ground turkey may also be used in this way.

Uccelletti di Campagna Senza Testa ("Crazy Birds")

These only look like birds. In Britain they are called "olives." Make them with tender cuts of beef, veal, or pork.

Cut slices of meat into strips about 1 1/2 in. (4 cm.) wide and a little over 2 1/2 in. (6 1/2 cm.) long. Beat them flat and on each piece lay a slice of ham and a sage leaf. Sprinkle with pepper and roll up. Thread these onto skewers with alternate pieces of bread and bacon.

Brush the meat and bread with melted lard or oil. Grill over charcoal, turning the skewers slowly until the meat is cooked and the bread and bacon nicely browned.

Stuffed Brochettes of Beef

For a taste of Provence cut thin slices of tender beef (fillet, rump, sirloin) and flatten them, being careful not to make any holes. Cut into strips about 1 1/2 to 2 1/2 in. (4 to 6 1/2 cm.) wide. Make a stuffing with bread crumbs from 4 slices of dry bread. Sprinkle with a little oil, enough to make a stiff paste. Add a good quantity of chopped, mixed fresh herbs—parsley, chives, chervil (only a touch of thyme), 2 or more cloves of garlic, crushed, salt and pepper, and if you like a few tablespoons of grated Gruyère cheese. Mix well with your hands. Press a little of this paste on the end of each piece of meat, roll up, and thread onto skewers. Cook gently, turning a few times and brushing with oil until done—about 10 to 12 minutes.

Neapolitan Kebabs

Flatten small thin slices of pork or other meats. Season with salt and pepper and sprinkle with raisins or sultanas (soaked in water until plump, then drained) and a few pine nuts. Roll up tightly and thread on skewers close together. Cook for 10 to 12 minutes, brushing with oil or melted butter to keep the meat moist.

FISH AND SEAFOOD

My fondest memories of Portugal are associated with the smell of sardines cooking. Most of the summer nights were spent walking on the beach, waiting for the fish to be pulled in with large nets, and watching it being auctioned in the marketplace. As the bidding continued, dozens of little fires were started along the sea front in clay braziers shaped like flowerpots. We watched the fishermen clean and wash mountains of sardines, and simply lay them on small grills fixed on the top of the pots, without oil or butter or anything else. Within minutes they were ready. We were offered an endless but irresistible supply of crisp "sardinhas" with a sprinkling of salt and pepper and vinegar on thick slices of bread, accompanied by a tomato and pepper salad with onion rings and black olives.

Grilling is a most delicious way of cooking any fish, but not all of them can be dealt with as summarily as sardines. Depending on size, plumpness, and oiliness, each type of fish needs a particular treatment. Most fish need frequent brushing with oil or melted butter or a marinade to prevent them from drying out, unless they are very oily, like sardines. They can also be floured or rolled in bread crumbs and then smeared with oil or melted butter, which forms a handsome crust that keeps them moist.

To Prepare the Fish

Thoroughly rinse and wash. Draw out the innards through the gills or by slitting the belly. Do not take off the head. It is not always necessary to remove scales, as they practically melt in the fire and there is sometimes an advantage in leaving them on. But if you want a charcoal-grilled skin, push the scales up the wrong way with the blunt edge of a knife.

For large and medium fish make a few incisions diagonally in two or three places on each side in the thicker part, with the point of a knife, so that it cooks more evenly. The cuts allow a sauce or marinade to penetrate and prevent the bare skin from bursting.

To Cook the Fish

A very large fish may be roasted on a spit or cooked on a grill. A double grill or basket makes it easier to turn over without breaking or damaging the skin. Otherwise use a spatula and be sure you oil the grill, or the skin will be torn off, taking some flesh with it.

If the fish is very large (more than 3 1/2 lb./1 1/2 kg.) place it 6 to 8 in. (15 to 20 cm.) from the fire. If it is medium size place it 5 to 6 in. (13 to 15 cm.) away. Splitting the fish in half through the back cuts the cooking time and gives the smoky taste to a larger surface. If you like a crust roll the fish in flour.

The cooking time varies depending on the size and type of fish—from about 15 minutes for a 2- to 3 1/2-lb. (1- to 1 1/2-kg.) lean fish to 45 minutes for a 10-lb. (5-kg.) oily one (the oilier the flesh the longer it takes). Judge the time according to the fire. Give the first side longer than the second, or turn over a few times if the fish is firm enough, brushing frequently with olive oil, melted butter, or a marinade.

For fish cooked en papillote in foil see page 207.

For small fish you need a well-oiled double grill to hold them while you turn them over. Gut the fish and wash the cavity. Oil and place 4 to 5 in. (10 to 13 cm.) from the fire. Grill one side, sprinkle with salt and pepper, then

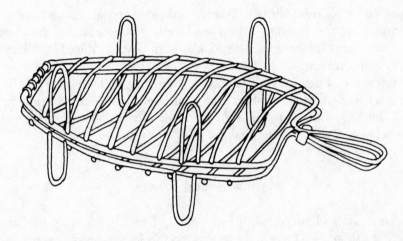

turn over on the other side and season this one before serving. As a rough guide small fish take 6 to 7 minutes, medium ones 8 to 12 minutes (2 to 3 minutes longer if oily).

Fish Steaks

Large fish with a firm flesh (tuna and swordfish are particularly good) can be cut in thick steaks. You can use fillets, but they must be thick or they have a tendency to dry out.

Sprinkle with olive oil, salt, and pepper or leave in a marinade (see pp. 203, 264) for an hour. Drain, dredge in flour if you want a good crust, then sprinkle again with oil or the marinade. Cook on both sides on a gentle fire, brushing again with the oil or marinade, until it just begins to flake and the crust starts to brown.

Serve with lemon wedges and a sprinkling of chopped parsley.

Eels and Elvers

On the East Coast Americans—especially those of Italian descent—relish eels. Clint Greyn, who has cooked them at Clevedon, not far from Bristol, England, where fishermen sometimes give them away free as part of the catch that they do not usually sell, says that for grilling it is best not to skin them.

Eels should be alive when you buy them and have the fishmonger kill them by chopping off or bashing the head. Cut the rest into 1 1/2- to 2-in. (4- to 5-cm.) pieces. Marinate in olive oil and vinegar seasoned with salt and pepper, or simply rub with salt. Thread on skewers or place on an oiled grill over a medium fire, brushing with oil and turning often until the flesh separates easily from the bone. Serve sprinkled with olive oil mixed with lemon juice or wine vinegar.

Bay leaves threaded on the skewer alternately with the fish give it a delicious flavor, and so do embers from a burnt-out bundle of vine prunings.

Clint has found that a mild soy marinade or the classic Japanese marinade below also suits eels admirably.

Marinades and Sauces

Though steaks and cubed fish benefit, it is not usually necessary to marinate whole fish at all. The delicate taste is too precious to mask, and skin and scales act as a barrier to the fire. But aromatics in the basting oil give it a subtle perfume and turn the marinade into a sauce. Use olive oil, gently flavored, to sprinkle the fish, inside and out, and brush frequently during the cooking.

An herb oil. Season with salt and pepper and beat in some chopped herbs such as rosemary, fennel, thyme, bay, tarragon, basil, oregano, marjoram, parsley, and coriander leaves. If you let them macerate for a few days the flavor will have infused even better. Prepare a jar and add a crushed clove of garlic if you like.

A spice oil. Flavor the oil with spices such as cumin, coriander, paprika, and cayenne—a pinch of the last and a teaspoon each of the others for 2/3 cup (150 ml.) of oil. Add salt to taste.

A sharp oil. Oily fish do better with a sharp taste to cut the richness. Add lemon or wine vinegar in the proportion of a vinaigrette or in equal quantities.

A delicious specialty of Orleans is grilled herring served hot with a peppery vinaigrette. Split the fish in half and grill just until flaky. Pour the sauce over it while it is sizzling hot.

A classic Japanese marinade is a mixture of equal quantities of soy sauce and mirin, a sweet rice wine, for which you can substitute a medium or dry sherry, and vegetable oil. You may please your fancy and add to taste: sugar or honey, fresh ginger root squeezed in a garlic press, lemon juice or vinegar (2 teaspoons of each may be right with 2 tablespoons of each of the main ingredients), and a crushed clove of garlic.

Try it with salmon, halibut, turbot, and bass.

Harra—a peppery sauce. I shall never forget the hot spicy taste of the sauce which was painted on a large fish for me by a man at Sharm el Sheikh. A few tables and chairs were set around a fire where a variety of fish were being cooked. They were brought wriggling from the sea by a young boy who ran into the water and picked one from a large basket for each order. We had chosen a large one because of our ravenous appetite and it seemed to take hours to cook. Its name sounded like "loukoz," and when I asked again, the man replied with a mock Jewish intonation: "Family name Berkovitz!"

"Loukoz" is the Arab name for bass, and I have tried to re-create the sauce from memory. Put all the ingredients in a blender: 2/3 cup (150 ml.) olive oil, a small onion, 2 cloves garlic, the juice of 1 whole lemon or more, salt, pepper, 1 tablespoon paprika, 1 tablespoon cumin, 1/4 teaspoon cayenne, and 1 good bunch of fresh coriander leaves.

A flavored butter prepared in advance (see p. 297) makes an excellent sauce as it melts over a sizzling hot fish cooked with little or no embellishments. The most appropriate is one combined with fishy things such as soft poached fish roes or the coral, eggs, and creamy parts of shrimp, crayfish, or lobster. Smoked salmon bits may also be used. Caviar makes a very grand sauce and mashed anchovy fillets a strongly flavored one. The amount you need will depend on what you choose and the intensity of flavor, but the principle is the same. Pound to a paste, soften a good amount of unsalted butter, and beat in the fishy paste, a little at a time.

You may add condiments to taste: lemon juice, a little Dijon mustard, black pepper, paprika, a pinch of cayenne, salt if necessary, fresh grated horseradish. Tomato paste gives a fine color.

Beurre meunière, the most common butter sauce, can be made on the spot. Cook some butter in a saucepan until it is slightly brown, then add a squeeze of lemon juice.

Thick whipping cream, seasoned with salt, coarsely ground black pepper, and lemon juice, and heated up in a pan with a sprinkling of herbs such as tarragon, parsley, or chives, makes the easiest sauce and also the most delicate.

Wine Butter Sauce to Serve with Fish and Shellfish

3 medium shallots, chopped
1/2 small onion, chopped
1/2 lb. (115 g.) unsalted butter,
    allowed to soften

1/4 bottle red or white wine
Salt and pepper

Soften the shallots and the onion in 2 tablespoons of the butter. Pour in the wine and simmer until reduced by a quarter, then add the butter bit by bit, whisking constantly, until it is properly incorporated. Season to taste with salt and pepper.

Barbecue Sauce for Shrimp or Fish

2 tablespoons butter
Juice of half a lemon
2 cloves garlic, pressed

1 teaspoon paprika
Cayenne pepper or chili powder

Melt the butter in a saucepan and add the lemon, garlic, paprika, and a good pinch of cayenne or chili powder. Blend well together.

Fish with Only Its Natural Flavor

A fish can be cooked as it is with its scales on. Put it straight onto the grill with no oil or butter or anything. Do not slash the fish; simply put the thickest part on the hottest part of the grill, and turn it over a few times until the flesh is done. The scales will coalesce and keep the flesh soft and juicy, and the salt deposit which they contain will intensify the tangy flavor of the sea. Make a little cut with a knife to see if it is done. If the flesh is opaque close to the bone it is ready.

Fish and Shrimp Flamed in Aromatic Herbs and Spirits

The method is worthy of sea bream, bass, salmon, salmon trout, and red mullet, but any other fish will gain in flavor.

Clean, wash, and score the fish in 2 or 3 places. Stuff the cavity with sprigs of fennel, parsley, thyme, or rosemary and roll it in flour. Season with salt and pepper and sprinkle with olive oil. Grill on embers, prefer-

ably using a double grill, for 3 to 5 minutes on either side, then turn over
again and cook both sides until the flesh has only just become opaque and
flaky. Brush frequently with oil. (Turn only once if there is a risk of breaking the fish.) Lay on a bed of dry fennel branches or bay leaves, or a mixture
of dried rosemary, fennel, and thyme, which may be placed in a serving
dish or on a rack. Top the fish with additional herbs. Pour a little heated
Cognac or other spirit such as marc, armagnac, or calvados over them and
ignite. Alternatively, if the twigs are moistened slightly you will get a good
smoky flavor.

Shrimp are especially good grilled in their shells then laid on a bed of
dry fennel twigs. Ignite Pernod in a spoon and pour it on the twigs.

If you have no herbs but a good supply of spirits, heat some up, throw
it on the fish as you serve, and ignite.

Masgouf

At night the banks of the river Tigris in Iraq sparkle with the twinkling lights
of little fires. The seductive smoke of a burning camel thorn bush, plucked
from the desert, mingled with the aroma of roasting fish entices passersby.
The fish, split open as they come out of the river, are held upright with stakes
like a fleet of double-masted sailing boats encircling the fire, flesh side toward
it to absorb the smoke.

Fried onions and tomatoes, highly spiced with curry and pepper, bubble
in pans on the side of the fire. When the fish are almost cooked by smoking
they are laid skin side down over the glowing ashes into which the bush has
crumpled. The sauce is spread on the browned flesh and gentle pricking allows
it to seep in.

Fish Wrapped in Leaves

A good way to cook fish. It gives a distinctive sharp lemony flavor.

Scale fish carefully and wash. The entrails of most very fresh fish (unless
a scavenger) are considered a delicacy and should not be removed. If you have
time marinate the fish for an hour in olive oil with bay leaves, parsley, thyme,
chives, and cracked peppercorns; otherwise it is enough to rub inside and out
with garlic-flavored olive oil. Sprinkle with salt and pepper. Wrap in vine
leaves and grill on a low fire for 7 to 8 minutes, turning over once.

If you are in a vine-growing region pick as many vine leaves as you can
keep for later use. Blanch for a minute in boiling water, pack in a jar, and cover
with brine.

Banana leaves and lotus leaves are also good as a wrapping for all kinds of fish. Cabbage and lettuce are more readily available alternatives.

Cooking in Cornhusks

Good for small and medium fish. Pull back the husks and remove ears of corn by breaking them off at the stalks, leaving husk ends intact. Carefully remove all silk threads and soak husks in water for a few minutes, then place a cleaned fish inside each and tie the husks up securely at the silk end. They can go straight into a bed of hot embers. Turn them once. Medium-size fish require 15 minutes.

Steaming in Seaweed

A most delicious way of cooking on the beach. Wrap the fish in layers of wet seaweed and place on a grill over a gentle fire. Cockles, mussels, and crustacea are also excellent cooked in this way. A fish weighing about 1 3/4 lb. (800 g.) is done in about 20 minutes; smaller fish, shrimp, and shellfish, in much less time. For details about a New England clambake, see page 343.

Fish Grilled with Salt in the Japanese Way

The Japanese cook sea bream in salt alone, but most other small whole fish can be treated in the same manner. Clean, wash, and scale the fish. Sprinkle very generously with salt inside and out (Peter and Joan Martin suggest 2 percent of the fish's weight in salt in *Japanese Cooking*), and leave for 30 minutes. Wipe the fish dry just before grilling and sprinkle again with salt (especially tail and fins) for a white powdery finish. Cook on an oiled grill for 5 minutes on each side or until golden.

Sole Meunière

One large sole will do for two. Cut heads off, remove the gray skin from the back, scale the white underskin, and score it diagonally with a sharp knife. Cut the fins off with scissors and cut open the stomach to remove the insides. Wash under cold water. Brush with oil and sprinkle with salt and pepper. Put on an oiled grill, white skin side down, for 4 minutes, then turn the fish over and grill a further 4 minutes.

Lift the fillets in 4 unbroken pieces by cutting along the length of the backbone with a knife and sliding the blade between the flesh and bones to loosen them.

Serve with unsalted butter heated in a pan until it is light brown. At the last moment add salt and pepper and a good squeeze of lemon juice.

Fish Kebabs or Brochettes

Large fish, skinned and cut into cubes, and smaller ones, cut into slices, make good kebabs. Salmon, turbot, swordfish, and tuna are best, but other firm fish such as monkfish, cod, halibut, sturgeon, shad, gray mullet, and mackerel can also be cooked in this way.

Cut the fish into cubes or slices 1 1/2 in. (4 cm.) thick. Marinate in a mixture of olive oil and lemon juice with salt and pepper, a little grated onion, and finely chopped parsley for an hour—fennel, oregano, rosemary, or marjoram may also be used. Other marinades are given on pages 203 and 264.

Thread onto skewers or reeds with a bay leaf between each piece. Turn over a gentle fire, brushing from time to time with the marinade, until only just done—about 8 to 10 minutes.

Tuna en brochette—with bacon fat to lubricate—is very good.

Barbecued Lobster

Cut the lobster in half with a sharp knife and a hammer or meat mallet. Split it from end to end, starting at the head. Remove the stomach and the intestinal vein but not the green liver (the tomalley), which is delicious, nor the pinkish red roe or coral in the female.

Brush the flesh with melted butter or oil and sprinkle with salt, pepper, and lemon juice.

Grill the lobster shell-side down 6 to 7 in. (15 to 18 cm.) above the source of heat for about 10 to 20 minutes, until it is almost done. Turn and grill the flesh side for 1 or 2 minutes more. Remove the claws and drop them for 2 or 3 minutes into the embers.

Serve sprinkled with melted butter and a squeeze of lemon. Or make a sauce by mixing 1 tablespoon mustard with 1 tablespoon oil and 2 tablespoons melted butter; add a little salt, cayenne pepper, and/or paprika and some finely chopped parsley. A tablespoon of heavy cream may also be added.

Take a nutcracker with you to crack the claws.

Fish en Papillote

Cooking in foil with seasonings and aromatics suits nothing so well as fish, especially since foil has replaced old-fashioned oiled paper.

The fish cooks in its own juices. Nothing is lost, and herbs, wines, and flavorings are most effective. There is no risk of drying out and the more fragile fish are not damaged.

Big fish like turbot, salmon, bass, shad, pompano, flounder, etc. can be cooked whole or split in half and each piece wrapped separately. Medium ones like trout, red mullet, and mackerel are wrapped individually, as are fillets and steaks.

You must have a large enough piece of foil to enclose the fish loosely, and brush it well with oil or melted butter so that the skin does not stick.

Clean the fish and slash the skin diagonally in the thicker part if left whole or cut into 1-in. (2 1/2-cm.) steaks or fillets. Place on the foil, season with salt and coarsely ground black pepper, and sprinkle with a chopped fresh herb: parsley, chervil, tarragon, or bay leaf for the more delicate flesh, rosemary, thyme, or marjoram for the stronger-tasting fish. It is a good idea to fill the cavity with butter and herbs for extra flavor. A few tablespoons of bread crumbs will absorb and hold the juices.

You may moisten with dry white wine, or try any of the following: salmon is worthy of champagne, and a drop of pastis or vermouth goes well with trout (so does the juice of a piece of fresh ginger squeezed through a garlic press), while a few tablespoons of thick cream go extremely well with either. White wine vinegar and cider suit mackerel. Sometimes a teaspoon of Dijon mustard is an advantage, as is crushed garlic for those who like it. And of course there

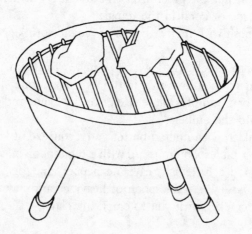

is the usual squeeze of lemon. The art lies in flavoring subtly so as not to mask the delicate taste of the fish.

Fold the foil around the fish, making a loose parcel, with the edges tightly closed by folding and twisting into a firm seal (see p. 207).

Put on the grill near the fire. Allow roughly 5 to 7 minutes each side for steaks and medium fish such as trout and up to 45 minutes in all for a very large one, turning over once.

Pass around some lemon wedges and let everyone open his own parcel. Some people might like to pour a little heated liquor over the fish and set it alight.

Variations: Parcel the fish with sliced mushrooms or a few sharp gooseberries if it is mackerel.

An unusual stuffing for foiled fish: fill the fish with a sprinkling of raisins or sultanas and pine nuts or coarsely chopped walnuts and hazelnuts or some flaked almonds. These are best toasted first on a piece of foil over the grill. This is not as strange as you might think. It is popular in the Middle East as well as Sicily and south of the Mediterranean, and worth trying with a variety of fish such as sardines, mackerel, and trout. I have even added chopped dates successfully.

A good idea popular in France is to toast some almonds lightly on a separate piece of foil placed on the grill and to sprinkle them on the fish when you are ready to eat.

Alice Water's Charcoal-Grilled Shellfish with Red Wine Butter Sauce*

The shellfish should be very fresh. The amounts given are approximate and may vary according to availability and taste. This recipe serves 12. Rock and Jonah crabs (Maine) would grill up fine; so would Florida stone crabs, Alaska king crabs, Alaska tanner or "snow crabs," and the Atlantic blue crab, *Callinectes sapidus Rathbun*.

THE SHELLFISH

1 live lobster, about 1 1/2 lb. (675 g.)	2 dozen mussels
1 large live Dungeness crab, about 2 lb. (1 kg.)	1/2 to 3/4 lb. (1/4 to 1/3 kg.) scallops
2 dozen oysters	

*From Alice Water's *Chez Panisse Cookbook* (New York: Random House, 1983).

Bring a large pot of salted water to a boil and cook the lobster and crab in it for about 2 minutes. Remove them from the pot, cool enough to handle, clean them, and disjoint them with a sharp knife. Leave the shells on and cut the lobster tail into about 1-in. (2 1/2-cm.) rounds; leave the crab legs as they are and divide the body into 4 to 6 pieces, depending on the size of the crab. Reserve the tomalley and coral for another use. Scrub the oysters and mussels and debeard the mussels.

THE RED WINE BUTTER SAUCE

6 medium shallots
1 small onion
1 lb. (1/2 kg.) and 3 tablespoons
    unsalted butter

1/2 bottle light red wine (chianti
    or Beaujolais)
About 1 tablespoon red wine vinegar
Salt and black pepper to taste

Fine-dice the shallots and onion. Cook them in 3 tablespoons butter over low heat for about 10 minutes, until they are translucent. Cut 1 pound butter into tablespoon-size bits and soften slightly. Add red wine and red wine vinegar to the pan. Reduce over medium-low heat until the liquid is syrupy and about 3/4 cup remains. Taste for acidity and add a little more vinegar if necessary. Increase the heat to medium-high and whisk in half of the softened butter bit by bit. When the butter has been incorporated, lower the heat, and add the rest of the butter in 4 or 5 additions, whisking constantly. Season the sauce with salt and lots of freshly ground black pepper. Keep the sauce warm in a double boiler.

Prepare a charcoal fire that is very hot in one area, flames just licking above the grill, and medium-hot in another area. Put the oysters and mussels over the hot fire and cook for about 5 minutes, until they are about half open. Remove them from the fire and finish opening them with an oyster knife if necessary. Put them on warmed platters or plates and spoon a little red wine butter over each. Cook the crab and lobster pieces and the scallops over the medium fire for 3 to 5 minutes, turning frequently. The cooking time will vary, the lobster and scallops taking less time, the crab legs more. Arrange the lobster, crab, and scallops on warm platters, and brush them lightly with a little red wine butter. Serve the rest of the sauce in small bowls.

BARBECUED FRUITS

It is sometimes fun to take advantage of a lingering fire to give the fruits of the season a different savor. You may prepare those that are to be cooked in foil at home and wrap them up ready for the fire.

Caramelized Apples

Stick hard eating apples on the end of a skewer and hold them very close to the fire, turning them, until the skin blisters and comes off easily (about 8 minutes). Drop in a bowl of sugar and return to the fire until the sugar melts and caramelizes.

Apples in Foil

You may use large tart apples or dessert apples. Wash and core them and place each on a piece of foil large enough to cover them well. Fill the centers with sugar and a dusting of cinnamon, or flavor if you like with a small piece of vanilla pod. Dot with butter. Wrap up well in the foil so that the package is leakproof. Put on a hot grill for 40 to 50 minutes or until they feel soft, turning over once.

You may put the apples straight into the ashes if you wrap them in a double layer of foil. They will need less time, about 25 minutes.

As an alternative, put a few raisins and sultanas in the center or some apricot purée (see p. 89).

Bananas

Bananas cook very well in their skins. A Creole way is to slit them open and press in a teaspoon of rum and a sprinkling of cinnamon. Put them on the grill for 10 minutes, turning once.

Stuffed Pears

Carefully core 4 large pears from the base. Fill them with a mixture of 1/4 cup (60 g.) ground almonds, 2 tablespoons sugar, 1 tablespoon butter, and 1 large egg yolk worked to a paste (you may add 1 or 2 drops of pure almond essence if the almonds do not have much taste). Wrap each one in foil so that the package is leakproof. Put on a hot grill for about 30 minutes, or until they are soft, turning over once.

Mixed Fruit Skewers

Thread onto skewers alternate pieces of fruit such as quartered peaches, halved apricots, unripe banana slices, chunks of pineapple, orange segments, apples and pears cut into wedges (sprinkled with lemon juice so that they do not darken), pitted plums, or cherries. Cook over a medium fire, turning for 5 to 10 minutes. Sprinkle with sugar and let it caramelize over the fire.

A very attractive alternative to the caramel is to brush frequently with a mixture of 1/4 lb. (115 g.) melted butter, 1 tablespoon sugar, and 1 teaspoon cinnamon or powdered ginger or the seeds from a cardamom pod. Or squeeze lemon or orange juice into the melted butter.

Serve with a little of the basting sauce poured over.

Oranges with Rum

Peel large oranges, removing the pith. Cut in slices and re-form, sprinkling with very little brown sugar and cinnamon. Wrap in 2 layers of foil (to avoid leakage), with a sprinkling of rum, and put on the fire for 10 to 15 minutes.

Chestnuts

Make a slit in each chestnut with a sharp knife and put them on the grill. Turn them over and roast until they are done and nicely colored—about 10 to 15 minutes. Otherwise you can wrap several together in foil and let them cook 20 minutes in the ashes. Chestnuts can also be served as a vegetable and are particularly good with game and duck.

A TEXAS BARBECUE

Here is a beautiful description of a barbecue feast from William Humphrey's *Home from the Hill:*

The oaks in the front lawn were just leafing out, and in their flickering and lacy shade a long trestle table had been set up on sawhorses. Four large unopened cartons labeled *Potato Chips* were spaced along it, alternating with shiny new number 3 galvanized washtubs filled to the brim with creamy white potato salad dotted with green specks of chopped pickle. On four big turkey platters in the center of the table there must have been six gross of deviled eggs, yellow as a bed of buttercups in blossom. There were columns of paper plates; as for silver, each family was to come bringing its own. Underneath the table, with their rims touching, were tubs packed with ice, sweating cold already, some filled with bottled beer, some with colored sodawater for the children. Your mouth watered and your teeth were set on edge so that you knew from a distance of ten feet that the two barrels beneath the biggest tree were full of sour pickles. On the outdoor fireplace a wash-pot of pork-and-beans slowly bubbled. Rows of folding chairs belonging to the Baptist Church were stacked spoke-wise against trees. Half the ice cream freezers in town had been borrowed for the occasion and half the Negro boys hired to crank them. The freezers were covered with wet towsacks. The boys took turns cranking. Two boys went from freezer to freezer sprinkling rock salt from a bag onto the ice. Two others brought buckets from the garage, where a man was busy chipping the second hundred pound block in a flying spray.

The barbecue pit—eight feet long, three wide, and six feet deep, to judge by the mound of dirt alongside—had been dug the day before; the fire had been lighted and through the night fed half a cord of green hickory, so that now a close view gave you the sensation of looking into the crater of a live volcano. Two tall slingshot-shaped poles had been driven into the ground at the ends of the pit.

At seven a.m. six men brought the boar down from the garage. He was spitted on a length of water pipe to which at one end was fitted a crank. The ends of the pipe were lowered into the crotches of the two posts. The carcass sagged over the fire. The skin at once puckered and shriveled in the heat, and in another moment the fat began to drip onto the coals, sending up little explosions of smoke.

Then down from the house came two more assistants carrying a washtub between them. Behind them came Chauncey in a chef's hat made from a grocery sack, carrying a floor mop over his shoulder. The tub seemed to be full of fresh blood; it was the barbecue sauce, Chauncey's recipe, famous at every Juneteenth, as the Negroes call Emancipation Day, for thirty years. He dipped the new mop into the tub, and while a boy turned the crank, gave the boar his first basting. When he was turned belly-up he was seen to be stuffed and sewn with wire. Some said he was stuffed with the parts of a dozen chickens, some said with a barrelful of sausage meat and bread crumbs. Chauncey smiled knowingly; he wasn't saying.

GRAVEYARD BANQUETING
IN CHINA AND
BARBECUING IN HONG KONG

Feasting at the graveside is the happiest part of ancestor worship in China. I learned about the late spring picnics in honor of ancestors, which villagers call *hek saontu* (eating on the hill), from the sinologist Hugh Baker. In the New Territories of Hong Kong these events are financed by the income from trust land set aside by the ancestors. Whole pigs are brought already boiled, or roasted and glazed to a beautiful brown, and when the family clan is a thousand people strong there may be as many as seventeen pigs, as well as cooked chickens and ducks, squid, duck eggs, and green-yolked "one-hundred-year eggs" preserved in ashes and lime.

When the ancestors have extracted the spiritual content from the offering, the worshipers can eat it. After the ritual ceremony, they either take it home or cater on the spot. The cooked meat is chopped up into morsels and stir-fried briefly with vegetables and flavorings in woks set up over fires between the graves, while people squat on the grass around large wooden serving tubs waiting with little porcelain bowls to help themselves.

Though the Chinese do not generally much like sweet things, they bring little cakes made out of almond and lotus paste and glutinous flour stuffed with chopped peanuts, colored in lurid reds and pinks, and often leave them on the graves for the birds.

Another traditional occasion for bringing out food is the outing to watch the full harvest moon on the fifteenth day of the eighth lunar month, when special sweet and savory moon cakes with a duck egg inside are given away as presents and passed around as an expensive currency. The little brown pies are taken to the top of mountains, out to sea, or on the lakes, where a perfect view of the moon is assured.

For the Dragon Boat Festival on the fifth day of the fifth lunar month people take a pudding of glutinous rice and chicken, cooked in lotus leaves and tied with multicolored thread, to eat during the Dragon Boat races.

Ritual and ceremony apart, taking out food simply for the pleasure of eating it in the open is not part of Chinese life. It is more usual to purchase it ready cooked in the street. Popular foods available from stalls are squares of bean curd which can be smelled four blocks away when they are fried, green peppers cut into four pieces, each stuffed with glutinous rice and bits of fish. There is also beef and offal such as colored intestines and tripe, steamed or boiled with aniseed flavoring. In Hong Kong there are those extraordinary floating kitchens called sampans, as large as a small car, that specialize in seafood. They pull out live crabs, shrimp, or fish from a tank and cook it in front of you, usually steaming it with fresh ginger and spring onions, and serve it in a soy sauce with a hint of sugar accompanied by black beans and cooked peppers.

It was on a trip to the Seychelles islands, where the most popular meals at the hotel were the Creole barbecues, that I discovered grilled meats with a Chinese flavor. A look into the kitchen having revealed a giant drum of Heinz Sweet and Sour Sauce, I took myself to the island restaurants which advertised local foods. These were a mixture of French and African with Indian and Chinese overtones. The Chinese fishermen who have settled in the islands since the last century brought to many dishes their ways of flavor-

ing, most notably to the spare ribs and morsels of pork and the fish which people grill outside their corrugated iron huts.

Although barbecuing is not a traditional Chinese method of cooking, the delicate mixtures of soy sauce and sherry, minced ginger and garlic, vinegar, and sugar make excellent marinades and sauces, while the traditional mixture of honey and water makes an excellent glaze for grilled foods.

With the influence of Western culture, barbecuing has recently become very fashionable in Hong Kong, and not only with the rich. On Sundays there are queues of people waiting at the bus stop to be taken to the countryside half an hour's ride away, with bundles and bags hanging on poles balanced on their shoulders. They carry chunks of chicken, pork steaks, and spare ribs marinating in soy mixtures and the soft sweet yellowish bread rolls introduced by White Russian bakers. And they bring charcoal or wood for the stone pits and the brick barbecues that have been built out there especially for them.

Marinades and Sauces

These, more than anything else in Chinese cooking, are a matter of individual inspiration and taste, and though the elements do not vary much, the proportions do. Here are a few suggestions which will give a special Chinese fragrance to your barbecued foods. Use them for king-size shrimp (see p. 287), for bass and other fish, and for pork. Read about marinades (p. 203).

Soy sauce. Mix 6 tablespoons soy sauce with 4 tablespoons dry sherry, 2 teaspoons sugar, 4 tablespoons sesame or other oil, and a 1-in. (2 1/2-cm.) piece of fresh ginger root crushed in a garlic press or with the flat of a knife to extract the juice.

You can vary this by adding 4 crushed cloves, 1/2 teaspoon cinnamon or aniseed, a sprinkling of salt, and 1 dried tangerine peel cut into pieces.

For a garlicky flavor add as much as 5 cloves of garlic, crushed.

And if you like the stronger taste of Szechuan, you can have a good pinch of black or chili pepper or roasted and crushed Szechuan peppers.

Sweet-and-sour sauce. Mix 3 tablespoons each of soy sauce, tomato ketchup, and vinegar with 1 1/2 tablespoons sherry, 1 1/2 tablespoons sugar, and 1/2 teaspoon salt.

For a glaze to paint on the food toward the end of the cooking time, mix 2 tablespoons honey with 2 tablespoons water, and if you can get it from a Chinese store, 1 teaspoon five-fragrance spice.

Spare Ribs

There is not much meat on spare ribs, so if they are the main part of the meal you may need 1 1/8 lb. (1/2 kg.) per person. Back ribs are meatier. It makes things easier not to separate the ribs, which need a long slow cooking (over an hour) on a very gentle fire. Place the whole racks, rubbed with salt, bone side down, on the grill for about 20 minutes, then turn the meat side down for 10 minutes until nicely browned. Turn again and continue to cook with the bone side down for another 30 minutes at least, brushing frequently with one of the marinades, then turn a few times until well browned.

Pork Kebabs

Cut fillet or leg into 3/4-in. (2-cm.) cubes and leave for an hour in one of the marinades (see p. 278). Thread on skewers and turn over the fire for 7 to 10 minutes, brushing occasionally with oil until crisp and brown.

Or cut pork fillet into slices like large flat coins, marinate, and put on the grill.

Spicy Pork Meatballs

To 2 1/4 lb. (1 kg.) ground pork add 3 tablespoons sherry, 3 tablespoons soy sauce, 1 1/2 teaspoons sugar, salt and pepper to taste, 4 spring onions, finely chopped, and a 3/4-in. (2-cm.) piece of fresh ginger root, crushed in a garlic press to extract the juice. Work well together and roll into small round balls or flat cakes (which are more practical). A basket grill is useful to turn them over. Cook until they are crisp on the outside but still tender inside.

Vegetables Stir-fried in a Wok

If you want to bring a wok along, you can stir-fry any number of vegetables to accompany your meats. You can have Chinese lettuce, cabbage, celery, cauliflower, peas, snowpeas, broccoli, spinach, bean sprouts, or mushrooms, or a few of these.

Wash and drain well, slice thinly, cut into little pieces, or divide into flowerets, as required. Sauté quickly in very little oil on a high flame until the vegetables are done but still crisp. Do not overcook.

You need season with only a light sprinkling of salt or you may flavor with a little crushed garlic, grated fresh ginger, and a few finely chopped spring onions.

You may also add some canned vegetables such as baby corn, grass mushrooms, or bamboo shoots and cook them through.

A SOUTHEAST ASIAN
SELECTION

Where Islam has taken root at the confluent of India and China, the Arab art of the grill and the skewer has attained a special subtlety in the form of saté foods. Nowhere has an amalgam of culinary tastes and ways come together so successfully to the advantage of the barbecue as in Southeast Asia. The cooking of Indonesia, Thailand, Malaysia and Singapore, Burma, Laos, and Vietnam is full of variety and reflects the mixed cultural heritage of their multiracial and multireligious populations. A wide range of regional styles of cooking has combined with the influence of Arab traders and Islamic scholars to produce a variety of interesting sauces and marinades in a region where the basic cooking apparatus is still the open charcoal fire. Dishes bear the imprint of the old civilizations of India and China in varying degrees as well as a touch of the scents of Holland, Spain, and Portugal.

Inspired and guided by Rosemary Brissenden's *South East Asian Food* and Alan Davidson's *Seafood of South East Asia,* I have taken the liberty of borrowing and adapting the varied flavorings of the region. People there have been doing just that from each other for centuries. The selection I include is merely an introduction to the local blends of soy sauce and chilies, rice wine, tamarind, fish paste, and coconut milk. Those who wish to discover the true culinary traditions of the area must refer to these books as well as to Sri Owen's *Indonesian Food and Cookery* and Phia Sing's *Traditional Recipes of Laos.* The last was written by the man who was in charge of the royal kitchens in Luang Prabang until 1965. He was also court doctor, poet, choreographer, and architect. Although *Modern Thai Cooking* by M. L. Taw Kritakara and M. R. Pimsai Amranand does not have much in the way of grilled foods, there are some delightful accompanying dishes.

I have drawn on these books and simplified many dishes. The marinades and sauces have many ingredients, none complicated, and making them with an electric blender or food processor is a very simple and speedy matter. If you want to make the ingredients yourself as they are prepared locally this may take a little time and effort but it is not impossible. Coconut milk is made by soaking freshly grated or desiccated coconut in water (about 2 1/2 cups/600 ml. for 1/2 lb./225 g.) for 20 minutes and passing the liquid through a fine sieve. Tamarind juice is made by soaking the dried fibrous pod in water and straining. However, creamed coconut and tamarind paste are now available in Oriental stores and need only be diluted with water. Fish sauce and paste can be bought in cans or packets or substituted with shrimp or anchovy paste. Several types of soy sauce can be found everywhere. The spices are those on the shelves of most supermarkets. I have used nut oil instead of coconut, and peanut oils and lemon zest instead of lemon grass. Medium dry sherry is the nearest thing to rice wine. You can use crunchy peanut butter instead of fried and ground peanuts. Fresh ginger can be found in many grocers throughout the year. You obtain the juice by squeezing a piece in a garlic press. For the purpose of a marinade and a sauce, these things will be good enough. Use the measures given as a rough guide to improvise with what is available, combining the ingredients to taste and making them as hot as you like. (Read about marinades on p. 264.)

A Well-Chosen Platter of Mixed Saté

Prepare a meat or a fish platter, or both, and make a peanut sauce (see p. 283) to be reheated in a saucepan on the barbecue. Accompany with a large salad of raw vegetables cut up and set out in a manner that also pleases the eye and with plain rice (p. 74) if you like. Follow with a selection of exotic fruit.

Meat and Chicken Saté

Use tender cuts of beef (preferably steak), lamb (preferably leg), pork (fillet, leg, or chop), or chicken. Remove skin, bones, fat, and gristle and cut into 1/2-in. (1 1/4-cm.) cubes. Thread onto wooden saté or thin bamboo sticks or small skewers. Soak in one of the following marinades for about an hour. Grill briefly on a hot fire, turning often and basting with oil so that the meat does not dry out. To serve, arrange the skewers on a large heated platter. You may pour peanut sauce (p. 283) over them or use it as a dip. Garnish with lime wedges and, if you like, some finely chopped or minced fresh chilies.

Fish and Seafood Saté

Prepare a large variety of different kinds of fish and seafood. Chunks of firm fish, cockles, clams, mussels, shrimp, and cuttlefish can be threaded onto skewers and marinated. Whole fish must be cleaned and gutted but not necessarily scaled. If you want to marinate the fish, remove scales and make a few incisions on the side. Grill quickly, turning over once and basting frequently with oil and the marinade until it is done and lightly colored.

Marinades

For pork combine 4 tablespoons oil, 4 tablespoons soy sauce, 2 tablespoons honey, 2 tablespoons vinegar, 1 teaspoon aniseed, 2 crushed cloves garlic, salt, and pepper. You may add a little ginger juice by squeezing a piece in a garlic press.

For lamb blend an onion with 4 tablespoons oil and 4 tablespoons soy sauce, adding salt and pepper to taste.

For beef mix the juice of half a lemon and 1/2 teaspoon pure tamarind extract diluted in 2 tablespoons water, with 4 tablespoons soy sauce, 1 teaspoon sugar, 3 crushed cloves garlic, 1 grated onion, and salt and pepper to taste.

For chicken (1) combine 4 tablespoons dark soy sauce with 1 tablespoon honey, 2 tablespoons sherry, 2 tablespoons ginger juice, salt, and a pinch of ground chili or black pepper.

(2) Or try a spicy coconut milk paste made by adding 1/3 cup (85 g.) creamed coconut to 2/3 cup (150 ml.) hot water. When it is soft, beat well to a thick cream. Add 1 teaspoon pure tamarind extract and the following ground spices: 1 tablespoon coriander, 1 tablespoon fennel, 2 teaspoons cumin, 3/4 teaspoon turmeric, 2 teaspoons cinnamon, the seeds of 3 cardamom pods, and a good pinch of nutmeg and chili to taste. Beat well and add 1 tablespoon ginger juice, 1 grated onion, and 2 crushed cloves garlic.

For fish and seafood (1) mix 5 tablespoons soy sauce with 1 tablespoon ginger juice, 3 tablespoons dry sherry, salt, and pepper. If you like you may also add 2 crushed cloves garlic and 2 minced chilies. For a sweet-and-sour taste, add 2 tablespoons vinegar and 2 tablespoons honey or sugar.

(2) Dissolve 1/4 cup (60 g.) bought creamed coconut in 1/3 cup (80 ml.) hot water. Put it in the blender with 1 small onion, 1 clove garlic, 2 small fresh red chilies, a little grated lemon zest, and salt and pepper to taste.

(3) Dissolve 1 teaspoon tamarind extract in 1/3 cup (80 ml.) water. Add 5 tablespoons nut oil, salt, and pepper.

Peanut Sauce

There are many versions of this peanut and coconut sauce which accompanies grilled meats and fish alike. Spoon it over the skewered pieces when they are ready to serve, or serve as a dip. For this, provide a pile of lettuce leaves to wrap the grilled morsels, and dip them in the sauce before eating.

It is worth making a large quantity at the risk of having some left over. All the ingredients need not be used. Make your own selection to suit your tastes.

Put through a blender or blend to a paste in a food processor:

2 onions	1–2 tablespoons shrimp paste
4–6 cloves garlic	2 teaspoons ground coriander
2–8 fresh hot chilies (or more depending on how hot you like it)	2 teaspoons ground cumin
	1 teaspoon fennel

Fry the paste in 4 tablespoons oil in a large saucepan until the aroma rises. Then add:

3/4 cup (180 g.) creamed coconut, dissolved in 1 cup (1/4 liter) boiling water in a saucepan	2–4 tablespoons soy sauce
	1–2 tablespoons sugar
	Grated zest of 1 lemon
2 teaspoons tamarind extract dissolved in a few tablespoons of water	1 1/2 cups (340 g.) crunchy peanut butter
Juice of 1 lime	Salt and pepper to taste
2 tablespoons ginger juice	

Stir well, add a little water to thin it down, and simmer gently for 6 to 10 minutes until the sauce is thick and homogeneous. Heat it up again when you are ready to serve.

A Large Salad of Crisp Raw Vegetables

Use any of these which are available: cucumber, water chestnuts, bamboo shoots, long white radish, celery, fennel, and snowpeas cut into thin sticks or slices. Shred Chinese cabbage and romaine lettuce and add sprouts, blanched if you like. For color you may add carrots, red radishes cut into slices, and firm tomatoes cut into thin wedges. For a sharp note you can have tart fruits such as green papaw or mango, pineapple, gooseberries, or Granny Smith apples finely sliced (dip in acidulated water to prevent tarnishing).

Before serving toss in the traditional dressing: the juice of 1 lemon, 2 teaspoons sugar, 1 tablespoon fish sauce (or salt to taste), a pinch of ground chilies or freshly ground black pepper to taste. Try adding a small grated onion or 1 or 2 cloves of garlic, crushed. Or you may prefer a vinaigrette.

Garnish with sprigs of fresh mint, coriander leaves, watercress, or parsley very finely chopped or minced fresh chilies or preserved ginger and slices of garlic fried in oil.

Exotic Fruit

The best possible conclusion to a Southeast Asian meal is a selection of exotic tropical fruits such as mangoes, papaya, guavas, pineapple, lychees, and bananas. Serve them in a large flat basket on a bed of leaves.

Otherwise have a fruit salad of the same fruits, canned.

INDIAN OUTDOOR
COOKING FEASTS—
A RELIC OF THE RAJ

In India, eating is a private affair not to be witnessed by onlookers, and it is regarded as improper to eat in the open. Besides, it is often too hot, and flies and wasps, monkeys, and dangerous animals are familiar intruders. It is only the poor who have their tables and their pots and pans beneath the sky of necessity.

But there are a few occasions when eating outdoors is socially acceptable and a matter of pleasure. Traveling is one of them; hunting expeditions in the mountains are another. For both, people bring their servants, who cook the usual everyday foods over charcoal stoves with all the necessary kitchen equipment. At the pavilions, where large parties spend the night or several days, and where men and women are segregated, the women supervise the preparation of the meals in the open while the men go hunting deer, partridge, quail, and rabbit.

Picnics as such are not part of Indian life but a relic of the Raj, an Anglo-Indian inheritance. The British introduced picnics as a form of festivity in India in the seventeenth century in the early days of the East India Company. During the Raj they gave private parties in their gardens and occasionally rode out to a picnic in the cool of the morning. They made themselves comfortable under the shade of a mango tree, spreading out carpets, cushions, and mattresses and hanging out mosquito nets from branch to branch. They returned in rickshaws and palanquins, happy with food and lulled to sleep by the swaying of the palanquins and the soulful chant of the bearers.

Denis Kincaid describes Anglo-Indian picnics in *British Social Life in India, 1608–1937,* as stately formal affairs with squadrons of horses riding out and: "Being arrived and alighted a curious cold collation is orderly set forth on large Persian carpets, under the spreading shade of lofty trees, where a variety of wine and music exhilarate the spirits to a cheerful liveliness and

render every object divertive." There is also a description by Macdonal, a literary footman, of how his master Colonel Dow set off in a large sailing boat with

> . . . a vessel following us with all the necessaries for an empty house, servants, two havaldors or sepoy sergeants, twelve sepoys with their arms, four flanakins, with eight men for each, four saddle horses, with their keepers. We had plenty of provisions for us for two days in the boats. I was greatly delighted and thought it was a pleasant thing to live under the East India Company.
>
> As the boat sailed up the wide creek towards Thana, the gentlemen drank punch together while two musicians played French horns. In those quiet backwaters where an occasional dhow mooed softly over the smooth, white water and a warm sea-wind sighed over the reeds stirring the landward leaning palms and sending the white egrets flapping slowly over the terraced paddy fields, it was delightful to recline on cushions while servants filled and refilled one's glass; and the gentlemen's spirits rose and they burst into song; but after a few more rounds of punch they fell asleep. . . .

When the romantic tastes current in Europe spread to Anglo-Indian circles, nature itself became fashionable, at the same time as did sham Orientalism. Everyone talked of leaving the stuffy cities for the rest and refreshment of natural scenery and the profound reflections inspired by it. As in England, every young lady brought her easel and painting materials. And though the idylls were sometimes marred by attacks from monkeys or swarms of bees, the participants enjoyed themselves.

Miss Emily Eden, author of *The Semi-Detached House*, describes a party popular in Simla society in her 1839 diary:

> Our aides-de-camp gave a small "fête champêtre" yesterday in a valley called Annandale. The party, consisting of six ladies and six gentlemen, began at ten in the morning, and actually lasted till half-past nine at night. Annandale is a thick grove of fir trees, which no sun can pierce. They had bows and arrows, a swing, battledore and shuttlecock, and a fiddle—the only fiddle in Simla; and they danced and ate all day.

The food they served must have been the type described by Grace Gardiner and Flora Annie Steel in *The Complete Indian Housekeeper and Cook*, which they dedicated to "The English girls to whom fate may assign the task of being house mothers in our Eastern Empire": chaudfroid, crous-tade, mazarin, kromesquis, game pie, snipe pudding, and tapioca jelly.

These days the meals served in the hillside pavilions are a different story. Samosas and pakoris are handed around; dry vegetables are served. Vindalu, the hot delicacy of southern India, is especially popular because it does not have much sauce and because the vinegared curry keeps a very long time if covered with oil in a jar. But most popular are meats roasted on spits or grilled on skewers. The most elaborate, legendary hunter's meal consists of several animals, one smaller than the other, stuffed inside each other and cooked slowly on the spit.

One type of cooking which comes from the Northwest, predomin-antly Muslim India, and derives its name from the tandoor, the clay oven built out-of-doors in which it is usually cooked, is especially popular. Similar results can be obtained over a wood fire, and a variety of kebabs cooked on skewers and grilled fish make a large selection to choose from if you want to plan a barbecue with the flavors of India. (Read about the grill on page 241).

It is the yogurt marinade which tenderizes the meats, and the mixture of spices which makes tandoori foods and kebabs so good.

King-Size Shrimp

Peel and devein 1 1/8 lb. (1/2 kg.) shrimp. Marinate in a mixture of the following, blended to a cream, for at least an hour:

1 small onion	1 fresh hot green chili or a good
2–3 cloves garlic	pinch of cayenne pepper
3/4-in. (2-cm.) piece of fresh ginger	Salt
Juice of half a lemon	Chopped fresh coriander or
4 tablespoons vegetable oil	flat-leafed parsley

Drain and skewer or place on a grill over a medium fire. Cook 10 to 15 minutes, turning over once and brushing with oil until slightly browned.

Serve with a sprinkling of chopped fresh coriander or parsley.

Variations: Tamarind juice instead of lemon will give a tart flavor. Pour a teacupful of boiling water on a small lump of dried tamarind pulp and soak for an hour. Strain the liquid, squashing the soft pulp out of the fibrous material. Or dilute 1/2 teaspoonful of paste in a little water.

Swordfish, tuna, and other firm fish may be flavored in the same way and cooked on skewers.

Tandoori Fish

A tandoori paste is a symphony of tastes for which you must use your flair in mixing spices and flavorings.

Marinade for a large (2 1/4-lb./1-kg.) fish or for smaller ones. Blend the following to a paste—spices must be ground, the rest grated, crushed, or minced, or put through a blender or food processor.

1 medium onion	1 tablespoon coriander
6 cloves garlic	1 teaspoon cumin
1-in. (2 1/2-cm.) piece of fresh ginger	2 teaspoons fennel or aniseed
	5 cardamom pods
1 fresh hot green chili or a good pinch of cayenne pepper (more to taste)	1 teaspoon cinnamon
	Salt and black pepper
	1 teaspoon orange food coloring
Juice of 1 lemon	

Beat 2/3 cup (150 ml.) of either yogurt or oil into the paste.

Clean and scale the fish and make a few diagonal incisions in the skin. Rub the paste inside and out with your hands and leave for at least 2 hours. Roast on a spit or cook on a moderate grill, basting with oil or clarified butter (see p. 297) until the flesh begins to flake and the skin is crisp.

Serve with onion rings and lemon wedges and sprinkle with chopped coriander, mint leaves, or flat-leafed parsley.

Tandoori Chicken

It is so hot in the tandoor that a whole small spring chicken takes only 5 to 10 minutes to cook. It takes longer on an open fire and needs constant brushing with oil or melted butter to keep it from drying out. Whether it is plump or small, cut it into pieces. If it is a small spring chicken allow a leg and a breast for each person. Skin and make a few incisions in the flesh with a sharp knife to allow the marinade to penetrate better. Leave it to soak in the marinade for 24 hours.

Marinade for 2 chickens. The mixture is highly individual, but here is a list of usual ingredients to try. Mash them to a paste in a blender before adding the yogurt (in India a few papaya leaves help to tenderize the meat).

1 large onion
6 cloves garlic
2-in. (5-cm.) piece of fresh ginger
Juice of 1 lemon
1 tablespoon ground coriander
1 teaspoon garam masala (p. 191)
1 teaspoon ground cumin
1 teaspoon ground turmeric

6 cardamom pods
1 teaspoon ground cinnamon
A pinch of cayenne or chili pepper
  or to taste
1 teaspoon orange or red
  food coloring
4 tablespoons oil
Salt

Beat paste with about 1 cup (235 ml.) yogurt in a bowl and turn the chicken pieces in this to coat them well. Leave, covered, in the refrigerator, turning the pieces a few times.

Cook on the grill (see p. 241), basting often with the marinade as well as with oil or clarified butter (see p. 297).

Serve with quartered lemons and garnish with onion rings, softened and rendered mild by soaking in cold salted water for about an hour.

This is a beautiful dish to serve. You may vary the shades of orange and red obtained by the combination of spices with varying amounts of red and yellow coloring.

For chicken tikka use chicken breasts alone. Cut them into strips and leave them in the marinade for as long as possible. Thread on skewers and grill, basting often with clarified butter.

Seekh Kebab

Use lamb or mutton free from skin and tendons but with a good amount of fat to keep the kebab moist and juicy. The secret is to work the ground meat to a paste so that it sticks well together around the skewer. Mince it twice and work it with your hands or put it through a food processor.

For 2 1/4 lb. (1 kg.) ground meat add the following flavorings to taste (sample the meat raw to test their intensity). The spices must be ground. In India they are usually freshly roasted or fried to bring out the best of their flavor before they are ground.

1 tablespoon coriander

1 teaspoon cumin

2 teaspoons cinnamon

A good pinch of nutmeg

A good pinch of mace

A pinch of cloves

1 teaspoon garam masala (p. 191)

Seeds from 3 cardamom pods

1 large onion, grated

1-in. (2 1/2-cm.) piece of fresh ginger, crushed in a garlic press

3 cloves garlic, crushed

A squeeze of lemon

3 tablespoons yogurt

A few sprigs of fresh coriander leaves, chopped

A few sprigs of fresh mint leaves, chopped

A few sprigs of parsley, chopped

1–2 hot green chilies, minced, or 1/2 teaspoon or more cayenne pepper

Salt and black pepper

Leave to stand, covered, in a cool place for 2 or 3 hours.

Take lumps of ground meat and press into a sausage shape about 1 in. (2 1/2 cm.) in diameter around skewers (with a wide flat blade so that the meat does not slide). Place on a grill over medium heat. Cook gently, turning over once (basting with oil or clarified butter—see p. 297—is necessary only if there is not enough fat), until they are brown but still tender and juicy inside (see p. 256).

Serve with lemon wedges and slices of raw onions softened by sprinkling with salt for 30 minutes.

Accompany with chutneys (see p. 310) and a yogurt raitas (see p. 291).

It requires experience to hold the meat on the skewer, as it tends to fall off if you do not work quickly. It is easier and just as good to shape the meat into round cakes (like a small hamburger).

Bhoti Kebab / Cubed Lamb or Mutton

Cut 2 1/4 lb. (1 kg.) lean lamb or mutton into cubes (see p. 254). Leave in a marinade prepared with the following ingredients—preferably turned to a paste in a blender. The spices must be ground and the yogurt added last. The quantities of spices are large, but the marinade is not too strong.

1 onion

1-in. (2 1/2-cm.) piece of ginger

8 cloves garlic

2 green chilies or 1/2–1 teaspoon cayenne pepper

1 tablespoon garam masala (p. 191)

1 tablespoon coriander

1 tablespoon cumin

2 teaspoons cinnamon

Seeds from 4 cardamom pods

A pinch of nutmeg

A pinch of cloves

Juice of 1 lemon

Salt and pepper

2/3 cup (150 ml.) yogurt

Put in a bowl with the meat, turning the cubes so that they are well coated. Leave in a cool place to marinate for 3 or 4 hours.

Drain and thread on skewers and cook over a medium fire until all sides are nicely browned, basting frequently with oil or clarified butter.

Serve with lemon wedges, softened onion rings (by sprinkling with salt and letting them lose juices), chutneys (see p. 310) and raitas (following recipe).

Yogurt Raitas

To balance spicy Indian grills there is nothing better than a refreshing yogurt sauce. Beat into 2 cups (1/2 liter) yogurt in a bowl the juice of half a lemon, 2 crushed cloves garlic, a few chopped mint leaves, and a finely chopped fresh green chili.

Variations: For a spicy raita add one or more of the following to taste, a pinch at a time: 1 teaspoon paprika, a good pinch of cayenne, 1/2 in. (1 1/2 cm.) ginger, squeezed in a garlic press to extract the juice, a good pinch of garam masala, a good pinch of cumin, a good pinch of coriander, and a few coriander leaves, chopped.

Other ingredients which are ordinarily added to yogurt for a raita include: grated carrots with chopped almonds, sliced bananas with sultanas, diced boiled new potatoes and roasted eggplant pulp (see p. 218).

You can turn it into a salad by adding raw vegetables such as 1/2 cucumber, peeled and grated or finely chopped, a tomato, finely chopped, 1 onion, finely chopped or grated, or 4 chopped spring onions and 1 green chili finely chopped or minced (optional).

Suggestions for the Traveler's Galley Kitchen and the Camp Cook

THE VAGRANT COOK

The food of expeditions has usually been a matter of sustenance. But for those who are as devoted to good food as to adventure, the challenge is no longer in traveling tough but rather in the opposite—in making it smooth and pleasurable. As Bradford Angier, the author of *Wilderness Cookery*, said: "We come to appreciate that making it easy on ourselves takes a lot more experience and ingenuity than bulling it through the tough way." Today many sailors and campers see cooking and eating as a way of enhancing their holidays, tasting local produce, and exploring new ways of preparing.

The job of the sea cook even more than that of someone traveling in a camper is one of planning and organization, of calculating quantities and numbers of meals and of deciding what must be done ahead of time. Menus must be worked out with regard to the type of vacation, its length and facilities, and local resources, so that meals may be adapted to eventualities such as delays due to weather conditions or an exhausting day when one is too tired to cook. Make lists of necessities, remembering that your provisions can be augmented by fresh local produce.

There are limitations which make vacation catering, whether on land or sea, different from cooking at home. The restrictions are those of space, equipment, fuel, and fresh water, and it is often difficult to keep perishables. A pan of boiling water or a frying pan of hot oil is a dangerous thing at sea, or even in port where a passing motor launch will rock your boat. But there are many advantages for those who travel with their cooking apparatus close at hand, not least that the cook is freed from serving everyday food and following recipes too closely.

The usual repertoire of vacation cooking is based on one-pan specials suitable for a single burner, on quick and easy meals and food that needs no cooking. For a brief weekend trip all that may be needed are picnic meals prepared in advance; if you are camping or plan to run your boat in a sheltered cove, it is from the section on barbecuing that you can draw inspiration, while on the move, or in open waters, sandwiches and finger foods or instant meals are required. For the lazy hours spent around camp or in settled moorings the preparation of the meal is the highlight of the day, when everyone joins in the catering and the cook is seldom abandoned to do all the work alone. Then is the time to embark on a sumptuous feast.

PROVISIONS AT SEA
OR IN A CAMPER

If you can buy fresh food as often as you like you will need only a few standbys, with your basic essentials of tea, coffee, sugar, marmalade, olives in oil, and the usual condiments, herbs, spices, oils, store-bought mayonnaise, butter, and alcohols which are necessary for good cooking. If conditions are uncertain you had best take with you as many good things made to last as you have room for.

It is difficult to keep perishables, especially in hot weather; an electric refrigerator is a rare luxury on a boat or in a camper, an ice box not always practical. And although the old and simple method of cooling by evaporation is effective, the capacity of a "wet box" made of porous cement or clay, kept wet in a reservoir or wrapped in wet towels, is limited. So buy little; take fruit and vegetables underripe, and check meat and chicken for spoilage.

Stow the provisions with a system so as to be able to find them easily in order of their keeping properties.

You may use stoneware or porcelain preserving jars, but soft plastic containers are best, as they are unbreakable and easily stacked. Smaller ones are better than larger ones as, if they are open for too long, there is a risk that the food will deteriorate. Tubes are better than bottles for condiments and sauces. At sea mark your jars and boxes with nail polish, as damp will cause paper to come off.

I have been told by an English yachting friend that he always uses dehydrated onions and potato flakes because of the time saved and the rubbish produced with the fresh variety. Powders and cans are the usual travelers' stocks these days, but it has not always been so. I wonder what has become of the great repertoire of preserved food amassed by nations of voyagers. Born of necessity, to store the abundance of one season against the scarcity of another and as a result of the gradual separation of country from town, these provisions were nevertheless something of a delicacy; smelling of alcohol and brine, vinegar and spices, swimming in oil, encased in pastry or set in butter or pig's feet jelly, salted or smoked, dried or pickled. A few such preserves still make nostalgic appearances in specialty foodstores, evoking memories of oiling, waxing, oatchaff and wheatstraw, baking paste and clay, and burying in sawdust.

Hams, swathed in a crust of muslin, used to be given several coats of whitewash for long keeping; fish was salted and hung up to become hard as wood on racks at the yardarm of sailing boats. Roast chickens were preserved whole in salted butter with spices; their legs were stewed for hours with veal bones to provide a liquor which, when reduced and strained, cooled into a hard jelly. This was cut into squares and dried out on a flannel to make an instant broth when dissolved in water. There was hung beef and beef cheese and cooked meats preserved in pots, set firmly with plenty of butter or suet to exclude the air, and sprigs of aromatic herbs laid on top to keep the flies away. Salt bacon, pickled mackerel, soused herrings, and potted salmon were taken to sea.

All these store foods were infinitely more interesting than the dehydrated and canned foods for which they were abandoned when the canning industries came into their own.

Mass production may be of vital importance, but it has nothing to do with gastronomy. Although we may not now wish to preserve our meat by burying it in pits or drying it in the wind, it is better to salt and spice it and surround it with fat than to buy it in cans. It is worth returning to some of the old methods of preserving food, for they produce delicacies which are hard to better.

Oil and Vinegar Sauces

To keep fresh herbs in oil, finely chop a bunch and cover with olive oil in a jar. This turns into a convenient sauce for pasta with the addition of salt and pepper and crushed garlic. Parsley makes the most common sauce and basil the much loved pesto.

Sami Zubaida flavors a mixture of olive, walnut, and nut oils with a piece of ginger, cut into thin slices, and a few sprigs of fresh coriander leaves.

Piri-piri, a hot Portuguese sauce which originated in Africa, is made with dried chilies. Fill about a third of a bottle with chilies and cover with olive oil. You may also add a few cloves of garlic and some lime juice. Leave for a month for the flavors to be absorbed before you use it. It is very strong, so use it discreetly. It makes a good sauce to brush on grilled chicken as it cooks. Two tablespoons are enough for 1 chicken.

A large quantity of vinaigrette may be prepared in advance for instant use (for basic recipe and variations see p. 79).

My friend Ans Hey keeps a jar of vinegar which she fills with lemon slices, garlic cloves, and bunches of the herbs that grow wild around the house, and occasionally a strong chili.

Agro Dolce is an unusual Italian sweet-and-sour sauce to serve with cold meats and fish. Dissolve 1/2 cup (100 g.) sugar in 1 1/4 cups (300 ml.) good wine vinegar in a pan. Add 1/4 cup (60 g.) ground almonds and 1/4 cup (60 g.) currants or raisins. Other possible additions are cherries, pine nuts, and candied peel, and a few mint leaves will give a refreshing flavor.

Bring to the boil and stir occasionally until it thickens.

See the section "Cold Sauces and Relishes" (pp. 79–90) for other sauces that keep well.

Butters

Unsalted butter does not keep as well as salted butter, but rid of its sediment it keeps perfectly well for months and does not burn brown during frying.

To clarify butter, heat slowly in a pan until thoroughly melted and frothy, then chill in the refrigerator for a few hours until the thick layer of clarified butter sets firm on top of the undesirable residue. Transfer the butter carefully to another pan, leaving behind the residue. Melt the butter again, and when it froths strain the clear liquid through a cloth into a jar. Make a large quantity; it will come in handy.

The French make a variety of flavored butters which they call *beurres composés.* They last as long as butter does and can be drawn upon to spread on a sizzling hot steak or grilled fish and to make an omelet. If they will need to last long they should be made with *clarified* butter.

Herb butter. Beat some unsalted butter with a spoon until it is light and creamy and add any fresh herb that you like—parsley, tarragon, chives, basil, mint, chervil, cress, blanched or not, and finely chopped. Season with salt and pepper and a squeeze of lemon. You can please yourself about quantities, but usual proportions are 2 to 3 tablespoons of herbs and the juice of a quarter lemon for 1/3 cup (85 g.) butter. With tarragon it is pleasant to substitute Madeira or port for the lemon juice. With basil a touch of crushed garlic is appreciated.

Garlic butter. Add 2 crushed cloves garlic to 1/4 lb. (115 g.) softened butter. You may like to boil the garlic for a few minutes until its taste has mellowed.

For anchovy butter beat 2 to 3 anchovy fillets, minced or pounded, with a squeeze of lemon and some pepper into 1/4 lb. (115 g.) butter.

For a mustard-flavored butter simply mix 1 or 2 tablespoons Dijon mustard into 1/4 lb. (115 g.) butter.

Flavored butter can include ground bitter almonds, chopped hard-boiled eggs, Roquefort cheese, chopped spring onions or mild grated onions, chopped capers, and gherkins. Some people add red or white wine or meat juices, or color the butter with paprika. Recently, flavored butters with the strong taste of cayenne, curry powder, or Worcestershire sauce have become popular in France.

   Whichever you choose to make, press it in a container, cover with paper, and keep it cool.

Special Mustards

Condiments attain a high degree of importance when facilities are limited. Here are two ways of making special mustards.

For a French moutarde aux anchois, chop and pound 8 anchovy fillets and combine with about 3/4 cup (180 ml.) Dijon mustard. Keep it in a little pot.

For an Italian mustard sauce, put a glassful of white wine in a saucepan with a small onion, stuck with 5 or 6 cloves, and a sprinkling of salt and pepper. Strain and stir gradually into about 1/2 cup (120 ml.) mustard. It will keep for months in a corked jar. White wine vinegar diluted with water can be used instead of wine.

Tomato Sauce

In Italy many people keep this sauce at home in a jar as an instant topping for spaghetti and as a useful base for various dishes. It keeps a long time if a good layer of covering oil is replaced every time it is drawn from. Make a large quantity.

   Fry 4 large chopped onions in 5 tablespoons olive oil, stirring until they are soft and golden. Add 3 1/2 lb. (1 1/2 kg.) tomatoes (skinned and quartered) or two large 1 lb. 12 oz. (800 g.) cans peeled tomatoes and crush them with a wooden spoon. Add a 2-oz. (60-g.) can of tomato purée, a carrot, and some celery leaves, all finely chopped, 5 large cloves garlic, crushed, a good pinch each of thyme, basil, and oregano, 2 slices of lemon, 3 bay leaves, a small bunch of chopped parsley, salt and pepper, and 1 or 2 tablespoons sugar. Cook slowly for 30 minutes, stirring occasionally and adding a little dry white wine or water if necessary. Pour into a large glass jar when slightly cool, covering with a thin layer of oil.

You may use this sauce to poach eggs in or to cook ham or bacon or chicken livers previously fried in butter.

If you are by the sea and find clams, make spaghetti alle vongole. Clean and soak the shells. Put them in a large pan with very little water. They will open after a few minutes of steaming. Take them out of the shells, add them to the tomato sauce, and heat it through. Cover the sauce again with oil every time after use.

Vegetable Pickles

Pickles play an important part in the sensual life of the Middle East. Greek grocers encourage prospective buyers to taste from their barreled selections, and cafés display them prominently in their windows. One childhood memory which evokes particular longing, since its delights were debarred from me for reasons of hygiene, is that of the pickle vendor installed on the street with a row of glass jars of the most alluring colors. Those of his customers squatting around him who could not afford pieces of vegetable seemed ecstatic only to soak up the liquor, usually colored pink by bits of beets, with a piece of bread. But we made our own variety and kept a constant supply, as did most other homes, to cut up into little pieces as mezze to accompany a glass of beer or ouzo, or as ready provisions for the picnic basket.

It is well worth investing in some large pickling jars and embarking on this most easy and rewarding activity, which provides wholesome holiday provisions.

The following recipes use old-fashioned methods and have a long enough life for a vacation but will generally not last indefinitely.

Mixed Pickles

It is a good idea to pickle several different vegetables together. They give taste and color to each other and provide a selection to choose from in one jar. Use a mixture of any of the following: turnips, carrots, cabbage, green beans,

cauliflower, cucumber, melon, sweet peppers, small pickling onions. Red cabbage and beets will give the pickles a beautiful red color. Trim or peel and thoroughly wash 2 1/4 lb. (1 kg.) vegetables. Cut into small pieces and pack tightly in jars with 2 or 3 small whole chili peppers, 3 or 4 cloves of garlic, slivered, and a few celery leaves. Bring to the boil salted water and white wine vinegar in the proportion 4 cups (1 scant liter) water to 2/3 to 1 1/4 cups (150 to 300 ml.) white vinegar and 2 to 4 tablespoons of salt, and pour over the vegetables while still hot. With the lesser quantities of vinegar and salt the vegetables taste more of themselves and are much better, but they do not last as long. The pickles will be ready to eat in about a week and will keep for about 2 months in a cool place.

Variations: For a Chinese flavor add 2 pieces of fresh peeled ginger root.

For an Indian one add 2 tablespoons mixed cumin, coriander, cinnamon, and cayenne pepper with a pinch of turmeric for its yellow color.

Another good alternative is to replace the chilies, garlic, and celery with 20 peppercorns, 20 juniper berries, a good pinch of mustard powder, and one of cayenne pepper.

Pickled Turnips

A Middle Eastern favorite. Trim, peel, and wash 2 1/4 lb. (1 kg.) small white turnips. Cut them in halves or quarters. Pack them in a clean glass jar with a few celery leaves, 2 to 4 cloves garlic, slivered, and 1 large sliced raw beet, placed at regular intervals.

In a stainless steel saucepan bring to the boil a solution of 4 cups (1 liter) water, 2/3 cup (150 ml.) white wine vinegar, and 3 level tablespoons salt. Pour over the vegetables to cover while still hot. Close tightly and store in a cool place.

The turnips should be mellow and pink right through within a week.

Eggplant Pickle

Pickles in oil last indefinitely and make an excellent salad.

Slice 2 1/4 lb. (1 kg.) eggplant. Sprinkle layers with salt in a colander and allow 2 hours for the salt to draw out the bitter juices. Wash the slices and poach for 5 minutes in about 1 cup (1/4 liter) wine vinegar and a little water to cover.

Drain and arrange in layers in a large glass jar, sprinkling each layer with a little crushed garlic (use 4 to 6 cloves) and a pinch of oregano. Cover with olive oil and close the jar tightly.

The pickles are ready to eat in a few days and can be kept for months.

Green, Red, or Yellow Pepper Pickle

Grill peppers as close to heat as possible, turning them until the skin is charred. Peel, core, seed, and slice into thick strips. Put in a jar with a few anchovy fillets and slices of lemon and cover with oil.

Pickled Fish

One of the things that Egyptian village folk brought back to Cairo from their visits home was *fessih:* fish that had been salted and buried in burning hot sand to dry. Every civilization has developed a way of curing fish to preserve it. It has been salted and hung like clothes in the wind, laid on stones in the sun, and smoked over slow fires in sheds and barrels, resulting in a wide variety of tastes, much to the advantage of travelers and nomads. Although in the past the rock-hard kite-shaped board of salt cod has gone on many a long journey all over the world, today the problem of cooking it in a camper or under canvas is that water is usually in short supply and too much of it is required to desalt and freshen the fish. It is better to take along good-quality cans of sardines, tuna fish, and anchovies in oil to serve as part of a mixed hors d'œuvre or simply with bread and butter and a squeeze of lemon. It is better still to take fresh or mildly cured fish soaked in a preserving marinade, which also gives it a most delicious taste.

Marinated and Pickled Kippers

My parents keep a constant supply of kippers in oil which they bring out with olives and cheeses for a snack luncheon. This is their recipe. For 1 1/2 lb. (3/4 kg.) plump juicy kippers mix the juice of 1 1/2 lemons and 1 tablespoon sugar with enough light vegetable oil to cover the fillets in a jar. Sprinkle layers of fillets with the marinade and some chopped onion. Make sure the kippers are properly covered with oil. They will be ready to eat in 4 days and will keep for a long time. For me they are lovely as they are, but you may also use wine vinegar instead of or with the lemon juice as well as cayenne or black pepper.

Salted herrings can also be treated like this, but soak them in water to remove some of the salt first.

Kippers marinated in white wine. A popular French method. Clean and bone
6 fat kippers. Place the fillets in a container, sprinkling each layer with
a little finely chopped onion, black peppercorns, a bay leaf, thyme,
and a few drops of wine vinegar (another version also uses a clove of
garlic, a tablespoon of Dijon mustard, and half a dozen cloves). Cover
with white wine and leave to marinate for at least 5 days. This will keep,
closed, for many weeks.

Soused Herring or Mackerel

In France dry white wine is used, in England it is malt vinegar or dry cider,
and in Denmark a sweet-and-sour flavor is given to fish by adding a good
amount of sugar as well.

Cook the fish whole if they are small, simply beheading and cleaning. Or
you may split them and pull out the backbones. In England the fillets are
rolled up lengthwise and packed closely in an earthenware pot; in France they
lay them flat on an ovenproof dish.

For 6 fresh herrings or mackerel, cover the fillets with a large onion,
thinly sliced, 1 tablespoon pickling spices, 1 dried chili, 3 bay leaves, a sprinkling of salt and pepper, and 1 cup (1/4 liter) dry white wine or dry cider or
a mixture of 2/3 cup (150 ml.) wine vinegar and the same amount of water.
Cover with foil or a lid and bake in a 285°F (140°C) oven for about 1 1/2 hours.
Let it cool and set in its jelly. It will keep for a week.

For a stiffer jelly to hold in hot weather, make a stock with the fish heads
and flavorings. Strain it well and reduce it quite considerably before mixing
with the wine.

Serve dressed with a vinaigrette or sour cream mixed with the fish liquor
or a horseradish and fresh cream sauce (see p. 86).

The fish can be cut into pieces as an ingredient of many a salad with such
companions as potato, tomato, apple, beets, hard-boiled egg, and gherkins.

Potted Things
and "Sailor Savories"

The manufacture of potted meats on a commercial scale had its origin in
England. They were so named because they were traditionally preserved
in earthenware pots with a thick layer of suet or butter set stiff to exclude
the air. For three centuries, potted meats were present on the breakfast and
tea tables of the genteel and discriminating. Cooks employed in large private households spent much time chopping and pounding cooked meats,

poultry, and game as well as fish and cheese, with butter and a variety of spices.

During the nineteenth century, potted meats began to be produced in bulk. Many firms went into the business, which became a very important and competitive branch of the preserving trade. The principal raw materials used in the manufacture of "sailor savories," as the traditional fare for seamen and travelers became known, were salmon, anchovies, shrimp, lobster, herring, chicken, turkey, ham, and tongue. They were used alone or in combinations such as salmon and anchovy, salmon and shrimp, chicken and ham, ham and tongue.

Now that potted meats are regarded more in the nature of delicacies and their price is accordingly high, it is well worth preparing them yourself. They are easy enough to make in large quantities, especially for those who have a food processor. A delicious ready meal to serve cold, cut in slices or spread on bread, accompanied by a salad or pickle, they also keep for a long time.

Potted Meats

Use cooked meat, preferably pot roasted or boiled. Beef, veal, lamb, and pork, as well as chicken, turkey, and game birds, rabbit and hare, make good potted meats.

Remove any bones, skin, gristle, and fat. Cut meat in slices against the grain, finely chop or mince, then pound well, or put in a food processor. Add a quarter of the weight in butter (more if the meat is dry) and beat or pound together to a smooth paste, adding salt and pepper and flavorings to taste. The usual spices to add are mace (an old English favorite but not mine), nutmeg, allspice, and cayenne. Cinnamon, cumin, coriander, cardamom seeds, and cloves are less common but equally good. All must be finely ground. Add one or two of these a little at a time and taste before you add more. You may also add a little dry sherry or port, by the spoonful (but not gravy or it will not keep as long), and prepared mustard.

Pack into pots or jars (plastic will do) and cover with melted clarified butter (see p. 297) to seal from the air. Press a piece of greaseproof paper on top and close with a lid.

It will keep for many weeks in a cool place, but every time you take some, you must seal the top again with clarified butter.

Serve with pickles and brown bread.

In the old days they liked to mix meats such as veal and tongue or chicken and ham, which gave a marbled effect when it was cut in slices. The combination of flavors is also good.

Potted Fish

Trout, salmon, char, and grayling are old favorites for this popular English conserve, but there is no reason why you should not use any fleshy fish.

Lightly poach in a stock or court bouillon (see p. 73) or bake it in the oven wrapped in aluminum foil. Remove skin and bones and break fish into pieces. Season with salt and pepper, mace and nutmeg, or spices of your choice. Put into small pots and cover with melted clarified butter. Stir it in between the pieces. When it is cool and firm add more clarified butter if necessary to cover the fish entirely with a 1/8-in. (1/2-cm.) layer. Cover with greaseproof paper or foil and a lid. It should keep for weeks in a cool place. Cover with butter again as you use it.

Serve with brown bread and butter, a salad, and dry white wine.

Fish Pastes

Smoked fish pastes are one of the most delicious things to have benefited from the present revival of old English food, and no one should be happier for their return after almost a century of neglect than vacationers who have to cater for themselves.

Kipper, finnan haddock, and bloaters should be jugged before they are used. Leave them in a pan of water, which has just boiled, for 5 to 10 minutes. Drain and remove skin and bones. Smoked mackerel, trout, and salmon are used as they are. Simply skin and bone, then mash and pound the fish with an equal quantity of butter, or put it through a Mouli, or into a blender or food processor together with the butter. Add lemon juice and cayenne pepper to taste; it is better strongly flavored.

Variations: Try adding a little port, dry sherry, or Cognac and spices such as ground cloves, nutmeg, and black pepper. Add a pinch at a time and keep tasting. Salt is not usually required.

Put the paste into little pots and seal by covering with melted clarified butter (see p. 297). Covered with foil or greaseproof paper, it will keep for a few weeks in a cool spot.

For a paste that will keep just a few days, you can use cottage or cream cheese or whipped cream instead of butter.

Potted Shrimp

Melt 3/4 cup (175 g.) clarified butter in a saucepan. Throw in 1 lb. (500 g.) cooked and shelled shrimp; add a good pinch or two of grated nutmeg and cayenne pepper and just a touch of salt. Heat up not quite to the boiling point. Pour into little pots, chill, and when the butter solidifies, add a little more melted clarified butter to seal the shrimp entirely from the air. This will keep for a few weeks in a cool place.

Serve with thinly sliced buttered brown bread or toast with dry white wine.

Potted Shrimp Spread

Finely chop or mince 1 lb. (500 g.) cooked and shelled shrimp. Add the juice of half or one whole lemon and its grated zest, salt and pepper, and a good pinch of nutmeg. Spoon into little pots and cover with melted clarified butter (see p. 297).

Potted Cheese

Hard cheeses last longer than soft ones, and a good old-fashioned English way of making cheese last even longer is to combine it with butter.

Use matured Cheddar, Cheshire, Stilton, or Roquefort. Pound the cheese in a mortar with about a quarter its weight in softened unsalted butter, adding a little brandy, port, or red or white wine to taste. Otherwise you may put everything in a food processor.

If you wish, add a sprinkling of pepper or cayenne, nutmeg or mace, or a little prepared mustard, and if necessary a little salt. You may also mix in a few chopped almonds or walnuts. Press into pots and seal with a thin layer of melted clarified butter (see p. 297).

Cheese in Oil

In the Middle East cheese is kept in oil. Feta and other soft cheeses are cut into cubes and covered with olive or a light vegetable oil in a jar. Yogurt, left to drain in a cloth until it is as firm as cream cheese, and mixed with a little salt and pepper and dried mint, is rolled into balls and treated in the same manner, to be spooned out as an appetizer with drinks or as part of a light meal.

I recently discovered in the Vaucluse, Picodons marinés, small rounds of goat cheese kept in olive oil flavored with the herbs of the region. They are quite a delicacy and worth trying with an ordinary chèvre.

Preserved Meats (Confits)

My father remembers summer expeditions to the mountains of Lebanon where a whole lamb was prepared for the family to bring back to Egypt. It was called *kawarma* and was treated as a delicacy throughout the winter months. These are his instructions for young tender lamb.

Separate lean from fat. Cut the meat into medium-size cubes. (You must have lumps, not slices, so that you can take them out easily.) Salt the meat. For 2 1/4 lb. (1 kg.) meat use a tablespoon salt and a pinch of saltpeter. Add a teaspoon of cinnamon and one of allspice or one each of cumin and coriander and some black pepper. Leave covered for 24 hours.

Chop up the fat, adding the fat of two other lambs (in Lebanon the tail, usually wobbling with fat, was rendered down) and melt it down in a large pan over high heat. Add the meat and turn the heat down very low. Stir with a wooden spoon and cook until the meat is just done and its juices are no longer pink. Allow to cool before putting the meat, well covered with its fat, into clean glass, earthenware, or plastic jars (well washed in boiling soda water). No refrigeration is needed.

The French make delicious confits on the same principle with pork, goose, turkey, duck, and rabbit. Jane Grigson gives detailed instructions for all of these in *The Art of Making Sausages and Pâtés, and Other Charcuterie.* They are easy enough to make in large quantities and will keep for a year if it is not too hot, as long as you are careful to keep the meat always entirely covered with fat.

Use boned pork from the hind loin, cut into large pieces, and cut up the birds and rabbit but do not bone them. For 4 1/2 lb. (2 kg.) of meats prepare a mixture of 1/4 cup (50 g.) salt and a good pinch of saltpeter with a teaspoon of thyme, one of mace, nutmeg, or allspice and 1/2 teaspoon black pepper. Rub it into the meat and leave it for 24 hours.

Melt down 2 1/4 lb. (1 kg.) fat from the meat augmented by lard in a large heavy saucepan. Add the pieces of meat and cook them very slowly for about 1 to 2 hours until tender and no juice comes out when you pierce with a knitting needle, but be careful not to overcook or the meat will be hard and dry (the saltpeter keeps it deceptively pink). In the meantime wash some plastic containers with boiling soda water so that they are perfectly clean. Pack the pieces of meat in, leaving 2 in. (5 cm.) at the top, and pour the strained fat to the brim (it will contract as it sets). Allow to cool and solidify, then press a piece of greaseproof paper down on it.

Serve cold or reheated.

Rillettes

This shredded belly of pork mixed with fat was one of the bright spots of my boarding school days in Paris. It takes time but not too much effort and is well worth the patience. For 3 1/2 lb. (1 1/2 kg.) belly of pork you will need 2 cloves garlic, salt and pepper, a good pinch of nutmeg or mace, 2 bay leaves, and 1/2 teaspoon thyme.

Cut the meat into pieces. Put them in a large, heavy saucepan with the rest of the ingredients and with pieces of pork rind at the bottom and sides so that the meat does not stick to the pan and burn. Add 3 or 4 tablespoons water and cook on the lowest possible heat, turning the pieces occasionally, until all the fat has melted and the meat is cooked but still soft and juicy. It can take up to 4 hours, so be careful that it does not reach the point when it begins to fry and becomes dry and crisp and hard. Do not be tempted to raise the flame. Pour everything into a sieve over a bowl. Remove pieces of rind and bones. Chop the meat and pull it into shreds with your fingers and adjust the seasoning. Now mash and pound it with enough of the fat to make a smooth paste. Press into plastic pots and pour over them enough melted fat to cover the meat well. When it has cooled and set, press greaseproof paper on top and cover with the lid.

Eat rillettes spooned onto a slice of bread. If you want a pot to last for weeks you should melt some fat or clarified butter and pour it in to reseal every time you use it.

Spiced Beef

Mostly a matter of waiting, curing meat is as much a gastronomic event as a method of preserving it. This is Jane Grigson's recipe, which appeared in the *Observer* magazine.

Buy a 2 1/2–3 kilo (5–6 lb.) joint of silverside or round of beef, cut and tied for salting. Rub it over with 100 g. (3 oz.) dark brown sugar, and leave it for two days, turning it several times.

Mix together 115 g. (4 oz.) sea salt or pure rock salt, a heaped teaspoon of saltpeter, and 30 g. (1 oz.) each crushed black peppercorns, allspice berries, and juniper berries. Rub this mixture into the beef and leave for 9 more days, turning it over once or twice a day and rubbing it with the dark liquor.

To cook, dab off the bits of spice, or rinse quickly. Place in a close-fitting pot—this is important—with a generous 1/4 liter (1 cup) water. Cover the top with shredded suet. Jam the lid on the pot with a double layer of foil or a flour and water paste. Bake in the oven at 140°C (285°F), for 45 minutes a pound. Remove pot and leave undisturbed for 3 hours to cool down. Take off lid, drain meat, and place on a board. Cover with greaseproof paper and put a 2-kilo (4-lb.) weight (or heavy tins) on top. Leave for 24 hours, before carving into thin slices. Serve with avocado and potato salad and horseradish sauce, or with orange and olive salad.

Salamis and Sausages

Salamis and sausages keep very well and make a substantial nourishing meal.

The Italians are the world's best makers of dried and smoked sausages, and the French excel in the fresh sausage which keeps for more than a fortnight at least. (If you are tempted to make your own, Jane Grigson's *The Art of Making Sausages and Pâtés, and Other Charcuterie* has everything that needs to be known for the making of sausages, blood pudding, salt pork, and hams.) A good delicatessen department will also sell Moroccan mergez and Central European boiling sausages as well as English pure pork luncheon sausages.

Elizabeth David gives a few suggestions for hot sausage dishes in *French Provincial Cooking* which make a quick meal on a camp stove: A saucisson à la Lyonnaise is simmered in water or red wine and served with a well-dressed potato salad. In Alsace the boiled saucisson is served with a horseradish sauce made by stirring 1 tablespoon grated horseradish into 2/3 cup (150 ml.) thick cream seasoned with salt and pepper and a squeeze of lemon juice.

Blood sausage, boiling sausage, and saveloys may be cut into thick slices and gently fried in pork fat, oil, or butter and served on a bed of fried apple slices or fried onions and accompanied by mashed potatoes.

If they are very good they may deserve this delicious sauce from Normandy: after frying the slices of sausages pour a glass of cider or white wine into the frying pan; let it bubble, then add 1 or 2 tablespoons of calvados or brandy and stir in 2/3 cup (150 ml.) heavy cream. Heat through.

Fruit Chutneys

Fruit chutneys are one area of Indian culture that has been well and happily absorbed into Western cooking. They have found their place with cold meats particularly. Recipes vary considerably in strength and fieriness, in sweetness and sourness, as well as in the complexity of their ingredients, so follow your preference especially in the flavoring. They will keep unrefrigerated for a few weeks.

Mixed Fruit Chutney

Use apples, plums, pears, apricots, peaches—all or two or three—cored, pitted, peeled, and cut into small pieces. Put them in a large, heavy saucepan. For 2 1/4 lb. (1 kg.) fruit add 2 tablespoons sultanas, 3/4 lb. (350 g.) sugar, 1 cup (1/4 liter) cider or wine vinegar, 1 to 2 teaspoons garam masala (see page 191), 8 large cloves garlic, crushed, salt, 1 teaspoon ground ginger, chili or cayenne to taste (from 1/2 to 2 teaspoons). Simmer gently for at least 45 minutes, stirring constantly, until the mixture is soft, sticky, and thickened.

Cool before you put it in a jar.

A Tomato and Apple Chutney

Green tomatoes are traditionally used, but here you have to grow them yourself. Red ones will do just as well. Skin 1 lb. (1/2 kg.) by covering with boiling water and chop them. Peel, core, and chop 1 lb. (1/2 kg.) tart cooking apples. Put in a heavy-bottomed saucepan with 1 large chopped onion, 4 cloves garlic, crushed, 2 tablespoons raisins, 4 prunes, seeded and chopped, 3/4 lb. (350 g.) brown sugar, 1 tablespoon salt, 1 1/2 cups (355 ml.) wine or cider vinegar, 1 teaspoon each ground ginger and allspice. Simmer very gently for more than an hour until the mixture has the consistency of jam, stirring often as it begins to thicken and become sticky.

Add a pinch of cayenne pepper toward the end of the cooking time if you like it fiery. Let it cool before you put it in a jar.

Banana and Date Chutney with Tamarind

To extract the sour juice from dried fibrous tamarind pods obtained at Indian shops is a messy and arduous business. The same shops now sell a concentrated tamarind paste which is not as good as the real thing but will do quite well for this purpose.

Dissolve 2 teaspoons tamarind paste in 2/3 cup (150 ml.) boiling water in a saucepan. Add 1 tablespoon sugar, 1 1/2 teaspoons powdered cumin, and 1 teaspoon salt. Throw in about 9 dates, pitted and chopped, and a small handful of slivered almonds, then slice into the saucepan 3 green (unripe) bananas. Stir until the liquor has been absorbed, adding a good pinch or as much as you like of cayenne pepper.

Cool before you put it in a jar.

Preserved Fruits

A good way of keeping fruit ever at hand is to preserve it in syrup or with wines or spirits. It makes the most delicious quick dessert to be served alone in its juice or with cream, yogurt, or cream cheese. Sliced or mashed to a purée, it can also be used as a filling for pancakes and sweet omelets or as a topping or sauce.

Pears in Red or White Wine

Peel 4 1/2 lb. (2 kg.) small hard pears, leaving their stalks on. Put them in a large pan with a bottle of wine and 2 1/2 cups (1/2 kg.) sugar, and simmer for about 45 minutes until tender. You can also flavor with 4 or 5 cloves, a stick of cinnamon, and the zest of a lemon.

Transfer the pears to a large jar. Reduce the syrup until it is thick enough to coat a spoon and pour it over them. You may add a few tablespoons of a pear brandy or a fruit liqueur such as cassis.

Serve the pears as they are or with cream, yogurt, or cream cheese.

Variations: Try other fruits cooked this way: peach halves, sour cherries, or apple slices (for these add the juice of half a lemon).

Port makes an excellent alternative to cooking with wine.

Fruits in Alcohol—a Mixed Pot

In the countries where spirits or eaux de vie, alcohols between 45° and 55°, are not too expensive, fruits are commonly preserved in them. Cheaper alternatives are vodka, gin, rum, and some brandies. Start the preserve early in the spring and you will be able to take it on your summer travels to savor after cheese or when coffee is served. It is very pleasant and not that extravagant.

Different methods find advocates who discover little tricks for perfecting them over the years. Some start with raw fruit, pricking the tougher-skinned varieties with a needle or blanching them first. The preserve is usually ready after 2 or 3 months.

A large pot of mixed fruit will provide an exciting selection. Use peaches, skinned and halved, melon, peeled, seeded, and cut into large chunks, apples and pears, peeled and quartered, cherries, grapes, and plums, pricked all over with a needle, pineapple chunks, apricots, strawberries, figs, and raspberries —whatever is available—all sound and ripe and well washed. Pack all the fruit tightly in a large pot or jar. How much sugar to use is a matter of some controversy and usually varies between a quarter of the weight of the fruit to the same weight. The fruit is less likely to ferment if you use more sugar. There are various ways of combining spirit and sugar. The simplest is to sprinkle layers of fruit with sugar and then to pour the spirit straight out of the bottle over the fruit. But it may be more effective to warm up the alcohol in a saucepan with the sugar until it is dissolved.

Make sure the fruits are well covered with liquor and seal well.

For a preserve which is ready within a month, poach the fruit in very heavy syrup with its own weight of sugar and half the volume of water, until it is slightly tender and rather sweet. Drain and reduce the syrup, then pour over the fruit and cover with alcohol in a jar. In Apt, the center for fruits confits in the south of France, where I stopped for *confiseries comme autrefois* (crystallized fruit as in olden times) from the makers, people were queuing to buy small whole fruit by the kilo while they were in the sticky syrup stage.

There were very tiny oranges, tangerines, pears, figs, and other fruits ready for taking home and soaking in armagnac, calvados, the apple brandy, guillaumin made from pears, Kirsch from cherry stones, or mirabelle from plums.

Apple Butter

Peel, quarter, and core 4 1/2 lb. (2 kg.) apples. Cook them in cider or white wine to cover and 2 1/4 lb. (1 kg.) sugar, to a very thick pulp (about 45 minutes). Pour into jars and seal.

Variations: Spice the apple butter with 2 teaspoons cinnamon, 6 cloves, and a small piece of fresh ginger, or add a few tablespoons of calvados or brandy at the end of the cooking time.

An alternative, called apple rum, is to cook the apples with sugar and about 2 cups (1/2 liter) water for 30 minutes. Then add 2/3 cup (150 ml.) rum and cook the paste for a further 15 minutes.

Spoon out when you feel like something sweet, or use as a sauce for dessert.

Dried Fruit and Nuts

The chosen picnic fare for William Cobbett, who toured the countryside on horseback in the early nineteenth century, was nuts and apples. He urges their merits with great fervor in his book *Rural Rides, with Economical and Political Observations:*

> At Gloucester we furnished ourselves with nuts and apples, which, first a handful of nuts and then an apple, are, I can assure the reader, excellent and more wholesome fare. They say that nuts of all sorts are unwholesome; if they had been, I should never have written Registers and if they were now, I should have ceased to write ere this for upon an average, I have eaten a pint a day since I left home.

Nuts and apples were his way of avoiding the exorbitant prices charged by the innkeepers along the road.

Many people who eat to "fill up" for sustenance would agree with him, and add dried fruits. These have been esteemed from time immemorial by the peoples of the Near East and the Mediterranean countries. Ever since the crusaders brought them back to Europe they have been the special diet of travelers, their instant sustainers and revivers.

There is now a large trade in all types of dried fruits—figs, pears, peaches, dates, apricots, apples, prunes—either whole or pitted and halved or cut into rings. The choicest are the ones dried naturally in the sun. The best figs and sultanas come from Smyrna, the best dates from Persia, Morocco, and Tunisia. Muscatel are the finest table dessert raisins. They are produced in the south of Spain, chiefly in the Malaga district. The largest and the ones that retain a bluish tinge are the best. Other excellent raisins come from Valencia, California, South Africa, Greece, and Cyprus, and the loveliest currants, rich blue-black and both sweet and acid, from Greece. Sweet Jordan dessert almonds come from the Malaga coast of Spain. Valencia almonds and those from Sicily are also sweet, while Barberry ones from North Africa are bittersweet. California is now one of the biggest producers of dried fruit and nuts, and their varieties are as good as any.

STREET FOOD

When traveling by camper or by boat you may be able to find all you need on the spot in the street or in port. Street food has to be discovered. Each country has its own. Where there is no restaurant tradition, this is the only way that foreigners will get to taste local food; the alternative is the cosmopolitan cuisine served in hotels. I have always found street food irresistible for the alluring displays and enticing smells, as well as for the cries of the vendors, which are able to rouse even a dormant appetite.

As a child in Cairo I was fascinated by the cries of peddlers and street vendors, itinerant sellers of all types of foods. I waited for each familiar voice to pass under my bedroom window to allay the boredom of my enforced siesta. Sometimes the cry was accompanied by the rattle of pieces of paper twisted around bicycle spokes or by the clinking of glasses or the clanking of brass plates. One man called out every day at two o'clock with a plaintive nasal voice "Aha awaw!" For a long time I wondered what he sold. With the shutters down I never had a chance to see him. When I escaped the siesta and finally saw him, he was selling nothing at all. Perhaps he liked the sound of his cry.

Vendors plying through the streets or standing in the market, carrying their wares on trays placed on tightly coiled cloths on their heads, or in baskets or barrels strapped to their shoulders, were a source of endless fascination. The more perishable the food, the greater the need to dispose of it quickly, the more pressing their cries.

I was impressed by the speed at which they peeled oranges and separated the segments, sprinkled salt on a cucumber, and cut a square out of a watermelon before a prospective buyer had made up his mind, eloquently praising the honey-sweet virtues of their fruits at the same time.

Each place had its specialties. Outside the open-air cinemas sesame bread rings called *semit* were sold with Greek cheese. The sea breeze on the corniche in Alexandria carried the smell of corn cobs roasted on charcoal. On the beach you had to toss a coin with the vendor to win a sesame crunch or lose it and still have to pay. Anyone who has taken a walk in Cairo knows the smoky smell of lamb fanned into their face, and that of the mashed white beans that make up falafel, turning brown in sizzling hot oil. And who has not been tempted by the pickled turnips, swimming in brine made pink by beets, by the deep-fried eggplant slices soaked in oil and lemon juice, or by the crisp round fritters soaked in syrup?

The smells of Baghdad are only a little different. They are spicier. Here too pickled turnips are sold in the streets, but they are often sweetened with dates. Boiled chickpeas, sprinkled with oil and pennyroyal mint, are offered steaming hot. Carts are laden with a decorative assortment of hard-boiled eggs, pickles in vinegar, beets, tomatoes, spring onions, young lettuce hearts, and bunches of fresh herbs. The vendor will cut everything up for you into slices or little cubes and drop it into the pouch of a flat round hollow bread. Kebabshi (kebab vendors) sometimes turn their barrow into a small restaurant by providing a few chairs to sit at and eat all manner of grilled meat and offal.

In Morocco, meat is cut very small and flavored with a greater variety of spices. Vendors squat over small braziers on pavements, browning their *mechoui* together with little spicy sausages called *mergez*.

A Tunisian street favorite called *brik* is a meal in itself. Paper-thin sheets of pastry, each wrapped in a parcel around a filling composed of an egg and a choice of other ingredients, are deep-fried for passersby.

In Tehran, those who get to the bazaar before 7:00 A.M. are able to sample *calepache*. This is a lamb's head rich with creamy brains stewed slowly in a large cauldron together with feet, tripe, and stomach. During the fasting month of Ramadan a meaty porridge called *halim* is the breakfast food which fills the cauldron with breast of lamb and oats sweetened with sugar.

The anthropologist Ahmet E. Uysal wrote in an article on "Street Cries in Turkey" in the *Journal of American Folklore* (1968) that the list of goods sold in the streets and open-air bazaars of Turkey from pushcarts, baskets, and directly off the ground would cover the entire range of human needs. Apart from the usual fruit, vegetables, meat, and fish, cooked foods are also available; soups at breakfast time and sweet pastries during festivals. You will also get metaphors, puns, exaggerated descriptions, earthy and salty humor, practical wisdom, and frequent appeals to the medicinal properties of the foods. Ped-dlers enjoy a good deal of license for insolence and can often be heard pouring

outrageous insults onto passersby or making rude retorts and using words with double meanings. Some set up a lecture platform and demonstration table to attract prospective buyers.

The best of Israeli food is also in the street, a legacy of the Ottomans reinforced by the ways of Arabs and Oriental Jews. It is here that national styles are forged, that young Israelis from different backgrounds form their conception of the food of their land. They have got used to grabbing a cheap snack on their way somewhere at all times of the day, and it is the different foods, which start at the initiative of the vendor and spread quickly into a rash of kiosks, that bring the tastes and ways of the different communities into the common national pool. Often, they are better than the food provided by the trendy restaurants which open one day and close the next. The cactus peeled for you with art, the sesame bread rings sold with the spice mixture *zahtar*, fish grilled at the harbor, *sanbusak* and *borekas* produced at the back of gasoline stations, and homemade hummus or falafel offered in the market-

place are the joys of the country which tourists often miss for fear of food
poisoning and because they are strange. For obvious reasons the warmer and
the poorer countries are richest in open-air culinary activities.

In recent years there has been a renaissance of street fairs in U.S. cities
and towns, where a melting pot culture produces Italian, Greek, Middle and
Far Eastern, as well as Pennsylvania Dutch foods.

It's more than thirty years since the Kutztown Pennsylvania Dutch
Festival was initiated by Franklin and Marshall College near Allentown,
Pennsylvania, to give American visitors an outdoors ethnic food treat. New
York's St. Anthony street fairs have featured not only Italian sausages and
calzones, but Argentine barbecue, Middle Eastern gyros, Korean and Philip-
pine satray. California friends speak fondly of the Danish town of Solvang,
south of Santa Barbara, which holds open house in September and people
drive for miles to picnic on Danish smorgasbord. The Ethnic Festival is the
big summer event in Butte, Montana, where twenty-one different immigrant

groups take over the streets to celebrate the cooking of their forebears. As early as 1938 Dothan, Alabama, gained fame for its annual Peanut Festival with contests for special peanut recipes, and fun and games and feasting for all comers.

At one time "frost fairs" were frequent all over England during exceptionally cold weather. The seventeenth-century diarist John Evelyn describes the tents and booths that were erected over frozen rivers. Oxen and sheep were roasted whole (they were called Lapland mutton) and "hot codlins, pancakes, duck, goose, sack, rabbit, capon, hen and turkey" were sold as well as mutton pies and hot black puddings. In the nineteenth century there were itinerant vendors with baskets, especially at coach-side and railway station. Lord Macaulay describes the hazards of a coach journey:

> I travelled to town with a family of children who ate without intermission from Market Harborough, where they got into the coach, to the Peacock at Islington, where they got out of it. They breakfasted as if they had fasted all the preceding day. They dined as if they had never breakfasted. They ate on the road one large basket of sandwiches, another of fruit, and a boiled fowl: besides which there was not an orange-girl, an old man with cakes, or a boy with filberts, who came to the coach-side when we stopped to change horses, of whom they did not buy something.

IMPROMPTU MEALS

One of the best ways of discovering regional foods when traveling is to stop at small shops and markets and purchase local specialties for an impromptu roadside picnic or a cheap meal in a city park. In most countries some of the bigger towns have a permanent market, while smaller ones have a street market once a week. In France they are a feast of color, scent, and bustle, with stalls beautifully laid out with shiny fresh fish, cooked meats, fruit and vegetables, and a multitude of cheeses, a song of praise for local produce; quayside stalls sell seafood and shellfish ready for eating with only a squeeze of lemon and a piece of bread.

Remember that you are expected to take an interest in what you buy, so take your time, handle the food, and ask the merchant how to cook or use it. You might even be encouraged to taste before you decide to buy. For many people, the spur-of-the-moment meal from the market or the little shop is the most exciting, not least because it requires no work. Buying it provides half the fun. A sturdy shopping basket will be useful; a can opener, a corkscrew, and a good knife invaluable. It does, however, need inspiration and taste to assemble good things from visits to the grocer, the baker, the wine merchant, and the fruit seller. Lay out separate little dishes of whatever has tempted you —radishes, olives, knobbly tomatoes, spring onions.

Some Well-Tried Combinations to Assemble

Parma ham or other raw smoked hams are as good with ripe figs as they are with melon. There are many varieties of figs fruiting in various colors ranging from purple to whitish yellow, the rich golden yellow being the most prized.

Anchovy fillets, tomatoes, and olives are excellent arranged on a slice of good bread softened by moistening with a little water and sprinkled with a vinaigrette dressing. A little chopped onion, capers, and some fresh chopped basil if you happen to be in Italy make it even better. In Liguria they use hard dry biscuits (galette), instead of bread, in what is called caponata alla Ligure.

All cheese is good with olives and with a thick slice of country bread to break into pieces and soak up the oil or liquor of the olives. In Greece buy feta or Halumi; Halumi is good with a squeeze of lemon. In Italy try fontina with mild green peppers cut into thin strips. Cream cheeses such as Amari in Greece, Petit Suisse in France, and ricotta in Italy can also be eaten with sugar, honey, or jam. The blander ones can be mashed with a drop of brandy or spirit. A good English or American combination is tart apples with a hard crumbly cheese such as Lancashire, Cheddar, Colby, or Monterey Jack, and fresh walnuts.

Smoked fish—trout, mackerel, salmon, and eel—need no accompaniment other than lemon and bread and butter, except perhaps a little finely chopped onion.

Cod's roe mashed into a paste with olive oil and lemon juice is excellent with hot toast.

Tuna and artichokes in oil are excellent together, canned sardines good with hard-boiled eggs. Some grocers sell artichoke hearts. You may like to fill them with mayonnaise and chopped-up hard-boiled eggs, spring onions, or radishes.

Radishes are lovely with bread and butter and a sprinkling of salt.

Salami and bread and butter take a lot of beating, and mortadella is good with fennel.

You can make up a little salad with salt herring, cooked white haricot beans, black olives, quartered hard-boiled eggs, and thinly sliced onions—a meal in itself.

A Genoese hors d'œuvre combines small raw broad beans, rough salami sausage, and salty sheep's milk Sardo cheese. Another Italian favorite is tuna fish piled up on a bed of haricot beans or French beans dressed with oil. So is a plate of shrimp with green beans seasoned with olive oil, lemon juice, and a dash of salt and pepper.

Hors d'œuvres and Crudités —a Ready-Made Party Meal

A well-chosen hors d'œuvre platter, simply presented with taste and an eye for color, can also make a satisfying complete meal. The French present a selection of anchovy fillets, pâté de campagne, sliced sausage, raw ham, hard-boiled eggs, shrimp, herring tidbits, sardines, and olives. Coupled with crudités (see p. 91), you cannot want for anything else, except perhaps a well-flavored mayonnaise or an aïoli in which to dip them. (Various recipes for these are given on pp. 81–3.)

Antipasto

You can easily assemble a typical Italian antipasto platter.

An antipasto magro is without meats and usually consists of tuna, hard-boiled eggs, tomatoes, boiled potatoes, and beets—all set out on a large platter, quartered or cut in slices, accompanied by a vinaigrette dressing or a mayonnaise.

A complete antipasto platter consists of slices of Italian salami, mortadella, and raw and cooked ham placed on a bed of lettuce leaves with a few tomatoes cut in wedges, sliced fennel, pieces of tuna fish or sardines, a few artichoke hearts in oil or brine, some fat firm radishes, and a few ripe olives. A special dressing enlivens the dish. Make this with olive oil beaten with 2 to 3 chopped and mashed anchovy fillets. Add lemon juice, salt and pepper to taste, and capers if you like.

Steak Tartare

Clint Greyn suggests this as a dish to make in France where suitable meat is easily obtainable: perfectly lean beef, free from every bit of fat and connective tissue, absolutely fresh, and chopped rather than minced. A knife to chop up the accompaniments is the only piece of equipment required to make up this ancient Mongolian nomadic classic. Clint makes it up for two on the plate and eats it just as soon as he comes out from the butcher's.

For two, 1/2 lb. (250 g.) raw minced beef will be enough. Shape it into mounds on two plates. Make a well in the middle and drop an egg yolk into each. Make a ring of finely chopped garnishes—2 onions, 2 tablespoons capers, 2 tablespoons pickled gherkins, and 2 tablespoons parsley—around the meat.

Present with salt and pepper, Tabasco if you like, and lemon wedges. Each person can season and mix in the garnish ingredients as he likes. Have a plate of thin slices of brown bread and butter.

An American "steak tartare" is sirloin, tenderloin, or T-bone steak chopped or ground fine, seasoned with salt and pepper, and eaten as it is on crackers. It is sometimes mixed with raw egg and perhaps some chopped onions or nuts.

Using the Local Baker's Oven

Years ago an uncle in Egypt made a habit of buying a good piece of meat and taking it to the local baker's oven when he was on vacation in Alexandria. He ran with it, sizzling and succulent and wrapped in brown paper, to the restaurant where he had invited some guests to a meal, ordering only drinks and salads. He reckoned this was a cheaper and delicious way of entertaining.

There may not be many restaurants left that would allow this, but there are still country places where the local baker obliges customers with the use of his oven and will let them put in a piece of meat to be collected when it is ready. It is worth finding out and making use of this special service for a party in the country. For cooking a whole baby pig or lamb see the instructions on pp. 228–33. They will need less time in the oven than on the spit—about three-quarters of the time.

LIVING OFF THE LAND

"What is sweeter than honey?" The answer to this Arab riddle is "Free vinegar." Food that you do not have to pay for has a special charm.

In the Seychelles islands I discovered that it is possible to live quite happily on food caught or found growing wild without recourse to the Indian shops. According to local lore, cultivation of the fruits and spices planted in the eighteenth century by French settlers arriving from nearby Mauritius was abandoned when slavery was abolished. The emancipated slaves, preferring to enjoy their newly acquired freedom, refused to work any longer on the plantations. Most things have managed to grow without attention, the multitude of birds obliging by chewing the berries and spitting the stones in appropriate places. It is always easy to wade into the sea and hit a fish on the head without having to go far out beyond the coral reef where sharks might be waiting. And the coconuts fall by themselves.

The flesh of one species of coconut is a translucent jelly when the fruit is less than a year old and still young and tender. It is delicious eaten chilled with sugar and a liqueur such as maraschino or anisette. Apart from its gastronomic virtues this coconut has other attractions; it is believed to be a powerful aphrodisiac. For centuries, since it was washed ashore on the beaches of India and Africa, this fruit, which grows only in the Seychelles, has excited

the imagination of generations. If you see the coco de mer you will understand, for the female nut, affectionately called coco fesses (fesses meaning buttocks in French), is like a curvaceous pelvis from one side. From the other it is like a belly framed by rounded thighs complete with what looks like pubic hair. The male trees produce nothing you can eat. They grow phallic catkins 2 1/2 in. (6 1/2 cm.) thick and 2 ft. (60 cm.) long with a heavy scented pollen. Legends tell of their nightly visits to the coco fesses. When the nut is old, the jelly dries hard like ivory. It is ground to a fine powder by the bonhomme du bois (the herbalist) and by the sorcerer who specializes in love potions and aids for revenge, with bits of wood, strings, animal bones, seeds, and old newspapers with photographs of famous lovers.

There are many things besides coconuts that you can pick, such as mangoes, papaws, guavas, pineapples, yams, breadfruits, sweet potatoes, and bananas. With all this natural bounty it is not surprising that the government drive for "growing your food" in the form of pop songs on the radio and visits from agricultural advisers was encountering more than a little resistance. Remembering distant days in Sicily where a tall tower in the middle of an orange grove was pointed out as being constantly inhabited by a marksman ready to shoot down anyone bold enough to pick an orange, I was relieved to find that things were different here. In accordance with biblical law, the law decrees that picking food on another man's land is not an offense as long as you eat it on the spot.

Marching armies, like pilgrims and explorers, have always relied to some extent on game and food growing wild when they could not seize a sheep from a farmer or ransack a store on the way. Legendary heroes, when resting from conquests, sought diversion in games nearly as formidable and imitative of their combats, which often placed their lives in danger. Diversions far tamer though no less absorbing were obtained simply by picking fruits and vegetables. The loss of the battle of Waterloo by the French has been attributed to wild strawberries. According to the famous chef Pierre Lacam, when the war was well under way in 1815, General Gérard, hurrying to the assistance of Napoleon, found Maréchal Grouchy in the village of Sart-a-Wachain, on the route to Namur, eating strawberries. The Maréchal refused to move.

All those who have dreamed of vast empires—Tamerlane, Timur, Genghis Khan, Charlemagne, Clovis, Napoleon—have of necessity wrenched all they could from trees, fields, rivers, and skies. For some it was not only a matter of survival.

For Babur, the first Mogul emperor, who spent twenty years in the early sixteenth century confirming his position in Afghanistan, regaining the Central Asian empire of Tamerlane and finally conquering within a few months half of Hindustan, it was a continuous gastronomic adventure. A robust and valiant warrior, he was also a joyous drinker and a generous one, a lover of poetry, backgammon, and food, who recorded everything in his famous diaries. The engaging conqueror, who combined an incessant activity at war with an extraordinary personal vigor, wept with delight on seeing the cattle on the hills of Fargana, the profusion of fruits in the orchards, the grain in the autumn fields, a duck shot during an excursion on a boat, a deer impaled near a roaring fire. . . .

Here is an entry for the year 1520 translated from the Turki text by Annette Susannah Beveridge (1921):

> Marching next day from that ground, I made an excursion up the valley-bottom of the Barik-ab towards Qurinq-sai. A few purslain trees were in the utmost autumn beauty. On dismounting, seasonable food was set out. The vintage was the cause! Wine was drunk! A sheep was ordered brought from the road and made into kebabs. We amused ourselves by setting fire to branches of holm-oak.
>
> Mulla 'Abdu'l-malik dïwâna having begged to take the news of our coming into Kabul, was sent ahead. To this place came Hasan Nabïra from Mïrzâ Khan's presence; he must have come after letting me know. There was drinking till the sun's decline; we then rode off. People in our party had become very drunk; Sayyid Qâsim so much so, that two of his servants mounted him and got him into camp with difficulty. Muli Baqir's Dost was so drunk that people, headed by Amïn-i-Muhammad Tarkhan and Mastû Chuhra, could not get him on his horse; even when they poured water on his head, nothing was affected. At that moment a body of Afghans appeared. Amïn-i-Muhammad, who had had enough himself, had this idea, "Rather than leave him here, as he is, to be taken, let us cut his head off and carry it with us." At last after 100 efforts, they mounted him and brought him with them. We reached Kabul at midnight.

Babur could tell of the most extraordinary and savage exploits and at the same time rhapsodize about the bounty and splendor of nature and its offerings. When he was not conquering, chopping off heads, fighting relatives, and protecting himself against intrigues, he was catching fish, hunting deer, eating, and drinking amid the falling petals and fruit blossoms and the flaming fire of autumn leaves. Pomegranates, oranges, and grapes were picked, confections were lovingly prepared, and there was continuous wine drinking and reveling throughout all the bloody campaigns. From time to time prayers were said to the prophet Muhammad and forgiveness was asked for the drinking of wine.

Babur also described in great detail all sorts of ingenious traps for animals. In one entry he tells of catching a bird:

Another of the curiosities of the Nijr-âû mountains is the lûkha bird, called also bû-qalamûn (chameleon) because between head and tail, it has four or five changing colours, resplendent like a pigeon's throat. It is about as large as the kabg-i-darï and seems to be the kabg-i-darï of Hindûstân. People tell this wonderful thing about it: When the birds, at the onset of winter, descend to the hill-skirts, if they come over a vineyard, they can fly no further and are taken.

Nowadays it is the ordinary vacationer who is more likely to make use of the local wild produce and discover that it is the best way to get to know a country.

The spoils of the European wilderness may not be as rich or as exotic, but they are there and it is worth keeping your eyes open for them, as do the children on their walks to school in Flora Thompson's *Lark Rise to Candleford.*

After the first mile or so the dinner baskets would be raided; or they would creep through the bars of the padlocked gates for turnips to pare with the teeth and munch, or for handfuls of green pea shucks, or ears of wheat, to rub out the sweet, milky grain between the hand and devour. In spring they ate the young green from the hawthorn hedges which they called "bread and cheese" and sorrel leaves from the wayside, which they called "sour grass," and in autumn there was an abundance of haws and blackberries and sloes and crab apples for them to feast upon. There was always something to eat, and they ate, not so much because they were hungry as from habit, and relish of the wild food.

There are many edibles growing wild, from barks and fruit, tender leafy greens, vegetables, and herbs to small game and seafood. Almost every animal, and every fish or bird, is good to eat. For a description of what the American wilderness has to offer, see page 357.

Wild berries. They are abundant and widespread in woods, hedgerows, and fields. Raspberries, blackberries, wild strawberries, blueberries, gooseberries, and bilberries, depending on their ripeness and sweetness, may be eaten off the bush or need only sugar and fresh cream. If they are too acid, a little simmering with sugar will turn them into an excellent compote. Hawthorn may be cooked with crab apples, which are unpalatable raw. Other fruits are less common, but you may come across cherry plums, wild cherries, and red or black currants.

I first discovered the joys of wild strawberries in the moist woodlands at the foot of the Italian Dolomites. The flavor and fragrance of this tiny species is greatly superior to the best strains of cultivated ones. They grow wild in many parts of Europe as well as in England, so be prepared for them on your country walks with basket or plastic bag. If you have neither, large thick leaves rolled into cones make good containers.

Eat them as soon as possible. They do not really need washing, but if you must, wash them as swiftly as possible without letting the water soak out the best of their flavor. They are so good that they can be eaten as they are. Dipping their point into a little salt, pepper, or a drop of vinegar brings out the flavor and sweetness.

Otherwise, dredge with sugar and if you can afford to be grand, pour wine (claret for instance) or champagne over them and smother generously with fresh cream. Our hotel at Cortina d'Ampezzo served them up to us with that light-as-a-cloud whipped cream they call *panna montata*. Wild blackberries, raspberries, and bilberries received the same treatment.

Sweet chestnuts are fairly common in woods and parks in the British Isles. The nuts are ready by October and November and may be gathered in the late autumn. Split the prickly husks underfoot and take out the beautifully polished brown nuts. Slit the skins and drop them in the hot ashes of an open fire. Do not try to eat horse chestnuts, which have thicker and more widely spaced spikes.

There is a large variety of green leaves which you can eat raw in a salad, such as watercress, white mustard, chicory, lamb's-quarters, dandelion leaves, and some unusual types of lettuce. Others must be cooked. Wood sorrel with cream makes a magnificent sauce for fish, and wild spinach or beet may be cooked in its own juice with water and butter or oil.

Mushroom hunting is one of the most enjoyable ways of passing the time in fields and woodlands after the first rains, but it is important to get a good field guide to make sure you know that they are not poisonous.

To pick mushrooms, twist gently to break them free. Cut off the base of the stem and remove any blemishes. There is no need to peel or wash them unless they are very dirty, and then do so very briefly. Grill them, brushed with plenty of oil or melted butter, or sauté quickly, small ones whole, large ones sliced. Season with salt and pepper when they have

exuded their juices after 3 or 4 minutes, and add some herbs if you have
them and a little lemon juice.

A MEAL IN A SKILLET OR A POT

There are many quick and simple meals which are as easy to make at camp
as on a boat or a camper using a frying pan or a saucepan. A few memorable
summer weeks spent camping with a group of Dutch artists in the French
village of Lacoste, of Marquis de Sade fame, taught me that the possibilities
are unlimited.

Sculptors, painters, and potters were helping their colleague, my friend
of art school days, Ans Hey, to build a house before the winter set in. She
repaid them with a constant and plentiful supply of local food, wines, and
pastis acquired on excursions to the markets held daily in different villages of
the Vaucluse.

In between laying bricks, plastering, and cutting wood everyone took
turns at cooking. The firebed was large and constantly replenished from a
stack of firewood. It was covered by a wire mesh grill, the wooden frame
resting on a low brick wall, large enough for several pans to sit on at once.
Heavy frying pans and large saucepans and casseroles were used as well as spits
and skewers. We fried and sautéed, grilled, toasted, and stewed. Children
were sent to collect wood and herbs and any wild fruits and edible plants they
could find. We cooked the most wonderful fish soups I have ever eaten and
dishes of the Midi smelling strongly of garlic and wild thyme and the local
wine. We made pancakes and fritters, pots of beans and spaghetti. There was
little we did not attempt, but some dishes were more suitable and more easily
prepared.

The following recipes make use of ingredients which should be bought
locally not very long before use, so that they are fresh and do not require
refrigeration, as well as standby provisions that keep well.

Sautéed and One-Pot Dishes

Sautéing is the best and simplest method of cooking in a galley kitchen on
a boat or in a camper because it is fast and requires little fat. Fuel is econo-
mized, and the risk of danger from hot oil and boiling water is eliminated.
All you need is a source of heat and a deep, heavy-bottomed frying pan.

For sautéed fish, see page 353.

To Sauté Meat

Cut thin slices and pound them flat or take large steaks or chops and cook them for a little longer. The principle is the same: sauté quickly in a mixture of butter and oil, searing the meat first so that it remains tender and juicy inside. Turn over once and season with salt and pepper.

To make a sauce, add a few tablespoons of wine or sherry or a dash of Cognac to the pan juices with a sprinkling of herbs and perhaps some crushed garlic, or use fresh or sour cream.

For a pepper steak use tender beef and press some very coarsely ground or crushed black peppercorns, about 1 1/2 to 2 teaspoons for each steak, into each side and cook as above, 3 minutes on each side over fairly high heat for rare meat. Turn the heat down and cook 2 minutes more for medium steaks.

For hamburgers, make as the recipe on page 249, but work the ground meat less. It is best when it just holds together softly. Make plump cakes and give 4 minutes to either side on high heat and 2 minutes more for each on lower heat.

Beefsteak Smothered in Onions

This recipe comes from Maria Parloa's *Camp Cookery.*

Fry brown four slices of salt pork; when brown take out the pork, and put in six onions sliced thin. Fry about ten minutes, stirring all the while; then take out all except a thin layer, and upon this lay a slice of steak, then a layer of onions, then steak, and cover thick with onions. Dredge each layer with pepper, salt and flour. Pour over this one cupful of boiling water, and cover tight. Simmer half an hour. When you serve, place the steak in the centre of the dish, and heap the onions around it. Serve the same vegetables as for broiled steak.

To Sauté Calf's Liver

Cut liver in very thin slices. Dust with flour if you wish. Sauté quickly in a mixture of butter and oil until colored on both sides but still pink inside. Add salt and pepper, a squeeze of lemon, a little vinegar, or a few tablespoons of Marsala. Cook a minute longer and serve with chopped parsley.

A Venetian version is to soften and lightly color several sliced onions. Place the seasoned liver slices on top and cook with the lid on until just done.

Another Italian way is to dredge the liver in flour and sauté in butter flavored with fried crushed garlic and chopped sage.

To Sauté Chicken

Use boned chicken or quarters (without the wings). Sauté in a mixture of oil and butter for about 5 to 8 minutes until barely golden on both sides, then reduce the heat, add salt and pepper, and let it cook slowly for another 10 to 20 minutes (legs require more time than breasts), shaking the pan occasionally and turning the pieces over.

You may add a little wine or sherry, port or Madeira, lemon or tomato juice, and an herb such as parsley or tarragon when the chicken has already colored. Add a little cream if you like, just before you are ready to serve.

An Egyptian way is to flavor the chicken with crushed garlic, lemon juice, a cracked cardamom pod, and a sprinkling of spices—either cinnamon and allspice or a touch of turmeric for color.

I particularly like the Creole flavors obtained by mixing a piece of grated ginger with 2 chopped cloves garlic fried in the oil or butter and adding a few peeled and chopped tomatoes.

Chicken with vegetables. Fry the chicken briefly on both sides, then add to the pan any of the following: chopped spring onions, sliced or chopped onions, tomatoes, cut into pieces, sliced zucchini, diced peppers, mushrooms, whole or sliced.

Egg Dishes

Cheap, nutritious, and tasty—much can be done in a frying pan besides the usual omelet and fried, scrambled, and boiled eggs.

With ham and a sweet-and-sour sauce. Fry 4 thick slices cooked ham in butter or oil. Remove from the pan. Add 1 tablespoon sugar and let it brown slightly. Pour in 5 to 6 tablespoons wine vinegar and let it bubble for half a minute. Return the ham and slip 4 eggs over it. Season with salt and pepper and cook gently until eggs have set.

With cheese. Fry a small onion or a crushed clove of garlic in a little butter
until it colors. Put in slices or cubes of a cheese that becomes thready
when it melts, such as provolone, mozzarella, or fontina or the Greek
Halumi. Add a pinch of nutmeg or spread with a teaspoonful of mild
mustard. Break 4 eggs over the top and cook until they set and the cheese
bubbles. You may beat the eggs instead of leaving them whole.

A Tunisian dish—Chakchouka. Fry a coarsely chopped onion in a little oil
until golden. Add a green pepper, seeded and cut small, and fry until soft.
Add 3 or 4 tomatoes, peeled and cut in half, seasoning with salt and
pepper, and cook gently for a few minutes. Drop the eggs in whole and
cook until set. You may also stir the eggs in if you like a creamy texture.

Pasticio

Years ago, walking through a pine forest along the sea front at Forte dei
Marmi, we were amazed at the number of families sitting at tables eating
spaghetti under the trees. Surrounded by chopping boards, sieves, frying pans,
and Primus stoves, they had evidently prepared it on the spot and must have
started early with the sauce. The Italians, I thought, cannot live without
spaghetti.

More recently, and very far from Italy, I spent a night by Lake Tiberias
in Israel at a site where campers rented huts and did their own cooking. Here
too, among the kebabs and steaks and eggplant salads, were mountains of
spaghetti. Obviously, everybody likes them enough to make them on vacation
and even if you have only one burner you can make everything (sauce and all)
with one pot and a sieve.

All there is to know about cooking pasta is to throw it in a great deal of
salted and fast-boiling water, to stir well, and to leave it in until it is only just
tender—with a bite still. It must not be soft, mushy, or sticky. Drain quickly.
We use 1 lb. (1/2 kg.) for four people.

The simplest way of serving pasta is also for me the tastiest—with plenty of
butter, salt, and pepper, sometimes topped with grated Parmesan or
crumbled ricotta.

Al olio e al alio, dressed in olive oil with plenty of crushed garlic and finely
chopped parsley, is just as easy.

Another quick sauce is light cream with chopped cooked ham, seasoned with
pepper and with salt if the ham is not too salty.

For a very good tomato sauce, simply chop up fresh ripe tomatoes and put them in a bowl with olive oil, salt, and pepper. Toss the pasta in as soon as it comes out of the water. To this you can add little leftover bits of ham or pork or veal or a can of tuna with a can of anchovies, chopped up.

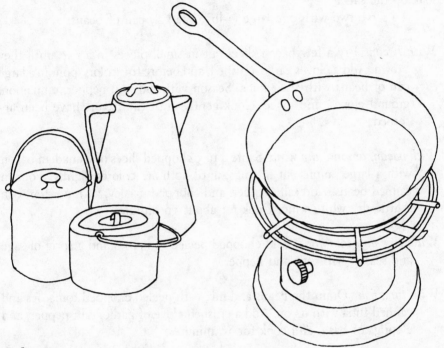

Polenta

This popular Italian cornmeal mush makes a perfect campsite food to accompany grilled meats. Depending on how soft you like it, boil 3 or 4 cups (1/2 to 3/4 liter) of water or milk or a mixture of both with salt to taste in a saucepan, and sprinkle in 1 cup (100 g.) cornmeal, stirring constantly to avoid lumping, until the mixture thickens. Then cook gently over low heat, stirring frequently so that the mixture does not stick, until it is thick and smooth and comes away clean from the sides of the pan. Stir in lavish quantities of butter and, if you like, some cheese—grated Parmesan or small cubes of Bel Paese or mozzarella.

Beans

When you are busy and hard up and have hungry people to feed, canned beans are a godsend. And you can improve on the usual way of heating them up in their can, with inspiration from Italy. (A famous Tuscan outdoor bean dish has them cooking in a large wine flask, such as a chianti bottle with the straw removed, in smoldering ashes for about 3 hours.) You can use canned beans —kidney, butter, garbanzo (chickpeas), or haricot—in their natural juice, with the following embellishments, and serve hot as a meal in itself with bread to soak up the sauce.

To serve two with one large (1-lb. /1/2-kg.) can of beans:

With bacon. Fry a few bacon slices cut in small pieces in a pan until they brown. Add 2 cloves garlic, crushed, and before this colors, pour in a large can of beans with their juice. Season with salt and pepper, cinnamon, ground cloves, and mace. Cook gently until the flavors have been absorbed.

With bacon, onions, and wine. Sauté 4 to 5 chopped slices of Canadian bacon with a large onion, cut in rings, until both are colored lightly. Pour in canned beans. Add salt, pepper, and chopped parsley, and moisten with a little dry white wine. Cook for about 10 minutes.

With sage and tomatoes. Add chopped peeled tomatoes and a sprig of sage and season with salt and pepper.

With tuna fish. Drain the beans and mix with peeled chopped tomatoes and canned tuna with its oil. Add a crushed clove of garlic, salt, pepper, and 2 sprigs of basil, and cook for 10 minutes.

With pork sausages intended for boiling. Cook sausages, throw out the water, and put them aside. Put a little oil in the pan and fry a small chopped onion until it is golden. Add a chopped clove of garlic and barely let it color. Stir in 2 to 3 tablespoons tomato paste, then return the sausages to the pan and add the beans with their juice and some chopped parsley. Cook for about 10 minutes.

For a Middle Eastern meal buy canned Egyptian brown beans. For a large can, add 2 cloves garlic, pressed. Heat thoroughly and serve in bowls with a hard-boiled egg for each person. Pass around olive oil and lemon quarters, salt, and pepper for each person to season as he wishes.

Chickpeas to eat as a salad. Drain canned chickpeas of their juice and season to taste with salt and pepper, lemon juice, and olive oil. Add plenty of crushed garlic or grated onion and some chopped parsley.

Pan Haggerty

For this filling potato (1 lb./1/2 kg.), onion (9 oz./250 g.), and cheese (1/4 lb./125 g.) dish-in-the-frying-pan from Northumberland, slice the vegetables very thin. Put alternate layers of potato, onion, and grated matured Cheddar or Lancashire cheese in a well-oiled pan, seasoning each layer with salt and pepper. Cover with a lid and cook gently for about 30 minutes until the vegetables are very tender.

Sautéed Fruits

For a change from eating them raw, you can make a dessert of sautéed fruits. Apples, peeled and cut in rings, pears, cut in halves or slices, or whole bananas can be sautéed in unsalted butter with a little oil to prevent burning. Sprinkle with sugar and let it caramelize slightly. Cook until tender, then pour in calvados, Cognac, or rum and set it alight.

Fruit Fritters

One way of enjoying wild berries such as bilberries and for that matter any other fruit, is to make them into fritters. To make a batter, gradually add 2/3 cup (150 ml.) milk or water to 1 cup (140 g.) plain flour—enough for a thick cream. Add 2 tablespoons oil and 2 eggs (to add the egg whites stiffly beaten at the last minute is nice but not always practical), a pinch of salt, and if you like a tablespoon of sugar. Beat vigorously until smooth. Leave for 30 minutes. The fritters should be fried in shallow oil or butter.

Small berries. Add enough washed and dried berries to make the batter quite heavy with fruit. Drop the batter in hot oil by the spoonful. Turn over once and when nicely browned, drain and sprinkle liberally with powdered sugar.

Larger fruit. Apples, cored and cut in rings, apricot halves, pineapple slices, bananas, and orange segments can be marinated for an hour in lemon juice with a sprinkling of sugar or Grand Marnier, Curaçao, rum, Kirsch, or wine. Drain well before dipping each piece in the batter to coat it evenly. If the fruit is too moist for the batter to stick, dust first with flour or fine biscuit crumbs. Fry in hot oil.

Sweet Omelet

Make a light omelet in the usual way by beating the eggs and pouring them into a tablespoon of hot butter in a large pan, but flavor with sugar instead of salt and pepper: 3 to 4 tablespoons for 8 eggs is about right.

Or make it fluffy like a soufflé if you have a hand beater. Separate the yolks and whites, beat the whites stiff with a pinch of salt until firm, then add sugar gradually. Fold into the yolks. Cook by the ladleful in hot foaming butter, turning over with the help of a plate. Serve at once sprinkled with sugar and, if you like, a spirit such as Kirsch, Cognac, or rum, which may be set alight in a tablespoon over a flame.

You may garnish with fresh whipped cream, or top with warmed-up jam.

Omelette normande. Make an apple sauce: sauté sliced apples in hot unsalted
butter for about 7 to 10 minutes, stirring and turning them over. Add
sugar to taste. Moisten with calvados or rum and set aflame. Shake and
remove from the heat. Add a few tablespoons of heavy cream. Spoon a
generous amount over each omelet as it is ready to serve and fold in half.
Heat some more calvados or rum and pour over the omelets. Set alight.

LONG SLOW COOKING

Camacho's Wedding Feast

The first thing that met Sancho's sight there was a whole steer spitten on an entire elm, before a mighty fire made of a pile of wood that seemed a small mountain. Round this bonfire were placed six capacious pots, cast in no common mould, or rather six ample coppers, every one containing a whole shamble of meat, and entire sheep were sunk and lost in them, and soaked as if they were pigeons. The branches of the trees round were all garnished with an infinite number of skinned hares and plucked fowls of several sorts: and then for a drink, Sancho told above three-score skins of wine, each of which contained above two arrobas, and as it afterwards proved, sprightly liquor. A goodly pile of white loaves made a large rampart on the one side, and a stately wall of cheeses set up like bricks made a comely bulwark on the other. Two pans of oil, each bigger than a dyer's vat, served to fry their pancakes, which they lifted out with two strong peels when they were fried enough, and then they dropped them into as large a kettle of honey prepared for that purpose. To dress all this provision there were above fifty cooks, men and women, all cleanly, diligent and cheerful. In the ample belly of the steer they had stowed twelve tender little sucking-pigs to give it the more savoury taste. Spices of all sorts, that appeared to be bought by wholesale, were visible in a great chest. In short, the whole provision was indeed country-like, but plentiful enough to feast an army.

Sancho Panza beheld all this with wonder and delight. The first temptation that captivated his senses was the goodly pots; his bowels yearned, and his mouth watered at the dainty contents: by-and-by he falls desperately in love with the skins of wine; and lastly his affections were fixed on the frying-pans, if such honourable kettles may accept of the name. So, being able to hold out no longer, he accosted one of the busy cooks with all the smooth and hungry reasons he was master of; he begged his leave to sop a portion of bread in one of the pans. "Friend," quoth the cook, "no hunger must be felt near us today, thanks to the rich Camacho. 'light, 'light, man, and if thou canst find ever a ladle there, skim out a pullet or two, and much good may it do you." "I see no ladle, sir," quoth Sancho. "Sinner o' me!" cried the cook, "what a silly helpless fellow thou art!" With that he took a kettle, and sousing into one of the pots, he fished out three hens and a couple of geese at one heave. "Here, friend," said he to Sancho, "take this, and make shift to stay your stomach with that scum till dinner be ready." "But where shall I put it?" cried Sancho. "Here," answered the cook, "take ladle and all, and thank Camacho's wealth and bounty for it all."

—Miguel de Cervantes Saavedra, *Don Quixote*

Whether cooking outdoors, in the wilderness or over a camp stove, the contents of the stewpot are most likely to be potluck, as the availability of ingredients cannot always be guaranteed. It may take at least 3 hours and maybe 5 or 6 for the meat to be tender and the flavors absorbed, but waiting for the stew to be ready is one of the pleasures of camp life. You will need a large heavy pot or casserole with a close-fitting lid; otherwise you can seal the lid on with a stiff flour and water paste. Stand it firmly on a grill over a constantly replenished fire, smoored (covered with sods) to remain aglow for hours, or in a pit (see p. 362).

Meats cooked long and slowly with vegetables in a pot tend to be homely dishes, but you can make them as grand as you like by putting wine, cider, or beer in the pot instead of water. For a stew, a great deal of license is allowed and you can improvise with the following recipes. Make a large amount. If there are not many of you it will do for more than one meal. Serve in soup bowls over a thick slice of toasted bread, to eat with a fork and a spoon.

A Flemish Carbonnade   *(for more than 6)*

4 1/2-lb. (2-kg.) cheap cut of beef
Oil
2–3 tablespoons flour
2 large onions, sliced
2 bay leaves
A few stalks parsley
1 bottle of beer (strong ale, pale
    or brown)

A pinch of nutmeg
1 teaspoon allspice
3 cloves
2 tablespoons vinegar
2 teaspoons sugar
Salt and pepper to taste
A few sliced carrots (optional)
2 cloves garlic, crushed (optional)

Trim the fat off the beef. Leave the meat whole or cut in pieces of any size. Fry meat in a little oil until browned and take it out of the pot. Add the flour and let it brown. Add the onions to the pot with the bay leaves and parsley stalks. Cover with the beer, bring to the boil, remove any scum, then add the spices, vinegar, sugar, salt, and pepper. You may also add the carrots and garlic.

Cook for several hours until the meat is very tender. Taste and adjust seasonings.

Serve with French bread cut in thick slices, lightly toasted over the fire and spread with butter and Dijon mustard.

A French Daube   *(for more than 6)*

5 slices bacon
Oil
4 1/2-lb. (2-kg.) piece of beef (brisket
    will do)
5 peeled tomatoes
2–3 cloves garlic, chopped
12 pearl onions

Parsley and its stalks, finely chopped
1 teaspoon thyme
2 bay leaves
A handful of quartered mushrooms
Salt and pepper to taste
1/2 bottle red or dry white wine

Fry the bacon in a little oil in a pot. Remove bacon and sear the beef. Return the bacon, put the meat on top, and surround with the vegetables and herbs. Add the wine and enough water to cover.

There is nothing to stop you from adding other vegetables such as celery, carrots, leeks, and little turnips cut into pieces. A slice of lemon or orange gives a delicate perfume.

Put the lid on tightly, seal if you like with a flour and water paste, and cook very gently for 4 or 5 hours or more, depending on the method, until the meat is so tender that you can pull the portions apart gently. Before serving, adjust the seasonings.

Serve in bowls with potatoes, boiled separately or cooked in the ashes (see p. 216), and a thick slice of French bread, lightly toasted on the fire. You will be happy to have anything left over next day.

For a bœuf bourguignonne cut the beef into bite-size pieces and dredge them in flour. Fry the diced bacon in a little oil with the vegetables until they brown before sautéing the meat. Add wine and flavorings as above and cook for several hours in a closed pot.

Bœuf à la Mode

This makes an admirable hot-pot. Use the recipe on page 64, but without the calf's feet, which provide the jelly for the cold version.

Hunter's Chicken *(for more than 6)*

2 small chickens	1/2–1 teaspoon thyme, basil, or
2 tablespoons flour	marjoram or all three
4 slices bacon	A few sprigs of parsley
3–4 tablespoons oil or butter	1 cup (1/4 liter) dry white wine
3 cloves garlic, crushed	2–3 tablespoons tomato purée
Salt and pepper	1/2 lb. (225 g.) mushrooms
1 bay leaf	

Make this in a large, heavy pot.

Cut the chicken into quarters, remove the skin if you like, and dredge with flour. Chop the bacon and fry gently in oil or butter and remove onto a plate. Fry the chicken pieces in the same fat and brown lightly all over. Add the garlic, salt, pepper, and herbs and cover with white wine. Stir in tomato purée and add the mushrooms (cut in two or four if they are large). Cover the pot and simmer 45 to 60 minutes in the ashes or over a low flame.

An Irish Stew　*(for more than 6)*

Serve this with hot toast or put toast in the bowls before filling them with stew.

2 1/4 lb. (1 kg.) mutton or lamb	Salt and pepper
2 1/4 lb. (1 kg.) onions	Pinches of nutmeg or thyme
2 1/4 lb. (1 kg.) potatoes	

Trim off all the fat from the mutton or lamb and cut in largish chunks. Peel and slice the onions and potatoes. Alternate layers of each in a large pot, sprinkling each with salt and pepper, occasionally with a pinch of nutmeg or thyme. Cover with water and simmer, with lid on, for at least 2 to 3 hours, until the meat is very tender and the potatoes melted.

STRAIGHT FROM THE WATER

As everyone knows who has tasted it, a fish just out of the water is quite different from the one bought from the fishmonger.

The ancient Romans, who idolized fish as much as the Greeks before them, were particularly fond of cooking fish live. To indulge in these refinements of pleasure they constructed fish ponds on the roofs of their houses and built canals bringing river water into their dining rooms. The fish swam in tanks under the table and it was necessary only to stoop and pick them out the instant before eating. The greater sensualists sharpened their appetites by watching them agonizing in boiling water or on the grill. There was no better stimulant than an expiring mullet, blushing red in its agony and turning lighter shades during its passage from life to death. Our own sensitivities allow us greater pleasure in the more sporting activity of fishing and looking for shellfish on the wet sand when the tide has gone.

Though we do not now wish to see a fish die in its sauce, it is certainly at its very best when freshly caught, and no one must miss an opportunity of tasting it still smelling of the sea or just out of stream or lake.

If you are on a fishing vacation, cruising in a boat, or camping near a fishing port or on the beach, you may not fulfill the dream of many yachtsmen to furnish all the meals by means of your own fishing prowess, but you can at least purchase good fresh fish from local fishermen or at the quayside market. Amaranth Sitas writes in her book *Kopiaste* published in Cyprus: "Fish tastes better if caught with a spear or prongs because it is killed instantly. Second best is fish caught by angling or in snares, and last when caught by trawlers or nets because then the fish dies of suffocation." I am unable to confirm that, but certainly it is only by the water that you can taste fish and shellfish at their very best, absolutely fresh. (Fish caught in muddy waters does not taste very good, but it can be improved by soaking in strong brine for an hour or two.)

Collecting shellfish and crustacea can easily become a passion, and the excitement lies as much in the hunt and the rituals of preparation as in the food itself. Although sometimes, as with winkles, it is more an absorbing distraction than a matter of good eating, nothing is more agreeable than a platter of gathered shellfish and other seafood including clams, cockles, mussels, scallops, crabs, and shrimp. They are treasures that you find in clusters strewn across the sand just after the tide has gone, or simply feel when you wade barefooted into the water. You can pry them off a rock as with sea urchins or dig them out of the sand with shovels, rakes, hoes, or trowels, or you can hammer them out of their homes in rocks. Razor clams leave holes in the sand as a clue to their presence, and crabs hiding in shallow pools can be caught at low tide. Poke around with a stick and use a rake to pull them out of the swaying seaweed where they lurk.

Dealing with Shellfish

There is only one danger when you gather your own: polluted water. Not all shellfish, and particularly mussels, are edible; some are even poisonous, so you must seek advice from locals. Make sure that you never collect them in parts of the sea that may be contaminated by sewage. Always wash them well in several changes of clean fresh water and leave them in a bucket of clean sea water for at least 6 hours or overnight so that they disgorge any sand. Remove beards with a knife or scissors and discard those too heavy, too light, broken, or open. Make sure that they are all alive by gently forcing them open. If they stay open they are likely to be dead.

Boil cockles and winkles in clean sea water seasoned with pepper, thyme, and a bay leaf. Use pins to extract them from their shells with a curling motion so that they do not break.

Purists rightly prefer to eat shellfish alive and raw. Pry them open with a special knife or let gentle heat do it for you. Serve with lemon and slices of buttered brown bread.

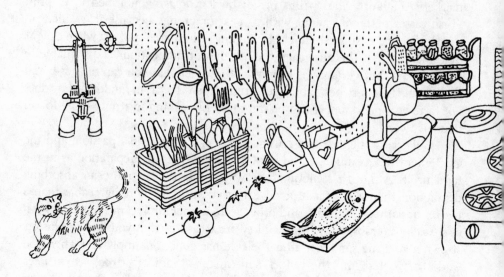

If you prefer to cook them, throw scallops, clams, and mussels into a bucket
with a little sea water. Cover the bucket and bring to the boil. The shells
will open within 5 minutes. Shellfish will also cook on a grill or sheet of
foil over a bed of coals in the same time. Serve with melted butter or oil
and lemon juice.

In France in the Charente they have a very dramatic way of cooking mussels
on the beach which is called an *éclade.* Place the shells close together
pointing toward the center on a bed of leaves or a wooden plank. Cover
with a thick blanket of dry pine needles and set alight. Blow off the
charred bits and eat the opened mussels with fat slices of country bread,
buttered and sprinkled with salt and pepper.

If you have a frying pan and facilities you can take the shellfish out of their
shells, dip them in beaten egg, then flour or fine bread crumbs, and fry
them quickly in oil or butter, turning them over once until golden (about
4 minutes). A squeeze of lemon and black pepper is all you need.

For a special treat sauté large scallops in butter with a touch of crushed garlic.
Add salt and pepper and a little white wine and cook for 10 minutes. Or
pour in a few tablespoons of brandy. Heat it for a few seconds and set
it alight.

Mixed Seafood Salad

Open shellfish by placing them on a hot grill or heating them in a pan or metal pail with very little water. Follow the instructions on page 354 for cooking an octopus and cut it into small pieces. Poach shrimp for 10 minutes and shell them.

Put everything in a large bowl and dress with plenty of olive oil and about half this quantity of lemon juice. Add salt and pepper, and a touch of Dijon mustard if you like. Leave for an hour or so before serving, sprinkled with finely chopped parsley.

Clam Soup

This clam soup is as delicious as it is simple. Serve it with soda crackers.

3 cups (3/4 liter) milk
2 cups (450 g.) minced clams
3 tablespoons butter

Salt and pepper
Chopped parsley (optional)

Bring the milk to the boil, add the rest of the ingredients except parsley, and heat through. Sprinkle with parsley if you wish.

Chowders

There is much controversy about the way you make clam and other chowders. Opinions are divided about whether the onion should be fried before the salt pork or put in to simmer with the potatoes or left out altogether, whether to use hard or soft clams or a mixture of both, and whether to have milk or tomatoes. Some like a thin chowder; others prefer to make it thick and sustaining, adding flour thickener or noodles, and there are different flavorings. It is usually a regional matter.

I have picked two of the simplest recipes that I also find the most appealing. They can easily be made up on the beach, and you can substitute any sort of seafood, including scallops, oysters, crabs, and lobster meat for the clams or fish.

Fish Chowder

Use any firm fish you can find for this easy version of the famous American fish stew. Serve with crackers and butter.

1/2 lb. (1/4 kg.) salt pork
2 cups (450 g.) sliced onions
2 qt. (2 liters) milk
1/2–1 1/2 lb. (225–675 g.) potatoes
2 1/4–3 1/2-lb. (1–1 1/2-kg.) fish: one
     or a choice of several such as

cod, haddock, hake, halibut,
     flounder, grouper, etc., skinned
     and boned and cut into good-size
     serving pieces
Salt and pepper

Fry the salt pork slowly in a large pot. When the fat melts and the scraps are brown, add the onions and cook until they are soft and transparent, then pour in the milk and add the potatoes. Cook for 5 minutes, then add the fish and cook for 10 to 15 minutes until the fish is translucent, removing any scum as it appears and seasoning with salt and pepper (taking into account the saltiness of the salt pork). Add water if the chowder seems too thick.

Jim Beard's Old Western Clam Chowder

This is made with razor clams, and a most delicious chowder it is. Our family recipe—given here, and the recipe of most of our friends—was different from the run-of-the-mill chowder and considerably better.

5 or 6 rashers smoked bacon, cut
    thick, or salt pork (they give
    entirely different flavors,
    both excellent)
1 small onion, finely chopped
3 to 4 smallish potatoes, peeled
    and diced
1 teaspoon salt
1 1/2 cups (355 ml.) clam broth

Water
1 teaspoon freshly ground pepper
1/2 teaspoon thyme
1 quart milk or half and half
2 to 3 cups (450 to 675 g.) minced
    razor clams or other clams
Butter
Chopped parsley

Cut the bacon or salt pork into small squares and try out in a large, heavy skillet till crisp. Remove, add the onion, and sauté in the fat until just wilted. Transfer to absorbent paper, and pour off the fat from the skillet. Add the potatoes to the pan with the salt. Combine clam broth with enough water— or use additional clam broth—to just cover the potatoes. Cook until the potatoes are quite tender. Transfer to a 3- to 4-qt. (3- to 4-liter) saucepan and add the onion mixture, pepper, thyme, and milk or half-and-half. Bring to the boiling point, add the clams, and cook just long enough to heat them through. Correct the seasoning. Serve in chowder bowls or large cups with a small piece of butter and a sprinkling of chopped parsley.

A New England Clambake

Monumental piles of seashells that archaeologists call kitchen middens once marked the mouths of rivers along the New England coast. Left by Algonquin Indians who came down to the sea not only to fish but to dig clams, which they often baked, these hills of discard signified the abundance of shellfish that awaited itinerant tribesmen for centuries before the Pilgrims arrived at Plymouth Rock. The Indians passed on their intricate knack of heating stones to cook food from the sea with food from the land, and a truly aboriginal American institution became one of the gastronomical glories of Yankee summers.

A genuine clambake exemplifies the age-old ritual of eating out-of-doors. "One of the most memorable meals I can remember," Evan Jones once told me, "was eaten beside a driftwood fire while a flat wind raced in off the water, blowing soft rain across the pebbly beach." Evan said he couldn't forget the vast quantities of fish and crustaceans, "and the flavors still rise to my tastebuds as I think of those shells that came sizzling hot, then popped open to fill one's nostrils with such an appetizing aroma."

Such memories as Evan's are not surprising to people who know the pleasure of a clambake. As he said, "The word would not have become an American synonym for a joyous musical jam session, or great doings of any kind, if it weren't true that cooking clams outdoors is as exhilarating a summer frolic as man has so far contrived."

Clambakes, Evan points out, begin with driftwood fires. A veteran bakemaster will have dug a shallow ditch and in it started a huge blaze. While it burns for several hours it is stoked periodically while those who have come to feast collect dry boulders, about the size of a man's head. Any that are damp and therefore might explode are rejected, as well as any previously used in a fire because such rocks won't stand the heat twice. The fire's fiercely hot coals will turn boulders white-hot in about an hour.

Meanwhile in further preparation for the clambake rockweed is collected from the water's edge. A bushel or more of soft clams is thoroughly washed to remove as much sand as possible, and all other items for this seaside menu are made ready. Only the soft-shell, longneck, or steamer clams *(Mys arenaria)* are acceptable, because those called quahogs or hard-shells turn tough in this kind of cooking. The Indians also ate quahogs raw (as do many people today), and they used the purple parts of quahog shells for money.

In typical clambake procedure, the white-hot stones are swept clean with leafy branches and are covered by a thick layer of wet rockweed, then by chicken wire. The clams are spread over and covered with more dripping rockweed, with as many potatoes as there may be guests, with twice as many ears of corn and small sausages, chickens, and lobsters. The entire "mixed grill" is buried in seaweed, covered with a thick wet canvas, and more water may be splashed over it during the baking. Steam from the clams and tangy seaweed intermingles and permeates everything, salting it with the essence of the sea. Picnickers love to watch the seething of the seaweed, under the canvas, as it spatters against the heat of the stones. "Let the wind off the water be as cold as it is damp—it will increase the appetite," Evan told me.

A clambake professionally set up to feed hundreds of guests at a time demonstrates vividly how the basic wilderness method has been adapted to modern facilities. In some permanent locations commercial bakemasters have erected concrete-and-stone pits at counter height as substitutes for seaside fires. Along the Maine coast there are sheet-iron stoves to take the place of the Indians' heated boulders. The most common twentieth-century accommodation, however, is said to be the so-called barrel bake, in which a saturated wooden drum, its bottom covered with sand to prevent burning, serves as a pit and scrap iron is used in place of rocks to carry the heat. According to Evan, a bakemaster must listen at the side of the barrel until the sound of growling can be plainly heard; only then is a perfect feast sure to follow.

In the opinion of habitual participants, a clambake is truly a feast.

Traditionally, menus include accompaniments of sliced cucumbers, sliced tomatoes, onion rings, brown bread or homemade white, butter, pepper, vinegar, and pepper sauce. The feast may begin with clam chowder. "Have some beer," Evan said. "When the steamed clams hit your paper plate in an aromatic mist, spread the shells apart, take the clam by the snout, and dip it in molten butter laced with vinegar or a hot condiment, if you like. In any event, don't hesitate to down all that arrives on your plate as quickly as possible. No doubt, the white man has elaborated the clambake, but its essentials and the fundamentals of cooking it haven't changed from the ways of the Indians. It is still the best of picnics, perhaps the most American of them all."

Washtub Clambake for Twelve *(for more than 6)*

1/2 bushel rockweed
6 small broiling chickens
12 small lobsters
12 baking potatoes, scrubbed but
    not peeled

12 sweet potatoes
24 ears of corn, silk removed and
    husks retained
3 pecks soft clams

Build a hot fire, preferably in an outdoor fireplace. In a clean washtub or galvanized garbage can put a layer of rockweed and a quart of water. Place a grill over the fire and the clambake tub on top. Wrap the chickens and lobsters well in cheesecloth and spread over the damp rockweed. Add some rockweed and distribute baking and sweet potatoes and corn. Top this with seaweed and spread clams, then add more seaweed. Cover with heavy canvas and the lid of the tub or can. Maintain a hot fire for about 2 hours, dousing the contents of the clambake with a little sea water from time to time. Serve with lots of butter, salt, and pepper.

Cooking Fish in a Wet Newspaper

Many an angler must have treated his catch in this manner: wrap the fish in several sheets of wet newspaper and put it close to a roaring fire or over dying embers to cook slowly and gently, protected by the steam of the wet newspaper. As an added refinement you may sprinkle the newspaper with vinegar.

Fried Shrimp

The large ones are best. Fry them in their shells in sizzling oil or butter with crushed garlic, salt, and pepper. In the Seychelles I learned that fresh ginger suits them well. Add a little, grated or squeezed in a garlic press, or use a pinch of dry powder.

Spicy Prawns or Shrimp—a Moroccan Specialty

1 1/8 lb. (1/2 kg.) large unpeeled and
    uncooked prawns or shrimp
3 large cloves garlic, crushed
4 tablespoons oil
Salt
1 teaspoon paprika

1 teaspoon cumin
1/2 teaspoon ginger
A good pinch of cayenne
A bunch of fresh coriander or parsley,
    finely chopped

Prawns or shrimp can easily be found frozen. They are cheapest in Chinese supermarkets. Defrost if necessary and remove shells, heads, limbs, and tails and devein. Fry the garlic in oil until the aroma rises. Add seasoning and spices, stir, then throw in the prawns or shrimp. Fry quickly, stirring until they turn pink. Add the coriander and parsley, and keep on the fire a minute more.

Crabs

No crab can ever be as good as the one, fresh from the boiling pail, which you have just pulled out of a shallow pool.

Fill a large pot or a clean metal pail with fresh sea water and add enough salt to float an egg. Bring it to the boil over a fire and throw in one or more crabs at a time. Let the water return to the boil, then simmer for 10 to 15 minutes if the crabs are small (less than 1 lb./1/2 kg.), and 10 minutes more for each extra pound. It is hard to estimate their weight, but the time does not matter too much.

To eat you will need a sharp knife, a nutcracker, or a mallet to crack the legs and claws, and thin skewers or long needles to poke out difficult bits. Twist off legs and claws. Turn the crab on its back. Lift up and remove the pointed flap together with the intestinal vein and take out the central body part. Discard the feathery lung sections and scoop out the soft flesh.

Serve in the shell with a bowl of melted butter or some heated heavy cream and lemon juice, and some bread.

If you want to serve it cold as a salad, dress the chopped crabmeat with olive oil, lemon juice, salt, and pepper, garnish with parsley, and return it to the washed shell.

Feasting on Crabs

Along the shoreline of the Mid-Atlantic states it's not uncommon to discover beach parties at which live hard-shell crabs are steamed in giant lard cans in spicy vinegar vapor. Sitting at picnic tables spread with newspaper, crab enthusiasts break the shells with nutcrackers and lubricate the feast with cold beer. Stone crabs are found from the Carolinas to Florida, along with spider crabs, and both Dungeness and Alaskan crabs are flown from the Pacific to Eastern markets.

Louisiana Barbecued Buster Crabs

12 buster crabs (caught while in the process of molting)
Milk

Minced chives
Minced parsley

THE BASTING SAUCE

1 cup (1/4 liter) melted butter
1 teaspoon lime juice

Worcestershire sauce
2 tablespoons minced chives

Wash crabs in cold water, clean, and soak in milk. Stretch a piece of wire screen or heavy aluminum foil over hot coals. Arrange crabs and baste several times with butter sauce. Cook for 15 minutes, then sprinkle with chives and parsley.

Eastern Shore Deviled Soft-Shell Crabs

12 soft-shell crabs
Flour for dredging
Butter
Salt and pepper
2 heaping tablespoons minced parsley

2 tablespoons finely chopped onion
2 teaspoons paprika
3 tablespoons lemon juice
3 tablespoons sherry

Clean crabs and blot dry with paper towels or picnic napkins. Dredge in flour, and in a large picnic skillet heat enough butter to cover bottom of pan by 1/4 in. (1/2 cm.). Arrange crabs in one layer, sprinkling with salt, pepper, parsley, and onion. Shake in paprika. When butter begins to bubble around the rim, sprinkle crabs with lemon juice, and cover the pan tightly. In about 3 or 4 minutes (depending upon fire) turn over crabs, sprinkling again with salt, pepper, parsley, onion, and paprika. Cover and let crabs brown on second side. Add sherry and cook about 3 minutes more. Serve as hot as possible.

Charcoal-Broiled King Crab Legs

| 3–4 frozen king crabs | Melted butter |
| Lemon juice | |

Use one large middle section of the crab leg for each serving and split the shell with a sharp boning knife (a hunting knife will do), making a crosscut in the middle. Curl the edges of the cut shell a little outward to be ready to receive sauce. Simply squeeze a generous amount of lemon juice into the hot butter and pour into the shell's opening. Broil over glowing charcoal, basting several times, and serve with additional melted butter.

Oyster Feasts—Oyster Roasts

Winter picnics with oysters as the main ingredient have an old and elegant history in the South. Evan Jones writes in *American Food* about these informal alfresco entertainments in the early days of the nineteenth century.

> There was often a feeling of privileged informality when country people gathered to feast on oysters, or other seafood, as guests of the country gentleman who ran for political office—at least plantation aristocrats thought it was informality. Handymen carted big stoves onto the meadow and set them up in long lines facing each other. In between these lines serving girls set tables, also in long lines, impeccably decorating them with ancestral napery, fine china, and gleaming silver. When, at the appointed hour of one P.M., a hunting horn sounded from the portico of the great house, oysters by the barrelful were spread out to roast. A butler discharged his troops with whiskey punch for men and eggnogs for women. After the leisurely drinks, a guest once recorded, there came "battalions of pickaninnies bearing platters of sput-

tering oysters." And after an hour or so of feasting on oysters, there was an hour's rest while the linen was changed and order restored to the dining tables. Then crayfish in aspic, shrimp and watercress salad, red snapper baked whole with a wine sauce, terrapin stew and venison patty, pudding made of palmetto hearts, and yams "baked so tenderly they fell into the mold of any hand they touched." Not until sundown was there a hint of the real reason for the picnic; then the host announced to his sated guests that he was standing for office and would appreciate their votes.

There was a landed-gentry Englishness to scenes like this. Much of the colonial South had been founded by cavaliers, loyal to England's king. The average plantation owner was a man of the middle class who acquired land and devoted his energies to building a life of greater security and more evidence of affluence than he or his forebears had known before. Social status was of grave concern and was marked by emphasis on horse racing and fox hunting, six-in-hand coaches and ten-gallon punch bowls. Hospitality, above all, was *de rigueur*, not only because there were few taverns in the early days but because guests added interest to the isolation of plantation life. Entertaining was easy enough, with so many servants, easier because so many had an affinity for cooking well. The colonial South, said Sir William Berkeley, a Virginia governor in the seventeenth century, was "the land of good eating, good drinking, stout men and pretty women." With these planters' wives a good table was a point of honor. Meals on most plantations were prepared in detached kitchens and sped to the table under cover by waiters recruited from the slave population—"long trains of slaves," as an early traveler wrote, "passing to and fro, with the different viands."

These days ritual celebrations gather big crowds below the Mason-Dixon line where oysters are a staple plucked from the southern Atlantic and Gulf coasts. The village of Roadanthe, which is hemmed by the sea on the North Carolina coast, boasts of having the world's greatest oyster roasts. Plantation owners on such rivers as South Carolina's Combahee still entertain with oysters by the bushel freshly dredged from local streams. (One bushel for fifteen guests is the rule.) They are washed and scrubbed and shoveled onto iron mesh, or grills, or sheet iron over a hot crackling fire made of brush. A blanket of wet gunnysacking provides steam, and when the oysters pop and are spread out on a great table, the hungry fall to and devour them in typically informal American style.

Gargantuan feasts are part of Maryland Thanksgiving and Christmas celebrations, which may end up in a garage or hall when it is too cold to stand outside. The specially large and flavorsome oysters that arrive by the truckload are served in all sorts of ways: with milk or cream, in a stew, in a soup, pickled or in a mush, or simply steamed or roasted and served with bowls of melted butter and vinegar or lemon wedges and ketchup, Worcestershire sauce, or horseradish. It is easy to imagine that each of the 101 oyster recipes from May Southworth's book of 1907 would have been tried at one time or another at a roast. The roast beef, ham, and biscuits that are sometimes provided are obviously superfluous.

Oysters al Fresco

6 dozen oysters, well scrubbed | Salt and pepper
3/4 lb. (340 g.) butter, melted | Paprika

On a grill over hot coals arrange oysters with larger half of shell face down. Roast about 10 minutes, until shells open. Let everyone dip his and her oysters in melted butter and sprinkle with salt, pepper, and paprika.

In Praise of Raw Fish

Many people who try raw fish find it so good that they lose their enthusiasm for cooked fish, and it has become the fashion these days to search in old-established cuisines for traditional ways to serve it up. As fish has to be absolutely fresh to be eaten raw, the best time to start is with the fisherman's haul or your own catch while it is still full of the savor of the sea or stream.

Although the muddy taste of some fresh-water fish, such as carp, may be slightly tempered by soaking for a few hours in salted water, they are not the most suitable fish to be eaten raw. Most other fish are so delicious that they need few embellishments.

First you must gut, scale, clean, and wash the fish (for instructions see p. 262); then you must fillet it with a sharp knife.

The Dutch leave herrings sprinkled in a large quantity of coarse salt overnight. When you are ready to eat, remove the skin with a sharp knife. Split the fish down the center of the back, lever up the backbone, and carefully pull it out; the tiny fine bones will come off with it. All you need is some finely chopped onion and you have the best way of savoring herring.

Marinating in lime or lemon juice is a method which originated in Polynesia and has long been popular in South America and Mexico, where it is called seviche. It has recently become one of the fashionable foods with gastronomes around the world—rightly so, for it is delicious. You may treat salmon or humbler fish such as whiting, mullet, herring, bass, bream, anchovies, sardines, and smelts in this way.

Cut the fish in pieces or in slices 1/2 in. (1 1/2 cm.) to 1 in. (2 1/2 cm.) thick, and cover with lime or lemon juice for about 3 hours, by which time the flesh will be opaque. (You may also cut it very thin, like smoked salmon, and leave it to marinate for only 30 minutes.) Drain and reserve the juice. Use some of it to make a dressing with olive oil, salt, and pepper. You may add a sprinkling of chopped fresh herbs such as parsley, tarragon, oregano, basil, and dill. A good accompaniment is marinated mushrooms.

For a Latin American flavor add peeled and chopped tomatoes, finely chopped onions, a sliced or chopped fresh hot pepper, and a touch of crushed garlic. Spread this on top of the fish served on a bed of lettuce. A squeeze of lime juice may be added to the dressing.

For a Japanese way see page 184.

Gravlax

This Scandinavian way of treating salmon can also be applied to cheaper fish such as bluefish and mackerel. Buy a large middle piece weighing 2 1/4 or 3 1/2 lb. (1 to 1 1/2 kg.). Scale and wash it and cut off the head, then split it in two halves. Remove the backbone and pull out remaining bones as well as the brown strip of flesh down the middle. Put one piece skin side down in a bowl and sprinkle with a mixture of 4 tablespoons salt, 1 1/4 tablespoons sugar, 2 tablespoons crushed peppers, and a finely chopped bunch of dill. Cover with the second piece of fish, skin side up. Weight down with a plate and a stone on top and refrigerate for 2 or 3 days, turning over the piece of fish about twice a day so that all the flesh lies evenly in the juices that will be extruded.

To serve, slice as thin as possible at an angle (like smoked salmon) and accompany by gravlax sauce: Mix 4 tablespoons mild mustard, 1 tablespoon powdered sugar, 2 tablespoons dry white wine, then gradually beat in 6 tablespoons vegetable oil until the sauce has the consistency of mayonnaise. Stir in 3 tablespoons chopped dill.

There is a new French style of making gravlax: Mix 1/4 cup (60 g.) salt with 1 teaspoon sugar and rub onto the skinned fillets. Wrap in foil and leave in the refrigerator for 2 or 3 days, turning over once. Unwrap the fish and spread with 2 tablespoons soft green peppercorns, puréed with 4 tablespoons chopped fresh herbs such as thyme, tarragon, and chervil. Wrap the fish up again and weight it down between 2 trays. Leave in the refrigerator for at least half a day.

Plank-Roasted Salmon

James Beard gives the Indian way of plank-roasting a whole salmon, which is still done today on beaches along the coasts of Oregon and Washington:

You will need a hardwood board about 1 1/2 or 2 in. (4 to 5 cm.) thick, and a little wider and longer than the split fish. If you wish, cover the plank with foil. Nail the fish, skin side down, to the plank. Salt and pepper it, and spread it with butter, then prop the board at a slight angle near enough to the fire so that the fish will cook slowly. Brush it with oil or butter from time to time. When the fish flakes easily it is done. Serve with lemon and copious quantities of butter.

Fish Cooked au Bleu

This is a good way of cooking trout, carp, pike, or roach just as soon as it is pulled out of the lake or river. Fill a clean metal pail with 1 part vinegar and 3 parts fresh water. Add salt and pepper and put it to boil on the fire. Then toss in the fish unscaled, gutted quickly while still alive and jumping, and simmer for 5 to 10 minutes until it is just cooked through (and the trout tinged with blue).

Serve with butter and lemon juice and boiled new potatoes.

A Fry-Up

There is not much you can do with very small fish besides a fry-up, and for that you must be on firm land and in possession of a large, deep pan.

If the mountain stream has provided a collection of little fish at the end of your line, or if your net is full of a mixed bag from the sea, this is how you deal with an assortment of small fry such as sardines, anchovies, whitebait, and smelts:

Dry the fish in a cloth as it is, then roll (toss lightly) in flour. Heat plenty of oil in a deep frying pan, preferably one with a wire frying basket. Fry a few at a time, so that they do not stick together, in very hot oil. The smaller the fish, the hotter must be the oil. Whitebait need the oil to be smoking. They will be ready in a matter of minutes. Shake the basket gently if using one, or separate the fish with a fork. As soon as they are crisp and brown, drain and serve on paper napkins to absorb the oil. Garnish with sprigs of parsley and lemon wedges.

That is how the hotel Beau Rivage served us the result of a day's arduous fishing on the beach in Alexandria when we were children.

Sautéed Fish

Sautéing is the easiest way to cook a fish. Mark Twain describes frying one with bacon in *By the Camp Fire:*

They came back to camp wonderfully refreshed, glad hearted and ravenous; and they soon had the camp fire blazing up again. Huck found a spring of clear cold water close by, and the boys made cups of broad oak or hickory leaves, and felt that water, sweetened with such a wild-wood charm as that, would be a good enough substitute for coffee. While Joe was slicing bacon for breakfast, Tom and Huck asked him to hold on a minute; they stepped to a promising nook in the river bank and threw in their lines, almost immediately they had reward. Joe had not had time to get impatient before they were back again with some handsome bass, a couple of sun perch, and a small cat-fish— provisions enough for quite a family. They fried the fish with the bacon and were astonished, for no fish had ever seemed so delicious before. They did not know that the quicker a fresh water fish is on the fire after it is caught, the better it is; and they reflected little upon what a sauce open-air sleeping, open-air exercise, bathing, and a large ingredient of hunger make, too.

To cook fish à la meunière, clean and scale (sole is best skinned), cut it in steaks if it is too large for the pan, season, and dust with flour. Sauté quickly in a sizzling mixture of butter and oil or in clarified butter (see p. 297). For larger fish, reduce the heat and cook slowly until done (3 to 5 minutes for steaks and small fish, up to 10 minutes for a large trout). Season with salt and pepper and a squeeze of lemon and serve with sprigs of parsley.

You may also let the butter turn brown (which is called beurre noir) before putting in the fish.

As a luxury and for a sauce, stir some dry white wine with a few chopped fresh tarragon leaves in the pan drippings.

For a garnish, lightly fry slivered blanched almonds or sliced mushrooms in the same butter and pan and pour in fresh cream.

An Octopus

One summer I witnessed the demise of an octopus on the Greek island of Scopelos. A group of people were gazing into the sea. One was holding a pole with a white vest fastened on the end which he shook in the water. He pulled it out to a murmur of congratulations, for embracing it was an octopus which looked imploringly at the congregation. An onlooker carefully turned its ink sac inside out, gutted it and removed the eye and beak, then, holding it by its tentacles, beat it against the ground relentlessly. Another rubbed it vigorously with a stone. The entire process to tenderize the flesh took almost half an hour, during which time the others had started a fire. By the time the octopus was cut into pieces and threaded on skewers, the fire had died down to embers and was ready to receive it. As a foreign guest on the island I was not allowed to go without sampling a few pieces.

For those who are interested, octopus is as good boiled as it is grilled, but remember to beat it well; otherwise, however long you cook it, it will still be like rubber. Put it in a large pan of clean sea water and simmer for about 2 to 2 1/2 hours. Take it out and cut into small pieces.

Dress with plenty of olive oil and lemon juice, adding a little Dijon mustard, salt, and pepper, and leave to absorb this for 2 hours before serving.

Very tiny baby octopus like squid (cleaned of intestines and ink sacs) are delicious fried in oil with chopped onions or a little garlic, salt, and pepper. Cook over a brisk heat for 10 minutes. Sprinkle with parsley and lemon juice.

Bouillabaisse   *(for more than 6)*

If you are near the Mediterranean you must make this soup which accommodates whatever you can find. There is no better way to sing the praise of the produce of the sea, and you would be well advised to go armed with a copy of Alan Davidson's *Mediterranean Seafood*, which is a mine of information on all its edible marine life.

Bouillabaisse belongs to Marseilles and has the flavor of the Mediterranean. With aïoli and pastis, it is a main ingredient of the local *douceur de vivre*, without which you can never fully enjoy the blue of the sea and the sky, the mauve of the rocks, the pale pink and ocher houses, the forgotten ports, and the game of pétanque. As is to be expected from the Midi, local opinion is divided as to how the best bouillabaisse is made. Alan Davidson gives a simple and excellent version:

Buy fish* as follows:

a) a rascasse or two, depending on size
b) some other fish with firm flesh such as monkfish, gurnard, weever
or star-gazer eel or moray or conger
c) some delicate fish such as whiting or flatfish
d) a few small wrasse or the like
e) an inexpensive crustacean which might be squille or a petite cigale.

Have 4 1/2 lb. (2 kg.) in all. Gut and scale the fish, cut them in pieces where necessary and wash them.

Now heat a wineglassful of olive oil in a large cooking pot and brown in this a large onion, finely sliced, and 2 cloves of garlic. Add 1 lb. (1/2 kg.) of peeled and chopped tomatoes (or a corresponding amount of tomato concentrate) followed by about 3 liters of water (preferably boiling) and the fish from groups (a) and (b) and (d) and (e). Those from group (d) are intended to disintegrate in the cooking, adding body to the soup. Season with salt and pepper. Add chopped parsley and a pinch of saffron, a piece of orange peel, a clove, a bay leaf, and a sprig of thyme. Pour a wineglassful of olive oil over all. Bring to and keep at a vigorous boil for 15 to 20 minutes. Add the fish in group (c) toward the end of this period, allowing just enough time for them to cook.

When all is ready lift out the crustaceans and the fish which are still

---

*If you're not near the Mediterranean other fish you can substitute are: sculpin, bass, cod, cusk, flounder, sole, grouper, haddock, hake, halibut, pollack, perch, and snapper.

whole and serve them on one platter. Pour the broth over pieces of garlic-rubbed toast in soup plates (straining it in the process if you wish). Serve rouille alongside.

For the rouille: Pound 2 cloves garlic and 2 sweet red peppers in a mortar and pestle or purée in a food processor, add a chunk of bread, soaked in water and squeezed, and mix well. Then add 2 tablespoons olive oil and beat in some fish broth, about 1 1/2 wineglasses full for a thick sauce.

Rice for the Open Sea

Seychellois fishermen, who spend their days between the sixty islands of the Indian Ocean archipelago, bring only long-grain rice and a heavy pot with a lid for the traditional midday meal. When they begin to feel hungry they boil up some sea water in the pot over a fire, throw in an equal volume of rice, and when the water begins to be absorbed they lay a few fish, whatever they have got in their nets, on the top under the lid, to steam for the last few minutes while the rice cooks.

Arroz a la marinera. Alan Davidson gives this Spanish recipe in *Mediterranean Seafood* for a paella-type rice and seafood dish which is a little more elaborate. The small round-grain rice and the larger quantity of water give the dish the soft mushy quality of Italian risottos. You will need:

1 cup (1/4 liter) olive oil
1 1/8 lb. (1/2 kg.) in all of angler fish, squid, and cuttlefish, prepared and cut into chunks and strips
2 onions, chopped
4 tomatoes, peeled and chopped
Plenty of paprika

1 1/2 lb. (700–750 g.) rice (if possible Valencian)
Just over 8 cups (2 liters) fish stock
1 1/8 lb. (1/2 kg.) in all of Norway lobster,* shrimp, and mussels (or substitute any fish and seafood available)

*Alan Davidson says that Norway lobster is the same thing as Dublin Bay prawns and scampi.

Heat the olive oil and add the pieces of angler fish, squid, and cuttlefish. When these are golden add the chopped onion and tomato and paprika. Continue to fry all this for a few minutes, taking care not to burn the paprika.

Next add the rice and twice the quantity by volume of fish stock. (This will work out at just over 8 cups or 2 liters.) Three minutes later add the Norway lobster, shrimp, and mussels (cleaned but whole). Continue cooking for about 20 minutes until the rice has absorbed all the liquid.

Hot Smoking

Hot smoking is an idea that should appeal to anglers, for it cooks fish in 20 minutes and gives it a most unusual smoky flavor. Most things are enhanced by this method of cooking. It is quite different from cold smoking, which takes hours and days.

Little smokers for taking on a picnic have been appearing on the market in recent years, but the enterprising can make their own with a metal box, a baffle plate, and a grill.

To smoke fish, spread some sawdust at the bottom of the tin—hickory, elm, apple, ash, all these are excellent. Put the baffle plate over it, then the grill. Slash the fish diagonally so that it does not curl and season if you like with salt and pepper and lemon juice and put a sprig of herbs in the cavity. You may find this superfluous beside the strong perfume of the smoke from the smoldering wood dust. Lay the fish on the grill. If it is too big to fit in you can cut it into steaks. Shut the lid and light the fuel in the burner underneath. The fish will be ready to eat in about 20 minutes. Trout and mackerel are especially good treated in this way.

DINING IN THE
AMERICAN WILDERNESS

"These days you can dine about as easily and well in the wilderness as in the city. Matter of fact, you're likely to find yourself eating considerably better." Bradford Angier, the author of *Wilderness Cookery*, was talking about America, where thousands of edible herbs, vegetables, and fruits grow wild. He exhorted hunters to upgrade the meals made with their catch with these delicacies.

All outdoorsmen know that one of the delights of a hunting or fishing trip is the savory conclusion: barbecued quail or partridge, roasted wild turkey, elk chops, antelope and beaver steaks, or rabbit stew. In a country where hunting and fishing are much loved and prestigious sports, there has been a deluge of cookbooks on the subject. So much so that a great outdoorsman was moved to complain that some of the recipes must have been lifted from wives' cookbooks, so impractical were the methods and the seasonings "straight from Paris to disguise the taste of plain wholesome food." He lamented that "not one told how to bake bread, cook oatmeal and cornmeal, fry trout, roast meat, bake dry beans or stew prunes." Of course, when the only "store grub" you can take on a hiking or canoeing trip must weigh no more than 2 lb. (1 kg.) a day you had better try to rely more on the wild edibles you can procure and stick to basics of cooking.

Without the experience of the hunt I will restrict myself to passing on a few hints from some of the hunter-cook writers of America for preparing big and small game, upland birds, water fowl, fish, and a few of the more widespread fruit and vegetables that grow wild.

L. W. Johnson has this to say in his *Wild Game Cookbook*: Dress the game quickly and draw the birds. Hang them for a few days in a cool place if you like to "season" the meat. Pheasant, quail, and Hungarian partridge can be wet picked, prairie chickens and sharp-tails can be scalded and picked. It is easier to skin some birds but often better not to, as the fat under the skin imparts a more delicate flavor to the meat and also protects it. To skin, start at the breast, peel the feathers off, cut off the legs at the joint, and take off the wings. Then wash in cold water.

Young birds (bones are soft, beaks come off easily, and claws are blunt) can be roasted or grilled, preferably covered with bacon strips, but mature ones require longer, moist cooking such as stewing. A pheasant will serve three or four, a partridge one. With quail and woodcock, count on two birds for each serving. To remove a too gamy flavor or the fishy one of wild ducks, soak the birds in salted water acidulated with a little vinegar or lemon for a few hours.

Usual methods of cooking include cutting in pieces, dipping or not in flour and frying in bacon fat, wrapping in foil and pushing between coals for 30 minutes to an hour or longer depending on the bird, and simmering in a pot with vegetables. Here is an old-timer's secret for prairie chicken: Clean and season it inside, feathers still on, and wrap it in yellow clay mixed with water to make a paste, seal up the body cavity, then open up the bed of coals, put the bird down in the bottom, cover it, and leave it for a couple of hours. Crack the rock-hard clay open, and feathers and skin come off, leaving nice clean, tasty meat.

The best way to eat big game is roasted or cut in steaks or chops and grilled over the fire, but it can also be sautéed in sizzling fat and stewed with all sorts of vegetables in a mulligan. Other ways are baking in a pit or cooking the animal in its hide in a hole on hot stones or in ashes. Moose, venison, bear, antelope, caribou, beaver, mountain sheep, muskrat, lynx, and cougar all furnish good meat, each with its own special wild flavor.

Of the smaller game, the white gelatinous meat of beaver tail is a rare delicacy; opossum is the most prized and better for barbecuing after it has been aged a few days. Coon is excellent when slowly cooked, roasted, or braised. Brunswick stew is made with squirrel and all sorts of vegetables. Muskrat tastes like turkey, only better, rabbit and hare like chicken. All these things can also be made into a game soup or a huntsmen's stew or a fricassee.

The way to cook your fish depends partly on its fatness. Plump fish like trout, salmon, and white fish can be baked in a Dutch oven or roasted or grilled. Lean catches such as pike, bass, perch, and Arctic grayling must be basted frequently or should be poached, steamed, or sautéed or cooked in foil.

Everything can be greatly embellished by wild edibles. Vine leaves can serve as a wrapping on the grill or the spit, burning prunings and fruit woods impart a special flavor, and berries can be used for stuffing or as a sauce. Grapes and cherries and many different types of berries such as blueberries, gooseberries, cranberries, strawberries, raspberries, blackberries, and less common ones can be found all over America.

Wild mushrooms can be put in the stewpot or the frying pan or chopped up for the sauce. The inner bark of the birch, which can be boiled, is sweet and spicy, and pines, too, have an inner bark that you can eat. Many varieties of wild greens can be found growing nearly everywhere and can be eaten raw as salad or cooked, lamb's-quarters being the acknowledged pick of the edible greens, Bradford Angier lists these and many other edibles such as plantain, which is eaten like dandelion. He gives a recipe for a wild greens soup which also includes mustard greens and watercress slowly heated, but not allowed to boil, in milk with salt and pepper. Easily gathered mustard seeds make a good garnish for salads and give a delicious flavor to venison. The young leaves, stems, and flowers of fireweed can be eaten both raw and cooked, the young, red-stemmed shoots are an asparagus substitute, and you can steep the leaves for tea. Horsetail prospers about shaded brooks and in cool moist locations, and clover can be a salad garnish. All sorts of roots can be boiled or smoldered in ashes. Many types of seaweed such as dulse and kelp, which grow attached to rocks, are very good in soups and stews. There is wild cucumber which tastes like cucumber but looks like berries. Salal is a wintergreen fruit which is delicious in apple sauce. Glasswort, which is also called beach asparagus, makes a good boiled salad with a vinegar dressing. The young fiddleheads of brake ferns can also be boiled and dressed, and mountain sorrel has a delightful sharp flavor. Wild celery is good with fish; cowslip roots look like sauerkraut when they are cooked. It is no wonder that Mr. Angier's motto is "pick instead of pack." The "grub box" need be used only as a last resort.

Hints for Game and Camp Cooking

Here are some hints for game and camp cooking from Seneca's *Canoe and Camp Cookery* (1893).

Stuffed Game Roasted

Large birds (ducks or turkeys, etc.), rabbits, hares, woodchucks, porcupines, opossums, and the like may be stuffed with a dressing made of salt pork and bread or crackers. Chop the pork very fine, soak the bread or crackers in hot water and mash them smooth, and mix them with the chopped pork. Season with pepper, a little salt, sage, and chopped onion. Sew up the game after stuffing with wire in two or three places, and roast over hot coals. If wrapped in wet brown paper, it may be immersed in hot ashes and baked; if small, it may be baked the same as fish.

Opossums and Young Pigs   *(for more than 6)*

Are roasted alike. After cleaning the opossum or pig stuff him with bread crumbs, chopped onion and sage or summer savory for seasoning, boiled Irish and sweet potatoes (the latter especially with the 'possum) and whole boiled onions being pushed in among the dressing. Wire up the opening in two or three places, fold the legs down on the body and wire them fast. Then cut a strong, straight, hard-wood limb, and run it through the animal from stern to snout. This is to be suspended from two crotched stakes over the fire, and, if smooth, the 'possum or pig cannot be turned on it, as the limb will turn inside the animal. Therefore, in lopping off the twigs from the limb after it is cut, leave half an inch or so of each twig to act as a barb, insert the limb in the animal butt first, then give it a "yank" backward so that the barbs may hold when it is desired to turn the animal to roast all sides alike. Cut gashes in the thickest parts of the meat so that it may roast evenly throughout. A 'possum or pig prepared as above may be coated with clay and baked in the ground with plenty of coals in from two to three hours. When roasted over the fire the drippings should be caught and used to baste it.

Pork Hash

Cut salt pork or bacon into small dice, and while it is frying over a slow fire cut raw potatoes and onions into thin slices, put them with the pork, cover the frying pan and cook for ten minutes, occasionally stirring.

Pork and Beans

The right proportions are two quarts of beans to three pounds of pork. Pick over the beans at night, wash them, and put them to soak in cold water until the next morning. Then if only boiled pork and beans are desired, drain the beans, and put them with the pork in the pot, just cover with cold water, set over the fire (with the cover on the pot), and boil till the beans are tender, skimming the scum off as it rises. If baked beans are wanted parboil the pork and cut it into thin slices, then drain the beans and boil as above. Put half the beans into the bake-kettle, then the pork, then the remainder of the beans, and pour over them half a pint of boiling water. Bake among the coals till the top is crusted brown. If buried in the ground with a good supply of coals it is best to put them in at night when going to bed, and they will be done in the morning. If the bake-kettle is enveloped in hot coals on the surface of the ground they will bake on the outside quicker, but inside, where the pork is, they will not be baked at all. This latter method, therefore, should only be used when in a hurry, and in this case the pork should be scattered around in different portions of the pot, and the beans left may be re-baked for another meal.

Game Stew

Cut up any kind of game, whether furred or feathered, into small pieces, wash it, and put it in a pot with some pork cut into pieces three inches square, and rather more than enough water to cover it all. Let it boil for half an hour, skimming off the particles that rise to the top. Then add four or five sliced onions, some parsley or summer savory, salt and pepper, and boil slowly for an hour and a half. Half an hour before it is done put in a few pared potatoes, cut to a uniform size.

PRIMITIVE
WAYS OF COOKING

Pit Cooking

Kafupi Petrides, a painter who lives on the island of Evia in Greece, told me about her occasional oven: "I dig a hole in the earth or sand, line it with large stones and make a good fire on them for about half an hour. When it has died down completely I wrap fish or meat or game which I have seasoned with salt and pepper, rigani or bay and garlic, lemon juice or wine, as the case may be —in a large piece of foil and put it in the hole, cover it completely and heavily with the earth or sand and leave it to cook for 2 1/2 to 3 hours. . . ."

However primitive it might seem, this is an excellent and satisfying way of cooking still practiced all over the world in the countryside. Greeks call it klephti or robber cooking, and in Sardinia cooking in a pit is also known as brigand cooking. For in this way animal thieves can cook their stolen sheep or calf, pig or donkey, undetected. In the Middle East it is used mainly on festive occasions, but some villages in Libya still make large communal pit ovens to hold the food of all the households as well as that of occasional travelers.

There are different ways of cooking in a pit: over a fire or when it has died out, or with the fire on top, over ground.

Make a pit as large as you like to accommodate one item or a variety of foods; 2 ft. (60 cm.) deep and 3 to 4 ft. (90 to 120 cm.) across is a good size. Make a fire at the bottom and let it burn down to embers for about an hour. Any fruitwood gives the food a special taste. Place a wire mesh or other grid a few inches above the embers, supported by metal rods and bricks or stones.

Place the food on the grid, wrapped if you like in layers of paper or foil for cleanliness (this will result in a steamed effect). Cover first with branches, reeds, or such things and then with grass or hay.

The clambake in America is a form of pit cooking. For an account of this by Evan Jones, see page 343.

Cooking without a fire takes longer but the result is food of particular tenderness. Line the bottom and sides of the pit with medium-size stones and smaller ones or shingle in between. Build a large hardwood fire on top of the stones and let it burn for at least 2 hours so that the stones may store enough heat. Let it die down, then brush or rake off the embers and bits of charcoal. Cover the stones with a bed of succulent grass or better still with aromatic leaves such as papaya vine or beech (cactus leaves in the desert) and a few sprigs of any herbs that happen to grow around. Lay the food to be cooked (meat, fish, and vegetables, seasoned to your liking) over the leaves and cover with a second thick layer of leaves. Pile small rocks, stones, earth, or sand on top of the leaves to weigh them down and to retain the heat. If you have a tarpaulin or canvas lay this on the leaves first.

(You may also wrap the food in paper or foil with the seasonings of your choice. It will cook in its own steam but will not benefit from the special smoky flavor.)

Cooking time depends on the type and size of the food; it is difficult to give correct times and necessary to uncover and test if it is done. As a rough guide everything takes at least half as long again as in a normal oven. I have not tried it myself, but that is what my friends say. Overcooking in this way never seems to harm the food.

The brigands' way is to have the fire on top of the food (no doubt so as to put the animal out of sight as quickly as possible!). Put a metal sheet placed on a ridge halfway up the hole to hold the wood.

Beanhole Beans

Baking food in a hole in the ground is probably one of the oldest forms of cooking, and in America it is a pioneer tradition claimed by loyal State of Maine citizens as their own. In fact, the high repute of Maine lumberjack cooks is such that it has been said that Canadian lumber magnates sent scouts to investigate the method and then gave orders to their own logging camp cooks to serve real Yankee baked beans to their own workmen.

Anyone who camps out in brisk weather has a sense of how delicious beanhole beans can be. Long ago in a series of articles on camping that he wrote for the *Boston Post,* Howard Reynolds described the wilderness ritual:

First dig a hole in the ground, fairly free of rocks, 2 feet deep by 18 inches in circumference. In the hole kindling of soft wood is placed, and over the hole a cobhouse of split hard wood is built. When the fire is lighted in the kindling, the cobhouse catches fire, and as the air circulates freely through it, the hardwood sticks, being of uniform size, all burn down together.

In the meanwhile, over the campfire a pail of beans (about 2 quarts dried beans) has been parboiling so that their skins crack when dished out in a spoon and exposed to air. The water from these is drained off and they are poured into another pail on the bottom of which has been placed several thick slices of fat salt pork. On top of the beans is placed a piece of pork weighing about a pound, the rind of which has been well gashed. Over all is poured a teaspoonful of salt, 3 tablespoons of molasses, 2 of sugar and a dash of mustard, dissolved in hot water. The pail is then filled with enough boiling water to cover the beans.

Next the coals are raked out of the hole and the pail, covered tight, is placed in the hole. The live coals are then shoveled around it and over it, together with a few inches of earth tramped down tight and allowed to remain alone all night. In the morning, dig the pail out and serve.

Another Yankee bean enthusiast once wrote: "One admirable feature of this dish is that, besides enjoying the unapproached perfection of home baked beans, you can eat them from a bean hole with no pang of remorse for someone who had to keep a kitchen hot all day long in midsummer." Here is his recipe:

(for more than 6)

1 3/4 lbs. (800 g.) pea beans
1/8 teaspoon baking soda
1 tablespoon sliced onion
1 1/8 lb. (1/2 kg.) salt pork or
    bacon, sliced

1/4 teaspoon dry mustard
2 teaspoons salt
1 teaspoon black pepper
4 tablespoons molasses

Wash and pick over beans, and soak them in cold water overnight. Simmer 1 hour, or until skins begin to crack, in water to which soda has been added. Proceed as above. Let beans cook all day for supper, or all night for breakfast.

Chinook Method: Horace Kephart, an outdoorsman who wrote *Camp Cookery* in 1923, heated stones outside the pit and then threw them in the hole to steam his meat and vegetables. Here are his instructions: Build a large fire and throw on it a number of smooth stones, not of the bombshell kind. Dig a hole in the ground near the fire. When the stones are red hot, fork them into the hole, level them, cover with green or wet leaves, grass or branches, place the meat or potatoes on this layer, cover with more leaves, and then cover all with a good layer of earth. Now bore a small hole down to the food, pour in some water, and immediately stop up the hole, letting the food steam until tender. This, according to Kephart, is the Chinook method of cooking the outdoor feast called *camass*. Shellfish can be steamed in the same way.

Pit Cooking in Texas

From Evan Jones I learned that "Texans consider themselves masters of fire pits and scoff at outsiders who have the audacity to use the word barbecue in a competitive sense. In other southern reaches of the U.S.," Evan wrote to me,

the term is still used regularly in reference to specialized outdoor cooking, but when a plantation Southerner says he is going to eat "barbecue" he means he's going to eat pig meat that is slow-cooked— with or without sauce—by a pitmaster whose place of business is open throughout the year for that purpose alone. But only beef—some Texans will tell you—is "real" barbecue, and it must be beef brisket to satisfy the dedicated Texas aficionado. When a traveler in the Lone Star state catches the scent of burning mesquite logs or crushed pecan shells he has caught the signal that a bona-fide Texas outdoor cook is at work.

Professionally, the master of brisket barbecuing is an entrepreneur whose sights are set on the Texas lunch hour, and his work begins— of course—the night before. In the shank of the evening, when his place of business is devoid of customers, he goes to his walk-in cooler, sharpens his knife, and begins boning slabs of beef, slitting them expertly in order to save the fat that helps to lubricate his work. On the grate that crisscrosses his glowing firepit he spreads the briskets, rubbing each piece with salt, black pepper, and powdered sweet red pepper. Not until breakfast time will he raise the sheet metal lid that keeps the heat from escaping from the pit. His barbecue may seem tender at this point, but he knows that more logs are needed to provide even longer cooking. Only at high noon will it be so tender it seems to be falling apart.

Carolina barbecued pork takes even longer to reach perfection than

Texas brisket. Although oak is sometimes used for smoking pork, hickory coals are preferred by old-time Carolina cooks, and fires may be started about 8:00 A.M. in pits lined with bricks, stones, or concrete. When barbecuing a pig of, say, 65 pounds, the head is cut off and the body slit so it will lie flat. About noon the pig is placed skin side up on iron rods across burning coals in the pit. Periodically, while it slowly roasts for a dozen or so hours, it is basted with vinegar seasoned with red pepper pods. Then the skin is rubbed, in the traditional way, with lard before the pig is flipped over. Barbecuing continues while salt is added to the basting sauce for the seasoning of the cooked side. The cooked meat is allowed to cool, then is chopped coarsely and mixed with the basting sauce. It is reheated just before serving—often with corn bread as an accompaniment. A kitchen-made substitute may be taken on a picnic.

Here's the recipe.

Carolina Homemade Chopped Barbecue   *(for more than 6)*

3 1/2–4 1/2-lb. (1 1/2–2-kg.) pork
  shoulder with bone in
4 cloves garlic
3 cups (3/4 liter) cider vinegar

Fresh peppercorns
1 teaspoon red pepper
Salt

Put the pork shoulder in an iron pot with the garlic cloves left whole, 1 cup (1/4 liter) vinegar, and the unground peppercorns. Add water to cover meat, bring to a boil, and skim froth. Simmer, covered, about 3 hours. Meanwhile combine 2 cups (1/2 liter) vinegar with about a teaspoon of red pepper and a little salt. Put in screw-top jar and shake well.

Remove pork from pot and discard liquid. Place wire grill in bottom of pot with the pork arranged on it, and baste meat with some of vinegar sauce. Roast in 350°F (180°C) oven, basting often, for 1 1/2 hours; turn meat and continue roasting and basting 1 1/2 hours more. Remove pork and chop fine, then return to pot to transport to picnic site where it can be heated before serving.

An Improvised Oven in the Ground—Dutch Oven

Much like beanhole cooks in America, Basque sheep herders who spend months at a time high up in the Rocky Mountains use cast iron or aluminum pots buried in a shallow pit under the fire. All you need is a large can with a lid and a metal sheet.

Dig a hole in the ground large enough to contain it. If the ground is wet, dig it larger and line it with flat stones. Light a wood fire in the hole. When it has burned to embers push them to the sides of the hole and put the can in the center. Cover with the metal sheet or a piece of wood. For a more even heat, shovel some embers onto the metal sheet and let them burn on top of the hole. You can bake a cake or a large roast or the stews described on page 335.

A Built-up Oven

For a large permanent camp it is worth building a more elaborate kind of oven. F. Marian McNeill gives instructions for this in *The Camper's Kitchen:*

The materials required are bricks, turves, stones, or clay, with two pieces of sheet iron or tin, about 3 feet square.

With the bricks or other material build round three sides of a square the same size as the sheet-iron. When it is about nine inches high, insert one piece of sheet-iron, and continue building until the two sides are about eighteen inches high. The back, however, must be a little lower than the sides, so as to provide a draught. The second piece of sheet-iron is placed on the top, and is supported, of course, only by the sides.

The fire is lighted on the lower shelf. The space below serves as an oven for joints, puddings, or cakes, whilst soups, stews, vegetables, etc., are cooked on the top of the stove.

A Reflector Oven

A useful arrangement for cooking in front of a camp fire is a reflector also described by F. Marian McNeill. This consists of a shallow open-fronted box or screen, preferably of aluminum, with a sloping roof, and a shelf supported on ledges in the middle. The food to be cooked is placed on the shelf, and heat from the fire is reflected down from the top and up from the bottom in addition to the direct rays. With the concentrated heat from every direction, the food cooks evenly and quickly. The reflector can be made to fold and, with hinge-pins and rivets of aluminum wire, is rustless. To get the best results, the metal should be kept polished, and when not in use it should be protected with canvas.

A Haybox

A haybox is an old-fashioned method for long slow cooking which works very well. Some friends cook their meal in their car trunk in this way when they go out for the day.

Line a wooden or strong cardboard box tightly with a thick blanket or insulating felt or pipe lagging and fill with hay or straw or newspapers. Transfer a boiling pot straight from the fire to the box or wrap food in foil, then in a towel, and bury in the hay. Cover with more hay and lagging and secure the lid. If the food is boiling hot when you put it in, it will continue to cook slowly for many hours.

Cooking in Clay

In England this is known as a gypsy method of cooking hedgehogs, but it will also do very well with fish, birds, and any little animal. The advantage is that you do not need to pluck or skin; spikes, feathers, fur, and skin all come off with the clay, leaving the flesh perfectly clean and cooked in its own juices. Remove head, feet, and entrails and clean the cavities, and if seasonings are at hand, stuff with herbs, a small onion, a slice of lemon, and a sprinkling of salt and pepper. Cover with wet clay, coat after coat, to a thickness of 1 1/2 to 2 in. (4 to 5 cm.) and bury in hot embers. When the clay cracks it should be ready. Depending on size it may take between 1 and 3 hours. Remove from the fire and break open.

Lacking clay, an excellent alternative is a flour and water paste or a thick dough casing. Tortilla dough is used in Mexico.

Fish Baked in Clay

If you can find fine sticky clay (it may be with a red or a bluish tinge) it is worth trying this method of cooking fish which really seals in the flavor. If it is not already wet, work it to the consistency of a stiff dough. Encase the fish live if you can, stunned to keep it from wriggling. Otherwise simply gut the fish through the mouth and put a sprig of herbs or a slice of lemon in the cavity for flavor. Do not cut the belly or mud will get inside, and do not scale the fish or remove the head; leave it as it is. Simply cover it completely with a layer of mud pie clay about 1 to 1 1/2 in. (2 1/2 to 4 cm.) thick and place it on hot embers. There is much controversy over the length of cooking time: some cooks advocate 15 minutes only for a medium-size fish and 15 minutes per pound for a large one, while others believe that a 3 1/2-lb. (1 1/2-kg.) fish needs 2 hours. I have not tried it, and my informants were equally divided, but each said that when the clay cracks the fish should be done. Remove from the fire and break open the shell. Scales, skin, fins, and tail will come off, remaining stuck to the clay, leaving the steaming white flesh full of juice and flavor.

EQUIPMENT

Everyone seems to agree on the perfect spot for a picnic or at least those who have put their choice on paper do. It should be green, with green ground and leafy trees for the sun to shine through, small paths, hidden recesses, gentle hills, and above all water: a rushing stream, a smiling lake, or a bubbling cascade. Some like to sit on the grass and eat with their hands to commune more fully with Nature and be part of it all. Others like to lord it over her by spreading a tablecloth and bringing out their finest china, cut glass, and silver. My parents bring a folding table and chairs for the sunshine hours they spend under a tree on Hampstead Heath, a few minutes from their London home.

The necessary equipment for outdoor eating is a matter of taste. There are no rules. Lady Harriet St. Clair quotes a celebrated German cookbook in her own *Dainty Dishes* with suggestions for a shooting breakfast: "Gentle-men usually prefer eating this about the middle of the day, in the open air, with their fingers in order that they may lose no time; so it is not generally necessary to send knives or forks or tablecloths, but you must take care, in order not to make them angry, that the luncheon is there at the right time and place."

H. D. Renner in *The Origins of Food Habits* is another advocate of using fingers, especially for gnawing bones: "Many things are allowed outdoors which are not inside. One is gnawing bones." He says, "The meat is tastiest near the bone and can be smelt at the same time as eaten which exerts a far more intense effect as on the plate. The action of gnawing prolongs the pleasure and you can still recollect the pleasant feelings for a long time after by taking an occasional sniff at your fingers."

It is quite possible to eat in a very elegant manner without knives and forks. Flat pita bread is used in the Middle East to scoop up morsels of food and to dip into creamy pastes or soak up the last of a sauce, and leaves of all kinds make excellent plates and spoons. In the areas where they grow, banana and lotus leaves are commonly used; around the Mediterranean it is vine leaves, but it is easier and nicer to wrap the food up in lettuce leaves of the soft round variety which do not break when you roll them up.

To carry the food, the traditional lidded wicker baskets with handles on two
   sides are useful. Large old-fashioned ones like a suitcase, good for large
   parties, can be found in a few stores, but a small ordinary basket may be
   all you need, or a metal or plastic box. Nowadays you see a lot of plastic
   hampers, which are usually insulated, that come in a variety of sizes. Just

be careful not to overload them since their handles usually cannot bear much weight.

Whether you have a large cardboard box as a hamper in the car or only a backpack, it is important to organize food and supplies to save space and make transport easier. Equipment must be light and not bulky. Containers must be leakproof, especially if they contain liquids. Screw-on tops are best for these. Reinforce the closing if necessary with heavy masking tape. Use heavy-duty freezer plastic bags and plastic wrap. Wrap anything that bruises easily in soft paper before packing and breakables such as bottles in a cloth.

Make a list of what you need: deep plates or bowls to avoid spillage, plastic cups, ground sheet, rug, corkscrew, can opener, sharp knife, matches, cutlery, large plastic bags for rubbish and dirty crocks, salt, pepper, sugar, condiments, sauces, and relishes (Mrs. Beeton's choice was "a stick of horseradish, a bottle of good mint sauce well corked, a bottle of salad dressing, a bottle of vinegar, made mustard, pepper, salt, good oil and pounded sugar . . . and ice.") Please yourself.

Useful tips. Serve foods from the molds in which they have been cooked or the bowls they have set in. Don't bother to turn them out unless for a special occasion. Small individual timbale molds are attractive to present but a larger mold is more practical for transport. For easier serving, things may be carved or sliced and re-formed into their original shape and wrapped tightly in foil. Otherwise bring a good carving knife and a wooden board.

Keep perishables in the coldest part of your car and insulate food boxes with damp newspaper if it is very hot. Bottles may be cooled in a running stream but must be placed securely or tied to a tree. Or leave them for a while in a windy spot wrapped in a wet towel.

Keeping things hot or cold. It is possible and easy to carry safely a varied and elaborate feast.

Technical progress has gone far in providing us with all manner of containers for keeping things hot or cold, crisp and fresh, without letting them spill, crush, or crumble. You will find them in any camping department. There is a wide range of portable vacuum and insulated containers: bags, boxes, chests, buckets, beakers, tumblers, jars, jugs, and serving dishes in all shapes and sizes to keep solid and liquid foods hot for up to 4 hours or cold for 8.

If ice packs are put inside, foods can be kept really chilled for a whole day. These packs, which may be rigid or flexible, contain a gel substance that stays colder than ice for a very long time. Two packs used together are doubly effective. They must be left in a freezer compartment overnight until their contents solidify. Some packs can also be used for keeping things hot and must be put in boiling water for 10 minutes, but they are effective for only an hour or two. Plastic insulated boxes usually have a tray on the lid to hold the packs. In an insulated bag frozen packs should be laid on top of but separated from the food; hot ones must be put at the bottom.

Whatever the container and however many items, these must be frozen or chilled and kept in the refrigerator until the last minute or packed very hot straight out of the oven. Rinse the container before filling it. Stuff cloth or paper in between the items to prevent air pockets which make it less effective.

A version of the old haybox (p. 368) will also keep things hot for a long time.

Stoves and Other Cooking Equipment

The problems of cooking in a camper or galley or at camp are governed by cooker capacity and the necessity to economize on gas and by limited working space. They are easily overcome with a little thought and ingenuity and the right equipment, which usually has to be limited to a minimum.

For fuel, unless you rely entirely on the open fire, you have the choice of a bottled gas cooker, a kerosene-burning stove, or an alcohol one. With all of these there are usually one or two burners, a grill, and occasionally an oven.

Stoves burning kerosene are the most economical. Primus stoves are compact and easy to operate, but greater care is needed in handling the fuel. Cartridge gas stoves are the most expensive to run but the easiest and best to use, though they do not function very well at low temperatures. Different models have varying capacities, attachments, and extras. Mini light and collapsible picnic cookers using methylated spirits may be all you need for a brief cooking or for warming up food.

For a long vacation there is a wide range of gas cookers with two burners and useful parts such as wind breaks, cooker shelf, warming rack, and grill pan. Most valuable is one with a fine adjustment from fast burning to the slowest simmer. Rechargeable gas containers can easily be refilled. For average summer-time cooking a 10-lb. (4 1/2-kg.) container should last about 10 days.

You will need a canteen of one or more saucepans or frying pans that nest into each other for storage. If you cannot carry much, the French army kit and the G.I. canteen are ideal, but their aluminum pans are of necessity light and thin and you must be careful not to burn the food.

If you have space it is well worth taking heavy-bottomed pans (non-stick ones are useful) with fitting lids. High, narrow saucepans are best for saving heat and fuel.

An asbestos mat is a substitute for a grill and good for making toast. A griddle is excellent for making bread (see p. 220) and cooking steaks and sausages. The best is made of cast iron; it has a ribbed surface and a stick-resistant matte enamel finish. A heavy pot or casserole which can be left for hours in hot ashes is useful for stewing. A pressure cooker or a crockpot, if you have a battery, saves fuel and time.

Other necessary cooking equipment includes water carriers, lanterns, food boxes, can opener, corkscrew, and the basic necessities of the kitchen: sharp knife, wooden spoon, grater, fish slicer, rotary beater, garlic press. Add to these a campfire grill and heavy-duty foil and an ax and saw for cutting wood.

Barbecuing Chart, Bibliography, and Index

Barbecuing Chart

The cooking times suggested should be taken as only a very rough guide. In reality timing depends not only on the thickness and type of food, whether it is lean or fat, tough or tender, and the distance from the fire, but also on the relative efficiency of the grill, the size of the firebed, the quality of wood or coals (this especially varies widely) and their concentration, as well as the weather conditions. The time given is for cooking on both sides. You may prefer to give the first side a longer cooking time.

If the food is wrapped in foil cook for an additional 5 to 10 minutes.

The heat of the fire is measured by the distance of the grill or spit from the bed of embers:

Searing hot	1 1/2–2 in. (4–5 cm.)
Hot	3 in. (8 cm.)
Medium	4 in. (10 cm.)
Low	5 in. (13 cm.)

If you cannot adjust the height of the grill easily, simply change the position of the meat from the hottest part—straight above—to the edge of the fire.

For cooking on a spit, the distance should be measured from the fire to the food. To obtain medium heat place the spit 6 in. (15 cm.) away from the fire so that the meat is about 4 in. (10 cm.) away. Lower it for searing and raise it for slow cooking.

Type of food	Cut	Thickness or weight	Heat	Approximate (generous) total cooking time (for both or all sides)
Beef Best rare or underdone, seared and browned outside				After 1 minute searing each side and turning once, give the second side a little less than the first.
	Steaks	1 in. (2 1/2 cm.)	hot	6 minutes for rare, up to 10 minutes for medium.

Type of food	Cut	Thickness or weight	Heat	Approximate (generous) total cooking time (for both or all sides)
Beef (cont'd)	Steaks (cont'd)	2 in. (5 cm.)	hot	8 minutes for rare, up to 16 minutes for medium.
	Hamburgers	1 in. (2 1/2 cm.)	hot	6–10 minutes.
	Kebab	1 in. (2 1/2 cm.)	hot/ medium	5–10 minutes turning frequently.
	Small roast	such as fillet	low	Sear first. Cook 7 minutes per lb. (450 g.) for rare, 10 minutes per lb. (450 g.) for medium. Turn occasionally.
	Large roast	up to 9 lb. (4 kg.)	spit	Sear first. Cook 15 minutes per lb (450 g.) for rare meat, 20 minutes per lb. (450 g.) for medium.
Lamb Preferably pink and juicy but also liked well done.	Chops	3/4–1 in. (2–2 1/2 cm.)	medium	Cook 7–15 minutes. Bring closer to the heat to brown for the last 2 minutes. Turn once.
	Kebabs	3/4–1 in. (2–2 1/2 cm.)	medium	6–15 minutes, turning frequently.
	Minced kebabs	flat cakes or sausage shape	medium	5–8 minutes, turning over once or more.
	Butterfly leg of lamb	2 1/2–3 in. (6 1/2–8 cm.)	low	35–45 minutes for pink inside, 15 minutes more for well done. Turn occasionally.

Type of food	Cut	Thickness or weight	Heat	Approximate (generous) total cooking time (for both or all sides)
Lamb (cont'd)	Leg or rolled shoulder	3 1/2–4 1/2 lb. (1 1/2–2 kg.)	spit	1 1/4–1 1/2 hours (or 20 minutes per lb./450 g.).
	Whole baby lamb	21 lb. (10 kg.)	spit	4–5 hours, turning occasionally for well done.
Pork Should be well done but still juicy.	Chops	3/4–1 in. (2–2 1/2 cm.)	medium	15–20 minutes, turning once.
	Kebabs	3/4–1 in. (2–2 1/2 cm.)	medium	12–15 minutes, turning frequently.
	Spare ribs, whole rack		low	1 1/2 hours.
	Large roast		spit	25–30 minutes per lb. (450 g.) plus 25 minutes extra.
	Whole sucking pig	15 lb. (7 kg.)	spit	3 1/2–4 hours, turning occasionally.
	Sausages		medium	8–12 minutes, turning frequently.
	Boudin, andouillette		medium	20–25 minutes, turning frequently.
Veal Needs to be well done but not dry.	Chops	1/2–3/4 in. (1 1/2–2 cm.)	medium	8–10 minutes, turning once.
	Fillet thinly sliced	1/8 in. (1/2 cm.)	medium	6–8 minutes, turning once.
	Rolled loin or shoulder		spit	25–30 minutes per lb. (450 g.) (about 1 1/2–2 1/2 hours).

Type of food	Cut	Thickness or weight	Heat	Approximate (generous) total cooking time (for both or all sides)
Kidneys Browned outside, juicy and rare inside.	Calf's, sliced or cut in half lengthwise; or lamb's, whole or cut in half lengthwise		medium	5–10 minutes, turning once.
Liver Browned outside, pink inside.	Calf's, lamb's, or pig's, thickly sliced		hot	4–6 minutes, turning once.
Chicken Must be a young and tender one.	Boned breasts		medium	10–15 minutes, turning once or more.
	Legs or drumsticks		medium	25–35 minutes, turning occasionally.
	Wings		medium	10–15 minutes, turning once or more.
	Kebabs		medium	5–10 minutes, turning frequently.
	Whole, split open		medium	30–45 minutes, turning occasionally. Give longer to the bone side.
	Whole	(2 1/4– 3 1/2 lb. (1– 1 1/2 kg.)	spit	1–1 1/4 hours.
	Livers		medium	5 minutes.
Rock Cornish Hen	Split open and flattened		medium	20–30 minutes, turning occasionally.

Type of food	Cut	Thickness or weight	Heat	Approximate (generous) total cooking time (for both or all sides)
Rock Cornish Hen (cont'd)	Whole		spit	30–40 minutes, turning occasionally.
Duckling	Whole	split open	medium/ low	About 40 minutes. Turn occasionally, starting with the skin side down.
	Whole	4/5 lb. (3/4–2 1/4 kg.)	spit	1–1 1/2 hours.
Wild Duck	Whole	1/2–1 3/4 lb. (1/4–3/4 kg.)	spit	18–20 minutes.
Goose	Whole	small, young	spit	Allow about 20 minutes per lb. (450 g.).
Guinea Fowl	Whole	young, under 3 1/2 lb. (1 1/2 kg.), split open and flattened	medium	20–30 minutes, turning occasionally.
Pigeon	Whole	split open and flattened	medium	15–25 minutes.
Little Birds	Whole		spit or medium	6 minutes if very small, otherwise 12–15 minutes, turning frequently.
Rabbit	Whole	cut into pieces	spit	45–60 minutes.

Type of food	Cut	Thickness or weight	Heat	Approximate (generous) total cooking time (for both or all sides)
Rabbit (cont'd)	Young		medium	15–30 minutes.
Fish Must never be overcooked, as it dries out.	Large	whole	low	Allow 10 minutes per 1 in. (2 1/2 cm.) of thickness, turn at least once.
		split in half	low	Allow 10 minutes per 1 in. (2 1/2 cm.) thickness. (You need not turn.)
	Small	medium small	hot/ medium	8–12 minutes.
		very small	hot/ medium	5–6 minutes.
	Steaks	1 in. (2 1/2 cm.)	medium	6–10 minutes. Turn once (thinner steaks or fillets do not need turning).
		2 in. (5 cm.)	medium/ low	12–20 minutes.
	Kebabs	1 in. (2 1/2 cm.)	medium	5–8 minutes.
King-Size Prawns or Shrimp	In their shells		medium	8–10 minutes. Turn once.
	Without their shells, skewered		medium	5–6 minutes, turning occasionally.
Lobster	Cut in half		low	15–20 minutes shell side, turning for the last 3 minutes.
Shellfish	In their shells		medium	Until they open.

Type of food	Cut	Thickness or weight	Heat	Approximate (generous) total cooking time (for both or all sides)
Shellfish (cont'd)	Out of their shells or skewered		medium	5–10 minutes.
Snails	In their shells		medium	5–6 minutes.

Bibliography

Andoh, Elizabeth. *At Home with Japanese Cooking.* New York: Alfred A. Knopf, 1980.

Angier, Bradford. *Wilderness Cookery.* Harrisburg, Pa: The Telegraph Press, 1961.

Battiscombe, Georgina. *English Picnics.* London: The Country Book Club, 1951.

Beard, James. *Barbecue with Beard.* New York: Warner Books, 1976.

———. *Beard on Food.* New York: Alfred A. Knopf, 1974.

———, with Helen Evans Brown. *The Complete Book of Outdoor Cookery.* Garden City, N.Y.: Doubleday, 1955.

———. *Cook It Outdoors.* New York: M. Barrows and Co., 1942.

———. *Delights and Prejudices.* New York: Simon & Schuster, 1971.

———. *The James Beard Cookbook.* New York: E. P. Dutton, 1970.

———. *James Beard's American Cookery.* Boston: Little, Brown & Company, 1972.

———. *Jim Beard's New Barbecue Book.* New York: Macmillan, 1960.

Beck, Simone. *Simca's Cuisine.* New York: Alfred A. Knopf, 1972.

Boni, Ada. *Italian Regional Cooking.* Translated by Maria Langdale and Ursula Whyte. Sunbury on Thames: Thomas Nelson & Sons, 1969.

Brillat-Savarin, Jean Anthelme. *Gastronomy as a Fine Art.* London: Chatto & Windus, 1889.

Brissenden, Rosemary. *South East Asian Food.* London: Penguin Books, 1972.

Brown, Cora, Rose, and Bob. *Outdoor Cooking.* New York: The Greystone Press, 1940.

Child, Julia. *From Julia Child's Kitchen.* New York: Alfred A. Knopf, 1975.

Cobbett, William. *Rural Rides,* ed. E. W. Martin. London: Beckman Publishers, 1958.

Collin, Richard and Rima. *The New Orleans Cookbook.* New York: Alfred A. Knopf, 1975.

David, Elizabeth. *Elizabeth David Classics: Mediterranean Food, French Country Cooking, and Summer Cooking.* New York: Alfred A. Knopf, 1980.

———. *Spices, Salt and Aromatics in the English Kitchen.* London: Penguin Books, 1970.

Davidson, Alan. *Mediterranean Seafood.* Baton Rouge, La.: Louisiana State University Press, 1981.

———. *Seafood of Southeast Asia.* Singapore: State Mutual Books, 1977.

Farmer, Fannie, revised by Marion Cunningham with Jeri Lauber. *The Fannie Farmer Cookbook.* New York: Alfred A. Knopf, 1980.

Fisher, M. F. K. *The Art of Eating.* New York: Vintage Books, 1976.

———. *Two Towns in Provence: Map of Another Town & A Considerable Town.* New York: Vintage, 1983.

———. *With Bold Knife and Fork.* New York: G. P. Putnam's Sons, 1968.

Gardiner, G., and Steel, F. A. *The Complete Indian Housekeeper and Cook.* London: William Heinemann, 1904.

Gore, Lilli. *Game Cooking.* London: Penguin Books, 1976.

Grigson, Jane. *The Art of Making Sausages, Patés, and Other Charcuterie.* New York: Alfred A. Knopf, 1976.

———. *English Food.* London: Michael Joseph Ltd., 1974.

———. *Fish Cookery.* London: Penguin Books, 1975.

———. *Good Things.* New York: Alfred A. Knopf, 1971.

———. *The Mushroom Feast.* New York: Alfred A. Knopf, 1975.

Hargreaves, Barbara. *The Sporting Wife: Game and Fish Cooking.* London: H. F. & G. Witherby, 1976.

Hartley, Dorothy. *Food in England.* London: Macdonald, 1954.

Hazan, Marcella. *The Classic Italian Cookbook.* New York: Alfred A. Knopf, 1976.

Hill, Brian Merrikin, ed. *The Greedy Book: A Feast for the Eyes.* London: Rupert Hart-Davis, 1966.

Humphrey William. *Home from the Hill.* New York: Alfred A. Knopf, 1958.

Jaffrey, Madhur. *An Invitation to Indian Cooking.* New York: Alfred A. Knopf, 1973.

Johnson, L. W., ed. *Wild Game Cookbook.* New York: Benjamin Company, 1968.

Jones, Evan. *American Food: The Gastronomic Story.* New York: Random House, 1974.

———. *The Food Lovers Companion.* New York: Harper & Row, 1979.

———. *The World of Cheese.* New York: Alfred A. Knopf, 1976.

Jones, Judith and Evan. *The Book of Bread.* New York: Harper & Row, 1982.

Kephart, Horace. *Camp Cookery.* New York: The Macmillan Company, 1923.

Kincaid, Denis. *British Social Life in India 1608–1937,* second edition. London: Routledge & Kegan Paul, 1973.

Kritakara, M. L., and Pimsai Amranand, M. R. *Modern Thai Cooking.* Bangkok: Editions Dunag Kamol, 1977.

Lewis, Edna. *The Taste of Country Cooking.* New York: Alfred A. Knopf, 1976.

Leyel, Mrs. C. F. *Picnics for Motorists.* London: George Routledge & Sons, 1936.

Leyel, Hilda Winifred Wanton, and Hartley, Olga. *The Gentle Art of Cookery.* London: Chatto and Windus, 1925.

Mabey, Richard. *Food for Free: Guide to the Edible Wild Plants of Britain.* London: Fontana, 1975.

Magasawa, Kimiko, and Condon, Camy. *Eating Cheap in Japan.* Tokyo: Shufunotomo Co., 1972.

Marks, James F. *Barbecues.* London: Penguin Books, 1977.

Martin, Peter and Joan. *Japanese Cooking.* London: Penguin Books, 1972.

McNeill, F. Marian. *The Camper's Kitchen.* London: Alexander MacLehose & Co., 1933.

Ortiz, Elisabeth Lambert. *The Book of Latin American Cooking.* New York: Alfred A. Knopf, 1979.

————. *The Complete Book of Japanese Cooking.* New York: M. Evans & Co., 1976.

————. *The Complete Book of Mexican Cooking.* New York: M. Evans & Co., 1967.

Owen, Sri. *Indonesian Food and Cookery.* London: Prospect Books, 1980.

Parloa, Maria. *Camp Cookery. How to Live in Camp.* Boston: Graves, Locke and Company, 1878.

Renner, H. D. *The Origins of Food Habits.* London: Faber & Faber, 1944.

Roden, Claudia. *A Book of Middle Eastern Food.* New York: Alfred A. Knopf, 1972.

————. *Coffee.* London: Penguin Books, 1981.

Rombauer, Irma S., and Becker, Marion Rombauer. *Joy of Cooking.* Indianapolis: Bobbs-Merrill Company, 1975.

St. Clair, Lady Harriet. *Dainty Dishes.* Edinburgh, 1866.

Seneca. *Canoe and Camp Cookery: A Practical Cook Book for Canoeists, Corinthian Sailors & Others.* Forest & Stream Publishing Co., 1893.

Sing, Phia. *Phia Sing's Traditional Recipes of Laos.* London: Prospect Books, 1981.

Singh, Balbir. *Indian Cookery.* London: Mills & Boon, 1971.

Singh, Dharamjit. *Indian Cookery.* London: Penguin Books, 1970.

Sitas, Amaranth. *Kopiaste.* Limassol, Cyprus, 1968.

Smith, Michael. *Fine English Cookery.* London: Faber & Faber, 1977.

Sysonby, Lady. *Lady Sysonby's Cookbook.* London: Putnam, 1935.

Tezuka, Professor Kaneko. *Japanese Food.* Tokyo, Board of Tourist Industry, Japanese Government Railways, 1936.

Waters, Alice. *The Chez Panisse Menu Cookbook.* New York: Random House, 1982.

Index

Claudia Roden was born and brought up in Cairo, where she participated in the customs and cultures of the Arab world, and in the many small communities of the region—Armenian, Coptic, Jewish, and European. She left Egypt to finish her education in Paris and London, and traveled widely in Europe and South America. She then studied art in London and painted until 1965. Since then she has been involved with food and cooking and has written and contributed to several magazines and books. In 1980 she opened a Middle Eastern cookery school in London, where she lives.

A NOTE ON THE TYPE

The text of this book was set in Aster, a film version of Electra, designed by William Addison Dwiggins for the Mergenthaler Linotype Company and first made available in 1935. Electra cannot be classified as either "modern" or "old style." It is not based on any historical model and hence does not echo any particular period or style of type design. It avoids the extreme contrast between thick and thin elements that marks most modern faces and is without eccentricities that catch the eye and interfere with reading. In general, Electra is a simple, readable typeface that attempts to give a feeling of fluidity, power, and speed.

W. A. Dwiggins (1880–1956) began an association with the Mergenthaler Linotype Company in 1929 and over the next twenty-seven years designed a number of book types, including Metro, Electra, Caledonia, Eldorado, and Falcon.